Other Books by Michael J. Kiser:

"A Journey into the Spiritual Quest of Who We Are"
4 Book Series
(Current Story of this Time Frame 1966 - 2005)

Book 1
~ The Reawakening ~
Book 2
~ Why Were They Called Gods? ~
Book 3
~ The Knowledge That Was Once Forbidden By Some Of The Ancient Beings ~
Book 4
~ The Quantum Leap into Consciousness ~
~~~

Other books by Michael J. Kiser

~~~~~~~

Battling Guillain Barre Syndrome / Acute Relapsing CIDP
(Auto-Biography – A personal experience)

~~~~~~

The End Time – What is it Really About?

A Journey Into the Spiritual Quest of Who We Are
Complete 4 BOOK in 1

By
Michael J. Kiser

Edited by
Stephanie Lyon
and
Heidi Erikson

DragonEye Publishing

A Journey into the Spiritual Quest of Who We Are:
Complete 4 books in 1
The Reawakening – Book 1
Why Were They Called Gods – Book 2
The Knowledge that was once forbidden by some of the ancient beings – Book 3
The Quantum Leap into Consciousness – Book 4

Copyright 2006
by Michael J. Kiser

All rights reserved. Reproduction of any kind is strictly prohibited without the written permission from the author and from the publisher.

Cover Design 2006 by Michael J. Kiser

Edited by
Stephanie Lyons
Heidi Erikson

First Edition
First Printing November 2006

ISBN 13: 978-0-9767832-5-1   (Paperback)
ISBN 13: 978-1-61500-079-1 (EPub EBook)
ISBN 13: 978-1-61500-175-0 (PDF)

Published by Ancient Civilizations, an Imprint of DragonEye Publishing

Website: www.DragonEyePublishers.com
email: Orders@DragonEyePublishers.com

DragonEye Publishing
753 Linden Place, Unit A
Elmira, NY 14901 USA

CONTENTS

Book 1 The Reawakening

5   Acknowledgement
7   Dedication
9   Foreword
11   Preface
13   Star Maps

Chapter 1
17   The Journey Begins

Chapter 2
24   The Contact - A Pleiadean Visit

Chapter 3
36   Dimensional Beings

Chapter 4
47   Artwork of Visions from a Distant Place

Chapter 5
56   Working with Crystals
60   Use of Crystals

Chapter 6
61   Views on Life in the Past and the Future
65   Views on the Pyramids
68   The Unknown World of Terra (Earth)
72   Changes of Our Past World Cycles

Chapter 7
99   Energy of the Ancients

Chapter 8
114 Atlantis

Chapter 9
120 The Fear Creators
123 The Time for a New Beginning... Is Now
132 Questions and Answers
133 A Message for All

Chapter 10
135 The Creation of Gods and Devils from Off-World Races
138 Battles with Off-World Races and Humankind
140 Dimensional Shifting

Chapter 11
145 The Final Battles

151 <u>Book 2 Why Were They Called Gods...?</u>

153 Introduction: A Search into a Forbidden Question

Chapter 12
163 The Terra Papers
(Story of gods-100, 000 years ago to present time - 1st-2nd stories of the creation- Creation of the Human race.)

Chapter 13
268 Beyond the Beyond
(Story of the gods-15, 000 years ago- 2nd-3rd - story of the creation- creation of the Human race.)

Chapter 14

285 The Elect as Elohim
(Story of the gods-6, 000 years ago- 3rd-4th story of the creation- creation of the Human race.)

Chapter 15
333 The Meaning of the Names of Gods

Chapter 16
358 Light Bearer and the Morning Star

Chapter 17
364 Abracadabra The Meaning of Names

Chapter 18
411 Names of Ancient Gods and Goddess
418 Names of Gods and Goddess Timelines
423 Mythological and Earth Events Timelines

Chapter 19
426 Claiming Who You Are

431 <u>Book 3 The Knowledge that was once forbidden by some of the Ancient Beings</u>

433 Kiazers' Quest
434 The Gathering
435 Zoroastrian Dualism
437 From the Beings of Beings

Chapter 20
441 The Thought

Chapter 21
446 Creations

Chapter 22

488 Ahriman The Destroyer

Chapter 23
499 The Ancient of Beings

Chapter 24
509 Watchers
513 Dolphins of Heaven

Chapter 25
518 The Knowledge

Chapter 26
530 Removing the Acknowledgement of Ancient Technology and Knowledge of Life

Chapter 27
535 Essence of our Existence
537 Removing the Veils
542 Ever going Forward

545 Book 4 The Quantum Leap into Consciousness

547 Preface

Chapter 28
549 The Creation of the Veils of Illusions
555 Breaking Away

Chapter 29
558 The Start of a New Age

Chapter 30
565 The Rite of Passage
572 The Next Step on the Ladder of Evolution
578 Becoming fully awaken Beings
Chapter 31

584 Into the Unknown but Known
586 Understanding the Living Force
594 The One Path of many Journeys

   Chapter 32
599 The Departure of Some of the Previous Guardians
603 The Return of some Ancient Beings

   Chapter 33
615 Entering the Halls of Cosmic Creations
626 The Unseen World

   Chapter 34
629 The Arrival of new Guardians

   Chapter 35
635 Time Ends
637 Meeting with the Beings of Beings
639 A Message from the Ancient Beings of Beings

647 Research Materials used

A Journey into the Spiritual Quest of Who We Are
Complete 4 Books in 1

A Journey Into the Spiritual Quest of Who We Are
Complete 4 BOOK in 1

Book 1
The Reawakening

A Journey into the Spiritual Quest of Who We Are
Complete 4 Books in 1

A Journey into the Spiritual Quest of Who We Are
Complete 4 Books in 1

A Journey into the Spiritual Quest of Who We Are
Complete 4 Books in 1

A Journey into the Spiritual Quest of Who We Are
Complete 4 Books in 1

Acknowledgement

Artwork by Michael J. Kiser

Photos by Michael J. Kiser / Cindy M. Kiser

This book is dedicated to everyone who is seeking to find his or her true self for these New Times that are approaching rapidly.

This dedication is also to all of the guides I have been learning from, and to everyone to whom I have passed my knowledge, in one form or another about Universal knowledge. I also dedicate this book to everyone who has taken part in making what this book is today.

I thank all Star Brothers and Sisters of all races. I release my love to all of you who exist in all the Universes. My heart is filled with the wonderful information you have shared with me and you have enriched my life.

A Journey into the Spiritual Quest of Who We Are
Complete 4 Books in 1

A Journey into the Spiritual Quest of Who We Are
Complete 4 Books in 1

Dedication

I dedicate this book to Cindy, my soul mate and wife. Even though it was only a short five years that we had together, we cherished and loved each other deeply.

In Memory of Cindy M. Green (Kiser)
2-4-1965 to 7-2-1993

A Journey into the Spiritual Quest of Who We Are
Complete 4 Books in 1

A Journey into the Spiritual Quest of Who We Are
Complete 4 Books in 1

FOREWORD

In this series of four books, you will embark into a journey that will unlock the deepest spiritual understanding of who we are in this vast life that we are part of. Since 1968, Kiazer has brought forth several questions, including but not limited to: Have we lived before? Along with who are we as human beings along with our duality of a spirit / soul being that co-exists within us? Is there other life amongst the countless numbers of stars? Kiazer has delved deep into these and many other questions in his search for the truth of our existence, in the vast universe we all live in.

At this time of August of 1987, Kiazer had decided to tell his experiences of his journeys that started in the summer of June 1968.

Michael was born on April 21, 1966, and he experienced a horrific event in June 1968. This brought forth a highly evolved being of pure energy named Kiazer. This started a physical journey unlike any other that Kiazer had ever experienced before.

Kiazer traveled his unique path into this quest of spiritual reawakening and learning who he is and what life consists of. He uncovers the answers to these questions and much more.

A Journey into the Spiritual Quest of Who We Are
Complete 4 Books in 1

This reawakening involves our next step in human evolution, going from our third dimensional existence into the fourth and fifth dimensional existence, as we learn to claim who we are as human beings, along with a spirit /soul being that co-exist within us for their own experiences, which are set apart for our experiences.

As the Earth, is making Her quantum leap into the next existence, I ask you, "Are you ready to make your leap with Her to a new beginning?"

It is time for all to learn who we are. A new beginning is in front of all of us.

I hope you gain the understanding of the knowledge that has been kept away from you for over twelve thousand years. When you are finished reading this series of books, I hope you will have a wider view on a part of life that has been somewhat of a large mystery and that is not fully understood. I hope you will grow in knowledge of understanding the universal language of the true knowledge of life, as Kiazer has come to unlock the knowledge that is within all of us.

A Journey into the Spiritual Quest of Who We Are
Complete 4 Books in 1

Preface

This is a true story about the journey of Michael (Kiazer) as he embarks upon the journey of universal knowledge travels down his path of destiny, which started back in the summer of 1968 when he was two years old. He had no concept of what he would be getting into at that time. He was drawn to learning the truth of our existence which, at that time; Michael had thought was common knowledge to all who live on Earth. While the years went by, Michael learned that the knowledge he had was not common knowledge. Nevertheless, this did not keep Michael from continuing to learn the knowledge of the origin of life, that he was becoming aware of.

The years passed and Michael delved deeper and deeper into the forbidden knowledge that had been, and still are considered forbidden by the world religions highest caretakers of the many religions of Earth's belief systems. These caretakers decided to keep this 'True Knowledge' about our existence and of the many off world beings and these beings knowledge about life, hidden from all.

In the early fall of 1968, Michael began to reawaken his knowledge within him, which consisted of the off-world beings and the multi-dimensional worlds that exist around the earth. This reawakening

A Journey into the Spiritual Quest of Who We Are
Complete 4 Books in 1

began the removal of the 'veils of illusions' and Michael came to realize that there are many, many veils. In addition, by the summer of 1977, he found himself drawn to continue on his path of destiny of discovering who he was to become, as his future became his present.

These are the journals of Michael's journeys as he reawakens the knowledge, which has been forbidden for anyone to delve deep into and to learn, what all those religious caretakers consider forbidden for all to look into or even to ask questions about.

Journey with Michael as he helps to remove the 'veils of illusion' that have been placed upon the human civilizations for many, many eons. Within these journeys all of you will understand the dynamics of your physical being and of your spirit / soul being, with a completely new awareness of the universal knowledge of yourselves.

View the star maps drawings on pages 13-14

A Journey into the Spiritual Quest of Who We Are
Complete 4 Books in 1

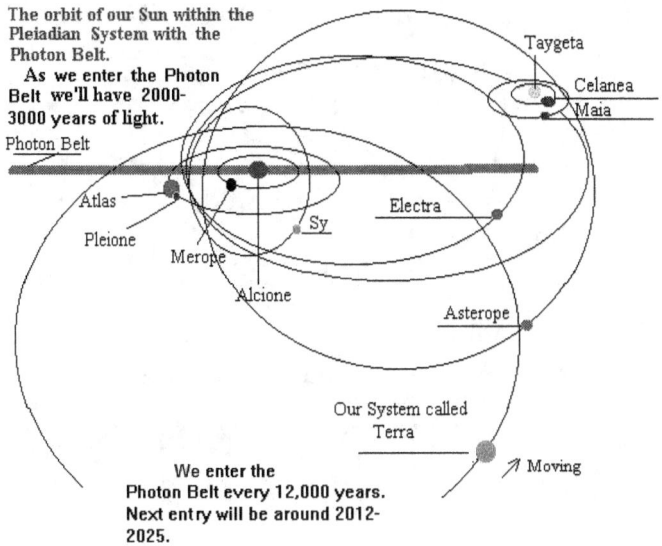

A Journey into the Spiritual Quest of Who We Are
Complete 4 Books in 1

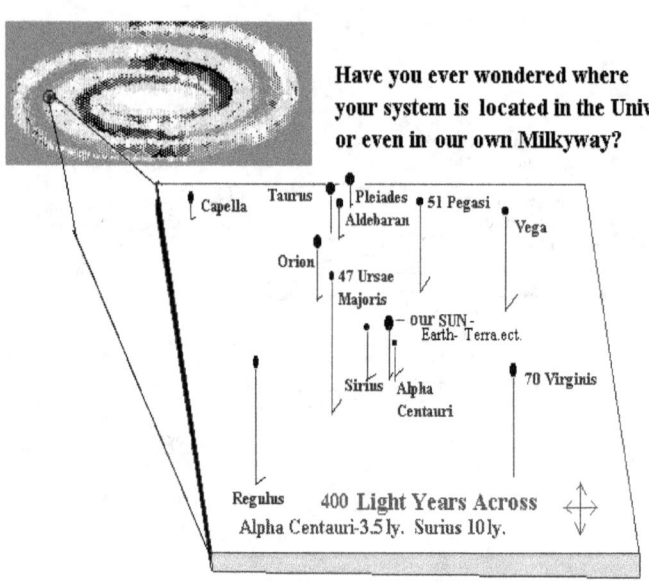

A Journey into the Spiritual Quest of Who We Are
Complete 4 Books in 1

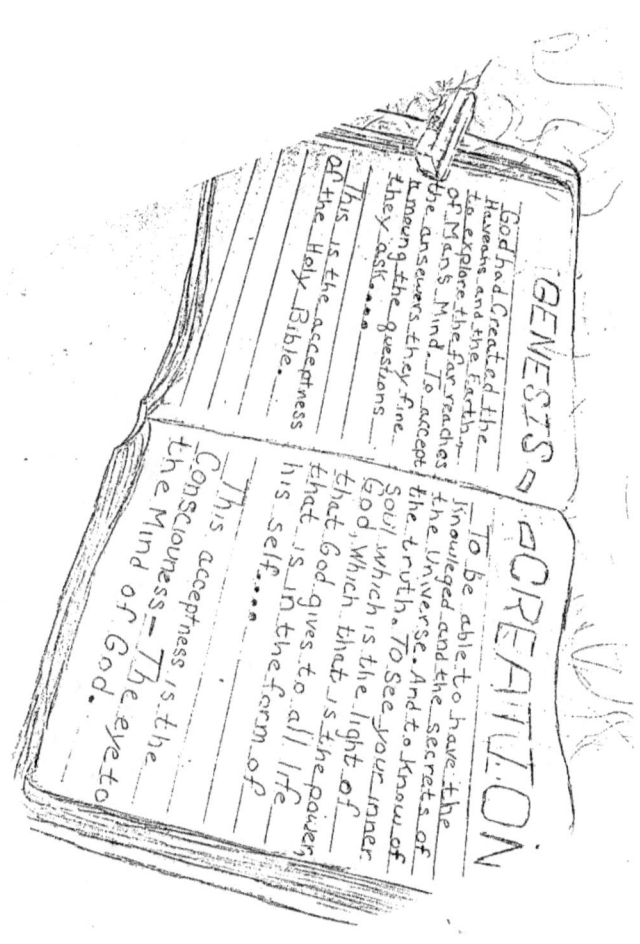

A Journey into the Spiritual Quest of Who We Are
Complete 4 Books in 1

Book 1 – The Reawakening

Chapter 1

The Journey Begins

At the last half of the twentieth century and before the beginning of the second millennium, there are several highly evolved beings choosing to re-incarnate at this time. This is one story of one of those beings that had returned to help the civilizations of Earth to evolve spiritually and to learn of the truth of what had been kept in most secrecy by all the religions of Earth. On the eastern region of the continent of North America, in the city of Elmira, New York, on the eastern region, nestled in a valley surrounded by rolling hills, on April 21, 1966 about 5:30 p.m., a male being named Michael was born to, Judy and Garry. Little did they know of Michael's life path, that the physical being of Michael had chosen to experience on this physical plane of Earth at this time.

Sometime around two years and two months later, around the morning of June 18, 1968, Michael's mom was taking care of his little sister Tammy who was about three months old, Michael mentions to his mother, "mom… I am not feeling good." So his mother Judy told Michael in a soothing voice, "Go on up to your room and lay down and rest for a while, and come down when you want!". Michael went upstairs to his room and rested for a while.

After about four and a half hours of resting, around 2:15 p.m. Michael decided to get up and go downstairs to where his mother and sister are. Michael stood up from his bed, made his way to the stairs, took one step down the stairs, and tumbled down thirteen steps to the bottom. A loud crashing noise of glass was heard and Michael's mom looks over to the steps, she could see from the chair that she was sitting in that Mike's head was sticking out through the glass door. Judy said in a frantic voice, "Oh my God!". Judy jumped up from the chair and ran over to the closed door that closes the downstairs from the upstairs. Michael's head was sticking through the glass door that was shut with Mike on the other side. Judy began to have tears, and she was fearful as she looked around the floor and had noticed how Michael's head was in the door. She ran to Michael and she saw that the glass around his neck was like daggers all the way around his neck. All of the glass shards were about a half inch or less and Judy said to Michael, with fear, "Stay still… And try not to move." Michael was on his hands and knees on the steps with his head sticking through the closed door. Judy took a few steps into the kitchen, grabbed a towel, and tried to put the towel between the glass shards and Michael's neck. Then Michael's Mom mentions to Michael with fear, "Stay still. I'm going to get help…" Then Judy ran out the front door with fear, in her voice, yelling for Ida

Book 1 – The Reawakening

from next door to come out and help, "IDA… Ida… call for help Mike's head is sticking through the glass door and the door is shut…"

About 2:30 p.m., with-in seconds of Judy running outside for help, Michael's arms gave away and Michael died within seconds. Seconds after Michael had died… time had stopped.

Michael's body was removed from the glass door and all the blood was cleaned from the glass door, by the means of teleportation by a clocked starship that was in the area. And another being named Kiazer Wilhelm was on board of this ship. He was similar in appearance and age to Michael, he was then teleported into Michael's place of having his head placed into the glass door, like Michael was seconds ago. Then time started again. Judy ran back inside, and checked on Tammy, Michael's four-month-old sister. Judy noticed that Tammy was still asleep during all of this, and then Judy went back over to where Michael was. Judy still with fear in her voice mentioned to Michael, "Your still alright, Ida is calling and getting help." Two minutes later Ida came over and watched Tammy. With in another two minutes, Del, Ida's Husband shows up first. He worked at the City yard of Elmira, just about four blocks away from them. As Del arrived at their home, Ida yelled at Del as he was getting out of his car, "there is a ladder next to Judy and Garry's house on the side by the patio." Del ran outback of Judy and Garry's home and climbed the ladder to the patio roof. He then pulled off the screen from the window that was open. He climbed through the window and down the steps to be on the side of the door where Michael was to hold him to make sure that his arms would not give out. About ten minutes later, the firefighters and ambulance arrived around 2:35 p.m. to remove Michael's head from the door.

After they remove all the glass shards from around Michael's head, they removed his head from the door. They were able to open the door and Judy was sitting on the floor to the side, Del lifted Michael from the steps and took him over to his mother and Judy held Michael close to her and in tears with a frantic voice she said, "Your OK... Your OK...!" She kissed him on the head and said, "I am glad that I did not lose you. I love you!" The paramedics checked Michael out and by all of their amazement; Michael did not have any scratches of any kind on his head or around his neck where the glass shards were. The paramedics handed Michael back to his mother, then the paramedics picked up their equipments, and they left. Judy went into the front room and held Michael and his sister Tammy close to her, with tears. Del, cleaned up the broken glass, and Ida stayed with Judy for a while until Garry made it home from work around 3:15 p.m. Judy and Garry did not notice anything different about their son Michael, that is that Michael was not really Michael. All of the events of Michael dieing that day were removed by those beings in that invisible starship above the area at the time of this event happening. They were highly evolved beings and they knew how to control and to stop time for they had stopped time for several minutes to clean up the event of Michael dieing and as Kiazer Wilhelm placed himself in Michael's place.

Enters a being from a distant place and time

At this time, Kiazer Wilhelm began his unique destiny that was laid out before him as Michael. Kiazer's journey begins on earth as being Michael at the age of two. By the time Kiazer/Michael reached the age of two and a half years, he took interest in the star traveling beings that were from other star cultures within the Milky Way Galaxy.

Michael began to see how the people of earth were viewing the other life forms that were visiting this world and how the people of earth viewed these off world beings. During the many centuries past and through the 1960's there had been many people reporting what has been termed Unidentified Flying Object (UFO) sightings. Some of the reports were made into television series such as *Project Blue Book* in the year 1968-1969, to explain this UFO phenomenon away. Other shows were made into movies for television and the silver screen. In the late 1960's came a TV series called Star Trek created by Gene Roddenberry along with his Star Trek films that followed.

Kiazer also noticed that during the years between the1950's and 1975; various religions and sectors of the public were saying that any person who is involved in metaphysics was considered to be working with the devil and the energies of the super natural.

When Michael came of the age of five in 1971, his parents started taking him to church Sunday school at Christ's United Methodist Church, and it was here that Michael was taught about one of the earth's religions called Christianity. It was here that started Michael's learning's into the origins of life as he was taught through the Church. As months and years went by Michael began to ask questions about life and about the two so-called beings that are termed as God and the Devil. He asked why they were called God and the Devil and he continued to ask about the past civilizations on earth, to his Sunday school teacher's through the years. His Sunday school teachers answered those questions the best that they could. However, Michael knew that there was more than what they were teaching.

As the year 1977 approached, Michael began to notice a pattern within the many governments along with the many world religions they were trying to cover-up and hide the truth from the people about other life forms, which are about those star beings that have been amongst the people of Earth for the past 100,000 years and longer.

At the age of eleven in sixth grade, Michael also took interest in writing and reading ancient Egyptian hieroglyphs, along with learning about other cultural beliefs system such as Hindu, Buddha and many other religious beliefs that are spread across Earth.

Book 1 – The Reawakening

On May 25, 1977 a completely new approach to this higher spiritual awareness was presented in a film that also combined vast starships, aliens, humans and psychic powers. For the first time in this modern age, the public began to view psychic ability differently, including Michael, as he watched this particular film. This film was George Lucas's third film released on May 25, 1977 called 'Star Wars IV: A New Hope'. Michael witnessed how this helped the public begin to understand psychic ability. Shortly after the next two Star Wars films were released, the public was more spiritually involved in their understanding of the messages of these films.

In the early 1980's, some of the population around the Earth that had been negatively viewing those who were spiritually and metaphysically aware began to see things differently and were beginning to accept them, to some degree.

It was at this time that about a quarter of the people of Earth started to shift in their understanding about life and to become aware of their responsibilities as humans on Earth. People began to wake up to the understanding of all life in the Universe that is within every one of us. However, only few of us had learned how to tap into this knowledge and we were able to teach how they can awaken this knowledge within themselves.

Book 1 – The Reawakening

Chapter 2

The Contact

During the year 1980, Michael was fourteen years old and on Friday, November 14, a slightly warm late fall day, Michael went for a walk by Newtown Creek that runs through the city of Elmira, New York. As Michael walked along the creek, he thought to himself, "For the past twelve years I have believed in starships and beings from other worlds and the existence of other dimensions all around us." In addition, as the day went on, "I feel I will experience something extraordinary today."

As the day ended Michael went to his bedroom and as he lay in bed, he said in a whisper so low that nobody in the house could hear him, "I cannot wait until I have my first contact." He reached for his watch, which had a stopwatch on it that he set to zero. He wanted to record the time from when the craft would first appear until the craft flew out of sight. Michael went to bed that night around 10:30 p.m. Later that night, he was awakened from a deep sleep by a strange sound. It sounded like the huge engines for Earths' spacecrafts, except that it was silent; the sound of the craft was projected out only to Michael.

Michael reached for his watch and watched out his west window in the direction of the light tower, on Harris Hill three miles west of the city of Elmira. For a minute or two, he looked out his window and there was nothing to be seen. Seconds later, out of nowhere, two bright red lights appeared, shining over the hill.

As the craft turned the two large, red lights disappeared and a large blue light shined in Michael's direction. At that moment, the craft flew toward the house. As the craft approached him, Michael pushed the start button on the watch. He was able to see what the craft looked like in the front as the craft flew overhead. He turned around to look out his south window so that he would be able to see the underside and the backside of the craft. As the craft disappeared in the east, he pushed the stop button on the watch. Five seconds had passed.

He continued to look out his south window hoping that the craft would return. As Michael gazed out his window, he made some mental notes about his experience with the craft:

Michael thinks to himself, "I had never seen such a craft before. Its shape was like a boomerang, with one wing longer than the other was. There was a rectangular box shape on the underside, three-quarters the size of the ship. In the front of the ship, there was a giant blue light, located in the center of the rectangle. The craft flew about eighty yards over the tops of the trees. I was able to see a few beings in the windows that lined the rectangular box of the craft. On the backside of the craft, there were two gigantic red lights, appeared to be engines, one on each end of the rectangular box. The length of the craft's wing was about one hundred and fifty yards long. The craft disappeared in the east over Watercure Hill in line with the power lines there."

As he returned his gaze out his south window, from where he could see East Hill he hoped that the beings in the craft would return so he could meet them in person. Nothing happened for the next fifteen minutes, so Michael lay down in his bed and fell asleep.

The next morning Michael awoke between nine and ten o'clock to ensure that what he had seen the night before was real, he checked his watch and sure enough, five seconds still showed on the watch. He said to himself, "I *did* see a craft!" After he set the watch back down on the nightstand, he noticed some kind of mark on top of his right hand that had not been there when he went to bed the previous night. At that time, he did not remember how he was given the mark nor had he seen who had given it to him. Michael had a suspicion about where this mark had come from and from whom. Therefore, he thought it was best not to say anything to anyone about the experience at this time.

Now after five months had passed it was April 1981, and Michael was still trying to find out what happened to him that night of November 14, 1980. As he went for a walk along Newtown Creek he began to ponder to himself, *"Why was I chosen to have this contact or meeting with them, the beings of that craft back in 1980? Ever since I was 2 years of age, I had been having visions of who I am and ever since, that night of November of 1980 I have been having clearer visions of Earth of the past and present and of the future. Why was I made aware of all these powers and abilities within myself and to see of my future and along with the future of the earth?"*

Now, it had been five months since Michael had seen that craft. Since that visit of 1980, these visions had started to become more vivid then in the past years. That was when Michael's visions of his past and of his future life started to become much clear than several years past. He had been having visions of his next girlfriend that he would meet five years later, of exotic places like pyramids and lost cities like Atlantis. He was also seeing the future of the earth, which had been through several small wars, and the birth of the new and second sun of our solar system. He also saw the children that he would have. First was a daughter with his first wife that would have medium blonde hair, then a son with another lady with dark brown hair and that he would end up having a very limited time with due to his mother's behavior. In addition, Michael would have twins through yet another lady with light blonde hair, a girl and a boy. By this time, Michael was becoming pretty frightened and overwhelmed by all of this information and knowledge of his life in the past, present and of his future life that would manifest in this lifetime.

Book 1 – The Reawakening

During one night in late April of 1981, the time came for Michael to remember what happened after seeing the craft back in November of 1980 and after falling back to sleep from seeing that craft after it flown out of sight.

Michael was finally allowed to remember what happened to him after he had went back to sleep that night. Sometime later that same night of November 14, 1980 the beings in that craft returned, exactly when they returned is not known, Michael was awakened again this time not by the sounds of the craft's engines, but by a voice. He had heard his name being called from the back yard of his parent's house.

The calling voice sounded so peaceful. It was soft and soothing. He woke up and saw the soft blue light shining through the shade and curtains of the south window of his bedroom. When he began to reach out to open the shade to look and at that same time he mentioned, "the beings have returned for me for some reason."

He pulled the curtains apart and saw a young lady standing on a device that was floating a foot above the ground in the neighbor's backyard. There was also the soft blue light that he had seen earlier projected from the ship, and this time the light was directed down towards the ground where the young lady was standing on the device. Seconds later, he was out in his parent's backyard. It was like being transported, as one might see in a Star Trek episode. As he walked closer to the fence that separated the yards, he was able to see more clearly the young lady in the light.

She stood about five feet eight inches tall, slim and she had brownish blond hair that lay on her shoulders, and she had beautiful blue eyes. She wore something that resembled a uniform. The shirt had long white sleeves. The neck collar and shoulder area were not quite a navy blue color. The pants were also the dark blue. This uniform was one piece. She wore black boots that came to just below her knees.

She spoke again and said, "Kiazer, I hear you want to get to know who we are and why we are here, along with who you are. Am I right?" There was a pause for a minute then Michael answered, "Yes. But who is Kiazer I am Mike." She asked him to come into the light and stand next to her. As he walked closer, he started feeling a high level of static energy crackling through his body as he entered into the blue light and through the fence that separated the two yards. He then took a step up and stood next to her on an antigravity platform device. It was about four feet round in diameter, and about one foot in thickness.

Book 1 – The Reawakening

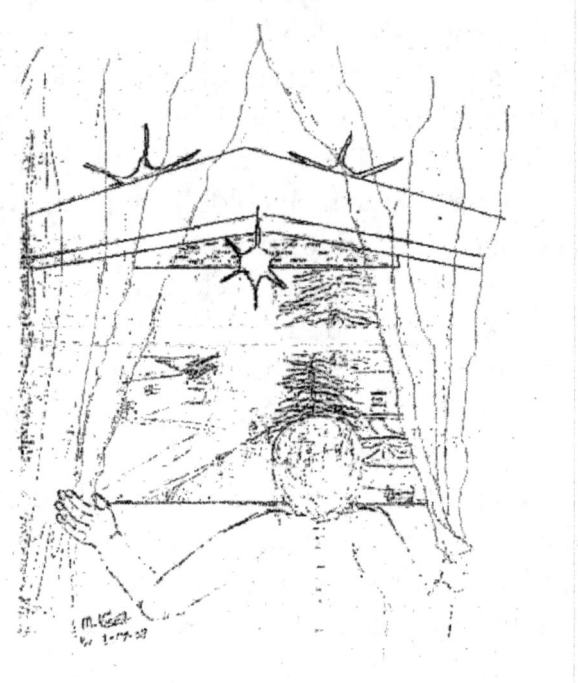

Book 1 – The Reawakening

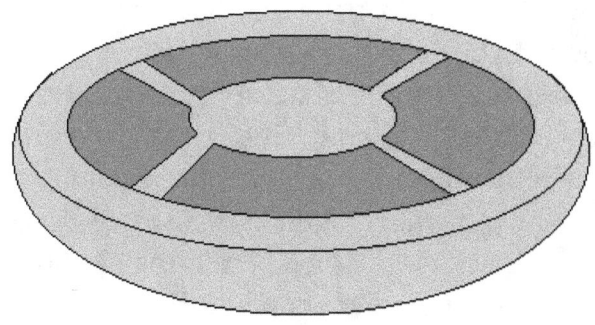

The platform - The anti-gravity device

They floated up to the craft, which was a shade akin to a silver black color, and had a surface texture like a mirror. The craft was hovering over the treetops, and Michael asked her if she could tell him her name. She replied with, "It is Victoria."

As soon as they arrived into the craft, Victoria said, "Your memory of who you are will be made known to you when the time is right for you to learn about your future and why we chose to meet with you and to make you aware of your knowledge and of your true identity, Kiazer. Later on this night before you leave our people, we are going to let you know your abilities and about whom you are. You will not remember them right away; they will be made known to you when it is time for you to reawaken the secrets of the Universe and about yourself."

"First Kiazer," she said, "let me show you around our ship." Therefore, she did. After Victoria showed Michael the Command room and the engines, they stopped at a lounging area as they sat looking out the row of windows. Victoria asks, "Kiazer what do you remember of your childhood?" Michael replies, "Why do you keep calling me Kiazer?" Victoria responds, "Because Kiazer, it is your true name. Now tell me what you remember of your childhood and how far back do you remember." Michael turns his gaze out the window for a minute then he returns his gaze back to Victoria. "I remember the age of 2 years old and falling down a flight of steps and putting my head through a glass pane door and having several glass shards pointing into my neck." Victoria replies, "I see. Kiazer that is a memory that is not yours and that did not happened to you. That happened to a 2-year-old boy by the name of Michael, he died which was part of his destiny, but it was not his parents destiny to have their child die. You Kiazer are a highly evolved being that exists in the seventh dimension as energy and you took on the form of Michael and we removed his body and you placed yourself in his place."

After a few minutes had passed Victoria led Kiazer to the medical room that is down the hall from where they were sitting.

Five other beings in the room were not of human origin. They were between five feet to six feet tall and slim, with longer fingers than humans have, and a large head with large black oval eyes, a small mouth and nose and a small hole where their ears would be. They had very little hair on their heads and their skin was bluish-gray.

Everything else about them seemed to be human but not in our way of thinking what human beings look like based on our human cultures of the past or current. Their clothing was similar to what Victoria was wearing. After Kiazer spent several minutes looking around the medical room, Victoria than directed him to go to the table that was upright, and to remove his clothes and to stand with his back firmly against the table. Kiazer removed his clothes and stood with his back to the table as Victoria instructed him. The beings and Victoria were talking in what Michael thought were whispers, but they was talking telepathically and all he could hear was, "He is in perfect health just like when he was with us twelve years ago, when he was chosen to be left here. It is time to reawaken his knowledge of who he is, along with his past lives from several thousands of years ago."

Seconds later Kiazer began to feel tired, but it felt like he was being hypnotized by the thoughts from their minds. After some time had passed he was awakened and there was only Victoria and himself in the room. She said, "Here are your cloths." Michael took his cloths and put them on. Victoria continues talking, "Kiazer, you have just been reminded of all the powers, abilities and the knowledge of the Universe, and of your past lives that you have had thousands of years ago, but have forgotten them when you came into this physical existence twelve years ago." There is something else, "We also gave you a mark on your right hand which you, Kiazer, will find out in time what it symbolizes."

An idea of what these other beings appeared to look like.

As Victoria escorted Kiazer from the ship, Victoria said to him, "Kiazer, you have to help the others and make it clear to them why they have the powers they bear within themselves, along with the knowledge of who they are, as well the purpose of it all. Kiazer, use the powers wisely, and be careful of the powers that are involved in the illusions, which are always present. Kiazer you will still go by Michael as you have been, now those that are of your soul group will recognize you as Kiazer, and they will call you by your true name. Other people in your life will only know you by Michael." Kiazer asks, "What is a soul group?" Victoria explains, "A soul group is the same souls that are at the same level of evolution that you are, you are a highly evolved soul of energy that exists in the seventh dimension. Earth and her people are in the third dimension - physical existence."

The craft that I saw on Nov. 14, 1980

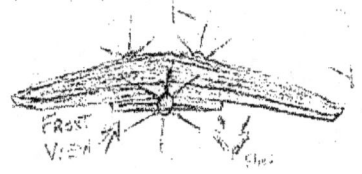

[The craft was about 150-200 yards long]

Direction of flight

A blue light on the front of the craft.
The rectangle box on the underside was where the control center and living quarters and other rooms are

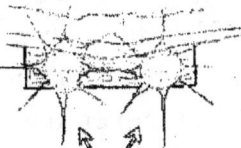

On the back of the craft are 2 red lights that are the engines.

Chapter 3

Dimensional Beings

Kiazer had never given any thought about becoming involved with psychic ability; it hadn't crossed his mind as he thinks back to February of 1981 when he realized what was happening to him. He was becoming more tuned in to the psychic world around him he began having recurring visions.

It was the summer of 1981, and Kiazer was out of school for the summer. As summer began, Kiazer felt compelled by someone or something with great powers up at the quarries. Kiazer decided to do some hiking around the stone quarries, which were up on Watercure Hill in the city of Elmira, only about a half-mile from where Kiazer was living at the time.

As Kiazer made his first adventure up to the quarries, he began to feel something different all around him. As Kiazer walked on the path he realized that he was feeling a strange presence, a high level of energy on this path.

As he reached the quarries, he still felt the energies that he had felt at the beginning of the path leading to the quarries. Kiazer walked slowly and then stopped at the first small quarry and looked around. He felt as though he was being watched by someone with the same energy that was on the path, yet somehow it was different. The energy he was feeling on the path was as if the energy knew him and Kiazer became a part of this energy. Kiazer knew this was part of the training that he would eventually be starting. During the walk, he felt himself to be in a different dimension and place. He also had to recognize the difference between the positive and the negative energies.

Kiazer then brought the positive energy into himself and blocked the negative energy to keep it a safe distance from him. He also had to find out who or what was watching him; and determine whether it was of good energy or of the darkness. Kiazer felt the coldness of the evil (as one might call it) that was being sent out, along with the warming of the good. Even though Kiazer felt as if someone was watching him while he was there, whoever it was did not make him or herself known. It was as if they were not there at all.

Five years later, in summer of 1986, Michael decided to talk to his mother about the psychic ability that he had been developing and becoming involved with. At that time, he found out for the first time that his mother and few of her friends were involved in exploring the psychic abilities in 1972. Then his mother and her friends decided to put it aside, because it was too much for them to handle at that particular time, in 1972 with the prevailing beliefs in place about such things.

Book 1 – The Reawakening

In March of 1987, Kiazer began to illustrate all of the visions he had been seeing since 1981. Some of those visions still return now and then. It had taken Kiazer six years to persuade himself to draw the vision shown on the cover of this book. Other visions became clearer after he drew them. This helped Kiazer to understand what was manifesting in his life.

One symbol was of a Double Sun Medallion, (here is a drawing of that), which Kiazer has been seeing in his visions since 1980.

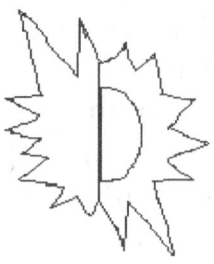

From 1980 through 1986, Michael had been having visions of himself wearing a sun Medallion and seeing planets that were unfamiliar to him at that time of his life.

Then one day during the late summer of 1986, Michael met up with his five lady friends that were of the same soul group which had known Kiazer since late fall of 1985, they knew Michael's real name as Kiazer. Everyone got into Kiazer's van and got ready to travel north to Buffalo, NY. Kiazer and his friends start on their adventure, Kiazer is driving his van and everyone is talking about the trip they are taking. Minutes later Kiazer is contacted telepathically by a lady. This female voice is mentioning, "Kiazer do you remember about the sun Medallion that you have been shown in your visions over the past years, it is now ready to be given to you, and you most stop at the small shop right up the street where you always go from time to time." Kiazer mentions to his friends, "I need to make a stop for a minute up here at this small shop." Everyone said at once, "That is alright Kiazer go ahead." Then everyone continued talking about the trip.

Minutes later Kiazer pulled into the shopping center and up next to the small shop, Kiazer parked the van facing the store as left the van running, he got out and headed into the shop. As Kiazer enters the shop the owner asks, "Can I help you with anything?" Kiazer knelt down, pointed to the one and only sun medallion in the glass case, and mentioned, "I will be interested in buying this sun medallion." The owner reached into the case and pulled out the Sun Medallion at the same time mentioning, "This came in this morning and there was no information in the invoice about this medallion. I have never seen this type of sun medallion and I opened this store in 1979."

Kiazer bought the sun medallion and headed out of the shop and into the van. As Kiazer entered the van, he mentioned, "Ok we are ready to continue on

Book 1 – The Reawakening

our trip." Sharon is sitting in the front seat and she asks, "Kiazer what did you buy?" Kiazer handed the bag to Sharon without telling her what he bought, and he started to drive. Kiazer replies, "You can go ahead and open and you tell me what you see." Sharon looks at Kiazer, knowing what is in the bag. She opened the bag and pulled out a plastic box and opened the box and at that moment Sharon says, "Its the sun medallion that you have been drawing. It is identically like your drawing."

In September of 1987, Michael went to see a psychic counselor in the city of Ithaca, north of Elmira on the eastern coast. Michael met with Robin, the counselor, to confirm his experiences and to further enhance his awareness. Michael knew that he still had more abilities within him which were to be unlocked, as he headed to the Continental Divide of

Book 1 – The Reawakening

the Rocky Mountains during the coming summer of 1988.

The abilities that Kiazer had already developed so far, were recreating his visions into helpful drawings to unlock the knowledge of his past lives from the times of Atlantis 100,000 years previously as well as another past life 6,000 years ago. He was also obtaining information from crystals that were used as record keepers during these times, and he was developing the ability to travel between other worlds that are all around us.

Friday, October 2, 1987, Kiazer had gone to bed after finishing one of his drawings that he had started the previous Monday that pertained to his future. Kiazer had known it for the past seven years. (The drawing is the one chosen for the cover of this book). The drawing below is a sketch of the actual medallion. This Sun Medallion has fifteen points; one-half of it has a raised half circle. Kiazer learns this particular medallion is to signify Kiazer's origin, which is within the three stars solar systems within the Pleiades star group. The Pleiades stars group consists of about 150,000 stars and our sun (star) is part of those Pleiades star systems.

On Sunday, October 25, 1987 at eight in the morning Kiazer, Mary and Cec awoke and had their breakfast and then Kiazer mentioned to Mary and Cec that he was going outside on the back porch for a couple of minutes, it was nine o'clock. While he was standing on the back porch of his home looking at Watercure Hill to the east he started to feel himself drifting into the fifth dimension as he traveled to the stone quarries where he went to do his vision quest at times and to experience the sun's energy. It is here at the quarries he absorbs the energy that the sun emits out to the solar system. Kiazer uses this energy from the sun to move between the multi dimensions that are around the earth. Kiazer had always felt that he was being watched every time he went to the quarries. Finally, after six and a half years from that first excursion to the quarries, the one that Kiazer had felt watching him without revealing itself, a being revealed itself as a pure silver wolf. When the wolf stands on all fours, his back is as high as Kiazer's mid chest, which is about five feet and five inches. Seconds latter the wolf transformed into an Indian medicine man. He told Kiazer that his name was Night Shadow, and that he is a changeling.

    After his introduction, Night Shadow changed back into a wolf and Kiazer ran with Night Shadow for a half hour around the quarries. After that event, Kiazer returned to the third dimensional world. Kiazer mentioned to Mary and Cec that he had just met with Night Shadow, his Spirit Guide. It seemed to Kiazer that he was with Night Shadow for only fifteen minutes due to him being out of body. But Mary and Cec indicated by their watch that it was actually an hour. Kiazer glanced at the clock, "It really was an hour that I was out of body."

    On Saturday, November 27, 1987, at 5:20 a.m. Kiazer was in his home in the den writing about his experiences to that point. Out of the corner of

Kiazer's sight, he saw a white flame that was about two inches tall and floating in the corner of the room. The pure white flame says to him, "Kiazer, you will be going to the Western Continental Divide area of the Rocky Mountains. When the time comes, in July of 1988, you will be taking a lady friend, whom you will meet two weeks before it is time to leave." At that point, Kiazer asked, "Where are we supposed to go when we are there?" In that moment, the flame left in the same manner as it had arrived.

On the Winter Solstice of 1987, Kiazer headed to the quarries for a Vision Quest to gather insight to a vision that he'd had back in 1981.

Kiazer once again sat on a small mound that allowed him to look upon the small quarry. Kiazer began breathing slowly to gain his focus so that he could alter his awareness so that he was able to move into the future. As Kiazer moved into this altered realm of existence, he was able to see the dimensional shift that this star system would be going through in the last part of the second decade after the turn of the century. The year 1966 brought the ending of the third dimensional existence for this star system. At this time, we began our slow transitional period from 1966 through 1985, of shedding those energies of the past age that existed for the past 4,000 years, as we come out of our transition phase we evolve as we shed those third dimensional experiences. We will start to receive the new energies that will start to enter into our star system from 1985- 2025. This will help us, the human race by bringing forth the fourth dimensional energy. This third dimensional world that we live on would only last through 2025, which at this time all life and the earth will be totally evolved to the forth and fifth dimensions. Kiazer was also shown earth existing in both fourth and fifth dimensions around the year 2025 simultaneously.

By March 13, 1988, Kiazer had been using his psychic abilities since early 1981. It was second nature to him. At this time, Kiazer began to see that more people around the world were becoming involved in this expanding awareness.

For the past seven years, Kiazer's spirit guide, Night Shadow had been teaching Kiazer how to alter his body's molecules and his state of consciousness so he could travel to the existence of the multiple worlds, which existed around the physical world. Night Shadow was also training Kiazer to look into the past, along with the possibilities of the near future as well as the distant future, which is based on the current events, the now.

During an early summer day of 1988, Kiazer headed out of his home for a walk up on the hill at the stone quarries. After Kiazer arrived at the quarries, he found a place to sit. As Kiazer relaxed, Night Shadow communicated with Kiazer. Night Shadow explained to Kiazer as he always had. Kiazer listened to Night Shadow's voice telling him, "To be in an altered state you need to be calm and cannot have anything around you that would distract you in any way. If there is any noise that you think would interrupt your concentration, try to block it out before you begin. Then go ahead and focus on the information that you seek."

Night Shadow asked, "Good Kiazer. What do you want to know about?" Kiazer entered into an altered state of consciousness, and he saw his surroundings in a different existence. Kiazer asked, "I would like to know more about my last life."

Within a second Kiazer was shown his second life, which was 6,000 years ago as Zoroaster and a glimpse of his death and his wife beheading him. Moments later Kiazer was shown his present and future life. Then several minutes later, returned from his altered state.

Night Shadow also mentioned to Kiazer, "There is another way of retrieving knowledge of the past and of the future, but this is bit different. It is set at a higher level of the altered state of the sub-conscious. For this you need to be in control of your mind; this particular procedure takes place during your sleep and is activated by your thinking of what you would like to have brought out, and made clear. Just before falling asleep, you ask the question in your mind, a thought, about what you would like to have more information.

When you begin to experience this event, it might feel as if you are in two different places at once, or you might look at it as a dream. It is real. Give it time and when you are ready to accept the answers, the answers will be brought to you. When you start receiving your answers, you will then be amazed and overwhelmed by the discoveries that you had found waiting for you."

Book 1 – The Reawakening

The sun medallion that Kiazer had been wearing around his neck since 1986 is a symbol to signify the guardians and protectors of the Star Systems. He understood that their main job in all the galaxies in the universes was to maintain the order in the sector of any galaxy that they oversaw. He discovered that the two systems that Kiazer was a guardian for are the planet that orbits the sun called Apsu, and a system located some 250 light years away known as Atlas. Atlas is one star system out of one hundred thousand stars that makes up the Pleiadean system, which is located in the Taurus constellation. These guardians receive information from what is known as the Essence of Life. From the information they receive, they make sure that this knowledge is revealed to all life that exists in all Universes. It is up to these guardians to help all civilizations to better understand themselves.

Chapter 4

Artwork of Visions from Distant Places

This chapter is specially designed to give the reader the opportunity to view the unique places that have been and still are a part of Kiazer's life, as mentioned earlier in previous chapters. Since1981 Kiazer had been seeing pyramids, planets, and Atlantis. He also saw the craft in 1980, along with Earth having two Suns. All of these visions have repeated themselves repeatedly, but with more detail each time around.

These are just a couple drawings to give you an idea:

Pages 49-51 - Atlas in the Pleiadean System.
Page 52 - Michael Kiser self-portrait with the planets in the Pleiades system.
Page 53 - One of the Atlantean cities
Page 54 - One of the Atlantean cities under the ocean after the last planet tilting that destroyed all civilizations 24,000 years ago.

Page 55 – A drawing of a temple for multi-dimensional transportation device and for the realignment for the energies of the body using crystals to be able to travel to other realms of existences.

Book 1 – The Reawakening

Book 1 – The Reawakening

Book 1 – The Reawakening

Book 1 – The Reawakening

Book 1 – The Reawakening

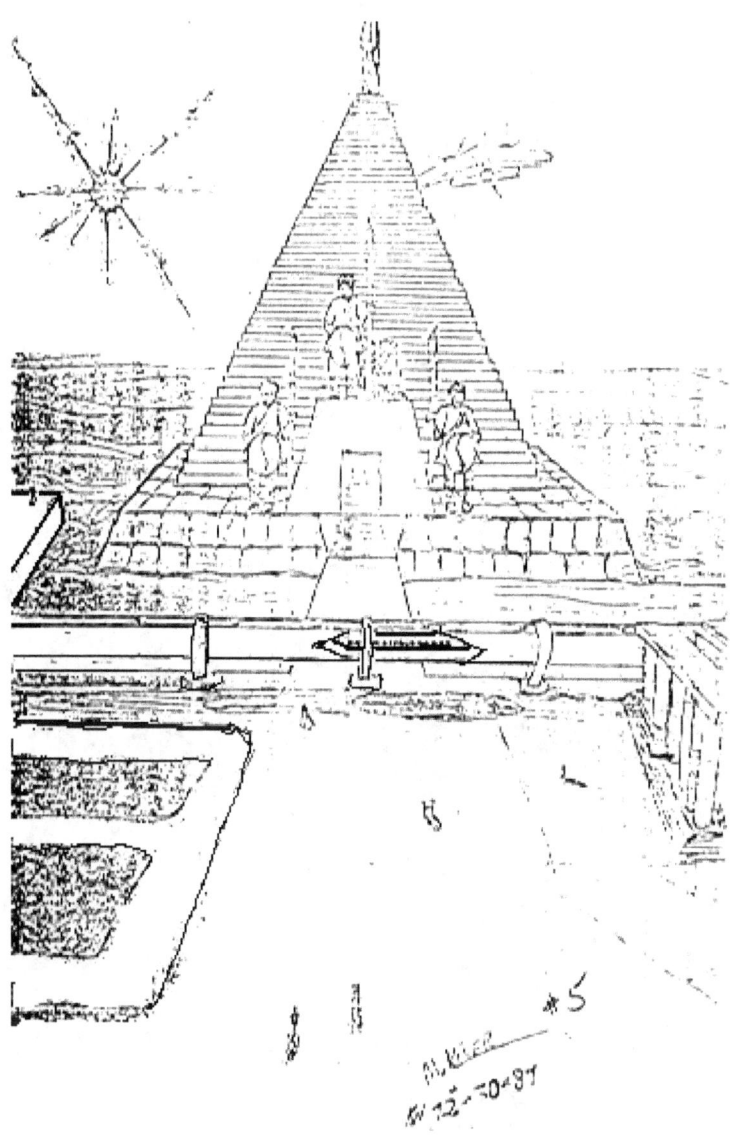

Book 1 – The Reawakening

Book 1 – The Reawakening

Chapter 5

Working with Crystals

Since the summer of 1987, Kiazer has spent a lot of time learning about the use of crystals and gemstones and what they are capable of doing. Kiazer learned that there everyday gem stones along with many types of crystals. These stones are able to help in all ways and in any form that these gem stones or crystals may be in. Many people around the world do not believe in the healing powers that these stones are able to perform. For instance, they can cure a simple common cold or can cure cancer of any form, which has been proven. Crystals also are used in storing information about past, present, and future events. All types of crystals and gemstones have all these properties in themselves.

The scientists of today's world are baffled by those strange phenomena that people say they experience from the use of these crystals and gemstones.

The offering of universal knowledge over the years has been overwhelming to Kiazer, including the information gathered from the other-world beings and about their culture and world which appears more advanced than Earth's technology by hundreds of thousands of years.

The beings from this ancient civilization have been visiting us as far back as 100,000 years ago. They have an advanced technology and a higher level of spiritual knowledge than those on Earth. Kiazer began to notice fear among the world governments and religious figures as they tried their best to keep the people from becoming involved with these highly evolved beings. He learned that the governments and religions do not want anyone to evolve, that this has been their way of controlling us. Regardless of the fears that all governments and religions created towards these other world beings, many know the truth about why these beings are visiting Terra.

The day before the summer solstice, Kiazer purchased candles and aromas so he would have them for a vision quest he was planning to do for the solstice. His purpose for the vision quest was to learn more about the star beings that have been visiting many people on Earth for the past twelve thousand years as it has been recorded in all religious texts around the world.

As Kiazer awakened the following morning, he prepared for his vision quest as the summer solstice began at noon. Kiazer lit the candles and sat on the floor to meditate. Within seconds Kiazer entered an altered state of consciousness as he brought forth his question, "Why are these star beings here? What is their purpose?"

Seconds later Kiazer heard a female voice, "These star beings are here because you, the human race are their children! You have the right to know this; they are your missing link to your evolutional transition. Kiazer pauses and he comes to understand why these beings are coming to earth.

The female continued, "some people use crystals to learn more about us, the star beings, the star travelers that are from your neighboring star systems and as far as on the opposite end of your galaxy and nearby galaxies. More people will begin to have physical contacts and that goes for out of body experiences with these beings. You all have the right to know about our knowledge, along with spirituality and our technology; it's not for any one group to know and to keep it to themselves. Then when you ask your religious caretakers about the knowledge of the origin of life and about the star beings you all come to hear about, they turn it around and tell you it is not for you, and it is the so called devils work (so they say). It is a way to keep you from evolving and to keep you in the dark.

The second reason why we come to Earth, is because the true knowledge of our very existence has been turned around, we have been made to look evil, when it should have been taught as of the good. It is up to people like yourself as guardians who have had physical contact and have become reawakened, along with the people who work with crystals to get this truth out to the people so they, too can become acquainted with it and use it.

Kiazer responded to the female voice, "I can clearly remember that I did not ask to be given this information and these powers. More or less, I was reminded about my knowledge and of its significance. I find it most interesting that people keep asking me if I believe in these aspects of psychic awareness. My answer is always going to be, yes I do believe in it. Then people turn around and say that they do not believe in it because it is a different belief system than they are accustomed to. Then a few days later they ask if we can talk about it. By this form of action, something had triggered an awakening in them." Victoria responds with, "You were told not too long ago by Robin, the psychic counselor in Ithaca New York, that she had never seen anything quite like the way you go about teaching people about spirituality and about who they are. She had also told you that this would be good for her your first wife when it comes her time to teach this knowledge to the public. You and your wife will have a unique way of getting a person's subconscious aware of something extraordinary. You will overwhelm them with the rewards of finding their answers to the highest mysteries and legends of all times of life and about the Earth."

USE OF CRYSTALS

Many people around the world in the multi-cultures are aware that crystals are able to assist in healing and they hold knowledge of past civilizations and of future civilizations. These properties are also contained within the common gemstones of the world. For example, different colored gemstones and crystals affect the different Chakras. Chakras are the soul centers of your being. All the Chakras absorb a special current of energy, or light, through its particular color ray for both the physical and the higher levels of consciousness.

This chart shows the seven rays, their Chakras, and qualities.

Chakras	Ray/color	Works on Quality
1) Crown	Violet	Spirituality
2) Third Eye/ forehead	Indigo	Intuition
3) Throat	Blue	Religious/Inspiration
4) Heart	Green	Harmony/Sympathy
5) Solar Plexus	Yellow	Intellect
6) Spleen/ Sexual Organs	Orange	Energy
7) Base of the spine	Red	Life

Chapter 6

Views on Life in the Past and Future

Around 8:30 a.m. on Tuesday, February 9, 1988 at Toshiba – Westinghouse in Horseheads, New York, where Michael had been working for the past year, Michael brought up a controversial subject with his coworkers to see what would transpire.

Michael asked John, "Do you think it is possible to be able to see into and to know of the future?"

John replied, "No It is not. The only way one is to know of the future is through God himself and that no one is to know of it, not even the Devil, whatever it might be."

Michael replied to John, "I know of the future, and what is to become of it, that we will be out among the stars with the help from the life that is out there. By that, I mean the extraterrestrials that have been watching us from the beginning of our time." Kiazer also shared that this event would take place in ten to twenty years from now, be around the years 1998-2010.

John said, "That is impossible and will not happen. It is written in the Bible that when the turn of the century comes, and as the destruction of the Earth begins, there will be no life to go to the stars. Anyway, we would not have that high of technology, and if we did, we will still destroy ourselves anyway, just to have more power over each other. I believe when we destroy ourselves, that God will destroy Earth; just as he gave life to us. I believe that God can take our lives away when he wants to."

Michael then asked John, "Do you believe in other life besides ours that is in our world, or do you think that we are the only ones amongst all those stars that we see at night?"

John replied, "It might be possible that there is other life besides ours, but I have to see them to believe it." Now, John asks Michael the same question, "What do you think, do they exist?"

Michael answered John, "I knew that you would ask me that after I asked you that question. Yes, I do believe in life forms other than our own in the Universe. This is because I encountered a UFO, as have many others. They often have been told by the government that the UFO's do not exist and that it was something else that they had seen. Nevertheless, the government is just now beginning to let the public know of their existence. For the past forty years they have been denying their existence."

Michael then asked, "How do you think life began on this planet thousands of years ago?"

Book 1 – The Reawakening

John replied, "Life began like this, I use the Bible as a reference guide." At that moment John pulled from his shirt pocket, a small condensed Bible and started reading Genesis. John then asked me if I believed in evolution because, he doesn't believe that we evolve to other life forms."

Michael says to John, "I believe we descended from a similar form not much like Ape's, but human Ape like forms."

At that time, another coworker, Joe, joined in on the conversation, Joe supported the ideas that Michael was stating. The three of them talked for twenty minutes more on descending from lower forms of beings. Michael and Joe decided to end that part of the conversation because John was becoming upset about it. Joe then asked Michael about the dinosaurs because John had asked him. Joe did not know that Michael was the one that started that topic as well.

Michael went on to tell Joe the same thing that he had told to John, "The dinosaurs were here on Earth first, and then humans evolved."

Joe replied, "I agree with you on that subject matter due to the destruction or change in the atmosphere that destroyed the dinosaurs, and humans evolved after that change."

John then spoke up, "I still do not believe in Evolution, or the Stone Age, because it is not written in the Bible."

Michael looked at John as he implores, "John, for a couple of minutes, forget about the Bible, and what has been passed down by religion and from generation to generation. Try to think about it in a different way." Michael said with sincerity, "John, I am not going to change what you believe in, I am only offering another viewpoint."

Michael continued with his questions, "What were the pyramids used for in Egypt during the time of the kings and pharaohs from 4,000 BCE to 0100 CE?"

John answered first, "They were used as tombs for the pharaoh and rulers of Egypt so they could have their belongings with them when they leave to go to the Heavens."

Joe replied right after John, "I have to agree with what John said about the pyramids."

With that, Michael explained to both of them about how the pyramids were used. Man has no known or written knowledge of why the large pyramids were built. For the past nineteen hundred years we have been told that these pyramids had been used as a portal for the souls of the kings, pharaohs to the afterlife. Michael went on to explain why these Pyramids were built. None of the secrets and knowledge of the Universe were put into the Bible.

Viewpoints on the Pyramids

Michael began to explain to both John and Joe that the pyramids hold the truth about all the secrets of all the Universes, and about the off-world beings that have been watching us. Most of the cultures, the people of Earth have not wanted to believe in them, these star beings, because their lives are so different from ours, and that they are so technologically advanced. Michael stated that the inscriptions on the walls of these pyramids hold the truth on how Earth began, and contradict the information passed down by our ancestors and in the Bible. Michael said, "I do not feel that everything was recorded in the so-called Bible of today as I see it, because societies of the religious sects during the Biblical times did not want people to know of the knowledge that the Universe holds for us. In addition, I see what people call the Bible is nothing more than stories of the ancient past and people are so involved in how people lived and how they believed. Along with how they were afraid of events, which were nothing more then natural events happening and not created by gods or devils, as we are all told through out all of those stories within all those religious books that are out there around the world. People believe these stories but they do not believe in past ancient civilizations older than 4,000 BCE, or 6,000 years age from the year 2,000 CE. Only because their Bible only goes back to a time of 8,000-6,000 years ago."

Now Michael continued, as there was no end to his knowledge. "On this next statement, I would like you to accept it as an opinion. It came from one of my past lives that are still a part of me today; this information is from the time when I lived 100,000 BCE – 12,000 BCE years ago on the continent called Atlantis.

As Michael began, he said, "I ask you to forget everything that you know, or everything that you think you know."

"The planets were not made in six days as the Bible states. It was more like thousands and millions of billions of years to get the planets the way they are today. There has been life on all of these planets of our star system at one time or another, except for Jupiter, which is not a planet. I will tell you about all six cycles of changes that occur, including the one that started in 1985 which you might have begun to notice."

"During any cycle or age, the civilization of that time, would come to think they had accomplished what they were set out to do in their lives and to live based on the Bible's of the world. Then the people will think everything will come to an end and a god or a devil will come to destroy their world and take the chosen ones to heaven and the rest will be taken to a forsaken place. At that moment the world is laid to waste to be claimed by time and for the world to be no more and to be recreated for another creation."

However, it really does not come to an end, it just appears that it does. During one of my past lives people from that time, which are referred to as Atlanteans, all had feared what you fear today what you call destruction, the End Times. All it really is, is the Earth undergoing changes to prepare for its next cycle of life. The civilizations of the past time were Atlantis, Mu and Lemuria. These civilizations are now submerged under the vast oceans of today and have been for the past 26,000 years ago. The Milky Way Galaxy goes through a dramatic transformation every 26,000 – 25,000 years. This brought changes that they never experienced, not of this magnitude that brought the tilting of the planet on its axis, which caused great floods. Also came a new energy to the planet that the planet had not experienced in well over one million years ago. I must state that the reason they had to go through that change was due to the misuse of some of their knowledge of the crystals. For creating this new energy, they created massive energy changes to the planets energy, which will last for the earth's next cycle of 26,000 –25,000 years. Which will end around our time of the year 2012 –2035 and we will witness a new beginning of life for ourselves and for the Milky Way Galaxy.

In addition, some of the scientists were involved in genetic alteration. None of this helped matters. During this event, some of us left the earth to return among the stars, but we also left behind our knowledge to be found by the next life that would evolve and inhabit the earth.

We know that some of the records of our knowledge have been found, but have not yet been deciphered because our buildings are beneath the oceans. Some of the newest cultures survived the changes and while some of the buildings are in ruins, most of them are in tack and are still in use. In time your people will find the secrets of our knowledge and learn to use them, that we once used, for good, but to do that, your people must learn to put aside the wars you all create and you need to make peace between all your countries and individuals as well. So do not attempt to seek out our wisdom in these pyramids, you will not find it because the time is not right for you to gain the knowledge of the Universe. This is the only way for this knowledge to be brought out at this time, until the true records are brought forth…

The Unknown Worlds of Earth

Michael continued explaining about the world:

"Let me ask you both, "How much do you know about our world?" John and Joe turned their heads to Michael with bewildered looks on their faces that went with the already overwhelming expression from the recent conversations.

Michael says, "I bet you are wondering what I am going to bring up next."

John, Joe and another worker named Larry are just amazed with all the information that Michael relayed. John replies, "We know everything about our world, all any one has to do is read the Bible and you have your answers!"

Michael continued, as he spoke of the unknown worlds surrounding Earth he looked in John's direction. "You are right by saying we know everything about our world of third dimensional existence only based on what we are told, what about all those other questions that are not answered, but we are told not to look into those questions?

Are you sure you know everything about your world? Now the time comes that you start thinking and looking back in your mind, your life about the things that you have been taught in your life. You are still probably saying there is nothing that is unknown about our world. You are probably right in saying that you know everything about this world of today that you live in. I can guarantee that you really do not know about the worlds within and beyond, of the ages past. We all witness mysterious events in our life that happen all through the history of humankind. You believe you know about your world that you live in today, but you or anyone else is stumped about the worlds, which exist within your world, including a world that is only looked upon as a legend, from what appears to be prehistory. For example, the superior civilizations that existed on Earth, such as the Atlanteans that lived on Atlantis, and on other continents like Mu, Lemuria and many other civilizations which date as far back as 100,000 years ago and older. The top scientists of today are baffled by strange phenomenal activity such as the Bermuda

Triangle, psychic ability, clairvoyance, places like Stonehenge, line drawings in Peru, the large pyramids around the world, and most of all, Atlantis (in the Bermuda Triangle). The list of unexplained phenomena goes on and on, and it does not stop. It includes the reports of the Starship that people around the entire world are seeing. The human race of our world today is trying to solve the mysteries of the unknown worlds that have been interacting with ours as far back as the human race can remember. Half of the people do not have any idea why these events are occurring in your world today. After all the research that has been going on over the past centuries, they still do not want to accept it.

    The people on your planet have been trying to find out and unlock the mysteries that have eluded you for thousands of years, and maybe as far back as hundreds of thousands of years. Humans of today do not look for the answers in the legends of today's life. The legends of the world today are looked upon as legends and myth in your time. People are afraid of finding out that these people of the past are really themselves going through incarnations, lifetime after lifetime. The time is now, this minute, not next week or a year from now, but this moment in time. It is now that you need to let the old Earth that you live on die along with your old Earth habits of the past. You need to start the changes in yourself, at the same time as your world is changing itself. It will be easier for you to understand at the end why you had to make this dramatic change. I and many others like

Book 1 – The Reawakening

myself can guarantee you, it is for the better, but during the beginning of this change, it will feel as if a catastrophic event has occurred.

Many people on our planet wish it were easy to solve the problems of today's life and find out about all the lives for which Earth has been a host. Why did your ancestors build those huge temples, pyramids and other structures, what were the reasons and why were they significant? Finding the answer for all those questions is what mankind is stumbling over in today's life. The answers cannot be found in the minds of yesterday's society."

"The answers are only found beyond the minds of the society, in those that do believe in other dimensions of existence that are as real as you holding this book, and as real as every soul that exists on this world and in all of the universes. Everybody knows Earth goes through changes from time to time and the cycles of life end and a new cycle of life begins. There are still many things unknown to the human conscious. People who are aware often ask why does this event have to occur and what purpose does it serve?"

"The second aspect to consider is what happens during the transition period between the two cycles."

Larry says to John and Joe, "It seems that Michael has been given all this knowledge for reasons unknown to us." As Larry turned to Michael he says, "Michael, I am intrigued by this information that you have." Michael acknowledged Larry with a nod.

Michael continued, "We all know that Earth always goes through all types of world changes. I would like to describe the cycles of the star system we live in. You are going to need the truth to survive the changes that will happen in our time."

Changes of our Past World Cycles

Now Michael mentions, "Some people know of the Biblical form of creation and accept it, but not all want to challenge how that information came into existence, or how the six days of creation were derived. I mentioned this subject earlier."

"The information that I am going to tell you is part of my knowledge as a guardian when I was on Atlantis over 100,000 years ago, and of which I am still a part. The information exists, but it has been hidden from human eyes and buried under the ocean floor for over 20,000 years."

"Now you and many others might or might not accept this information until the time comes for the records to be available once again. As I was a guardian then on Atlantis, I am still a guardian today. I still keep my promise. The time is coming and approaching fast."

Even to this day people of Earth still believe that this star system was created in a six-day period out of nothing.

Michael continued on explaining:

What you will come to learn here are the true definitions of the six cycles of life. With these definitions being formal, it should ease your soul in knowing that what is before you, is of good and that it is not your soul's first time going through these changes. Your soul has gone through this change hundreds or even thousands of times, but with a new physical body each time. More than half of Earth's population accepts the Bible, and a good majority believe that there has to be more than that, because of everything that is going on today. Let go of everything that you had learned through the years! Clear your mind of everything that you think you know.

Clear your mind of the questions that you have.

Prepare yourself, as you are about to go on a journey back several hundred million years ago, to a time of the structuring of the planets in this star system.

CYCLE 1~

During the beginning of the planets, there was a time of eternity that had existed. The planets were and always have been around, but in a different form of mass, not in the way your Sun is today.

The solar bodies that existed trillions of billions of years ago were forms of intense structures of living energy, without physical mass. Every planetary body was first a sphere of a high magnitude of an extremely powerful energy that attracts and brings organic mass to create the physical existence. The planets kept their own energy, which they were created from within and around the body structure, these spheres of energy then bind into the solid mass in which it shows that it does really exist there in a form of mass and energy. This began creating the form of energy into a solar body. The solar body was created in a period of a few billion years, but in that time, time did not exist, as we know it today. You might feel that it probably was a few days or years; in actuality, it was billions of years. The planets became a solid mass instead of the field of energy they once were. This brought forth a dramatic change. You knew that someone had to be behind the creation of a planet, which is there now, someone or something that has extreme power to create something out of literally nothing. When that event occurred, it ended one form of existence and brought forth a new form into existence.

This change, or phase, began a new cycle that lasted another several million years before it became suitable for physical form. This new cycle is also still in the time frame of eternity.

CYCLE 2~

The solar bodies that had been created thus far, are not of the dense mass structures that you know of today. The planet structures that were brought forth are of energy form, not yet solid mass but of semi-etheric. That is, if you were to actually touch such an object, your entire body would pass through it, even though that object appears to be solid to our perception. This cycle of creation took several thousands of years to bring the level of large amounts of energy to create a solid planetary body into existence. Even though you have several planetary bodies being constructed at once, they were not all created at the same time. The energy that is part of one creation is different from other creation that is taking place. Therefore, one planet might be constructed millions of hundreds or even thousands of years ahead of another planet. In addition, the one thing that was not in existence during the beginning of this course is life, as you know it to exist today.

Life, as it exists today would not come about for another several billion years on any of the planets that were forming at this stage. Life existed in the same form of energy patterns as the planets in the forms of ectoplasm, (also known as the souls and spirits), until the planet became a solid mass to support life of all kinds, as you know it today. From this time, it took several thousands of years of gearing up for the construction of the energies for atoms and cells for the physical structures that will exist on any particular planet. That planet finally became a solid living being on a large scale within the solar system, and the solar systems became a galaxy, and the galaxies made a universe, and so on.

All planets are alive and have some form of life even though you could not see or touch them. It was as real as everything around you now, but in a different existence. When that phase was complete, the planet was formed in a physical status, which became a solid mass like the Earth. This new planet was barren. Life did not exist at this time, but life could travel to these new planets, as one might travel from country to country on your current planet or even to the moon and were able to bring your own food there.

Nevertheless, it was not yet time for this new planet's own life to come forth.

Before life could come forth on the planet, the planet needed to go through a change of the structure appearance, so its own life could be sustained for a long period. This change was a dramatic geological reconstruction, which brought forth the atmosphere so that vegetation could begin to grow. The planet's own life would still not be present until millions of years had come to past. The beings that had encountered this planet in its early stages of energy before this sphere of energy became a physical body, had created their own cities of energy as these beings was also of energy that brought the Earth or any other planet into existence. It was only ten thousand years after these spirits/souls came to this planet. When they started to see the planet's first stage of transformation on the planetary scale, the earth became a physical structure and brought the attention to life forms that were of a physical form, as these souls and spirits continually watched as these physical beings arrived on this new world.

Book 1 – The Reawakening

CYCLE 3~

The planet's life might seem as though it was created in a blink of an eye to us. That is because time did not exist; in reality, thousands of years had passed to bring forth the planet's life into existence. Remember, the Earth had gone through several changes to make the Earth habitable for physical life, it took several thousand of years. The first of many physical humanoid beings, were as religion will call it the Adam and Eve race. The life that came to earth in physical form was from other planet from other star systems.

Several hundred thousand years later the life form which was in soul and spirit had gone through a metamorphosis stage. The life that existed then was so different to what you were brought up to think on how life was during this cycle. The life of these beings, energy and physical, lived as separate beings.

Some of the life forms that were on this planet, came from off worlds, were of mammals, reptilians, and humanoids.

After a million years of these beings living separately, all beings went through a metamorphosis stage, which was brought on to a great alignment with our star (Apsu) and with several other stars aligning with the center of the Milky Way Galaxy, which also aligned with the known center of our universe, which occurs once every 325,000-year cycle. When this cycle occurs all beings physical and soul, go into a dormant sleep and the physical, soul and spirit beings will merge into each other or they will become separate depending on the cycle they are in. As these beings fell asleep, and some of their technology was left on but most of their technology remained turned off. Building structures stayed intact during these beings long slumber.

After about one hundred years, these beings of both energy and physical had reawakened from their metamorphosis slumber and started their new life. No one had knowledge about these large buildings and they knew not of its technology, so they went on with their life anew.

At this time, these two types of beings of energy and physical were merged into an existence unlike anything that they both had ever experienced.

The life that was in existence on this world was of all types, small and extremely large reptilians and mammals along with the humanoids that roamed the land, sea, and air. These beings had existed there for about five thousand years without their sleeping technology and without any other forms of life. That is until other beings decided to inhabit this world as well. This new inhabitant did not start its growth on Earth either, but on another planet in a different solar system. This other planet was much like your solar system but thousands of years ahead of Earth's first inhabitants whose technology still lies mostly dormant.

The new life I am mentioning here is the human race, which was created in the Lyra constellation several thousand light years away. Keep in mind, this

Book 1 – The Reawakening

race was different; they were not what you would think of as your Adam and Eve. The beings that came to Earth arrived here to help step up the planet's physical energy and to pass along their knowledge to the life that might exist on this planet, if any, (they were surprised to find buildings and technology, and inhabitants that had no conscious knowledge of this sleeping technology). These humanoid beings knew that this technology had to belong to these inhabitants, because there were no other life forms among these beings. Their buildings and starships remained intact, it was as if they were asleep and upon awakening, they had no knowledge to their own technology. This race of humanoid beings was more highly evolved than you can imagine, by hundreds of thousands of years. Imagine this race on your world right now with all their knowledge and technology.

This race had also established several colonies on this world that were called Lemuria and MU and lived with the original beings. After some time had passed the original beings had grown accustomed to these humanoids, and some of the original beings that were here on Earth were willing to have their memory reawakened so they could use their own technology that had been turned off for about six thousand years. During the next four hundred thousand years, these three civilizations coexisted on this planet in peace and in harmony. All of these beings worked together and one civilization did not expect more or less cooperation from the others than each would give.

After those four hundred thousand years passed, their cycle was ending and life changed.

Then the Earth tilted on its axis, and life that was large and heavy was destroyed by means of being trapped by water, lava, and earthquakes. The life that could not adapt to the changes in climate, temperature, and most of all land, that life died off. The other most severe changes were the shift of the direction of the energy patterns on the planet. For this destruction did not happen overnight or even in a year or two, instead it took about a hundred years to bring this cycle of life to an end.

Therefore, what life did escape death and managed to adapt to the new way of living on this world, helped bring in the new cycle and changes. The ones that survived also struggled in keeping their technological knowledge alive, so they would have it after the changes were complete, unlike their last experience. As during the last cycle other civilizations came from across the stars to see if they could offer assistance to raise the new vibrations and to help heal the beings and the earth in their next step of existence.

Some beings that came to assist the inhabitants of the Earth were human, humanoid and humanoid dolphin (the grays but with more human structure). These beings came from AL-AN-RA, a group of stars in the Orion constellation. They helped in creating new colonies such as Mu, Lemuria, Easter Island and many others, except Atlantis - which came later.

This new energy change came around 100,000 years ago and lasted for a couple thousand years.

However, life was so different for them that you might find it difficult to imagine what it was really like. All of the beings that survived interacted with each other in ways you would not bring yourself to imagine. It was during this epoch that the half-man and half-animal was created along with the combining of off-world half-man-animal beings. These beings of half human-animal were not to be looked at by today as being devils. Churches imply that the devil is half human-animal, but THEY ARE NOT devils or demons. They had a mishap because of all the energies of the solar system that were turned around and they were not accustomed to that much energy alterations. Unlike the last cycle, the change was planetary. This next cycle of energy vibrations had encompassed several light-years across space. All these beings were created out of good. I ask you to accept this form of life as being good, and NOT THIS EVIL that the churches are making it look like. Evil is only negativity, and all life on and off the Earth is of positive and negative energy. Therefore, do you see why I ask you to accept these beings of the past and current times?

CYCLE 4~

The beginning of Atlantis was about 100,000 years ago. The beings that created Atlantis were from an off-world culture. They came from the Pleiades, which are in the Taurus constellation. This system consists of about 200,000 Suns and out of that, roughly 50,000 suns are considered wanderers and our Earth sun, known as Apsu, is one of them. The Pleiades consist of hundreds of thousands of cultures and beings. Some of the systems of the Pleiades were warring races; but most of them were of the peaceful type. Some of the peaceful beings were fleeing wars and set up colonies across the Milky Way galaxy on the wandering Pleiadean system worlds. The Pleiadeans knew exactly what was going on with one of their sister worlds because they too had gone through something similar in the last cycle thousands of years ago. Soon after the polarities had shifted and settled down, the Pleiadeans began to arrive and setup their colonies on Earth.

After several hundred years had past, some of those earlier scientists that arrived during the beginning of Atlantis had returned to Earth for their next embodiments. As some of the Pleiadean souls returned to Earth for their next embodiments, some of them were scientists and some began to become involved with altering the DNA as they started to create beings of half –human and animal.

Some of the scientists knew that using this technology was wrong and they joined with other Atlanteans to help separate these two merged beings with the use of the crystal device. Of course, these beings had the choice of free will to be separated and, nothing more. The process of separating the two trapped souls and physical beings in these merged bodies was long and hard.

After twenty thousand years had passed, when a new Atlantis race was being born, the souls that were reincarnating at this time were from the last energy shift. After they had been separated from their half human and animal bodies, they were still drawn to the intimacy with human and animal. In addition, the aid of new scientists did not help matters either during this time. Despite the warning that the guardians had put forth five thousand years previously to the scientists about the genetic alterations and their instructions to monitor the DNA and cell structure along with the energy polarity. Some of the original scientists that had helped during the last energy mishap were noticing something peculiar was happening.

The new reincarnating souls were still carrying the old energy with them into their new lives; some of them became scientists and started their own genetic alterations of the DNA and cell structuring. Therefore, the call went out to the guardians asking for their assistance in this matter.

In addition, the warning was given to the new reincarnating souls to stay away from this old pattern of energy.

This is what was told to the new beings:

A genetic alteration of cells and polarities of the two bodies beginning on the first day of conception, will have a dramatic conflict between the two DNA. You do not know what you are creating, nor do you know what it might do to you or us. You do not know what their actions might be towards us, or what dramatic destruction might happen just by having their energy polarities present on this planet. From their existence here and created by man himself, we know for sure that we are creating an event that we cannot live with. The karma that we ourselves create will stay here for the length of our cycle, and far ahead into the future. Life will have to deal with what we have created. They will feel our karma that started in our time. Nevertheless, we will feel the full force of our own karma that we created, as well as that of the future of this planet. We cannot take and alter the patterns of life to what we want on this planet or any other. By taking this action, to continue creating this form of human-animal life, and as we accept the true meaning of their existence on this plane of dimension that this planet is at, we need to stop these creations for our own good. Who is to say, that at a different time and dimension in the far future that the people of the earth will look at these beings in the same loving way, even though it was wrong to create them? Who is to say, that they would understand why we created these beings? Would they understand the truth about how that form of life really started, and why it came to happen the second time around?

The changes that this planet was experiencing at that time quickly brought forth the presence of energy changes, and from that created polarity patterns that the people were not ready to experience. Some of the beings cooperated in being removed from the pain and suffering they were experiencing while understanding that they were caught in an energy pattern of long ago. They knew it was from the displacement of energy at the end of the last cycle. The people of Earth were glad that these changes were finally complete.

Nevertheless, they did not consider this and did not heed the warnings from the Guardians; they had, had a whole lifetime of destruction from the misuse of the knowledge. What they had already gone through was only the beginning of a larger change that had yet to happen due to the misuse of crystals and the universal knowledge.

Similar to the first warning, the people did not listen to the Guardians' warning about interfering with the DNA.

The second warning was about the misuse of the universal knowledge and the use of the crystals and warring. Crystals had already been used for good to help the matadors during the previous ten thousand years. This stage started their second phase in their destruction, but they did not notice it for four thousand years. This was 75,000 years ago. The destruction that came at this time was more severe by a hundred times than what they witnessed during the first stage of their upheaval thousands of years before.

The first stage of their upheaval was mainly focused on them and their way of living, and some changes in the land they lived on, and changes in the environment.

The second stage was very dramatic, unbelievable, and breathtaking. This one series of changes lasted for about eight thousand years. It consisted of mainly changing the planet structures and the polarities of the planet, along with the energies of every being that existed on this planet at that time. This phase consisted of several changes including, a massive energy restructuring in the souls that were on this planet at that time. There was the destruction in some lands where they had misused the energy. There were massive changes for the polarities deep within and around Earth. There were slow changes of giant bodies of water moving over parts of the lands to cover them, so they could not be used again for several thousand years. This also included the beginning of the tilting of the Earth once again and the everlasting changes of the polarities as well. This affected all life, climates, as well as the water. The eight thousand years of catastrophes that all the world's civilizations had just gone through were far from being over. They now had the worse event of them all staring them right in their faces for their next fifty thousand years. For many souls knew that this time the destruction that was before them would destroy their civilization that was on this planet. The Guardians of the universal knowledge started making the necessary preparation to preserve their knowledge, for the future inhabitants to discover later. They did this so the universal wisdom that had once governed this planet would not be forgotten and lost forever.

In addition, there was the knowledge of what would happen if this knowledge was applied in the wrong way. Along with what the misuse of the energy could do to a civilization, or to the planet or even on a large scale, like the universes.

About 26,000 years ago, the Earth went to its new polarities position (the position the Earth is in now). There were large earthquakes and volcanoes activated that had been asleep for the previous four thousand years, along with very large tidal waves from two to four hundred feet walls of water crashing over bodies of land to cover them up for thousands of years. It was during this last phase of destruction that these civilizations made their preparation to return to their home worlds that they once came from, along with agreeing on returning to the Earth after these changes were complete. Not all the people wanted to leave their new home, some stayed just in case they had a chance of surviving this change. They would be here to assist in the new cycle along with the new life that would come about from this change they had created many thousands of years ago for themselves.

Twenty-four thousand years ago, after the Earth had settled down once again, and those that had survived, started getting their lives together and they had no memories of this great civilization of universal wisdom that they were once a part of.

This brings us to a point about 2,000 years after their last destruction. It was at this time that the humanoid ancestors had returned to Earth from their home worlds to see if any of their ancestors on Earth had survived.

When these star travelers returned to Earth they only found remnants of their cities standing and they had been abandoned. There were only about five to ten thousand different beings on the planet out of the original fifty million. The people that stayed behind for their own reasons appeared as they took a few steps backwards in their understanding of the universal knowledge about a couple hundred thousands of years that they lived with. These survivors had no memories of their own kind from the stars. Their own fate lay in their hands, and their destiny was to start from scratch in the universal knowledge, so they could learn from their mistakes. Therefore, once their ancestors arrived, they taught the survivors the universal ways of the ancient knowledge that had once governed this planet.

The star travelers settled in their old abandoned colonies. As the star travelers landed in their abandoned cities they found some of their people asleep in the cryogenic chambers, so they reawakened them, and as these beings begin to awaken they remembered who they are and about their technology. They started teaching the survivors about the universal ways of the ancient knowledge that once was part their old lives. This knowledge was introduced to the surviving beings through a slow process that expanded over the next twelve thousand years.

The beings that were in the cryogenics showed their star brothers and sisters what they had created which was in stasis. These beings were created were of humanoid human form, known from the means of growing humans genetically, similar to cloning. They do not have a bellybutton. As these beings try to explain their intentions to the returning star travelers, " we did this in case all of our lives were ended at least there would be a race of beings that would survive and life would continue on this Earth. This new race of beings will be capable of living for one to ten thousand years of age. Which will give this race a chance of creating a new human race that will have the bellybutton."

CYCLE 5~

In this one cycle, three events happened over a period of five thousand years.

The first event occurred at the end of the last cycle, three thousand years before Jesus' birth. This event consisted of the knowledge of what his mission would be. At this time, this mysterious soul will reincarnate onto Earth once again, to help reveal to the inhabitants, the knowledge of the universal law. For the next three thousand years, this new civilization waited and accepted the writings in their ancient text. Their ancestors said that this text was given to them by the star beings, which claimed and proved that they were their ancestors.

One thousand years ago from then, things began to change, once again. The priests became frightened about this because this being would be born shortly. The priests ordered for those texts that spoke about this highly evolved soul to be hidden and for a new text to be written. However, the new text was written in a way that told people that they should fear the one who will be born. When the time arrived, the priests ordered a massacre of all newborn males and boys up to five years of age. This went on for about couple of months. The priests did not want this being to have a chance to live and bring his knowledge into existence once again.

Despite the massacre, the parents of Jesus were able to leave the area prior to hearing a warning during their dreams, only to begin a journey for the rest of their lives. Although many years had passed, Emmanuel (Jesus) was able to elude the priest and the soldiers that were still trying to find him to kill him. Emmanuel (Jesus) was able to learn of the universal knowledge, and to begin his teachings to all those that followed him. Emmanuel (Jesus) learned of this wisdom from the ancient people, the ones who return to Terra from the star system known as the Pleiades.

Half way into teaching his followers Emmanuel (Jesus) was found by the soldiers and the priests had him murdered. They thought he died on the cross, but he was actually in a coma. After Emmanuel (Jesus) awoke from his coma, he lived to about 135 year, not the age of 32 when he has on the cross. Two hundred years after his death at 135, he was known by the name of Jesus.

The second event started right after Emmanuel's (Jesus') so-called death on the cross, which brought forth his disciples teachings, as they were instructed by Emmanuel (Jesus). Some teachings that Emmanuel's (Jesus) disciples were doing were the continuation from where Jesus left off. The disciples taught this teaching to millions of people about the ancient universal knowledge for about forty years. This knowledge went against what the church religion was teaching. The priests were trying to regain the church order after what Jesus' teachings did to the community. The church changed the true meaning of what the universal law consisted of. The original knowledge of the universal laws that is taught by the star beings is this; "Life is a constant in all forms weather it is energy or physical. There are no God's or Devil's. The physical body lives without a soul or spirit. All life is bound with both positive and negative energies; all life is created by energies, thoughts and evolutions. Above all there is no one to judge you for what you have done in your life. This is the true knowledge about life in the universes all around you." The knowledge that the original disciples taught and their followers would continue was the universal knowledge until about 800 AD, at which time the teachings would go into a recession, which lasted for eleven hundred years until it was reawakened around 1947 AD. During these years of recession of the ancient knowledge, the religions that were present during this time seemed to be of chaos or a backwards civilization in beliefs.

This view was only noticeable to the people that kept the universal knowledge to themselves, and only wrote them down and taught privately. They knew what would happen to them if the church heard what they were doing, and were involved in this forbidden knowledge. They would have been put to death by the means of being burned at the stake or stoned to death. After this recession of knowledge reached the end, and was reawakened so that the universal knowledge could be with a new generation of the true understanding of the universal law.

This reawakening began the third and final stage in the year of 1947. In 1947, an interstellar starship crashed in Roswell, New Mexico. This world would not be the same after this occurrence. From that first crashed ship, the North American government began to construct a special team to collect and hide this evidence from the public in any way possible. Cover-up stories were produced in hopes that the people would forget the incident after awhile.

However, the people did not forget. More and more people became interested and involved in it by the thousands. Many of them became interested by becoming contactees as the years went by. There were many investigations and the first hand contactees like myself, feel that our own government has been in the wrong by withholding this information from the public. For we know the same information as our so-called government plus more, and we accept our responsibility on what we think in our life, that we are the creators of what happens in them. It is hard to believe that our own government would do something like this, in hiding this important information from the public. The public has to find this information on our own, in a way of speaking. No one knows when the government and the religions will release the true information about these other beings that are amongst us.

They tend to release only a little of this knowledge at a time. The one thing that our government and the religions need to accept is that more than half of the population of Earth has had a contact with these beings in one form or another.

I know that there are many more people with the same thoughts as I have had. We want the government and the world religions to release all the information to the whole world on these beings. Their knowledge is not only for the government, but it is for every single being that lives upon this planet earth. We are all here on this planet to learn and progress on the evolutionary scale on the universal knowledge. No one government or religion has the right to hide this knowledge and wisdom from any being that wishes to learn of the off-world beings that are among us. This is a planet for all life to live on, to learn from, and to take responsibility in what we have created for ourselves to go through and learn from our mistakes so that we do not continue on that road of our past. We can make it better instead of making things worse for ourselves. Do you see, and understand now at the end, why this information must come forth?

The time is over for hiding this universal knowledge and the existence of other beings among us.

We accepted them a long time ago and everything they have to offer us, and they accepted what we have to offer to them. We all benefit from everything that we have to offer to every being that exists in or on, and off this planet, in one form or another.

CYCLE 6~

This event is one of the most important cycles that this world and the people in it will ever witness.

You have entered the null zone of your new cycle in the year 1985, which brought the beginning of peace making of the countries of this planet. However, the corrupted government is in charge, and this is not a united planet. Nevertheless, like all cycles, there is a period between the end and the new beginning that gives the planet time to change.

The time in between the two cycles might vary depending on what is coming for the inhabitants of the planet. You will see this new cycle in your life at the beginning of the year 2000, but, before then, there will be dramatic changes started in 1985 and becoming completed by 2025, which will start our new age. The changes that will be taking place are important in bringing the people together for peace and freedom, also the changes around the world will bring forth volcanoes, earthquakes and massive world coastal flooding. The world governments will change into one to end the world of multi-governmental jurisdictions that will come to bring the people of this world together. There will be massive upheaval in this world in the last decade before the new century comes into play. These changes are from floods and large earthquakes. Land that has been misused will be covered by large bodies of water creating new oceans and revealing new lands that were covered for the past twelve thousand years. These changes along with the tilting of Earth's axis and or the magnetic poles will be witnessed by the current inhabitants of the Earth.

You are all going to be part of the changes and not everyone will survive these changes. For those who do survive, it will be a new place, a new planet for the future. In this cycle, there will come the revealing of the universal knowledge that has been kept hidden from many of you for four thousand years. Through the change, learning of this wisdom will come as well as the everlasting peace that all people on this world have been waiting to experience. Besides having peace, there will also be eternal life for the souls. All beings have this choice to make if you want to take physical part in these changes or if you would like to leave through death so that you do not have to take part in these changes, this is freewill, it is there for everyone to decide on what you what to experience in your life.

Your new life within this era is really a step up in the physical and spiritual evolutionary ladder of unlimited knowledge of the universal wisdom. In this era, you will learn to develop into multi dimensional beings. You will use the knowledge that has been hidden within yourselves all these thousands of years. The missing link to human evolution has been inside each one of you for thousands and thousands of years. It never left, not even for a second; you just did not want to take on the responsibilities that you had been taught all through your life that there is a being that will take on your responsibilities for your thoughts, actions so that you will not burden yourself with them. So you burden another being with your responsibilities that has no right to your burdens, what gives you the right to do that? That is what you should be asking yourselves. It is our responsibility to finally take on our own burdens of our own creations of thoughts and actions. From doing this we will finally understand what life is all about and of our evolution in life.

This cycle is known by three names.

The first name is called the New Age. This is an indication of going into the unknown and not knowing what might be coming your way whether it's for the worst or for the better for your soul. However, either way, if you look at it now, you will benefit from your own experiences of these events that are in front of you. Of course, everything you experience will be a step up on the evolutionary scale of existence going towards becoming multidimensional beings.

This New Age is really a point in time where the soul of every being has the chance to start the beginning of their new life in another cycle of life, or another dimension of existence.

The other name for this cycle is the Second Coming of the Christ. This name indicates the awakening of the hidden knowledge that Emmanuel (Jesus) once taught and from those ancient star beings ages ago. We all have the same powers and abilities as they did all those ages ago this is the knowledge of the universal language that we all are part of since the beginning of time. Jesus showed the people of his time what they were able to do after a period of time that had gone by, but we will be able to perform more than what Jesus had shown us in the past. Therefore, the coming of the second Christ is not a single person who has the same powers that Jesus once had. Instead, it is the awakening of the souls of every being to show that they too are the creators of their lives, and no one else is, but themselves.

This is what the awakening of the universal knowledge is. This knowledge is about what binds all beings together, as all beings evolve into becoming multidimensional beings.

The third name that you will hear in time will be called the God Source. This is the involvement in the universal mind, all the souls acting as one, the ultimate creator. All souls will rejoin as one form of the universal mind. This is the ultimate universal knowledge that all mankind has been in search of for the past five thousand years, within this segment of the soul evolution, comes the light eternity, but only through the acceptance of the knowledge that comes from within the body, soul and spirit. All of these events are part of the universal plan of becoming perfect inter-dimensional and multi-dimensional beings. Meaning, up until now, you are only able to exist on one plane of existence at one time physically. You will coexist in any dimension, at your own free will of thought.

The meaning of the six-days of creation mentioned in the many texts and stories within the Bible as it is written, the stories in the accepted Judeo-Christian bible have been changed and mingled to suit the needs of those many cultures, religions and governments that create fear and work to control the masses.

The six days of creation is truly about the six cycles of our evolution and the transition of Earth, along with the human evolutional transformation as well that will be around or at the end of the year 2012.

December 21, 2012 will start our 7th cycle of life and a new beginning for all life on earth, the earth itself, and the Milky-Way Galaxy, as well for all life that is within the Milky-Way Galaxy. The old way of life as we all know it will end and there will be a new beginning for all of us.

Chapter 7

The Energy of the Ancients

Time passes and as the end of spring, 1988 approaches, Kiazer's dear friend of three years, Sharon, calls him to see if he is busy and if he would like to meet her for dinner. As the night comes Kiazer heads to pick Sharon up from college and they go out for dinner. Sharon is five feet tall, slim, with light brown hair that falls below her shoulders. As they began to eat about ten minutes after arriving at the restaurant, Sharon asks Kiazer a question, "Would you be interested in meeting one of my female friends?" Kiazer replied, "Yes... I would love to meet your friend."

A couple weeks later as May ended Kiazer headed over to pick up Sharon at her mother's home. Kiazer and Sharon went to meet with Cindy at her parent's home a couple of miles away on the south side of the city on the other side of the river that separates the city of Elmira. As they arrived at Cindy's parents home they learned that her father had passed away a month ago in April. Cindy and her two brothers had moved out of their parents home, and the whole family was blaming each other for their father's passing. Cindy and two of the three brothers went and rented a home together and Cindy's mother had no idea on where they moved to, since they did not want their mother to know where they had moved to until all had eased up from blaming each other.

A couple of weeks later on June 14, Kiazer headed over to see Sharon at her mother's home. Kiazer learned that Sharon had left to travel around the continent of North America. Therefore, Kiazer was left to find Cindy on his own. A couple of weeks later Kiazer stopped at a post office to see if he could find Cindy's address by using her mother's address and the postal clerk was able to find Cindy's address. Kiazer drove over to his friend Jeff's home to drop off his mail that went to Kiazer's home and then Kiazer headed over to see about meeting with Cindy on his own.

When Kiazer was one block from Cindy's house, he stopped at a red traffic light to turn left and there was a car in front of Kiazer, as Kiazer waited for the light to turn, he listened to a voice saying, "the lady in the car in front of you is Cindy your wife to be." He felt the presence of the lady in the car. I bet that is Cindy in the car in front of me, he thought to himself.

When the traffic light turned green, the lady turned left and then two houses down she turned into the driveway of her home as Kiazer pulled over and stopped in front of her house. Kiazer waited a couple of minutes, and then he got out of his van and headed up to the door. He paused for a couple of seconds before he knocked.

The door opened and a young twenty-two year old lady stood in the doorway. There was a pause for a second that felt like an eternity to Kiazer as his thoughts drifted. Cindy was exactly the way she was shown to him in visions years ago. Cindy is short, four feet eight inches tall, with light brown hair, and green eyes. As they met, both had the feeling that they already knew each another, yet this was their first physical meeting. When Kiazer saw Cindy, he knew that she was going to be his first wife from the visions that he had in the past.

Kiazer introduced himself, "Hi I am Kiazer. Are you Cindy?"

"Yes I am. Come in Kiazer. Sharon told me a lot about you."

As Kiazer entered Cindy's home he replied with, "Sharon did not mention a lot about you, I am glad that I found you. I searched for you on my own these last couple of weeks since Sharon has gone to travel around North America." Kiazer and Cindy spent an hour talking to one another and it was as if they had already known each other for a long time. Cindy had to get ready for work and she asked, "Kiazer I would love for us to get together tomorrow when I am off and we can spend all day with each other. Can we do that?" "Yes, we can. I would love that as well, Cindy, what time would you like to meet." Kiazer replied with excitement in his voice as they exchanged information for the time and place of their next meeting.

The next day arrived and at eleven a.m., Cindy showed up at Kiazer's home and he welcomed Cindy. Cindy entered into Kiazer's home and saw a couple of Kiazer's drawings on the wall and she walked towards two of the pictures and gazed as she said, "very interesting drawings that you do." "Well thank you, Cindy. These drawings are of visions that I have had of a distant world that is not of our star system." As Kiazer went into his bedroom and brought out a dozen of his other drawings, Cindy turned her gaze toward Kiazer's eyes and said, "Kiazer, I would be devoted to learn about the spiritual aspects of the metaphysical world. I am also twenty-five percent Algonquin Indian on my Father's side." Kiazer replied, "I would be honored to teach you about the spiritual world all around us."

Therefore, Kiazer began teaching Cindy about the metaphysical aspects of life, along with the use of crystals, and the worlds that are just beyond sight of the third dimensional world.

On June 28, Kiazer and Cindy had only known each other for two weeks. At this time, Kiazer was about to journey across the country of North America for the next two weeks. Kiazer asked Cindy, "Cindy I have two weeks off for my vacation and I am heading west. I have a question for you. Would you like to join me on this journey?" "I would love to go on this journey with you. I feel it is a journey for both of us. So, yes, I would be glad to accompany you." With this, Cindy hugged Kiazer and kissed him passionately.

Book 1 – The Reawakening

Cindy and Kiazer made their preparations as they packed their backpacks with their clothes, two boxes of food, and the tent as they loaded Kiazer's van to leave Elmira, on Wednesday, June 30, for the western Rocky Mountains of the Continental Divide. They had no idea where they would be heading on their adventure that was waiting for them. During these three days of driving, they found themselves drawn to the Pyramid Mounds of the mid eastern part of the country.

After three days of traveling, Cindy and Kiazer arrived in the town called The Garden of The Gods. Both connected instantly to the high level of energy that was attracting them to this area. The energy they were feeling was coming from within the Garden of the Gods and was welcoming them to a place of peace. This energy was the way things were hundreds of thousands of years ago around the planet and the way the future is to be. This was the peace that Cindy and Kiazer wanted to make for the Earth in the near future for the earth and for the people, with the powers that they both have within themselves that were given to them from birth and from their past lives. As the energies engulfed Cindy and Kiazer, the knowledge within each of them began to reawaken. They knew then that they had an important reason to move out to the Continental Divide to begin their work to help change the energy of the planet by bringing peace and to teach the people what is ahead of them and to understand the changes coming up between 1990 and 2025. Cindy and Kiazer had each been guardians to one of these inner earth entrances at The Garden of the Gods. It has been speculated for about two centuries that the earth has an existence of an inner world. Even the bibles of the world mention in the ages past, there were beings that came from within the world or that beings dwelt within the world.

As Cindy and Kiazer walked through The Garden of the Gods, they gathered energies with their own crystals and of their own Atlantean energy walking staff. These staffs were made of copper tube and to the person's height, with a crystal of the person's choosing that would be placed at the top of the staff as the bottom of the staff would be caped off with a copper cap. The staff would then be wrapped with leather or fur, this will help to insulate the staff for the person's grip and the staff will become warm from the energy collecting within the staff. They found themselves guided to several places to experience the energies that were created by a very large crystal far beneath the surface of the Garden of the God's, which protects information that is within these areas.

The light beings that are present in The Garden of the Gods are guardians or watchers of the many energy domes and of the crystal that holds the knowledge of an ancient civilization that once existed there. Kiazer and Cindy found themselves guided to these areas.

The rest of this chapter contains the photos in their original states showing energy domes and the light beings at The Garden of the Gods.

Book 1 – The Reawakening

    All of these pictures were taken with a 35 mm Chinon camera. These first four pictures were taken in July of 1988.

    The first picture was taken by Cindy Kiser, with the camera on a tripod at about 8 a.m. on a clear day with no clouds. The camera was pointed toward the west, thus there was no sun glare from the rising sun. The camera picked up a cloud formation behind Kiazer and an energy vortex in the area that, for

Kiazer, had bought forth a moment of non-existence of time and space.

At the same time, a gray type of being is seen over where I was standing. From where Kiazer was standing on that outcropping looking down at the camera, he could see a sealed entrance, and at that moment, Kiazer was out of his body and saw himself inside this cave wearing all white pants and shirt. Kiazer was looking out and seeing himself on the outside of this cave, which was a unique experience. Therefore, when Kiazer came down from this outcropping we went over to this sealed entrance and he told Cindy what he just experienced.

Cindy and Kiazer learned later that this entrance was sealed back in 1966.

Book 1 – The Reawakening

Also not too far from the sealed entrance, just a couple of minutes walk to the south we came upon another outcropping. Here we found a large stone head facing toward the north. This is a side view of the head that is about twenty feet in height.

Book 1 – The Reawakening

Book 1 – The Reawakening

A robed left arm can be seen vertically following the crack on the right side near where Cindy has her hand on the rock.

Book 1 – The Reawakening

This is a picture looking to the west towards Pikes Peak in Colorado Springs, Colorado in 1988, with the sun raising in the east around nine in the morning.

Kiazer and Cindy found themselves guided to two of these energy domes. As they entered the same energy dome, they immediately noticed that time and space were nonexistent and they entered into another realm of existence. They found a place to sit so they were both able to meditate to receive the knowledge of the dome. Kiazer and Cindy had brought crystals with them for storing the knowledge that they would come across on their journeys. They found that they could only be in the energy of the dome for no more than fifteen minutes, which was long enough to experience the dimensional shift to the fourth dimension that was present.

As they continued their journey, they were directed to an energy dome that was a short walk to the south from the first stone head. They came upon an area where they were able to feel an energy field.

This dome of energy appeared to be approximately 175 feet long and 40 feet high.

After spending the day at The Garden of the Gods, Kiazer and Cindy went to The Cave of the Winds and Pikes Peak just a short distance from where they were.

Their next destination was to drive over the mountain ranges of the Continental Divide to the western edge of Colorado through the Black Canyon of Gunnison, which is about mile wide, a mile deep and over seventy miles long.

Book 1 – The Reawakening

As Kiazer and Cindy spent a week camping at the Black Canyon of Gunnison, they journeyed around the canyon gathering energies within their own crystals and each of their Atlantean energy walking staffs. Their staffs were made of a copper tube wrapped with leather from top to bottom, with a copper cap on the bottom and a crystal of their own choice. Fur was wrapped around the part of the staff where they held on. The top of Cindy's staff was caped with a clear crystal, as Kiazer's staff was topped with an amber crystal.

After spending those two weeks together, they returned to Elmira. By this time they were experiencing deep affectionate feelings towards each other. They decided it was time to move in together. Kiazer helped Cindy move into his home. A few days later during the evening, Kiazer and Cindy were sitting on the couch talking about crystals and souls-spirits. Cindy looked into Kiazer's eyes while Kiazer returned her gaze she said to him, "Kiazer, ever since we met four weeks ago, I feel deep down within my soul that I have always known you. What does that mean?" Kiazer replied, "We are soul mates, and that means that we have spent some lifetimes together and that we are part of each other, as we come together through sexual union we feel our bodies merging." After a few minutes Kiazer stood up and he walked into the bedroom and brought out a crystal that he works with, to see if Cindy was able to tap into the crystals energies, since Cindy had never ventured into the metaphysical world until the past month.

Book 1 – The Reawakening

Cindy held the crystal in the palm of her right hand, and a few seconds later Cindy began to smile and blush with excitement. Kiazer asked her, "Why are you blushing with a smile?" Cindy replied, "The crystal is asking if I want to spend the rest of my life with you." As Cindy looked into Kiazer's eyes, Kiazer asked Cindy, "Would you love to be engaged and part of my life?" Cindy answered, "Yes, I would love to be your wife." At that moment Kiazer stood up and reached into his pants pocket and pulled out an engagement ring as they gazed into each other's eyes and Kiazer asked the question again as he placed the ring on Cindy's finger. Cindy responded again, with great joy, "Yes, I would love to be your wife." Kiazer and Cindy hugged and Kiazer stood up, as he picked Cindy up in the air as she wrapped her legs around Kiazer's waist. He carried her into their bedroom and they removed each other's clothes and made passionate love for a couple of hours before falling asleep.

Chapter 8

Atlantis

Since 1980, Kiazer had been researching Atlantis with the thought that one day he would travel to an area known as The Bermuda Triangle which through his research he learned was also known as the sunken lost continent of Atlantis in the Atlantic Ocean. Kiazer shared his years of research with Cindy, his new fiancée.

As the fall season of 1988 arrives on the continent of North America, Kiazer and Cindy began to make plans to travel to the Island of Nassau of the Bahamas that lies within The Bermuda Triangle. Kiazer and Cindy greatly anticipated their trip, even though they would be there for a week. They gathered the crystals that they planned to use to gather the information about Atlantis, which they could later retrieve when they returned home. As Cindy finished packing, her clothes and her crystals she asks Kiazer, "From what we both have read about The Bermuda Triangle, do you think we will end up disappearing like others in the past?"

Kiazer turned to look at Cindy and reassured her, "We will not disappear as others have in the past. The energies within The Bermuda Triangle are not active at this time and they will not become active again until after the year 2012. I assure you that we will be fine." Kiazer and Cindy sat on the bed together and Cindy was holding one of her crystals and asked, "I know that I have only been learning about the crystals for about three months, but how does the information become stored in the crystals and how will we be able to retrieve that information?" Kiazer placed his arm around Cindy as he explained, "The knowledge is transmitted by energy and the crystal stores all the information that it receives in that same energy form. Then when it is ready to be retrieved, that information is again sent to us in that same form of energy, and we then translate it into recognized patterns that we can translate into what we can understand. We can then teach others what we have learned."

As they prepared for their trip, Kiazer continued to tell Cindy about the continent of Atlantis, and The Bermuda Triangle. *"For the past twelve thousand years the strangest things been happening in the Bermuda Triangle that have not been explained nor does anyone on the day-to-day basis seem to understand the symbolism of the events that every individual experienced from the energies that they come in contact with from the continent of Atlantis."*

"People might say Earth is as old as history, but they cannot accept what is being found and carbon dated further than known history and they do not want any part of it to be true!"

"For instance, when things are spotted from the air in the Atlantic Ocean within the Bermuda Triangle where Atlantis once stood. The ocean claimed the city that was built on an already mystifying and beautiful, magnificent content well

over 14,000 years ago. The waves ocean floor sits two to three miles below the surface. At the Atlantic trench, the deepest canyons go to another two miles deeper below the surface and there is a sandy white floor bed waiting to be reawakened to be with a new generation. This generation desperately wants to reestablish the ancient code of universal peace among all of life on our world of earth along with all life in our Milky Way Galaxy and of other galaxies that are stretched across our known universes."

"In the years of 1968-1969 started the uncovering of the first landmass of the outskirts of Atlantis with structures on them, and even up through today, these structures are still becoming revealed a little at a time. There is another interesting thing about this landmass as it comes revealed above the sea level after twelve thousand years of being submerged."

Tuesday, October 11, 1988 arrived and Kiazer and Cindy set off on their journey to the Island of Nassau.

Kiazer and Cindy walked across the street to meet with Kiazer's mother, Judy, to let her know that they were ready to go to the airport and begin their journey.

Two days later after returning from the Island of Nassau, Kiazer began retrieving the knowledge of Atlantis from the two crystals that he had taken with him.

Throughout all the countries on Earth and for the past fifteen thousand years, there have always been countless fascinations about this continent of Atlantis along with the fear about this continent.

Kiazer thought about the continent of Atlantis as he held one of his crystals and he retrieved the insights of Atlantis, as he asks questions and receive answers. "Could these fears be brought upon by the disappearances of ships, planes, boats, divers, and along with other strange phenomenal events that date back to the last two thousand years and farther into the past?"

"Could this curiosity be brought forth by the early spotted pyramid structures beneath the shallow water around the new landmass that is beginning to reveal a continent called Atlantis?"

"Or possibly is it because the majority of people do not know what is waiting to be revealed to them? On the other hand, is it the curiosity of finding the truth about our universal origin, our true link in the universes around us?"

Kiazer continued to change the energy of his physical body to link with the crystal to retrieve the knowledge from Atlantis. Within moments Kiazer linked with his crystal and was shown what happens when a being or anything else entered the boundaries of the Bermuda Triangle when the energy was at it's highest in certain areas. Some might say people were incinerated by the energy or that they were stuck in a storm that killed them.

As Kiazer continued his connection with the crystal, he learned:

They were merely transported to another dimension within this world, or they were transported to another universe that lies within and beyond our comprehension of reality, or a parallel existence.

To find the answers to this place of the Bermuda Triangle, Atlantis, we would have to find the incarnated souls that lived during that era. On the other hand, we can find the people that were transported to these other alternative realities. The last place that we could look for this insight to Bermuda Triangle, Atlantis, would be the star beings that have been visiting our world Terra, for more than 100,000 years now.

As Kiazer mentioned earlier you could be transported into another dimension within our existence or any other in the universes that are around us. Let me take this moment to explain to you about this transportation. In this form of teleportation to another dimension on this planet, or to another you need two doorways. These doorways could take you to Terra past, to the future and even to a parallel existence, or even to the other end of this universe and beyond. Other dimensions within the one that you are living in at this moment can be explored. The reason behind the revealing of the land that is still known as Atlantis is to give us the information that is there for all people to know. Many have been trying to figure out about our existence in the Universe as well as the information about the starships that have been watching us for the past 25,000 years. Also revealing this information will explain more about things that are beyond most of the populations comprehension of life. It will help us to understand the spiritual aspects of life, the use of the pyramids, and how to heal with crystals. In the near future more of the lands will be revealed showing man that he is not alone in this Universe, and has never been and never will be alone.

These beings are not any different then you accept that they have been here thousands upon thousands of years before us. Their technologies are far superior to ours, including

Book 1 – The Reawakening

interplanetary travel, along with escaping the aging process as we know of it and many others feats that they have been capable of performing. People have been encountering these beings far back in our history have been keeping records of their visits here on Terra.

The Egyptians of your time looked at these beings as angels, or even at times, they were even looked upon as gods and devils. These beings are not gods or devils. They are as much human as we are. Because their physical appearance is different than ours does not make them any different from us. We have to understand that they are hundreds of thousands years older then us. Even though they are older then we are they are still of humanoid human form even though they do not appear as we do as humans.

As the people of earth enter into the New Millennium, we will learn about the many worlds of the Ancients, such as the time of Atlantis, Mu and Lemuria and many other cultures of those eras.

Will always be an opened question…

Chapter 9

The Fear Creators

Over time, Kiazer begins to learn about the fear creators. The fear creators are the gangs, riots, clans, and killings, this also goes for the governments and religions that control all in keeping the knowledge about certain documents that they see as secret on a need to know basis.

This fear is known as, the thought control over each other and over other countries; this is what they (the governments and religions) do to all.

As I said, I was going to be brief on the destructive THOUGHTS that create this powerful weapon that has been in existence before any other weapons on your planet was created. Now we are going to start explaining these THOUGHTS, which will be the most important and the most seen destructive THOUGHT, and how they are all related.

Government and religious control of keeping knowledge about certain documents secret on A NEED TO KNOW BASIS!!!!!

This has been the most important destructive force on the face of this planet for the past three thousand years. Within the power of this "thought weapon", the governments are the main destructive force. This one world government will tell you their story, and not the truth.

The story that they have been releasing to you is to have the people go about attacking one another. This secret one-world government is implicating their constitution and trying to bring forth martial law.

This is not limited to the continent of North America; it is also many other continents around Earth. There are military troops known as The New World Order that are ready to take control when the governments around the world are ready to call martial law amongst the people. This one world government is also in control of your modern religious figures. This government tells these figures how to run the churches and what information to release to their congregations. The information the religious figures have released confirms the information that the one world government released to the public at an earlier time, through the controlled news media.

Within this type of controlling the people, the churches that are being controlled by these foreign governments and some off-world beings, tell their people that these people that are involved in the paranormal, such as channels, clairvoyants, and others using supernatural abilities is the work of the devil and or the demons. From this view, the church congregation is being manipulated to think that the use of these gifts or powers are evil; that anyone who is involved in a higher awareness is to be considered corrupt, and that they should avoid contact.

The people who have this view towards the metaphysical should be considered corrupted because they are being controlled to think in that fashion because of how this one world government has corrupted the religion around the world. They do not want anyone growing spiritually and becoming free thinkers.

For the past several years, people have became aware that Earth is in danger of becoming destroyed by pollution, greenhouse effects, ozone depletion and waste materials that should be recycled. I would like to take you a step further.

Our world is in even greater danger than by thoughts and destructive habits of the people of Earth. Every thought and action by every person on our world is creating the future. Every thought and action a person puts out returns back to Terra tenfold. Many people do want to take responsibility for their thoughts and actions. For the other people who do not want to take responsibility for their lives, they will live lives of turmoil and self-destruction. The beliefs each person chooses to believe and how they live their lives determines how they will view their lives and Earth.

During the past few years, the world has seen more natural disasters than ever before. We must understand that Terra is going through major changes, and will continue to do so until after the turn of the century. The major changes on Earth affect every living thing and the world as well. Once we all accept this, we will better understand why people and every living thing are changing and acting the way that they are.

In these changes, there are realignments of the magnetic field around the planet and changes of the human DNA structure as well. These events are only the beginning of the major changes that Earth will experience. We all have to take responsibility for our own spiritual growth in our evolution.

This ends the current age, or cycle, of our life.

Our time has come... It is time for us to take that leap into the unknown.

It is time for our New Beginning.

The Time for a New Beginning is Now.

In the city of Elmira, on April 25 1990, two people began to prepare for their special upcoming event.

On May 5, 1990, Michael and Cindy gathered with their invited guests at their wedding at the Christ's United Methodist Church as they united themselves as one. After the service, they welcomed all to attend the celebration of Michael's and Cindy's amalgamation that follows.

Three days after their wedding, Michael and Cindy said goodbye to their families and prepared to go to the eastern side of the Continental Divide around the Garden of the Gods.

As fall began in their new home, Kiazer and Cindy learned about a group of people that had the same ideas that they did. They set out to meet with them to begin teaching their knowledge to this group of people. This group of people also had the same idea of sharing what they know with others.

During their meetings, Kiazer and Cindy shared their knowledge of what they have learned over the years and they spoke of particular events that they reawakened within themselves about the future of their star system and of the Milky Way Galaxy.

Kiazer said at one meeting, "Back in 1981 a vision of our star system showed that it was going to receive a second sun. At the time of viewing these events, I felt the world rumble like being hit by a strong force, much stronger than an earthquake. Our second sun would be seen in the northwest and it would happen around five or six in the evening one late summer day. I feel that it will take place around 2020-2025."

At the year 2030, we will be entering a field of magnificent light, which will last for about 2,156 years. During this, Age of Light will be the age of peace, unity, universal wisdom and knowledge and the unlimited or unconditional love, among many other spectacular events. It will be up to us to take responsibility for our thoughts and actions because no one else is going to be responsible them. There is no God, except the God that we are! Only we create our own destiny! Of course, there are other beings higher than our selves.

Cindy spoke at this time "Of course, there are other beings like ourselves, and these beings are ready to assist us in our spiritual journey to awaken our full

Book 1 – The Reawakening

awareness of who we really are! These other beings are not gods or devils but they are men and women like us on this spiritual road of reawakening. We will come across all types of beings, some more benevolent and some less, along with beings that are at the same level that we are at, at this time.

As time went on, Kiazer continued to learn the deepest knowledge of all life. He learned that we are all part of, and that we are all linked as, one being, yet at the same time we are individual physical beings in many ways. Along with our spiritual being that is within all of us, as this separate being is also experience a form of life through living within us.

As Kiazer met with one of those ancient beings, he learned the importance of all life in the Universe. This goes for all planets as well.

The ancient being said to him, "Within your destruction of humanity, you as a being on your world are going head-on into this destruction, which is a prominent one, unless, all of you change your ways and thoughts. This destruction will not involve nuclear or war-like weapons, but it will consist of a different kind of weapon. This weapon is far older and effective then any weapons that existed or will come to be created from any life on any planet including Earth.

Please, take this as a serious matter concerning this one weapon. This weapon is so dangerous and powerful and IT DOES EXIST ON YOUR PLANET. This weapon is capable of the destruction of life on Earth, as well as on other planets.

I want to mention that this weapon has been used on your world and on other planets that have had the same growth patterns that your world has evolved from.

This weapon has to become respected for truly what it is. Now, for only some of you that read this you will truly understand what I mean by this destruction. Everyone must take his or her responsibility for this one weapon, because it is your own thought. Thought is the destructive powerful weapon, which has been used many times on this planet and on many other planets in your solar system. For example, the planet (Mars) which when it was destroyed it created what you call the asteroid belt.

We would not indulge in the past destruction's since we already talked about them. We will mention to you about the destruction that is at hand, if not all Terrains must change their ways of life…

Kiazer continued to mention the destructive events that all of you are experiencing now and this needs to change NOW…

And Not Later…

Because Later Never Comes!

Kiazer and Cindy told the group about The Garden of the Gods' and what they learned there a couple of years previously.

Book 1 – The Reawakening

A couple of years later during the summer, Kiazer and Cindy made plans with the group to make a trip to The Garden of the Gods.

The next four pictures were taken in June 1992, around 1:30 p.m. The sun was behind us as we looked at the stone outcropping.

In these pictures are, light beings in the form of orbs of multiple colors of light, or energy. In this picture at the top of this ball of light, you can see what appears to be an arm appearing from the left that is also of the similar energy of the balls of light.

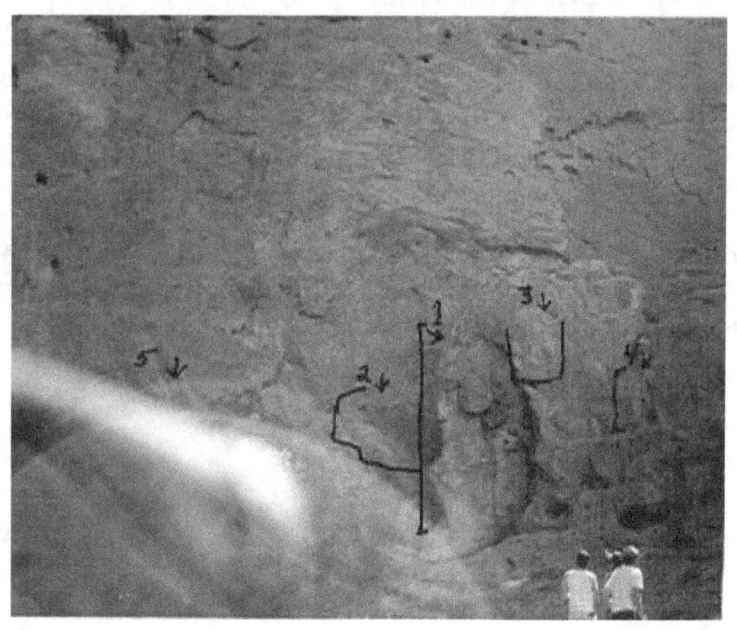

In this picture
#1 The stone head looking to the north.
#2-4 Other stone carved heads.
#5 The ball of light with a arm and hand.

Book 1 – The Reawakening

Book 1 – The Reawakening

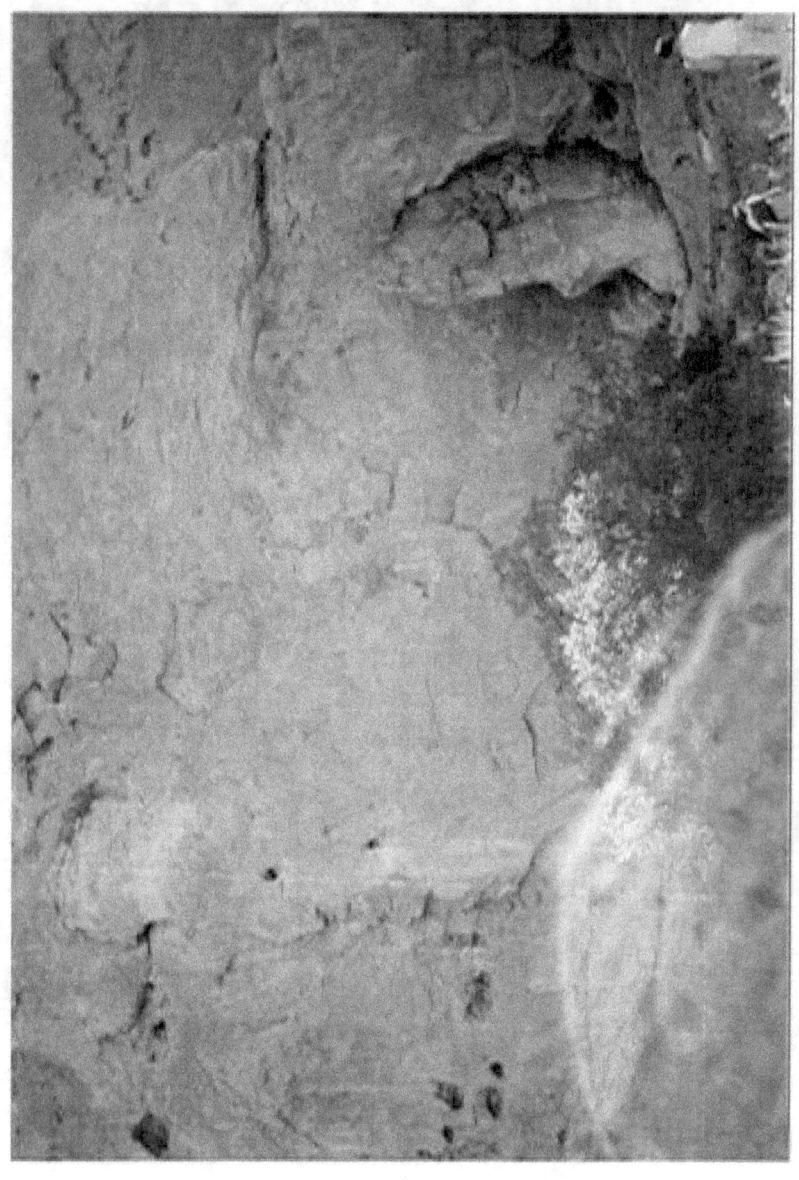

Book 1 – The Reawakening

Book 1 – The Reawakening

Questions and Answers

As Kiazer continues asking questions to the crystal, he receives the answers to relay to everyone.

Q. Why are we being visited? What is the importance behind it?

A. The reason for the visitations to Earth and making contact with certain spiritually awakened beings is because the contactees are awakened and ready for the truth that has been with them during their past lives and are ready to receive the Universal Truth. That way, they can pass on what they learn, and go on to the next level of existence, leaving the third dimension of reality behind and moving to the fourth and fifth dimensions.

Q. Where do these Star Travelers come from?

A. These beings are from your neighboring star systems such as the Pleiades, Zata 1, 2 Reticule, the Orion constellation, Sirius, Lyra, and many others as well.

Q. How should we look at the beings that are visiting our world and making contact with us?

A. Through all ages of time, all civilizations have looked at us as being gods. We are not gods. We are men and women like you, only more attuned and spiritually awakened. It had taken us several thousands of years to get to this place, like you.

A Message for All to Hear

An Ancient being is manifested in front of Kiazer. This being is of a human type; it is bald with bronze skin hues. The being wore a light tan hooded robe with a white rope tied around his waist. One end of the white rope was longer than the other end and had ten knots and gold tassels on both ends. This being sincerely told Kiazer, "Recently the human race has begun its spiritual awakening along with awakening new technology. You have been able to find out things that have been kept dormant for about twelve thousand years. This explains our interest in your species and your planet and star system. Your awakening is what has drawn us to you, along with the new technology that your scientists have been experimenting with for the last fifty to sixty years. If it is not used properly, it will destroy the star system and it will affect the surrounding star systems. That is why we are here, to help change your course of warring and destructive ways. If we cannot persuade you, then you leave us the only other choice, which is to intervene in your course of destruction. Since 1985 that is exactly what we had started, and will continue to do so, until all warring beings are removed from Terra. This process will go into the year 2020.

Therefore, by the year 2030, this planet will be in its full embracement of light that Earth is supposed to be. The New Era of Light will last for 2,156 years.

In 1993, another event was shown to Kiazer similar to the event when he was fourteen years old back in New York. This time he was shown the sun that we have today going through a restructuring so that the sun will die out for a period, restructure its crystalline body, and change its polarities at the same time. The sun would then shine again but will have a different light. This light is of positive energy. This event will take place around 2005-2015.

Chapter 10

The Creation of the Gods and the Devils from Off-World Alien Races

Kiazer continued to work with his crystals to unlock the knowledge of the Universes about the god and devil theories that had been passed down for the past twelve thousand years. He learned that the gods and the devils for the past twelve thousand years had been created by off-world beings.

Upon learning this, Kiazer asked aloud, "How can this be possible?"

For all, truth and knowledge are within...

There were no gods or devils mentioned in any of the cultures on Earth prior to the last global flood twelve thousand years ago. It was then, when the creation of your gods and devils were put into the minds of the inhabitants of this world. To this day, this is where these gods and devils remain alive, in the minds of the inhabitants. For the past twelve thousand-years there has been off-world influence upon the religions of Earth. Some of the alien beings looked into our thoughts and fears and used them against us to bring our fears into manifestation. These manifestations were of good and seventy-five percent were of the most terrifying events. From that moment on, the beings that took the appearance of these gods and devils have been programming the inhabitants and keeping them under the veils of illusion. Some of these off-world beings knew if they could manifest the thoughts of these inhabitants that they (the alien race) had a good chance of becoming these gods and devils. Through that magnifying thought, they increased the inhabitants thoughts tenfold.

    These beings and the inhabitants had their roles to play out from that moment on. Unfortunately, it turned out to be serious and the karma was to be played out to the end, until a future age where the inhabitants began to alter their thoughts and take responsibility for their thoughts and actions. Over the last twelve thousand years there have been hundreds of gods that people had come to pray under and to ask for protection from these so called devils, which are all part of the same being. The people have not been aware that these two beings of light and dark were the same. The beings that were acting as those gods and devils have been casting fear into the minds of the people by using natural world changes as the means of the End Times. Those beings were also bringing forth wars and disease. As long as we let this fear control us, then we will let it consume us. As long as the minds of the people contribute fear to their own creations of gods and devils, they will forever remain alive, and bring forth war and famine into the people's minds as they see it.

Those gods and devils have been given different names through the ages, but they are all of the same thought. Through the ages, the humankind has felt they needed some form of deity to represent good and evil, (light and dark / positive and negative). These gods and devils were to represent all events on and off Terra, or in other words (upon the Earth and in the Heavens / Space).

Those beings had no need for the concerns of the well being of the inhabitants of this world. They were mainly feeding off the fear, then acting out a play that was started several thousands of years ago.

Mankind had grown accustomed to the creation of these gods and devils that were created from their own thoughts without their awareness.

Even to this day people still believe in Gods and Devils and still do not ask any questions about their whereabouts, after their departure well over two thousand years ago, the people of today still fear their gods and devils return at the End Time...

Today we might stumble across an ancient cave or temple drawings of gods and devils being described as being benevolent or half-man –half-animal. Yes, these beings did exist, but not in the way, you have been taught to look at them. Those beings were of good as explained earlier. Those beings that were acting as gods and devils acted upon your thoughts and turned them into stories that you have been told and it was you that turned everything inside out, to look the way you wanted it to be.

The Battles with Alien Races and Humankind

Therefore, this begins the second epoch of the wars between the lower beings and the benevolent ones.

As Kiazer delves deep into earth's history through the many texts that are out there within the stories of the Bibles of the world he learns the following:

Several battles took place within the last seven thousand years including:

Seven Thousand years ago, the wars of the lower entities and the benevolent ones were waged against each another for this sector of this Universe. The survival of Light or Dark would reign over this Universe. The forces of Light had stepped back and let the forces for Dark create havoc. At the same time, the forces of Light had put aside their teachings and put the emphasis on the secret battle against the Dark forces.

Five thousand years ago set the scene for the Tower of Babel. This is where the so-called gods and devils began to punish the people for trying to learn of the Universal Laws and Truth, and of spiritual awakening. The benevolent beings would not have kept the people from learning the Truth.

During the same period as The Tower of Babel, the benevolent ones had brought forth the Ark of the Covenant, which was to aid in the battle of Light and

Book 1 – The Reawakening

Dark. The Ark of the Covenant was an off-world device, which amplifies the energy of Light to overthrow and offset the veils of illusion. Therefore, the people may have the chance to learn the Universal Truths.

Four thousand years ago began the wars of the lower entities and mankind.

2140 years ago, started an epoch of man against man, religions against religions, and still to this day we are under the veils of illusion, and are being controlled by the lower entities. The battle of Light and Dark is still being fought out in secrecy, as more and more people are learning about the Universal Truth, along with learning that we have all been lied to and controlled, and kept from our own right to grow and awaken to the full spiritual understanding of evolution.

Now, at the 21st Century we are going into a new beginning.

At this new beginning, for those who are ready to lift the veils of illusions from their consciousness, you will totally understand the truth of the meaning of the terms Armageddon and Judgment. This is your own undoing not the so-called gods and devils. This is where you and you alone, take the responsibility of your own judgments, along with your own battle of light and dark. No one is going to take the first step in your battle. It is totally up to you to take the steps to overcome the veils of illusions and become one with everything around you!

Dimensional Shifting

Since 1940, Earth's energy had been accelerated extremely to bring forth the Age of Aquarius. In doing this, Terra had started its dimensional shifting, which brought Earth to her next step of going from the third dimension to the fourth and fifth dimensions.

As of 1989-1993, the Earth had again accelerated her frequencies. This is where we noticed the weather and climate literally changed overnight. Things will continue to change through 2020-2035.

After the New Millennium, and around 2005-2020, we will be noticing a dramatic change in the planet. For instance, the planet becoming literally pulled apart, this is where Earth will separate and there will be two worlds. Remember in early chapters that I mentioned of a time that the earth would go through a time of darkness and a time of light for three days or so. This is part of that dimensional shift; this has been seen and has been called several names such as the End Times, the Photon Belt, and the Masonic Ring.

If earth needs to be pulled apart to create two earths, one planet will remain at the state it is in, in the third dimension, for the people that need more time to learn at a slower pace, to continue with war, conflicts and to find their place in life. This planet will have no knowledge of the other world that they had been separated. The third dimensional world will continue to develop and grow at a slower pace that they can deal with.

Then the third dimension world will also become fourth dimensional around 2100-2150 AD. At that time that world will become aware of their sister world that had separated from them previously, and will be allowed a limited interaction and returning back to their own world of fourth dimension.

For this third dimensional world, time will still exist, but in a different matter.

The second planet will have its Quantum Leap in Ascension, peace and light, of living in fourth and fifth dimensions simultaneously. The beings of this world will be aware of the third dimensional planet that they were part of earlier and can interact with those beings and continue to assist them in their spiritual growth, with a new belief system that would be structured before the separation begins. For this fourth and fifth dimensional world, time will no longer exist for these beings. These beings are free from linear time and space, making them the multi dimensional beings that they have been waiting for.

For the past several thousand eons…

I discuss the emergence process of Ascension.

Let me just say this, some will be in awe, a few will be spell bound, some will not know what to think about this, while the rest of you will know it to be the truth of things. The knowledge that you read is all true, and as mentioned through this whole book, the actual records of what I have said will be revealed to you, and to all life on Terra in time. That moment is approaching fast, faster then some of you can imagine and faster then some of you want it to be.

Others are waiting for this time to arrive…

…This knowledge has been awakened slowly, about 3,000 years ago; we were leaving the energies of Aries, then as we enter the age of Pisces, which ended not to long ago around the year 1900, which this time created conflicts, wars, and confusion. Now as the year 1900 comes about, we all start the protest of these wars. This event brought us into our next stage that started the Age of Aquarius, the age of peace, light and the emergence. Which would take about 150 plus years to bring humanity to this point, this point will be around 2010-2025, this is when the full consciousness of humanity would go to an Ascension, a Quantum Leap, in full Spiritual Awakening, overnight. This knowledge was brought into existence by several groups of highly evolved beings called Guardians, Keepers, Watchers or Overseers. These beings were enveloped in the Universal Laws, that Govern, or binds, all life and the Universes together.

This knowledge was assembled for one reason, which is that all life in existence would be taught the Universal Laws. These laws consist of information about the steps of evolution and evolution on all planes of existence. To make sure this information was available to the life on all planets and to all the dimensional planes and dimensions that exist, these Guardians of the Universal Laws would incarnate to these planes of existence. This knowledge could then be taught to the inhabitants to help them understand their importance in life. There are times that several Guardians will manifest upon a plane if the inhabitants need that type of effect to bring the Universal Knowledge to them. These beings can go about bringing their knowledge to any plane of existence on a planet or off the planet many ways.

You may recall in your bible of several beings living to be around 6-9 hundred years of age. Well, that is true for that time frame. This was a time when all beings lived several hundred of years. This era was 8,000 years ago. These beings came here from all corners of the universes to help all Star Civilizations, to awaken their Knowledge of Ascension that is within every being. The Knowledge of Ascension is still part of you. This knowledge exists in several places; one is the archive of the Vatican, where it has been distorted to hide the truth from you.

The Secret Vatican archive holds the truth about Ascension, along with many other secrets, that are considered forbidden information outside the walls of the Vatican. You have been told through the religions, through the ages, that no person has or can have Eternal Life (Ascension). Only the gods have the right to Eternal Life, or when you drink from the cup of Christ. That is not true at All! This is all part of the illusions! That the religions do not want you to know is that you, each one of you, have that decision within yourself to make! The way that is accomplished is by going within you and believing in yourself and knowing it is the master plan of Eternal Life.

Of course, you chose how long that Eternal Life would be. Ascension comes from using the universal energies and love, when used in unison with other key factors. You need to work with those energies and you need to know how to bring the energies into your being. Your physical Spiritual Teachers and out of body Spiritual guides, will show you the true way to Ascension. If you come across any beings that are claiming to be, the god, (your gods or devils) stay clear of them. They are part of the illusion that you need to get rid of. So, look within yourself to learn of the truth, ask who are your guides and teachers. Your guides and teachers will not claim that they are your gods or devils...

Nevertheless, they will claim that, we are gods unto our own selves and that there are no others over our own selves to answer to...

In addition, that we are one with everything and that we are everything around us and there is no separation of things and events!

We Are One With Everything!

Chapter 11

The Final Battle

What is this so-called battle of End Times all about?

Well, I am going to shine light on this topic. Some of you will not want to accept what I am going to present in this section. Some of you will, look into this to compare it to what you find. In addition, the other part of you, will know, that this is true and those things NEED to change, NOW, NOT LATER.

Like I mentioned earlier about the destruction of thought.

Well, here is a prime example, of just that.
I have talked to several people, to get their input on 'The End Times' - or this so called 'Armageddon'.

Most people who are of religious stature, say they live day in and day out by what their Bible says.

For centuries, the prophetic messengers on Earth have spoken of the ultimate climatic battle between good and evil. The prophetic writer, John, in the Holy Bible, writes in his Book of Revelation of the final battle at the end of the age, when the forces of good and evil clash. John calls this the Battle of Armageddon (Rev16:16)

Biblical writers reveal both mystery and lies concerning the Battle of Armageddon. Some claim this great battle to be a physical battle with thousands upon thousands of horses and men in hand-to-hand combat.

The combatants in this battle of Armageddon are to be god Jehovah and his forces and his 'chosen people' the Jews. They are to fight against the unbelievers and the forces of darkness. These are the infidels or gentiles, commonly called 'Goyium' by the Jews, meaning 'cattle'. Evil, of course, is to be defeated and destroyed and god Jehovah is to triumph. The gods 'chosen people' are to then lay claim to and occupy their 'promised land', the biblical land known as Palestine. From the "New Jerusalem" god Jehovah is to rule the world in peace-the kingdom of god of Earth.

Other prophetic writers claim the battle of Armageddon to be of spiritual nature rather than physical. The Angels of Light and the Angels of Darkness, he and his 'troops' are thrown into the 'Lake of Fire' and good reigns henceforth forever.

The truth is that there is to be an end of the age confrontation between good and evil upon Earth. Now Earth is making a great transition from third dimension through fourth and into fifth dimension at her request. In addition, by doing this, no evil is allowed in fourth, fifth dimension, all evil must be removed from Earth prior to this transition. Total harmony and balance must be restored to Earth. This is now happening.

This battle is both a physical and a spiritual battle and has been occurring on Earth for several millions of years now. It is nearly over. The forces of darkness have suffered great losses, the Draconian / Reptilian controllers have been leaving Earth recently. 'The Forces of Light' have placed a protective energy field around Earth to prevent these evil entities from ever returning. Along with the physical front hundreds of thousands of evil leaders in positions of authority such as administration, supervisors, attorney, bankers, judges, military commanders, doctors, teachers and clergymen have chosen to leave Earth. Look around you and discover for yourself who is 'missing'.

Who are the 'people of the lie'? Some are the adherents to the religion of Christianity and the believers in the infallibility of their 'holy' book the Bible. They believe the biblical tenants of god Jehovah being creator god and a just and loving entity. They believe that god Jehovah had a 'chosen people' the Jewish people, and that he gave these 'chosen people' a 'promised land' where they would live in peace and happiness. From their 'promised land' of Palestine and their 'new Jerusalem' with their god Jehovah, they would rule the world.

Christians the world over for centuries have believed this nonsense recorded in their holy bible by the KZB, without realizing that they (the Christians) are people of the lie. They are victims of the KZB joke. Those who wake up to the joke realize that their 'holy bible' is not so holy and that god Jehovah is not creator god after all.

And they all say, that their bible says that, god will come and destroy all evil and Earth... They also say that their god will do this and will do that, to those that do not believe in their god. In addition, everything that their bible says has come to happen.... In addition, the others will come to be.

I would like everyone to stop and look at this for one moment.

If someone from the future came to visit us in their past and told us this and was going to happen, 'only as an insight to our future'. In addition, someone writes all that down, not knowing that this person, from the future was telling him or her, "If you do not change, this is what will happen." In addition, someone in the near future finds those writings and reads what was written, at an earlier time... Then they might say, look, some of this came about, but as they read on, and learn about the other events, they might say that those other events do not need to come about. Then the people would say, lets change our THOUGHT, so the rest of these events do not come to be. Therefore, this event of changing our way of THOUGHT, changes what was told to the people of the past, of these events of the future...

You see, the Bible is using people to think a certain way. In addition, people are bringing these events into being, because of THOUGHT. In addition, people are not aware of what they are doing, mainly because, the way religions are teaching people.

All we need to do is change our way of THOUGHT and remove ourselves from this so-called bible, which uses us to bring these events into being from our THOUGHTS. In addition, people need to take responsibilities from their THOUGHTS, there is no god(s) bringing these events into being.... The human race is making all this happen.

We are entering the New Age. We have gone through this battle for eons. This battle is nearly over, and the Age of Light is upon us! After this new era of Light begins, Earth and the people will never again see evil play any part in life. Will you move with Earth and the Children of Light into the higher dimensions or return to a third dimensional planet for a continuation of your lessons in soul growth?

That choice is totally up to you.

But, if you chose not to change, and stay in the third dimension, you will no longer be part of this world... For we no longer need destructive thoughts, as Terra moves into fourth and fifth dimensions of peace, light, and balance, harmony.

Book 1 – The Reawakening

A Journey Into the Spiritual Quest of Who We Are
Complete 4 BOOK in 1

Book 2
WHY WERE THEY CALLED GODS..?

Researched and Assembled
by
Michael J. Kiser

Book 2 – Why Were They Called Gods…?

Book 2 – Why Were They Called Gods…?

A Search into the Forbidden Questions

For the past 27 years, Kiazer has been continuing to delve deep into the stories of those from many eons ago, which deals with the stories of the battles of the star beings, on Terra and amongst the countless star systems across the Milky Way Galaxy. As Kiazer continues down the path of destiny, he removes the veils of illusions to learn the Truth of the Universal Knowledge. This path takes Kiazer down many avenues.

As Kiazer continues, steadfastly down the path of destiny, his spiritual reawakening takes him down the many avenues of the various religious beliefs systems of Earth over the past 27 years. While Kiazer reawakens the countless knowledge within himself, during this time, he finds the same materials that correlate to his knowledge. This knowledge is no longer part of any society other than to those guardians, which are preserving the knowledge. Some day this knowledge will become a part of the entire world of Earth but only time can tell when the people of Earth are truly ready to learn of the truth. Because, presently the people of Earth are still not ready for what it entails and the responsibilities that come with the knowledge of truth. It's not an easy burden for those who possess this knowledge…

Book 2 – Why Were They Called Gods…?

In an earlier gathering, Kiazer has shared some of his insight / Knowledge about some of the aspects of life. Within this second Book, Kiazer continues to share his knowledge with you as he traverses down the path and learns who he is. While researching these questions of life, Kiazer learns of the Ancient stories that are often referred to as Myths of Creations and of gods and devils. This Book is part two, in the ongoing Journey series; it picks up where the previous one leaves off. Likewise, other books will follow. These Books are a journal of Kiazer's continuing search; of Who We Are and becoming that Being, we once were, in order to understand what life is.

So, it is up to the guardians, like Kiazer, along with many others as well to make sure this knowledge is preserved, in its entirety, so this knowledge can be put out to all Humans when the time is right.

What you are about to embark into -- are glimpses of what is about to become part of life on Earth once again, in due time. Because the humans on Earth cannot keep living the way they are today and have been for the past 5,000 years-.

There is a change. This change will come like the changes, of the past. The way that all humans have been living will end…

A New way of living will start A NEW WAY for all.

Book 2 – Why Were They Called Gods…?

Within this journal, Kiazer brings to light, some of these ancient stories, which correlates with what he brought to light within in Book 1. These materials are dated as far back as 7,000 years ago. Additionally, it tells about a myth, which dates back to around 42,000 years ago and possibly even older.

With writings taken from his journal, some of what you will learn about in connection with the Universal Knowledge includes:

1- The Ancient Battles of the past…
2- The True meaning of the word god(s) and devils…
3- The creating of the religions, of today…
4- The names of god(s), of the past…
5- Taking responsibilities for WHO WE ARE…

All research within these pages is just that for the researcher, 'myself', and this is the Truth. This is what I found during in my research, and it correlates to what I believe about the universes around us, seen and unseen.

For the reader this is just information? I do encourage the reader to go out and research on you own, see the scope of information that is available. You are about to learn the Knowledge of what life is really about throughout this entire series.

I will say this; do not believe everything that is told to you, unless you can prove it is true. This is what I have done and what I found.

To some of you that will receive this Book, you will feel that what you are reading has truth to it. As for the others… Well, you are not going to be convinced.

Book 2 – Why Were They Called Gods…?

Remember, always ask, WHY!

There is one more thing. Just when you think, you have all the pieces, to the puzzle of life... Well, think again, the puzzle never ends...
Never...

After gathering all materials, I had to figure out how to assemble it along with how far back into the Ancient knowledge I needed to go to show how everything started. I had to do this without putting too much information into each book. It would be all too easy to end up overwhelming the reader. I know it will end up overwhelming readers, because I experience this all the time and I have been researching this type of materials and many others on other topics for over 25 years.

At the end of this book, you will find an intense list of research materials. As I mentioned in the past and I'll say it again later, this is only a fragment of the Knowledge of the Ancients...

You will learn that Earth has a very old history that is not being told. This Knowledge has been guarded and considered secret by all world religions and governments along with the mainstream sciences.

Within this book, I am going to shine some light on this Knowledge that will help everyone understand our place here on this planet and also among the Universes, seen and unseen, which are all around us.

Remember, this is only the tip of the iceberg, and this is just the beginning. What you are about to embark on within this book, is only a fraction, out of several thousands of pages of the materials, I have explored in my search of, "The Universal Truth." There is still Knowledge out there that is waiting to be relearned or remembered.

This book is set up to start, somewhere in the Beginning..........

Even though there is no such thing, as the Beginning...

The time period I will start from is around 300,000 years BC. This seems to be a good time frame to initially explore from.
Well, on second thought, let's start at 100,000(B.C.E.) years ago... (BCE)= Before Current Era-True Meaning. I have to state at this point that no matter what you've been taught, there is a much of history not being told. Why is this? Well you will learn things within this book, in a way that you never have.
Are there really gods out there? On the other hand, are they merely beings that are not any different from us; beings that are merely more

Book 2 – Why Were They Called Gods…?

advanced, by thousands of years, in all aspects of life, such as Spirituality, Technology, and evolution?

Lets say, when these beings first came from the stars 50,000 – 5,000 years ago and even further back, they were looked upon and accepted as somehow superior to humans. Then centuries later and through time, these beings again visited planet Earth, but the people on Earth started calling them gods; merely because there was a new generation of people on the planet who had only read stories about these beings that came from the stars.

So, when people on the planet had their chance to meet these Star Beings, they started to view some of them as gods-even though they were not gods. Some of these Beings that came from the stars were also of their next generation as well. Thus, some of these Beings accepted the roles of being the god's of the people of the Earth and thereby started the god's theory through the centuries.

If before 4,000 years ago, these so-called gods were seen on a daily basis, then where are they now? And:

1) Why for the past 2-3 thousand years, have we not witnessed any "gods"? If they are truly gods, why are they not seen during these last 4,000 years?

2) If they really are gods, then why aren't they showing themselves openly in today's society?

3) Or, did the generation of Star civilizations that played the roles of god's die off? And, did their next generation of Star Beings realize what happened? Are these Star civilizations waiting for humanities next generation to evolve and move away from calling them deities? Instead, why not look at these Beings from the stars are more like us and do not mistake them as "gods"?

For the past 2-3 thousand years, no one had seen any of these Beings that are playing the roles of god's. But, now since the 1800s we are witnessing Beings with this advanced Spirituality and Technology that do come from the stars. Nevertheless, they ARE NOT gods. They are merely Beings. Not any different from us accept they are thousands of years ahead of us Spiritually, Technology and in evolutionary aspects as well. You will see how some of these beings took the word "god" and used it for their own benefits.

Some of these Star Beings manipulated the True meaning of life in a way to discourage humans from learning about whom we are and that they are our progenitors (creators). This is often used to control the masses with fear, by saying if you don't believe that these beings are 'gods' then you will be judged harshly and punished. This became a religion of positive (good) and negative (evil/fear). Then whatever these beings say to fear, is either good (positive/beneficial), or bad (negative/harmful),

All of this was adopted into modern society and it brought forth the religions of today. When will these religions end? It's past time for the older ways of the Ancients to come back into existence.

This will all come into the light around 2012-2025, which this will start the NEW AGE - A NEW CYCLE of life on Earth.

This Book is assembled in a way to bring readers the Knowledge about Life and to bring forth a vital missing link on how the evolutionary process started. You will be able to see how the religions theory of the so-called six-days of creation is false. You will also learn how religions were created in order to impose control over people.

You will learn why the religions have conspired to hide this truth from you and create their own so-called god's and devil's, and told the masses not to look at other aspects of life. People are told, "NOT TO ASK QUESTIONS," and that the masses need to do as they are told by religions. The religions have gone about changing the truth of Life, to fit their own needs.

You will see how all this came to happen!

Book 2 – Why Were They Called Gods…?

I have this Book laid out in a way so, you can see how things changed from a viewpoint of the beginning to the present...

Throughout this series you will find that the 'Earth' is referred to by many of her other names which are used by a variety of past civilizations. Be aware that the earth is also called, 'Terra', and, 'Gaia', along with 'Earth'. Just so readers are not confused.

Book 2 – Why Were They Called Gods…?

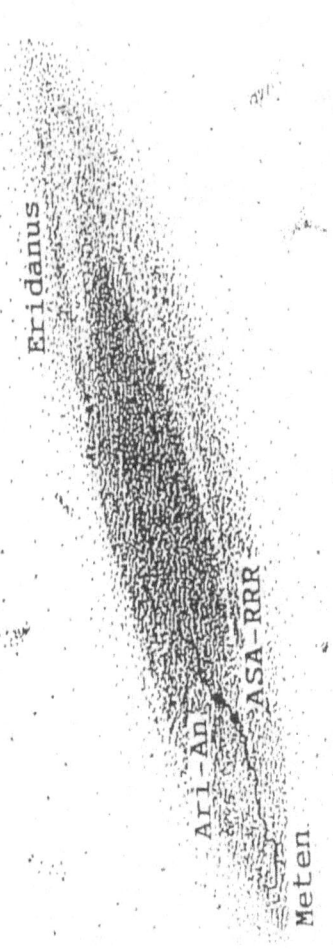

Chapter 12

The Terra Papers

Excerpts from The Terra Papers 1 & 2 By Robert Morning Sky

Italics are mine
This is a story that only a very few people know about. This is one story out of many, out of the so-called missing link of the beginning, of the evolution process. This Story takes us back to 100,000 years ago, to what might be the 1ST-2ND Stories of creation of the humanoids and of the creation of the Human race. You will see a lot of similarity in the story that parallels, with Star Wars, Star Gate the Movie and the TV series that followed with Star Gate Atlantis, and with Zecharia Sitchin Books 'The Earth Chronicles'.

3 July 1947 - Roswell, New Mexico ***

A bright, disc-shaped object was reported streaking over the skies of Roswell. Several callers reported seeing the unidentified object flying in a northwesterly direction before it disappeared over the

Book 2 – Why Were They Called Gods…?

horizon. The Army Air Force Field has confirmed the discovery of unidentifiable debris at a wreckage site in a location northwest of Roswell.

Therefore, begins one of the most infamous incidents in Man's history, the crash of a 'flying saucer'. Some say that this was the beginning of Man's contact with the enigmatic 'disk' and according to some, its occupants. Were there beings in the Roswell disk? Were these beings spirited away, to be studied and de-briefed?

On 13 August later that same year, another disk crashed in the night. Six young Indian Men who had been out camping saw the crash. Searching out the site, the six were able to find the wreckage before the soldiers arrived.

Amidst the twisted metal and charred desert bushes, they would make a startling discovery. There was a survivor! An unconscious being injured nevertheless alive, rather than abandon him to the soldiers, the youths chose to take the Being with them. The six spent the next few months nursing their Visitor back to health.

In time, the Star Being would come to trust the six. By using a small crystal to create images, the Visitor began to communicate with the young men. Calling him the Star Elder, the youths sat at the knee of their Friend, examining all of the crystalline images with great care, piecing together the incredible history of our Solar system and Mankind itself.

Star Elder's message was simple. Star Beings have been here since Earth was a barren rock. They were here when Men were created and they have been here throughout there evolution. In some cases, their involvement was benevolent in some times it was not.

This is the Story of Bek'Ti...

GENESIS
(300,000 B.C.)

The explosion rocked the Nothingness of the Void. Primordial 'essence' was thrown violently outward. Like a primeval ocean, wave after wave crashed out into the black pit of the Void. Nothingness beheld Chaos, Chaos poured out into Nothingness. As the primeval waters streamed outwards, rivers of dark 'essence' swirled together, forming huge whirlpools. As the whirlpools spun inwards, the 'essence' condensed into clouds of gas. Superheated from the compression force in the core of the swirl, sparks ignited the volatile clouds. Explosion after explosion formed enormous balls of fire, supernovas of brilliant red and dwarf stars of blazing blue. Like islands in the waters of 'essence', the stars formed from the swirls in the spinning

Book 2 – Why Were They Called Gods...?

galaxies. Time after time, the process was repeated in the Void...time after time, a galaxy was born.

In time, one of these galaxies would come to be known as 'ERIDANUS'; this is a history of one small part of ERIDANUS the Human species within, (The Milky Way Galaxy) and a tiny world that is known as Terra, 'EARTH'.

ERIDANUS
(100,000 B.C.)

In the swirling primordial 'waters' of ERIDANUS, many of the stars gave birth to worlds of their own. From the gases and dust thrown out from the suns, the planets condensed and cooled. Elemental gases combined to form moisture; the rain fell to form oceans. Thunderstorms raged, the oceans tossed and turned, crashing on the shores of the surface lands. In the midst of the lighting and fury, a single spark flashed, creating in one microsecond a single cell of life.

Single celled life form combined to create multi-celled creatures, multi-celled creatures became complex beings with billions of cells... fishes, insects, birds, reptiles, plants and mammals. As many different creatures as there are stars in the galaxy, came into existence.

In addition, in time, 'Humanoids' evolved. Fish humanoids, bird humanoids, Reptile humanoids,

Book 2 – Why Were They Called Gods...?

Mammal humanoids and humanoids of every kind, became the consistent outcome of evolution.

As primordial ERIDANUS MAN developed, his caves gave way to huts, gatherings of huts became settlements, and settlements became cities. The trapping and hunting of animals gave way to fur trading; fur trading gave way to markets... Moreover, so on....

Then ERIDANUS MAN looked up, up into the skies. In addition, he saw his moon. He created ships to carry him skyward, and his conquest of the moon began. As he stood on the moon, as he surveyed the lunar cities, he looked up and saw the stars above him. Seeking more, he moved skyward again. This time neighboring worlds were discovered. ERIDANUS MAN conquered the environment of the new world, and the cycle began again.

Therefore, it was that ERIDANUS MAN met ERIDANUS MAMMAL MAN, ERIDANUS REPTILE MAN met ERIDANUS INSECT MAN, and an ERIDANUS REPTILE MAN greeted them all. In time, they learned from each other and they lived together.

In addition... They went to War.

Primitive ERIDANUS MAN had become a 'civilized' ERIDANUS MAN; primitive war gave way to the Science of War. Death in all its horror became a tool of Progress. Galactic kingdoms in ERIDANUS rose and fell, civilizations prospered and died. A continuous series of wars engulfed the

Book 2 – Why Were They Called Gods...?

entire galaxy. No single Empire endured for long. None save one....

THE 'SSS' EMPIRE

In the galaxy of ERIDANUS, the way of things became war, violence and turbulence. Surfacing above other races as the Supreme Masters of War, the 'SSS' Beings, (so-called became of the hissing sound they made as they spoke), weathered war and chaos to seize and retain a sizable portion of the Ninth Sector of the galaxy. Through originally ruled over by Kings of repute, it was under the 'SSS' Queens that the Empire was to reach its pinnacle. Known as the 'SSS-T', the Queens and their techniques of rule became the very embodiment of Royal tribute to the deadlines of the reptilian Queens.

In a galaxy of chaos and war, the SSS beings had no peer or competition. Ruthless in command, and efficient in their cruelty, the SSS-T Queens were brilliant politicians and war strategists, using events to advantage and manipulating wars to their advantage and gain.

Providing the Royals with the power to conquer and reign over their foes was a powerful military force, unmatched and unequaled by any other. Comprised of tall imposing figures, the SSS Warriors were cold-blooded warriors with frightening dragon-like faces. Though evolution had long since removed their scale-like skins, the plates on the body armor gave an impression of fierce, dinosaurs beings. Only a long ridge of bone rising from the forehead and trailing back and over the head remained to hint at their reptilian ancestry. Known as the 'M-K' or 'M-G', the appearance of the SSS Warriors alone was enough to strike fear into an opponent's heart.

Countless wars over billions of years had taught the SSS Queens a vital lesson, an enemy of rebellious subject serves no purpose if executed. However, if the brain was re-programmed, resistance was eliminated and an able body was added to the labor force. Mind control was the SSS-T Science of choice.

Referred to by other races as the 'ARI' or 'Masters', in time they would become known as the 'ARI' of 'AN' (Heaven), or the 'ARI-AN'. Today it is known as ORION.

Though it had, became the epitome of power and might, a symbol of brutal ruler ship and unrelenting aggression, the fates would play a curious trick on ARI-AN. In their quest for galactic power, the SSS-T Warriors had looted the palace treasuries of their victimized worlds. The cultural riches of conquered worlds were placed on display in the museums of ARI-AN, making the Empire the center of Ninth Sector culture and wisdom. ARI-AN became the showcase world for Poetry and Music, Art and Dance. It was a step, however unknowing, for the evolution of temperance in the SSS-T psyche.

The following are Ancient Egyptian words of M-K/M-G origin:

Book 2 – Why Were They Called Gods…?

M'K - Name of a crocodile
MAG or M'G - Crocodile
Mek - Protector, protection
Mikh - Fight, to fight
M'Q - To slay, hack into pieces

In Ancient Egypt, the suffix -U indicates 'One of'. (Thus, M-K-U= 'of M-K' and M-G-U= 'of M-G')

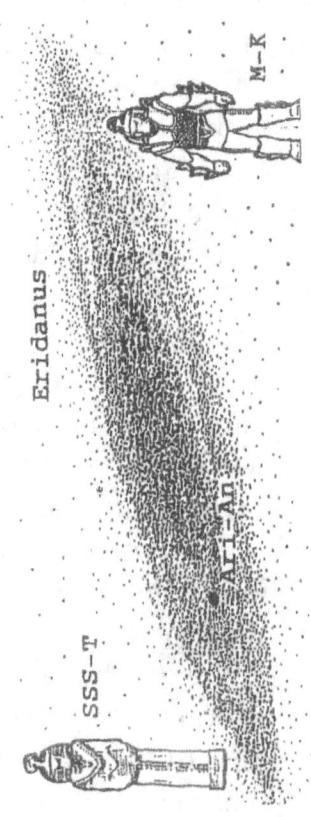

M'Ka - Brave, bold
M'Khai - To strike, fight
M'Khaiu - Fighters, foes
M'Khau - An animal
M'Ki - To protect, protector
M'Kiu - Protectors
MeKi - Protector
Mega - Crocodile
M'GA - Crocodile
M'Ga - Commandant, chief
M'GA - To command, instruct
Mgi - Brave
Mekhi - To beat, strike, fight

The following are various words of M-K/M-G origin:
Magha - Mighty, Great One (Hindu)
Mak - Great, superior (Sumerian)
Mactus - Glorified (Latin)
Mactabalis - Deadly (Latin)
Macto - Slay, smite, punish, afflict (Latin)
Magister - Master, chief (Latin)
Magnus - Magician (Latin)

The following are English words of M-K/M-G origin:
Amok - Chaos, turmoil
Image - Illusion (Re-programming the brain)
Imagine - Creating illusion (Re-programming the brain)
Make - To force

Major - Huge, greater
Mega - Huge, enormous
Majesty, Majestic - Royal, regal
Magic - Illusion (Re-programming the brain)
*MJ-12 (Majestic 12) - UFO investigations group (Re-programming the brain)

The following are various words of ARI-AN and SSS origin:
Aryan - The super-race of Adolph Hitler (ARI-AN)
SS - The elite military of Adolph Hitler (SSS)
ARI - Master, Keeper (Egyptian)
Ariz - Terrible One (Hebrew)
Ares - God of War (Latin)

The ASA-RRR

Though the reign of the SSS-T Queens on the Ninth Sector was seldom challenged, of great concern to the ARI-AN Queens were the movements and expansions of yet another race called 'RRR'. Evolved from vicious mammalian predators, the 'RRR' were still in the early stages of development, their thirst for expansionism unburdened by the softening that continual wars and time brought on.

For the RRR race, war was the entirety of existence all else was meaningless. Life itself meant obedience and total commitment to the RRR Kings, anything less meant death. So quickly did they create their Empire, so ruthless were their techniques that the RRR would become known as 'ASA' or Overlords. In the Ninth Sector, the worlds of the RRR would be known as ASA-RRR.

Led by the fearsome IKU warriors, a barbaric army with a fleet of deadly Starships of overwhelming firepower, the kings of ASA-RRR wreaked havoc on the worlds surrounding the Ninth passageway. The elite IKU forces descended on their unsuspecting targets with unmerciful and unrelenting attack, clearing the skyways of any potential resistance and totally decimating land-based strongholds, within moments, Warrior Ground Forces, the BEH, moved in to annihilate any remaining military forces. Renowned for their practice of devouring the flesh of their enemies, the IKU and BEH became known as the D-K or T-K, the Teeth of the RRR.

Aggressive and ravenous, unrelenting in their expansion, the RRR Conqueror Kings began the slow, methodical take-over of the PESH-METEN (Ninth Passageway), a crucial Star Lane. Seizing the Passageway would give the ASA-RRR Kings control of travel into and out of the ARI-AN Empire, and that possibility was one the SSS-T Queens could not permit.

But the ASA-RRR Kings were a formidable power. The Ways of War had been the driving force of their evolution. Every King had demanded much of their military forces. The Starship pilots, the IKU, possessed light beams, which could melt targets, cut them to pieces or disintegrate them. The elite Ground Forces, the BEH, used weapons which sounds that stunned the enemy, disintegrated solid objects or could be used to transport an object from one place to another.

Overall, the DAK forces had a short time to become an army of devastating power. The ASA-RRR Science of War was a Technology of Death called 'AT'. In addition, from this new science, the ultimate Warship was spawned. A planet-sized globe with the armaments of all other Starships... and more, the Warship was dubbed the 'RR' or 'AR'. A miniature world capable of destruction never before seen in the Ninth Sector, the AR of DAK forces made the Empire of force to be reckoned with. The rays of the sun glistening off the surface of the Death-ship made the AR shine like a bright star in the skies. Though a brilliant star was often a portent of wondrous things, this star brought death and destruction.

As the ASA-RRR Kings continued to expand their holdings, the SSS-T queens made careful gesture of peace towards the conquering Kings in the hopes of resolving the dilemma before War became necessary. The billions of years of conflict had taught the SSS-T an invaluable lesson; war brings death to a winner as well as a loser. There were other ways to win the conflict. Victory was, gained by taking the enemy into one's own folds. The DAK could be won over in a more clever and devious way.

The Queens of ARI-AN called for a meeting of Royals. If the Kings of ASA-RRR pledged their loyalty to the SSS-T High Throne and submitted themselves to the service of the Throne then they would be granted control of the outer stars of the Ninth Sector.

Realizing the magnitude of power in the offer extended, the ASA-RRR Kings quickly agreed to the Alliance. The DAK forces and mighty AR Death Planet were placed in the service of the SSS-T Queens; the outer Ninth Sector was made part of the ASA-RRR Empire. Catapulted to a place as super power by the Alliance, the Stars of ASA-RRR became known as the Empire of 'SSS-T.RRR, SSS-T' 'Empire born of the SSS-T, dying for the 'SSS-T' OR 'SS-RR-SS' (Sirius).

With the ARI-AN Alliance to back them, the ASA-RRR Kings began yet a greater effort to conquer and seize new systems, new worlds to add to their empire. Solidifying their power, levying heavy tolls and embargoes on travelers on the lanes of the Ninth Passageway, the SS-RR-SS Empire had soon become the ARI-AN Queens watched with a wary eye, the moment of betrayal must be carefully planned.

Therefore, for a time, a tenuous peace came to exist between the two Thrones. All was well, until the era of the Monarch known as the Great AN-AN, the Elder King of ASA-RRR.

In the era of the Great Elder King AN-AN, life on ASA-RRR was good. The luxuries and benefits that befitted a Conqueror race was theirs to enjoy and revel in. The alliance with the SSS-T Empire had made the Kings of ASA-RRR more powerful than ever before and had permitted the people of ASA-RRR an opportunity to enjoy a richer style of life.

However, the power of the Throne also made the life of the King more precarious. Treachery, lies and deceit surrounded the King. Assassination plots, military coups and alien invasions were the every day matters of the King. The Prince was expected to plot for his father's demise, distant brothers and illegitimate children pretended to the Throne Kingship. King AN-AN watched the skies for enemy attacks, and peered carefully over his shoulder at relatives and members of the royal court. Such was the life of a King of ASA-RRR, and such was the life of the Elder King AN-AN.

Seated in the Royal Court of the Great AN-AN, serving as Royal Cup-Bearer, was his brother, the Great AL-SHAR. Assisting in the governing of the Empire, the Great AL-SHAR served faithfully under his brother, the Great Elder King.

Peace reined, the Empire prospered, until the break out of war in the Central Stars. A series of major conflicts, known as the 'Galactic Great Wars', drew both the ARI-AN Empire and the Empire of ASA-RRR into its folds. The Great Elder King was summoned to the Palace of the SSS-T to render services as commander of the combined M-K and D-K Warriors.

Great AL-SHAR, acting on behalf of King AN-AN remained behind in the ASA-RRR Palace. Seeing is opportunity to betray his brother, Prince AL-SHAR decided to seize control of the Central ASA-RRR forces. The successful coup compelled the Prince to further action. He immediately dispatched an elite troop of assassins to hunt down and take the life of the Elder King. Historical documents would tell of the death in battle of the Great AN-AN, the Hero King who gave his life while in command of his armies. However, those who were in the Court of ASA-RRR knew why the King had died, and who was responsible.

Prince AL-SHAR, Royal Cup-Bearer, was now King AL-AL.

Lord Price AN-SHAR, son of the Hero King AN-AN and heir apparent, was captured and placed into exile by the new King of ASA-RRR, his claim to the throne stripped away forever.

To insure his personal safety, the Great King AL-AL made the grandson of the Great AN-AN his own personal Cupbearer. Deposed Prince AN-U was both hostage and servant to his King and Uncle. Revenge would have to wait.

For now, he would serve faithfully ... but he would learn. Someday the Throne of ASA-RRR would be his, this he vowed!

Book 2 – Why Were They Called Gods…?

In this time, yet another significant event would occur, one, which would change forever the fate of the Ninth Sector. A new star was beginning to mature, its young worlds cooling down to form inhabitable planets. King AL-AL, recognizing a potential for untapped precious ores, and the possibility of a strategic military outpost, immediately sent a trusted and faithful administrator to lay claim to the new solar system. Lord AL-AL-IM, Mater of Genesis Sciences, had an imposing task before him, to colonize and develop a primitive planetary system.

The young sun had originally formed with two worlds in orbit around it, one tiny inner planet, (now known as Mercury) and one large planet, its name to eventually be 'TIAMAT'.

In time, six more worlds would form, one pair of inner worlds (Venus and Mars), two central giants (Jupiter and Saturn), and a pair of twin planets, (Neptune and Uranus).

Nevertheless, TIAMAT, the tropical world would be the first planet to be developed by, Lord AL-AL-IM in his assignment. Already inhabited by settlers of numerous galactic star systems, TIAMAT was both a paradise and a frontier world of danger. The colonists and their families welcomed the presence of an ASA-RRR military contingency force and a direct link to King AL-AL and the Empire at ARI-AN. Protection and necessary supplies would now be available, TIAMAT would become a full-fledged world.

Lord AL-AL-IM began to immediately exploit the new solar system. The Sun was called 'Bad', 'where death is'. In the immediate proximity of the young sun, was the tiniest world, christened 'MUM-MU', 'first born traveler'. The next world would become a military outpost. Though possessed of super hot surface temperatures, its inner caverns gave comfortable shelter for the IKU and BEH forces. This world would become known as 'DAK-A-MU', 'place of DAK inside'.

The Red Sand planet, next in line, was a world with air and water, trees and an environment suitable for settlers to inhabit. A good site for colonists, it also provide a much need surface land for a central military fortress. This was the world of 'DAK-MU', 'place of DAK'.

Beyond the red sands world was TIAMAT, the center of the colonization efforts of Lord AL-AL-IM.

The largest of the system's worlds was a gigantic planet possessing gravitational forces that made it unsuitable for habitation but excellent for the production of super-metals. Under super-gravity conditions, metals could be forged into combinations impossible on other worlds. 'BAR-BAR-U' it was called, 'World of Metal Metals'.

The second titan world was the most dangerous. Internal forces were highly unstable. Possessing a constant cloud of dust and rocks circling around its furiously spinning center and with gravitational forces that pulled many ship into an uncorrectable spin, the giant would be known as 'TAR-GALLU', the 'Great Destroyer'. Of all the planets, the Ringed One' would prove the most dangerous.

Book 2 – Why Were They Called Gods…?

A distance past TAR-GALLU was a large cold swamp planet, poisonous gases in its skies. 'SHANAMMA' could be difficult to colonize but would be ideal for Genesis experiments. The outermost world was called 'IR-U', a near twin to 'SHANAMMA' in size. IR-U was a watery world with a misty covering.

Though the task was difficult, Lord AL-AL-IM would prove successful. The extremely high gravity forces on BAR-BAR-U simplified the manufacture of 'heavy' metals, unstable in an environment with low gravity. Military outpost on DAK-A-MU and DAK-MU proved secure and strong. Experimental farms on both SHANAMMA and IRU showed promise. The settlements on the moons of BAR-BAR-U and TAR-GALLU were thriving.

But TIAMAT was the crowning glory to the efforts of Lord AL-AL-IM. With the support of his King AL-AL back home, the Administrator was able to develop TIAMAT into a paradise far beyond expectation. Facilities to extract newly discovered ores were constructed; Atmospheric Conditioning Centers soon began the tedious task of transforming the skies into a more suitable environment. As a source of precious ores and a strategic control point of traffic on the Ninth Passageway star lanes, the new system further strengthened the strangle hold King AL-AL held on the outer Ninth Sector.

As his final project, Lord AL-AL-IM constructed a nearly perfect duplicate of the Palace of the ASA-

RRR Kings. Known as 'KI', its name literally meant 'In the Likeness of '. The new solar system of BAD had been conquered. In recognition of the efforts of AL-ALIM, the system was called 'ARI-DU', 'the Mastered place'. In addition, its Lord was AL-AL-IM, the EN-GI, and 'Lord of the world in the likeness of ASA-RRR'.

Under the premise of executing control of the star lanes of the Ninth Sector on behalf of the SSS-T Queens, AL-AL was able to control the travelers who entered the galaxy through the passageway. By refusing travel on the star lanes, King AL-AL could prevent potential alliance with the AR-AN from being formed. Negotiations with other galaxies were subject to the whims of King AL-AL, an intolerable situation for the SSS-T Queens. The ASA-RRR Empire could delay, or undo, all crucial SSS-T political and economic alliances. King AL-AL, had turn ARI-DU into an island outpost of phenomenal power.

And, though the Great AL-AL had further strengthened the ASA-RRR Throne, he had also weakened his position within the SSS-T Royal Court of ARI-AN. what the Great AL-AL could not foresee, what he could not suspect, was that his own future, his very survival, was hidden in the distant worlds AL-AL-IM had developed for him.

Lurking back in the Royal Palace was AN-U, the one time Prince and highly disgruntled grandson of the Great AN-AN, waiting patiently for a time in which to move against his Uncle. Choosing a day of

Book 2 – Why Were They Called Gods...?

High Celebration of DAK victories in battle, when AL-AL would not be in the Palace, the Prince acted. The Loyal followers of the Great AN-AN, still angry at AL-AL'S betrayal, joined with AN-U. Overwhelming force and lightning speed assured the Prince of an immediate success. King AL-AL, hearing of the war in the Palace, chose not to fight the Prince. Fleeing for his life, the Great AL-AL descended to his far-away Palace in the ARI-DU System. Here, a loyal following received the deposed King with the enthusiasm of thankful subjects. Refuge was found in the island outpost AL-AL had developed. Here he would be a King, still adored and still welcomed.

Back on ASA-RRR, the ex-Prince AN-U celebrated his long awaited revenge. The throne was his he was King AN-U.

Nevertheless, victory was not all complete. The Loyal Warrior forces of the Great AL-AL held fast to the new solar system. The efforts of AL-AL-IM and the resources dedicated by AL-AL to developing and exploiting the new outpost was to return a handsome reward to the Great AL-AL in the end. Consistency in the production of heavy metals on BAR-BAR-U and continual discovery and exploitation of precious ores, particularly an abundance of gold, made the new solar system indispensable.

The strength of AL-AL's hold on the solar system; a very strongly worded communiqué sent by the SSS-T Queens 'asking' that a civil war be avoided; and the vital resources brought in by the new system,

Book 2 – Why Were They Called Gods…?

all combined to give King AL-AL a very powerful position from which to negotiate a tentative truce, and a reprieve. With the SSS-T Queens looking over his shoulder, ASA-RRR King AN-U reluctantly accepted the agreement, for the while.

For a time, King AL-AL continued to provide a steady and abundant stream of precious ores and metals to ASA-RRR. The angry AN-U accepted the shipments on behalf of the Empire of ASA-RRR and the ARI-AN Empire, but continued to look for any sign of weakness, any trouble that might give cause to bring his DAK armada down on AL-AL.

AN-U placed his own elite IKU Star-pilots, the 'IKIKI', into orbits throughout the solar system. Any transgression, any mistake made by AL-AL, would bring down the wrath of his highness, King AN-U.

To further secure the solar system, King AN-U placed his own son, Prince AN-EN, in charge of the elite IKU Starships and a special group called the 'IKIKI', the 'Watchers'. His title would be 'EN-LIL', 'Lord of Command'. To insure shipments of crucial resources remained intact and on time, King AN-U appointed his eldest son, Lord Prince EA a Master of Genesis Sciences, to the position of EN-GI, the very same position once held by AL-AL-IM.

Lord Prince EN-LIL would be based on TIAMAT, as would be his brother Prince EN-KI. EN-LIL would travel the skyways; EN-KI would develop the system world and conduct continuing Genesis experiments on the watery world of SHANAMA. Mining, production and metallurgical operations would also fall into the realm of Prince EA's control. In this way, the King was assured his hand would extend over AL-AL's solar system.

Therefore, it was for many periods. Former King AL-AL would keep his word, producing the resources and maintaining order in the Ninth Passageway, while King AN-U reluctantly allowed a once hated foe to remain in power in the Ninth Passageway. Nevertheless, AN-U would never forget the injury he had suffered under the hands of his uncle AL-AL. When speaking of King AL-AL's duplicate palace, the Great AN-U always referred to it in an angry and disparaging manner. An 'Impure Palace', he called it, his own Palace on ASA-RRR was the 'Pure One', the ARI-DU Palace was the "Dark One'.

TIAMAT itself was the 'World of Darkness', regardless of its achievements.

King AN-U would never forget the torments his father had endured. The hatred of a lifetime welled up within his very being. King AL-AL would live, but he would pay for his sins against the family of AN-U.

But history was about to repeat itself. For in the very heart of ARI-DU, the grandson of King AL-AL, AL-AL-GAR, fear apparent to the Throne of the solar system, had become a far more powerful figure to the followers of King AL-AL than the King of ASA-RRR was comfortable.

Born to one of the IKIKI pilots, the orbiting 'Watchers' of AN-U, AL-AL-GAR learned early the ways of the Star-pilots and their warships. His piloting skills developed quickly, and in short time he was granted the status of IKU 'Master'. He, like his father, was IKU!

However, AL-AL-GAR had a plan. After IKU training, the Prince went to the High Palace of his grandfather, 'AM-BAHU', 'The Gathering Place'. He would make a strange request. Rather than rest on his laurels, the Prince asked to receive further training, only this time, in the military discipline of the elite BEH Warriors. Disciplined ground forces that were equivalent to the DAK Warriors of the skyways, the BEH were equally feared in the Ninth Sector. Exhibiting exemplary skills, the Prince once again completed his training in short time. Rising with quickness through the ranks, Lord Prince AL-AL-GAR would earn the title 'IKU-MAR-BEH', 'He is a Great One of the IKIKI and the BEH'. Nevertheless, AL-AL-GAR, an honored Master of both warrior disciplines, was to garner one more titles. He would receive the title of 'ZU', 'One who is Supreme Master', a status given only to the most elite of Warriors, a very select handful of fighters.

The Great AN-U was worried! A Master of War dwelled far away in the Kingdom of AL-AL. In addition, he was a Prince! The way in which IKU-MAR-BEH had pursued his military disciplines in such a brief time revealed much to King AN-U. He remembered what AL-AL had done to him when he was Prince. Now, the grandson of AL-AL, a Prince, had suffered the very same fate at the hands of King AN-U!

AN-U was sure he knew the young Prince's heart. He knew how angry IKU-MAR-BEH must be. King AN-U would have to take immediate steps to prevent IKU-MAR-BEH from rising to power, and possibly inciting the ARI-DU colonies to rebel.

Therefore, a worried King AN-U moved, as his uncle had moved against him long ago. IKU-MAR-BEH was made Royal Cupbearer. Summoned to the Palace of ASA-RRR, IKU-MAR-BEH was placed in the Seat of the Cupbearer, a position under King AN-U where he could be constantly watched.

In an effort to appease IKU-MAR-BEH, AN-U bestowed great honors on the young Prince, but to no avail. Still the King could sense the hatred of the Prince. King AN-U knew nothing would succeed; nothing would change the mind of IKU-MAR-BEH. Alternatively, this reason, he would always be on guard. King AN-U had no choice but be diligent in watching the Prince.

But there were more troubles for the King in the faraway solar system. Lord Prince EN-LIL, AN-U's son, the appointed Overlord of the new system, had protested his placement in a region so far from the ASA-RRR Palace. Perhaps he too would give thought to an attempt to overthrow his own father. The BEH Warriors were loyal, but they were also a powerful force and could not be ignored. A threat could arise from a group of rebels within the IKIKI. They were loyal to AN-U but all had families in the new solar system, and Prince IKU-MAR-BEH had once been one of them. They, too, could become a threat to his rule. The worries in the Kingdom of AL-AL were many.

AN-U had hoped that the presence of his sons would help, but the feuding between them had become worse while they had been in ARI-DU. However, Overlords of their very own domains, neither Prince was happy. Each had wanted complete control, total dominion over the entire AL-AL Kingdom of ARI-DU.

Both Princes made threatening, almost dangerous, noises. King AN-U could take no chances in ARIDU. Forced to descend to the distant faraway solar system, the King was determined to put things in order. To protect himself from a coup by a vengeful Prince IKU-MAR-BEH, King AN-U took the Prince along with him on his journey.

Feeling secure, the King AN-U made his way to the world's old discord, but as they arrived, Prince IKU-MAR-BEH asked a favor of the King. Many of IKU-MAR-BEH's family and friends within the IKIKI had planned a welcoming for him, the Prince, asked if he may be allowed to visit with them.

Distracted by the pending events, the Great King doubled the DAK guards around the young Prince and ordered the IKIKI ships be carefully watched. Perhaps this would placate Lord IKU-MAR-BEH for a time. Assured that the situation was well in hand, King AN-U agreed to the request.

Nevertheless, the dispute over dominion of TIAMAT, Throne World of the solar system, could not be settled. Prince ENL-LIL made it clear to his father, if he was to stay in the distant and primitive solar system, he wanted to reside in the Palace as the King of ARIDU. Prince EA argued that since he was older he was more deserving, and he was a Genesis Scientist, a Way of Discipline that was perfect for Kingship over ARIDU.

Seeing no resolution to the dilemma, King AN-U agreed to the choosing of lots to decide the fate of ARIDU. By chance, Prince EN-LIL became Lord of ARIDU, the world, and ARIDU the system. Prince EA would remain the EN-GI and would continue to organize the development and recovery operations throughout ARIDU. While the decision made little difference in the resolution of difficulties, but it gave the King respite for a short time... a very short time.

King AN-U boarded the small ship, which would take him up to his waiting flagship, the Royal 'AR'. As AN-U approached the converted planet-sized Death ship, he could not have been more proud. The gleaming ship was truly a Royal craft.

Nevertheless, an unexpected surprise awaited the King.

Overwhelming the Guards assigned to watch him, the young IKU-MAR-BEH and his loyal IKIKI Warriors had captured the AR Flagship IKU-MAR-BEH would have his revenge. As AN-U moved closer, the trap was made ready.

But a cry went out, a warning from a loyal AN-U Warrior. At the last moment, AN-U turned to flee. IKU-MAR-BEH struck quickly, damaging the ship of the King. The forces of AN-U, outnumbered and overwhelmed, struck back.

The battle was fierce in intensity, short.

The DAK Elite Royal Guard had little chance of victory; all they could only hope to do was create sufficient time to allow the King to escape. As AN-U fled into the stars on an escort ship, a final explosion and fireball marked the last stand of his loyal DAK defenders.

Lord Prince IKU-MAR-BEH moved quickly. With loyal IKIKI Warriors in the skyways and BEH Warriors on the planets, the takeover of the solar system was quick and decisive. Prince IKU-MAR-BEH found little resistance. The inhabitants of the AL-AL Kingdom supported his rebellion; they opposed the rule of the ASA-RRR Empire. Small pockets of AN-U loyalists were captured and neutralized. Prince IKU-MAR-BEH had won!

And in his victory, he had captured the mighty AR, flagship of the War armada of ASA-RRR. The cries of celebration were tumultuous! Long lives the Prince Long live Mighty ZU!

The Prince was victorious. As King of the rebel Kingdom, he would become known as King 'ZU-ZU', or 'ZUZ' (Zeus). The capture of the AR of AN-U would earn ZU-ZU yet another name, 'AR-ZU', 'Supreme Lord of AR'. In honor of his victory, the Palace of his grandfather, previously called 'AL-AMBAHU, was renamed 'AL AMBAHU ZU' or 'AL-AMBA-ZU' (OLYMPUS), 'Palace of gathering of AL and ZU'.

Book 2 – Why Were They Called Gods…?

The glory of the throne of ARIDU was his.

'The Battle of AN-U and KUMARBI', an ancient legend found on Babylonian clay tablets, describes a royal battle in the skies in which Prince KUMARBI fights with and defeats King AN-U, who flees into heaven. Before the battle is over, KUMARBI 'bites' AN-U in the genitals, hurting him. The story really says KUMARBI 'used his teeth' (DAK) on AN-U's 'ball of power' (The AR).

THE REBEL EMPIRE

King ZU-ZU (Zeus) knew he would not be able to savor his triumph for long. A new War was about to begin, a war, which pitted his young solar system and its inhabitants against an older star system that was the home of their ancestors.

Back in ASA-RRR, King AN-U stormed through his palace.

The specific event he had planned to avoid, a revolt led by Prince IKU-MAR-BEH, had not only happened, but also had forced AN-U himself, to flee in humiliation. AN-U lashed out in an almost uncontrollable rage. He ordered his second AR Death ship be made immediately ready for war! The rebellious Lord Prince IKU-MAR-BEH would pay dearly! Battle forces of elite BEH Warriors were loaded aboard the AR. The finest IKU star pilots were summoned, and the AR was armed. Escorted by

RRR Star fighters and Warships, the AR armada passed over the sky above the king's Palace. The sight lifted the spirit of the King; victory was sure to be his! Prince IKU-MAR-BEH would be punished for his blasphemous behavior!

Nevertheless, King ZU-ZU was ready. The captured AR was also made ready. Lord King AR-ZU (ZU-ZU) and his loyal IKU planned an unexpected welcome for the coming invasion force. Choosing not to await the arrival of the armada, AR-ZU and his forces planned to ambush the Death ship of AN-U while it was yet out of the ARIDU solar system.

As the Star fleet from ASA-RRR approached, AR-ZU waited. When he felt the moment was right, the IKU and BEH forces of the rebel Empire descended on the armada suddenly and with a fury befitting a galactic lightning storm. The escort ships that were caught by surprise exploded in huge balls of fire! The battle was engaged, flashes of brilliant white and green light crisscrossed through the blackness.

AR-ZU watched the progress of the battle carefully. The moment for unleashing his captured AR had to be precise.

As his attack ships struck with deadly accuracy, a sudden break appeared in the formations of AN-U's invasion forces. AR-ZU immediately summoned the captured AR Death ship.

For one brief moment, there was silence as the two large Warships faced each other. As two mighty bulls with lowered heads, the pause only preceded the headlong charge. Chaos, thunder and lightning filled the stairways. The weapons-fire was overwhelming. Lord King AR-ZU had to turn away from the blinding light and the deafening noise.

When the light flashes stopped, AR-ZU lifted up his visor and strained to see through the smoke. Fragments flew by his ship. As the haze cleared, AR-ZU realized what those final explosions had been. They had come from his captured AR Death ship. The enormous explosion hurled pieces of metal in every direction.

Shards of the AR outer skin bounced off AR-ZU's own ship. The mighty flagship of AN-U had defeated AR-ZU's Death ship and continued to move steadily forward.

AR-ZU watched in horror as the dying body the Warship hurtled flaming downward into the oncoming path of the world of KAKKAB SHANAMMA (Uranus), the planet where Prince EA was conducting experiments on plant and animal life. As the small moon-sized ship of metal entered the atmosphere, a shower of sparks filled the skies. Bolts of blue lightning flashed from the ship to the surface of the planet. The sky over KAKKAB SHANAMMA was in chaos even before the miles wide globe of burning metal collided with the world. Striking at an angle, the stricken AR careened off the planet, skidding, and bouncing, then catapulting into the black Void. KAKKAB SHANAMMA was tipped over on its axis. Shudders pulsed along the inner caverns of the planet; its quaking core was shaken and toppled. Once an upright world, it now lay on its side.

Lord AR-ZU watched helplessly as his valiant pilots fell into the dark void in the dying AR. They had struck a deathblow to a good part of the invasion forces but had given the ultimate sacrifice in doing so.

Turning away from sight, AR-ZU maneuvered his ship in an arc toward the still moving AR Death ship of AN-U. Imposing in its size, the AR was truly magnificent in its horror. As AR-ZU continued to watch, he noticed that the AR moved in an odd fashion, its path was erratic. The realization suddenly struck AR-ZU. The destruction beams of his IKIKI pilots had damaged the Death ship! The outcome of the battle was still undecided! AR-ZU could still win a victory!

With a renewed sense of hope, he ordered his Warships to descend on the AR Death ship again, with AR-ZU himself in the lead. Using Star fighters to occupy the escort forces, AR-ZU in his own starship, went after the crippled AR. Wave after wave of Starships attacked the damaged ship again and again, as it continued to move into AR-ZU's solar system.

With its own arsenal of powerful death rays, the Warship fought its way past distant IRU (Neptune) and the now fallen and tilting world of KAKKAB SHANAMMA.

Book 2 – Why Were They Called Gods…?

However, the constant fire barrage of AR-ZU's Starships began to take its toll. As the mighty AR moved into the proximity of TAR-GALLU (Saturn), the tremendous gravity of the ringed planet further pulled the shuddering Death ship away from its direct path towards TIAMAT. Almost out of control, the ship strained to stay its course.

Lord AR-ZU assembled his forces for one last attack. In one final decisive strike, Lord AR-ZU and his Starships gave there all against the AR. As each Star fighter descended and unloaded his arsenal, the AR shook and shuddered. The groan and creaks of the internal explosions sounded like ghoulish, demonic screams. Suddenly, the AR exploded in flames. Every part of the Death planet shook violently. Smoke and flames erupted from every crevice of the ship. Streaming clouds of blackness trailed behind the staggering ship, AR of AN-U was dying. AR-ZU sat back in his ship. He had successfully defeated the pride of the ASA-RRR Fleet.

Nevertheless, suddenly, he sat forward.

The valiant IKU pilots of AN-U took aim at the planet of TIAMAT with the only weapons they had left, the AR Death ship itself! Maneuvering the flaming and disintegrating warship, they hurled themselves directly at TIAMAT!

Book 2 – Why Were They Called Gods…?

The Great Palace of AL-AMBAHU-ZU was thrown into a panic. The alarm was sent out. Death was about to crash down from the sky. Starships, cargo ships, ship of every sort, were commandeered for the purposes of evacuation. However, it was too late! Nothing could be done! The inhabitants of TIAMAT had no chance, they could not be rescued, and it was too late!

Lord AR-ZU could hear the screams of his people over the beams of communication. Turning his head away, AR-ZU turned off the audio linkage. AR-ZU's pilots veered his ship away. Lord AR-ZU had to be saved! The collision was moments away!

As the dying AR Death ship struck the planet, the ship of Lord AR-ZU was enveloped in blinding light. In moments, the shock wave struck the ship, bouncing it around as if it were a leaf caught up in a tidal wave. Tumbling and twisting, the ship of Lord AR-ZU was thorn in the direction of TARGALLU, narrowly missing the stone rings.

When his pilots regained control of the spinning ship, an uneasy Lord AR-ZU looked back towards his beloved TIAMAT.

It was no more.

The collision had ripped the paradise world apart. Huge chunks of the planet were flying in every direction. Magma, metal, fire and lightning mixed to create a rain of burning death. Where once the proud planet had stood, only rock debris, smoke and dust remained. Pieces of TIAMAT were still flying by him as AR-ZU moved in to view the destroyed planet. Through a cloud of dust, smoke and gas, Lord AR-ZU, hoping for the best, maneuvered towards the place TIAMAT had once stood. As he pulled out of the dark mists, he saw it!

TIAMAT... or what was left of it.

The huge planet, with a gaping hole in its side, a smoke trail behind it hurtled away from him towards the sun. The Prince turned away again; TIAMAT was plummeting to its death into the sun below. His people were dead.

AR-ZU was silent. As he looked out, his gaze was met by a solar system that had been ravaged and decimated. The War left its mark on the moons and planets of ARIDU. The lives, the cities and the solar system itself were seriously damaged and possibly irreparably so.

Lord AR-ZU looked at the trail of rubble between DAK-MU, the red planet and the giant world of BAR-BAR-U.

TIAMAT was no more! Only the 'grave' stones remained.

Lord AR-ZU, and the IKIKI who remained, returned to DAK-MU, the central fortress. DAK-MU, a wondrous world itself, would become the new Royal planet. On DAK-MU, Lord and King AR-ZU would begin again, rebuilding the glory of TIAMAT and constructing a new Golden era, independent of ASA-RRR.

Book 2 – Why Were They Called Gods…?

As Lord AR-ZU, now King ZU-ZU, rested in his Palace on a mountain top of DAK-MU, an astonishing massage was received. The largest fragment of TIAMAT had slowed in its fall toward the sun; it would not disappear into the fiery abyss at all! It would come to rest in its own orbit just within the orbit of DAK-MU.

Lord King ZU-ZU wasted no time. Summoning his own teams of Genesis scientists, he ordered them to rebuild the burned skeletal remains of TIAMAT. Somehow, in someway, King ZU-ZU would bring the glory of the Paradise world to life again.

The success of the Genesis scientists lifted the King's spirits. He immediately ordered the construction of a large monument, a palace, to commemorate the loyal fallen Warriors of ARIDU. It would also be a monument to his father and his grandfather. In the Hall of AL-AL-U (Valhalla) on the world reconstructed, they would be honored, and never to be forgotten.

For a time, the destruction of the AR and its war escort along with the quick seizure of the ninth Passageway and its outposts, held the Great AN-U at bay. The strength of ZU-ZU and his brilliant war tactics had surprised the ASA-RRR King and his military forces. It would take time to re-evaluate, to plan for another attack.

Book 2 – Why Were They Called Gods…?

The Theology, a Greek tale of old, relates the tale of Zeus (ZU-ZU) and the Olympus Gods (AL-AMBAHU-ZU) who battle against the Olden Gods with **(OSIRIR or SIRIUS)** *The Theology reveals that when Zeus went to war* with the Olden Gods, Typhon, a great and hideous monster, was sent by Olden Gods to destroy Zeus: "When Zeus vanquished (Typhon), (Typhon) was hurled down a crippled wreck. The huge earth groaned. A great part of huge earth was scorched by the terrible vapor, melting as tin melts... In the glow of a blazing fire did the earth melt down." (Typhon was a name of the AR of AN-U.)

But King ZU-ZU knew this could not last forever.

King AN-U had suffered much. He would not remain quiet, not for long. AN-U had suffered personal attack and injury, he had lost his flagship in a coup take-over, and he had lost a second Death planet in battle. ZU-ZU had caused much damage and loss to AN-U, and he had taken away a key element of the Empire's hold on the Ninth Passageway. AN-U would be understandably angry. His Empire had been challenged!

But AN-U had much more at stake, the future of the Ninth Passageway was at risk, as was his hold on the throne. Loss of control of the Ninth Passageway system might give the War Queens of ARI-AN reason to side with the Rebel ZU-ZU, mining of precious ores and the production of heavy metals were most critical. The Queens would not tolerate this vital industry interfered with. Clearly, the King would have to act quickly before the ARI-AN Queens decided to allow ZU-ZU to remain in power as they had permitted his grandfather AL-AL.

Moreover, that was not all that concerned AN-U, Prince EN-LIL, also forced to flee the ARIDU system, had returned to sit in Royal Court of ASA-RRR. The potential threat he posed could not be ignored either. The King faced danger everywhere.

But before he could act, the King received word that the SSS-T Queens wanted his presence in the ARI-AN Palace. This worried AN-U. He knew they would demand an accounting. His defeat at the hands of the rebel Lord AR-ZU needed to have a resolution and recourse for alleviation.

AN-U presented himself before the Queens; a plan for the counter-attack had been drawn up by his DAK Commanders. The argument for immediate action seemed obvious to him.

The ARI-AN Queens listened in silence as AN-U spoke. In his words were his arguments for the continuance of assaults upon the rebellious star system. On completion of his talk, AN-U felt confident he had made his point.

As he sat down, he turned to see the Chamber doors open. To his dismay, the rebel King ZU-ZU entered the Court. AN-U stands to protest, but was commanded to sit quietly.

As the Rebel spoke to the Queens, AN-U could not remain seated. Leaping to his feet, he was again ordered to sit down.

Book 2 – Why Were They Called Gods…?

King ZU-ZU made his position clear. He was the rightful King of ARIDU and the people wanted him. The system had not been destroyed, production of metals and the supply of vital minerals could continue. The argument with his Grandfather would be fulfilled; AR-ZU would honor earlier promises...but WITHOUT the presence of AN-U.

The Queens did not speak a word. However, after a moment, an Elder Queen stood up. Her words were stern. The civil war, regardless of cause, had caused the destruction of TIAMAT, a world crucial to the ARIDU, ASA-RRR and ARI-AN Empires. The lives of millions had been threatened; countless warriors of both systems had died.

The SSS-T Queens demanded the cessation of hostilities! There would be no further destruction! The agreements with King AL-AL, in the guise of King ZU-ZU, would continue! The war was over!

To the horror of King AN-U, the Rebel would be permitted to live! Once again, a Royal member of the House of AL-AL-U had thwarted him!

King AN-U was furious. This he would not permit! There would come a day, he vowed, when the solar system would be a part of the ASA-RRR Empire again.

Therefore,... the Golden Era of ZU-ZU would flourish, if only for a short time.

The tales of the world under the hand of King ZU-ZU were many. Though a savior to his people, he was still a King.... and subject to arbitrary whims. Still things were well.

Fate would once again interfere with the future of the ARIDU (Earth's) solar system.

Shortly after the confrontation in the SSS-T Palace, the ARI-AN Queens would find themselves facing the looming specter of war with an ages-old enemy. Unfortunately for ZU-ZU, the threat came from a neighboring star system, not far from his ARIDU solar system.

Advised of the threatening situation, AN-U recognized an opportunity to remove the Rebel from power. Approaching the ARI-AN Queens, King AN-U made an argument for the removal of the young King ZU-ZU. The Ninth Passageway was vital to the ARI-AN Empire. ZU-ZU, in his ambition to expand his Empire, might be swayed to accept support from the very same enemies who threatened to battle against the SSS-T Queens.

If ZU-ZU had rebelled against the ASA-RRR Empire WITHOUT aid, why would he not rebel against the SSS-T Queen WITH the support of ARI-AN enemies?

The ARI-AN Queens paused, and agreed. They would assist the ASA-RRR King in his return to the Ninth Passageway solar system to subdue King ZU-ZU. Lord King AN-U was elated! In this venture, he would not fall. This time, the war armadas of both the SSS-T and the ASA-RRR Empires would join forces! By marshalling together his Starships and Warriors alongside the forces of the SSS-T Queens, AN-U had assembled an armada such as had never been seen before.

Book 2 – Why Were They Called Gods…?

The skies of the SIRIAN worlds were filled with Warships and Starships. The ASA-RRR people, the ASA-RR-U cheered as the King's mighty army made ready its departure.

Victory was written in the heavens!

Lord King ZU-ZU was told that a diplomatic entourage was on its way to his solar system Kingdom. By the time he was to learn of the trickery, it would be too late.

Cloaked and in silence, the armada of Warships arrived at the outer edge of the ARIDU system before they were detected. This mistake would prove to be fatal to the King and his young Empire.

The battle was quick and decisive.

The invasion forces poured into the solar system. The sheer number of ASA-RRR and ARI-AN warships overwhelmed IKIKI and BEH forces of AR-ZU. In short time, the invasion forces surrounded the War Planet. However, the orders of attack, issued by King AN-U, did not allow for prisoners, DAK-MU was to suffer total annihilation. The Star fighters were furious in their decimation of everything on the surface of DAK-MU. The fireballs created by the missile strikes reduced everything, including stone buildings, to cinders and ash. Final strikes with the destructive beams of light and the searing heat beams vaporized everything that remained. What was not blown apart was burned and melted beyond recognition.

Book 2 – Why Were They Called Gods...?

King ZU-ZU was captured and subdued, sentenced to return to the SIRIAN Star system for punishment. All rebel warrior forces of King ZU-ZU were summarily executed, as were loyal, faithful followers. The entirety of the empire's population would be brutally and cruelly punished... guilty or not.

The War Planet's surface was obliterated. All traces of life under King ZU-ZU were destroyed. Cities were leveled, forests destroyed. The beauty of the planet and its civilization was no more. All forms of life were destroyed. With no animals or plants to feed its atmosphere, the once living and thriving planet died. Only its red sands remained. The blood red dust became a fitting memorial to the bloodshed of the Solar System War in which billions perished.

Great Lord King AN-U was relieved. The Evil, rebel King ZU-ZU was vanquished. The Hand of the ASA-RRR was once again restored to the Ninth Passageway, and the realm of the ARI-AN SSS-T Queens was strengthened once again.

Therefore, it was peaceful for a time...

ERIDU

The Starship of Prince EA moved slowly over the land. He examined the surface carefully. Enormous glacial ice sheets blanketed most of the upper and lower hemispheres, an equatorial strip was the only part left untouched.

The Prince and his crew had analyzed the data carefully; the landing sight had already been selected. As the Prince emerged and examined the area, the words of his father, King AN-U were clear. Rebuild the devastated system, he ordered Prince EA.

The destruction of the world of ZU-ZU had been complete. The planet of Red Sands was reduced to dust and rubble. All traces of life were destroyed. Without life and plants, the atmosphere died. Ice sheets formed from the poles almost to the equator, DAK-MU (MARS) was frozen in its death. In addition, its sister world, DAK-A-MU, had been transformed into a planet of arid, scorched lands and deadly poisonous oceans. ARIDU,(Earth) the once rebuilt home of the Rebel ZU-ZU, was also devastated. Only IRU, TARGALLU, and BAR-BAR-U remained relatively intact.

The Prince could not imagine what it must have been like to be in the middle of it all, in the center of the battle. He, like his brother, had been forced to flee. He looked up into the heavens. The Prince knew his brother was overhead.

Somewhere, on an orbiting military cruiser, he was up above, looking down on him. Prince EN-LIL was Lord of the Airways.

Re-build, Prince EA was commanded. The Prince looked at the destroyed world. The task would be great; he would make sure to fulfill his father's orders. He would re-build, and he would establish a mining operation, extracting vital ores and precious minerals. He would re-build the paradise world from the war-torn planet... and perhaps, he would do a little more. EA revealed in the thought.

Therefore, they began, Prince EA and his volunteer crew, the ANUNNAKI. The chosen site for the initial compound had lots of water and fertile soil. Studies had revealed deposits of precious ores far below. It was the logical place to begin.

Each of the members of the Prince's crew had been chosen because of his or her special skills or abilities. Each one had been assigned the rank of Lord, each had been granted an amount of property in ARIDU, and each was given a fair share of future monetary returns from the new colonies.

The rewards were generous, the dangers considerable.

The Prince had taken his time in selecting his crew the stakes was high. But he was proud they were good.

The first assignment was the construction of the base of Operations. The compound would be built in stone, naturally durable and readily available. Nevertheless, the Anunnaki began to set up the cutting lights and sound carriers, the generators ceased to operate. The natural energy grid lines of energy, common to all worlds, were fluctuating wildly on the planet. The 'Great Collision', the event, which had created the world they stood on, had caused the inner core to become unstable, thus causing a constant wavering of the energy lines.

To produce a stable supply of power, Prince EA located a point where six energy lines naturally intersected. Here on the intersection, the Prince erected a large Energy House, a focusing center that would extract sufficient energy to run the construction equipment. Power crystals, specially grown for just such a purpose, were place in the Energy Chambers.

The Energy House would also hold the Re-animation Center within its walls. Fatally injured technicians must be taken care of immediately, Prince EA could not afford to lose even one of his carefully chosen crew.

And, because the irregularly pulsating energy lines made Star ship instruments unreliable, the Energy House was built with four highly reflective triangular sides that allowed an aerial orientation for pilots high above.

As the dreaded D-K were 'Destroyers of Life', so the Anunnaki were known as K-D, the 'Givers of Life'.

Slowly the power problems began to be resolved. But for much of the time, power anomalies made progress difficult in every aspect of the mining and construction projects. Field technicians were forces to perform unexpected physical labor to compensate for failed equipment. The Anunnaki were few, the labors many. The Anunnaki complained, Prince EA relayed the words to King AN-U, but the King would not hear of their problems. Production would still have to increase!

The Anunnaki felt overworked and ignored, they protested and threatened to cease their labors. Prince EA promised an increase in future rewards. Grudgingly, but with additional recompense promised, the Anunnaki returned to their labors.

Construction and mining/recovery crews switched to lower consumption cutting lights and sound wave movers. However, lower consumption meant lower output. Production was slowed down, causing King AN-U concern. To this end, Prince EA began the use of beasts of burden to assist the Anunnaki. Progress in the operation slow, but there was progress.

But in time, the operation was able to begin sending the gold shipments on schedule. Transport ships landed on ARIDU and departed with their vital cargoes. Gold was immediately sent back to ASA-RRR, other precious ores were sent right to the BAR-BAR-U and TARGALLU refineries. Even the tilting and erratic spinning KAKKAB SHANAMMA began to show signs of life on its surface.

Construction crews completed the stone structures of the compound, making the ARIDU settlement look more like a city, and not a mining camp. In addition, in the center of the compound, a magnificent Agricultural-Biological center was fast becoming the centerpiece of the stone city.

Book 2 – Why Were They Called Gods…?

The Prince had done well the Great AN-U was pleased.

Prince EA's Operation had allowed AN-U to retain control of the ARIDU solar system and keep his hold on the Star lanes in the Passageway. EA had succeeded beyond the expectations of his father. His talents as a Genesis Master were put to the test and he exceeded the task.

TIAMAT was re-born!

King AN-U immediately sent a dispatch. 'Old ARIDU', the 'Conquered Place', was dead! 'ERIDU', the 'Enslaved Place', was alive! No one would ever doubt the power, the might and vengeance of the ASA-RRR King again! The name of the colony would serve as a reminder and a warning to anyone who sought to challenge or question the might of the great AN-U!

The Hand of AN-U would always be upon ERIDU!

From ERIDU come the words for EARTH: Erde (German): ERDA (Old High German); Jordh (Icelandic); Airtha (Gothic); Jord (Danish); Erthe (Middle English)

Prince EA was assigned the title EN-GI, 'Lord of ERIDU'. The devastated world was a living place again! EA carefully manipulated and engineered animal and plant life forms that could endure in the harsh environment and poisonous nitrogen air of the planet. Atmospheric conditioning units began to make the air breathable and warmer. Often laboring

Book 2 – Why Were They Called Gods…?

for many time periods, the Prince gave little thought to rest.

However, the continuing efforts of Prince EA were not without their rewards. One of his ambitions, the establishment of a Center for Life Sciences, an agricultural/biological center, was actually achieved. An above ground laboratory, the Life Center produced and nurtured the hybrid seedlings and hybrid creatures, which would be transplanted around the globe. The Center became Prince EA's pride and joy, a Garden for Life.

Once again, the world began to take on the look and feel of a paradise world. Once again, the planet was alive! Though ERIDU was once again a harbinger of life, the planets of DAK-MU (Mars) and DAK-A-MU (Venus) were forbidden to have life once again on its surface. The Great AN-U decreed that both worlds would remain barren; they would serve as warning to any potential challenger. The Wrath of AN-U was great!

The Agricultural Center was also making great strides in creating new and unique life forms capable of surviving the atmosphere of ERIDU. But the experiments occupied Prince EA much of the time, taking him away from administration duties so necessary to a Lord.

The Great King AN-U was upset. The King of ASA-RRR had put Prince EA in charge of ERIDU because of his Genesis abilities. Prince EN-LIL, his second son, was to remain in charge of the airways and lanes of the ERIDU solar system. But Prince EN-LIL was once again making sounds of great displeasure in being placed so far away from the Royal Palace of ASA-RRR. This further upset the King.

And so, he moved to resolve the problems.
Prince EN-LIL was given administration control of ERIDU, the solar system, the planet and the city. But control over the development and exploitation of the planets would remain with Prince EA. Thus, dominion over ERIDU would be shared! In this way, King AN-U believed he could continue to keep an angry EN-LIL away from the court, fulfill his ambitions as a Lord of Power, and still utilize the abilities of Prince EA.
Prince EA, still EN-GI, was shattered and angry. All of his efforts and successes had been ignored, his place in the faraway empire stripped away. In anger, the Prince of Life left ERIDU, moving to a distant region in order to build yet another Agricultural-Biological Center. Here, in addition, he would develop a gold mining operation, but here, he would focus on his passion, the engineering of Life. Joined by his sister, Princess NIN-HUR-SAG, also a Genesis Scientist, both began a re-newel effort in the creation of life forms for the planet of ERIDU. In addition, in this effort, Princess NIN-HUR-SAG would be the creator of a 'hybrid' creature that would forever change the destiny of ERIDU and its ASA-RRR Masters.

In the meantime, Prince EN-LIL would use his own skills to streamline the Operation. Increasing production, calling for additional cargo flights, and demanding increased labors from the ANUNNAKI, Prince EN-LIL produced greater quantities of ore for less cost, and in shorter time. This pleased the Great King AN-U greatly.

But the demand for higher production stressed the worker ANUNNAKI to the breaking point. Fueled by the isolation and distance from loved ones the anger of the ANUNNAKI became a work stoppage, a strike. When threatened with punishment, a group of Anunnaki's attacked the palace of EN-LIL itself. His life threatened, Prince EN-LIL immediately called on AN-U to descend to the faraway Kingdom.

Angrily the King responded to the call from ERIDU. Both Prince EN-LIL and the Anunnaki demanded an audience with the King. The angry laborers asked for the immediate removal of Prince EN-LIL. Even the Prince himself, was asked to be removed, his desire was to return to the far away Royal High Court of ASA-RRR. Quietly yet firmly, Lord Prince EA added his voice to the requests for the re-assignment of his brother. Again faced with a serious situation, King AN-U was forced to make his way to the troubled outpost!

Arriving in the Palace of ERIDU, AN-U immediately held a hearing for the purpose of resolution of the situation. The voices were loud and

Book 2 – Why Were They Called Gods...?

angry. Everyone presented his case for the return of Prince EN-LIL to the court of ASA-RRR. No one asked for his continued rule. When the voices were finally quiet, the wishes of every member of the assembly was clear, EN-LIL must go.

Everyone turned to the King. He sat in silence he made no movement. He was sorely troubled, he had hoped that Lord Prince EN-LIL could somehow be kept in ERIDU. The Great and Wise AN-U found himself wanting, needing, a solution.

Seeing his opportunity, Prince EA stepped forward. With Princess NIN-HUR-SAG at his side, the Prince proposed to his Father and the Assembly, a simple solution. Within the Life Centers, he and the Princess had engineered many hybrids for use in labor in the fields. Utilizing genetic substances from the ASA-RRR people themselves and the genetic materials of ERIDU beasts created hybrid creatures of half ASA-RRR blood, the creatures retained their natural strengths but also gained sufficient intelligence to understand commands. The earlier success of the 'H-N' Lizard hybrid worker in the underground mines proved the worth of such an experiment. Other fabricated beasts, successful in specialized tasks only, were the "SEMT-UR", a half horse, half ASA-RRR hybrid, capable of carrying burdens long distances; and the powerful 'MENT-UR', a half bull, half ASA-RRR being with a capability of phenomenal feats of strength. The success of the hybrids had encourage Prince EA and Princess NIN-HUR-SAG to attempt yet another untried combination, one which would resolve the difficulty at hand.

King AN-U sat forward in his throne. The possibility of hybrid beasts as a solution to his problems was intriguing.

Prince EA, seeing the interest of the King, turned to an awaiting Princess NIN-HUR-SAG. He motioned to her; she made a gesture into the hallway. The show was about to begin.

To the surprise of everyone gathered, a huge hairy black beast came forward. It was the 'APA', a beast of the jungle, renowned for its strength and ferocity.

Cries of protest and fear went up from the assembly the beast was unchained! Nevertheless, before anyone could move, Princess NIN-HUR-SAG gave the beast a command, which the beast calmly and obediently followed. And in the next few moments, while everyone watches, the beast obeyed every command of the Lady Genesis scientist.

When the demonstration was completed, the Prince explained his idea to the King. The creature, a beast of great strength and limited intelligence could be genetically altered to become a laborer in the mines, taking the hardships away from the Anunnaki and freeing them for the more important tasks of construction.

The Great AN-U was impressed. Indeed the hybrid proposed seemed to be the solution. The murmurs of the Anunnaki seemed to be approving, EA felt. He smiled; sure, he had succeeded in removing him from ERIDU.

Book 2 – Why Were They Called Gods…?

King AN-U stood up.

Prince EA expected good news, ERIDU would be his now, EN-LIL would soon be gone. The dominion of the solar system would finally be rightfully his.

The King made his pronouncement. Prince EA would begin the immediate genetic changes needed to alter the beast! ALL Anunnaki laborers would return to their operations until the new creature was ready for work in the fields!

But to the horror of Prince EA, the King ended his words with an announcement that cut like a knife into his being... EN-LIL would remain in charge of ERIDU! The Beast of Prince EA would alleviate the situation and allow EN-LIL to stay!

Such were the words of King, so it would be!

Prince EA was shattered! He had once again been denied the Throne of ERIDU! EN-LIL, his life-long adversary, was a victor once again!

Storming from the Palace, Prince EA vowed he would never again enter the ERIDU Palace again until the throne was his! Though he had been the first-born son of King AN-U, he would never ascend to the Throne of ASA-RRR because Prince EN-LIL, the younger son, was born to King AN-U by his half-sister, a requirement in the ASA-RRR Rulers of Succession. Now the Throne of ERIDU had also taken away from him!

The enmity between the two had extended even to the very purpose of life itself. EN-LIL had believed the purpose of life was to give undying service to the Kings and the Throne of ASA-RRR. Nevertheless, the Genesis Sciences had revealed something highly different to Prince EA. <u>Life controlled was not life evolved, as blasphemous as that might be in ASA-RRR. Prince EA saw life as an opportunity for exploration of self.</u> Born of the same blood and world, no two brothers could have been further apart in their ways.

Therefore, the words of the Great AN-U added to the already raging feud between the two Princes. Prince EN-LIL would be Lord of the Word (Command) and continue his iron rule, while Prince EA would remain the Genesis Lord, developing ERIDU to the expectations of his father.

Prince EA resigned himself to his task; redesigning the beast, his sister had initiated to suit the needs of the work community of the Anunnaki. With his sister beside him, the Prince began the intricate procedures, nevertheless, his anger was in his heart, and would not leave his thoughts.

Thus the revenge of EA was born. Although directed to use the cellular material from one of the Anunnaki Lords, specifically chosen by Prince EN-LIL, <u>Prince EA substituted cells of his own choosing for the experiment. The time for the uncovering of the true identity of the beast would someday come, and he Prince EA, would have the last laugh.</u>

Book 2 – Why Were They Called Gods...?

Prototype after prototype was tried. Slowly, the beast was developed in intelligence without sacrificing strengths. Through experimentation in the field, the final product made its appearance. Rushed into service, the beast immediately proved itself. With strong arms and back, dexterity of hand and intelligent enough to follow instruction, the creature's versatility soon created a strong demand by the Anunnaki for additional beasts. The APA hybrid, known as 'ADAPA', was an able beast, ready to serve his masters.

Prince EN-LIL was unhappy with the beast from the first. He did not trust the temperament either of the creature, nor his brother. The beast was dangerous, controlling it was an undertaking he had no wish to do. There was a foreboding, a sense of trouble in EN-LIL's being, he could not rest easy.

But forced to use the beast by his father's Word, Prince EN-LIL decided to put the beast in the most perilous of work situations and in the harshest environments. The creature was an experiment and therefore, expendable.

Demanding that beasts that fell from their labors not be relieved, or tended to, the Prince was responsible for the deaths of many of the creatures. They were, after all, only beasts.

Prince EA received the news with horror! The creatures, His experimental ADAPA beasts, were being worked to death by his brother's orders. The creatures were not labor helpers; they had become slaves, inconsequential, disposable, and slaves.

Book 2 – Why Were They Called Gods...?

Prince EA had never felt such anger before. Everything, all of his efforts, were being systematically destroyed, his reclamation of ERIDU, the planet; his successful building of ERIDU, the city; and the creation and engineering of a beats of labor. There was wanton destruction of everything Prince EA had worked. His entire life's history was an on-going tale of submission to the whims of his brother.

Now it would come to a halt! Prince EA would strike back. He would make his brother pay for his sins... though a vehicle unexpected... the beast!

Returning to the Agricultural Center in ERIDU, Prince EA sought out the beasts in the Garden where they fed. Finding several of them alone, he approached them. Careful planning and precise breeding schedules permitted only certain beasts to mate, and only under the strictest supervision. No beast could mate without the approval of the Lord of the Word the results could be disastrous.

But Prince EA, in the Garden, introduced the beasts to a simple pleasure... the pleasure of spontaneous, unsupervised, sex Reacting from basic instincts, the beasts took to Lord EA's instruction quickly. Playful at first, then earnest in their enjoyment, the beasts frolicked in the Garden.

The Prince watched as the beasts reveled in the pleasure of intimacy. In a short life filled with agonies and labor, the brief moments of pleasure were a godsend. Moreover, with this new knowledge, the beast could be as his Masters, choosing a moment's pleasure without scheduling, without approval! The beasts looked back at the Prince, he had given them a little taste of true happiness. Their Creator, a Genesis Scientist whose mark was two intertwined strands of DNA, like serpents mating, had endowed them with the knowledge of 'knowing'.

In time, their Masters knew the clandestine 'behavior' of the beasts. Lord Prince ENLIL, informed of the furious. An immediate command was issued to round up all of the offending creatures, all renegade creatures were to be severely punished and instantly thrown out of the Life Center. Prince EN-LIL would tolerate no disobedience!

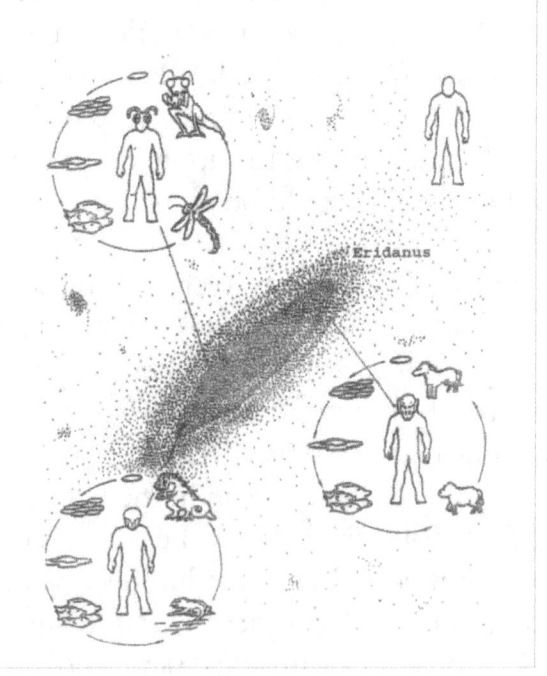

Book 2 – Why Were They Called Gods…?

Prince EN-LIL knew that somehow his brother had been the cause of the beast's horrendously criminal behavior. Only a Genesis scientist could affect the beast's temperament, only Prince EA could have had access to the creature. His brother was undermining EN-LIL he knew it! However, EN-LIL was not to be trifled with. To prevent further transgression, a new set of strict Commands for ADAPA beasts still within the Life Center and in the field operations was issued.

Thus were issued the commands of the Lord of the Word:

All beasts in the Agricultural Center must give complete and total obedience to Lord EN-LIL only! Loyalty to Prince EA or any other Lord Creator (K-D) was strictly forbidden!

All beasts in the Agricultural Center must give complete and total obedience to Lord EN-LIL! All traces of Prince EA and any other Lord Creator (K-D) will be removed. Any beast carrying any remembrances of Prince EA will be punished!

Remembrances of Prince EA will be punished!

All beasts in the Agricultural Center must give complete and total obedience to Lord EN-LIL! Any beast uttering evil sounds or angry sounds about Lord EN-LIL will be punished!

All beasts in the Agricultural Center must give complete and total obedience to Lord EN-LIL! Every beast must attend an obedience lesson every seventh period!

All beasts in the Agricultural Center must give complete and total obedience to Lord EN-LIL! Lord EN-LIL must approve the pairing together of beasts for mating! No beast 'my' mate outside of the pairing approved by Lord.

Such were the Commands of the Lord of the Word!

Prince EN-LIL would not be challenged! He would keep an Iron Hand over ERIDU. Let the beasts die in the wilderness! Let Prince EA care for them! They are 'MUS', 'Monsters' and deserve no assistance! Let the renegade beast henceforth be called 'ADA-MUS'! Let the females suffer in childbirth! No longer will the birthing chambers be available to them!

If the beasts of the Garden remain faithful, they shall be allowed to remain. They shall be called ADAPA.

Therefore, the beast was divided into two groups the faithful and the unfaithful, ADAPA AND THE ADAMUS.

Prince EA was pleased, however. For in the cast-outs, a chance to continue the experiment to create independent life still existed. His desire to fabricate a life form that was intelligent, yet independent of the 'System' that Prince EA, and Prince EN-LIL, had grown up in, was still possible. The beast would have a chance at freedom and independence, something that he, as a Prince of ASA-RRR, had not had.

The beast had been a testament to the Genesis skills of Prince EA, a Lord K-D. Engineering the combination of brute strength with some measure of intelligence had been tedious, but the Prince wanted more for the creature. Developing the beast's ability to speak had been a priority for Lord EA, it allowed communication with the K-D's and provided a means of measuring progress. Though the beast's vocabulary was minimal, it was understandable.

Locating pockets of the rejected beasts in the wilds, EA and his sister NIN-HUR-SAG began to teach them the skills of survival necessary in the cruel environment. From the first fire to the making of simple clothing, from making scratches on cave walls to the reading of symbols, both Lords of the Genesis Sciences took the beast along the path to a higher intelligence. The experimental 'prototype' of Princess NIN-HUR-SAG, had gone through several stages of development, but it had proven to be unique in its abilities.

In time, several of the beasts exhibited the exceptional ability of learning and communicating its knowledge to other beasts. Prince EA and his sister began to focus most of the attention on them, teaching them so that they might begin to spread the knowledge to others. These 'teachers', taught by K-D himself, became known as the 'SU', 'They who knew'. The 'EA-SU', the teachers spread the 'The Way of EA'.

Book 2 – Why Were They Called Gods...?

A later 'Teacher of Righteousness' would bear the name IESU (Jesus), a variation of EA-SU.

As the beasts in the wild progressed through the efforts of Prince EA, Lord Prince EN-LIL became further angered with the creatures. Though many of the ADAPA beasts still served loyally and faithfully in the ERIDU compound, still the Lord of the World felt hatred and distrust for the creature.

The AR Flagship, the ASA-RRR ship of State, was expected to arrive in ERIDU soon. Knowing that the massive Death ship cause an enormous gravitational pull, the Prince decided to steer the course of the AR into a path he could utilize. By changing the path over the icy poles, the gravitational pull would be strong enough to cause glacier to fall into ocean. This in turn would cause needed environmental changes. If a resultant flooding destroyed the beasts, then so be it! The Prince of the Word could justify the sacrifice of the beasts in exchange for the warming of the planet, the increasing of the amount of usable ocean waters, and the end of an ice age gripping the upper and lower hemispheres. All of that was of significantly greater import than the fate of the beast. When Lord K-D EA discovered the plans of his brother, he made immediate protest. However, the Lord of the Word would give no heed. In addition, to make matters worse, Prince EN-LIL forbade a single ADAMUS is spared; only the loyal ADAPA would be given shelter from the floodwaters. The renegade beasts would be sacrificed if necessary they had broken the commands. In addition, the Lord of the Word cautioned the Prince, giving warning to the beast was aiding an enemy of the state, a heinous crime!

Prince EA was trapped! To work with rejected creatures that was one thing, to give Royal aid was another. With not much choice in the matter, Prince EA gave his solemn oath to remain silent, giving no warning about the impending floods. Though reluctant to accept his brother's Word, Prince EN-LIL continued his plans for the ceremonial arrival of the AR.

Nevertheless, the Genesis Prince could not allow his beast to die. In secret, Lord EA made plans. Taking several of the beasts to the underground caverns of the 'HEN-T' hybrids, and other beasts to mountain highlands, Prince EA assured the survival of at least some of the beasts. As a final measure, Lord EA had a special cargo ship constructed that would sail far out into the ocean, away from the regions most likely to suffer. With these secret plans, Prince EA kept ADAMUS alive and his experiment intact. When the mighty AR returned, the floods began as EN-LIL had expected them to. He felt relieved; the beast would not be around to disturb him anymore.

When the floods subsided, and Lord EN-LIL discovered the deceit of his brother, his rage was uncontrollable. The two Princes confronted each other in the ERIDU Palace. Each had betrayed the other, Lord EN-LIL had attempted to destroy the prototypes of Prince EA's beast in its early stages, and Lord EA had tried to undo his brother's administration by tampering with the beast's breeding. EN-LIL had tried to destroy the beast with a flood; EA had broken a promise not to warn his creation, the beast.

Each Prince had committed a crime against the Empire, an act of deliberate sabotage of the assigned duties of a Royal Prince of the Throne. Neither would ever achieve the Throne if that kind of behavior continued. But Prince EA had never believed the Throne of ASA-RRR would ever be his, the Rights of Succession assured him of that. Prince EN-LIL, however, was the Heir Apparent. He could stand to lose everything!

Prince EN-LIL, Lord of the Word, had no choice. He made a decision. There must be a truce. Never again would he or any one of his Administrations interfere with Lord EA's duty, the development of ERIDU and all of its life forms. Lord EA had no alternative but to return the promise. He and all of the K-D's would never interfere with Lord EN-LIL again.

As a sign of his good intentions, Prince EN-LIL gave his brother agricultural implements for the beast, tools for him so that the beast could learn how to grow his own food. The Genesis Prince was surprised, but grateful for the gift from his brother, in exchange Prince EA promised to enhance the skills and abilities of certain special hybrids used by Lord EN-LIL in the administration of ERIDU.

Thus, for a time, the peace on ERIDU came to be. All the Beasts were, 'allowed to become educated and civilized; the Empire of ERIDU under EN-LIL grew and prospered. Genetic manipulation had given the beast the ability for minimal communication and understanding. Though engineered enhancement, the ADAPAS who remained in the Garden were made significantly stronger in analytic through processing. They became highly intelligent, capable of small-scale decisions, but remained docile and servile. Using ADAPAS and HEN-T servants, Prince EN-LIL and the ANUNNAKI were able to make dramatic progress in the ERIDU Operation.

The ADAMUS beasts, however, uncontrolled in their sexual activity grew quickly in number. Genetic manipulation would be more difficult in producing specific traits in them. Any genetic enhancement would be subject to random breeding, the desired results probably watered down. At best, only some of the beasts would retain the desired attributes, most of them would lose the hoped for traits entirely. But through personal contact and his EA-SU, Lord EA gave the ADAMUS beast what the ADAPA would never get, a chance to appreciate beauty. Teaching the beast how to enjoy and feel the wonders of art and music, the Prince in culled a sense of self and an awareness of the world around him. <u>Untainted by any influences of the ASA-RRR 'System', the ADAMUS</u>

<u>developed a sense of belonging to a family, and a sense of shaping and choosing his own destiny.</u>

The Prince was pleased. The System would not take hold, not with the beast. It had a chance, or so he hoped. In an effort to insure the beast would never again be desirable to system, Lord EA continued to enhance the sexual drive of the creature. If placed in a situation of choice, labors in the service of the System or pursuit of sexual pleasure, the beast would always choose sex. This would make the beast an undesirable in the eyes of his Brother EN-LIL.

Two distinct beasts, the ADAPA and the ADAMUS, were part of planet ERIDU. Lord Prince EA, a Master Genesis Sciences was 'Lord (EL) of the Beasts' (EL-EA or LEO). Prince EN-LIL Lord of the Command was 'Lord of obedient Servants'.

As word of Prince EA's beast spread to neighboring stars and galaxies, another group of Genesis Lords extended a gift to Lord EA. Known as the 'AKHU', they were descended from a bird-like ancestor. The Genesis Lords presented EA with the single strand of DNA filament that provided 'passion'. With this one single element, the invisible motivation force that gave a being intense feelings was passed on to the beasts of the Prince. In addition, with this gift, the ADAMUS beast would have even more passion, more feeling, than even the beings of the ASA-RRR Empire themselves. Taken from the cells of the AKHU, the offering became known as 'The Gift of the Feather'.

Thus, the paths of the two beasts, the ADAPAs of EN-LIL, and the ADAMUS of EN-GI or EN-KI, continued to separate. Of the same roots, initially for the same purpose, the two were now on different paths.

With time, Prince EA and Prince EN-LIL were able to make both groups work together. The ADAPA beasts completed their labors as obedient servants; the ADAMUS beasts completed the labors in exchange for food and supplies. As ERIDU expanded from one compound into many, the use of both beasts became a commonplace occurrence; ERIDU was a world of laboring beasts.

The World of ERIDU had become the new capitol of the far away solar system, a system nearly destroyed by the War with Lord AR-ZU and his rebels. Its restoration had strengthened the hold of King AN-U on the Ninth Passageway, assuring that his place with the ARI-AN Queens was secure. ERIDU, Capitol City; ERIDU Capitol World; and ERIDU, the solar system, had become a thriving, productive system.

But the way of the ASA-RRR always involved internal war. Offspring of both Prince EA and Prince EN-LIL made constant war with each other. Jealousy, envy and sheer want of power motivated members of the Royal families to attack each other and seize holdings. In addition, so long as Empire itself was in a way imperiled by the Royal wars, they

Book 2 – Why Were They Called Gods...?

were permitted. It was good for the young to test their war mettle against each other, from these things the way of the ASA-RRR was born.

Moreover, since Prince EA had given the beast the ability to learn and retain the knowledge, many Royals began to use the beast in the administration of their small kingdoms, using a beast to control other beasts. To the horror of the Prince, many beasts pledged fidelity to their Lords in exchange for an unending source of food and shelter. The one fear of Prince EA had been that the beast might return to the system if its survival was threatened, and now the fear had been realized. <u>But free will had been part of the experiment of the beasts,</u> if Prince EA interfered, he would defeat his own purposes in creating the beast. Therefore, the beast learned war.

The wars of the Royals were merely planetary chess games with pieces comprised of servants and beasts. Re-animation, a technique for bringing a dead being back to life, *(a good example is, Star Gate-Movie / TV Show)*, and medical transplants, were always available to the Royals in case of an injury or fatality. But crippling injury, wounds and death, that was for the lowly soldiers on the field that was saved for the beast.

But the beast proved itself, again and again. Loyal and intelligent, the beast had become vital participants in the running of ERIDU daily events. The ASA-RRR genetic background of the beast had a profound influence in its ability to learn and to adapt to the 'System'.

Book 2 – Why Were They Called Gods…?

Through the guiding efforts of Prince EA, the Royals and the ANUNNAKI, in time the beast was permitted to minister to its own affairs, to run its own small kingdom or territory... as long as it continued to pledge its loyalty and fidelity to one of the Royal Lords... and ultimately, to the Empire of ASA-RRR!

Therefore, ADAMA became part of ERIDU. From a role strictly as a slave beast of labor to a role as a contributing member of society (with an understanding of faithfulness to a Lord above), the ADAMA had risen to a place above other creatures of the world, second only to his Lord above.

The Wars of the Royals raged on, faithful ADAMAS serving on the battlefields for them. ERIDU Kingdoms rose and fell on the backs and the blood of the ADAMAS. Children of Lord EN-LIL and Lord EA constantly challenged each other over the rights of domain and power.

And so began the era that would see the War of the Great take-over, an attempt by Lord Prince MARDUK, son of Lord EA, King of the Beasts. An accomplished Master in the skills of the DAK Warriors Prince MARDUK wanted to become King of the system of ERIDU. Challenging other Royal family members for the Throne, including his uncle, Prince EN-LIL, and even his father, Lord EA, MARDUK would use war, works of intrigue and even the deadly art of betrayal to try to seize the Throne.

His father, EA, had been deprived of the Throne of ERIDU and ASA-RRR...he, MARDUK, would not suffer the same fate.

But in the midst of his rise to power, Prince MARDUK was wrongfully accused of the assassination of his own brother, Lord Prince DUMUZZI. Refusing to be imprisoned, MARDUK chose to fight against his accusers, taking refuge in a pyramid fortress. A hasty council was called, the decision made to end the war by sealing MARDUK into his stone structure. Trapped within, Prince MARDUK was doomed to death.

But fortune was with him. Several of his followers were able to tunnel up from beneath the structure, thereby giving MARDUK an opportunity to escape. With a bounty on his head, Prince MARDUK fled into the heavens,(Space).

And for a while, peace once again came to ERIDU... but as is the way of the ASA-RRR Empire, it would not last long.

High above within the stars of the ARI-AN Empire, MARDUK would find an ally, an ages-old enemy of AN-U and the Queens of the SSS-T Throne. Known as 'SSA-TA', 'underground ones', they were part of a reptilian rebel group who inhabited huge caverns within the worlds of the ARI-AN. Constantly threatening the Queens in power, they unceasingly searched for new ways to undermine the rule of the Queens.

Book 2 – Why Were They Called Gods...?

Despised and dreaded, the SSA-TA rebels gave audience to the Prince. Promising them great wealth and power, and full participation in his Empire in exchange for their support, a daunting MARDUL elicited their support.

Eagerly, the SSA-TA seized the opportunity to support an effort against the ASA-RRR. By weakening the DAK Empire, so too, the SSS-T Queens would be weakened. Perhaps enough so that their rebellion in ARI-AN would succeeds. Sending a communiqué throughout the ARI-AN Empire to their allies, the SSA-TA raised huge numbers of Warriors, each a dedicated and willing enemy of the SSS-T Queens.

By secretly supporting MARDUK, success in the take-over of the ERIDU colonies would give the SSA-TA rebels a tremendous stranglehold on the Ninth Passageway, (or STARGATE). The SSS-T Queens would have to negotiate with them. Should the rebellion not succeed, the death of MARDUK would satisfy both the SIRIANS, and the Queen? The Queen would tolerate the failure of a civil war far away from the SSS-T Empire.

Once again, the specter of a war loomed on the horizon of the ERIDU solar system.

But the success of another rebellion in ERIDU was remote at best. The Great AN-U had gone to great lengths to assure himself that another War of Revolution could not occur.

Book 2 – Why Were They Called Gods...?

To succeed, there would have to be yet another group who would have to give active support to Prince MARDUK, one that had a firm foothold within the ERIDU solar system itself and was part of the integral EN-LIL forces of Command.

Deep within the mining operations, the HEN-T hybrid had proven themselves as loyal servants. Long before the ADAMUS had done so, the HEN-T hybrid had risen to a position as one of the Royal families of ERIDU most faithful administrators. And, although many of the Royal off-spring families had used the ADAMUS beast as administrators over other beasts, Prince EN-LIL had continued to use only the HEN-T, considering them to be less of a threat and much more obedient. Key mid-level administration positions were assigned strictly to the HEN-T hybrids and never to an ADAMA beast.

Unlike the ADAMUS beast, Lord Prince EA had not altered, had not manipulated the HEN-T to a higher intelligence, thus making it more servile and less of a choice maker. But more crucial to the planned War of Darkness by Prince MARDUK, the HEN-T was created from the cellular materials of the lizards it was therefore a reptile! As distant relations of the SSA-TA rebels, they could be approached and possibly persuaded.

With the behind, the scenes of the SSA-TA, the Prince and an army of Masters of Deceit began their campaign to seduce the HEN-T servants of Lord EN-LIL. Promising the HEN-T that they would become his administrators, if the take-over were a success, MARDUK and the SSA-TA used every trick to swing the HEN-T over to the rebel side. MARDUK even offered shares in the wealth and riches of the Empire and future territory for their control. Their place in the Empire of MARDUK would be the best but the Prince himself.

Therefore, the secret take-over began. Using HEN-T hybrids, created and developed by the ARI-AN SSS-T for their use, the vengeful MARDUK secretly maneuvered his agents deep into the mines, the administrative offices and the Command Forces of EN-LIL himself.

As the HEN-T hybrids had moved up in the ranks of Prince EN-LIL's administration, they had become known as 'TCHET-T', 'Those of the TCHET-T (The 'Word'... the 'Word' being EN-LIL.)' Referred to as the 'SHET-I' or 'SHET' by the administration members of EN-LIL, they became trusted servants of both Lord Prince EN-LIL himself and the Royal families. His or her loyalty was never in doubt no one suspected the betrayal.

Slowly and quietly, the conspiracy began. The plot was simple, SSA-TA lizards, trained for subterfuge, and would infiltrate the ranks of the HEN-T workers. They would spread the word and recruit their distant cousins to the rebellion. In short time, the SHET were able to persuade the HEN-T lizards to enter the folds of the rebels. The HEN-T who joined with the plot became known as 'SHET-I', the Secret Ones'.

Following the initial infiltration of the ranks of HEN-T in the underground operations, the conspiracy moved into the inner core of the administration of Lord Prince EN-LIL. The command Forces, including the Communication and Logistic departments, were also targeted. Carefully and deliberately, the conspiracy gained a foothold in every department of Lord Prince EN-LIL's administration.

In time, Prince MARDUK and the hidden SHET-I were ready. Word was given to begin the attack. Invading ERIDU with his warships, MARDUK attacked viciously and unmercifully. ERIDU DAK and BEH forces were surprised. HEN-T workers in communication rooms disrupted messages of the invasion, preventing effective defensive action.

When finally notified, the DAK warriors responded in war hips that had been sabotaged, thus rendering them impotent. Many ships were detoured, or given wrong coordinates. ERIDU communications systems went silent. EN-LIL was undone. The SHET-I, and the turncoat HEN-T hybrids, had done well.

ERIDU, the island outpost of the ASA-RRR Empire, was now the seized empire of Lord Prince MARDUK, son of Prince EN-KI and grandson to king AN-U. MARDUK had been victorious, the 'War of Take-over', backed by the reptilian rebels, had been successful beyond expectations. The stealth and subterfuge, hid hidden deviousness, had prevented direct confrontation.

Prince EN-LIL and his followers fled back to the distant worlds of ASA-RRR. Prince EA took many of his followers and ADAMUS beasts to his star system, 'BAAL-EA-DAUS' (Pleiades) 'Place of BAAL (Lord) EA DA (The Creator)'.

The Royal offspring of both Lords EA and EN-LIL were also forced to flee. As MARDUK landed on the world of ERIDU his place on the Throne was unchallenged. To insure that no challenge might occur in the future, the Prince immediately ordered a search for any remaining Royal heirs. Their choice would be easy, total subjugation or death. The entire ERIDU Empire would bow to MARDUK, he would see to that.

SO IT BEGINS

This is where all records are destroyed and or changed. So, MARDUK thought. Then the Being 'MARDUK' saying he was the creator of all things and that you need to bow and to pray to him. If you did not then you were killed...

But, we just learned that, he is not the SO-CALLED one god, there were many before him. Nevertheless, MARDUK destroyed all the knowledge and history prior to him. MARDUK re-written all history, to suit his needs, of being this so-called 1st, and only god.

Book 2 – Why Were They Called Gods...?

This is the 2nd story of the creation of gods, and the creation of the Human race.

Once seated, MARDUK began his final campaign... to change or destroy any records, which attributed any heroic or kingly achievements to anyone other than himself. Stone monuments, obelisks and edifices were altered by stonecutters; tablets of clay or wood were burned or destroyed. No records of any other Monarch would remain. MARDUK had become the beginning and the end of all things; he had appointed himself Lord God and Creator of the Universe.

Henceforth, he was the 'Sun God RRA'.

Therefore, the records of ERIDU were changed. The Ruler ship of RRA MARDUK was total and retroactive.

Only one change remained to be made. Records were given a new face, but memories were left. Using the mid-altering techniques of his SSA-TA reptilian minions, the new King RRA ordered the systematic alteration of the minds of the beings of ERIDU.

To accomplish the monumental test, the SSA-TA converted existing structures with chambers for 're-programming', One by one or in groups, the colonists and the beasts, ADAMA and ADAPA, were promised wealth, property, power, sexual favors, any enticement which would draw the victims into the tunnels leading into the brightly lit <u>'re-programming' rooms. Once inside, memories were erased or altered</u>. 'Screen' memories, images designed

Book 2 – Why Were They Called Gods…?

to hide recollection of the events were often implanted. The Sun God RRA would be the one and only God of record, the one and only God of memory.

Colonists or beasts that refused voluntary treatment were seized and forcibly taken into the memory alteration chamber for adjustment, *(a good example of this is 'V' a TV / series in 1983).* Some EA-SU fled into the wilderness or high mountains, there to engrave in stone, clues to the secret of the 'Take-over', the Sun God RRA and the SHET... BEFORE their capture and re-programming. Somehow, the truth would become known again. The clues, however, would remain hidden, until uncovered and recognized or de-ciphered. ('The Face on Mars' and the 'Domed Cities on the Moon' are two examples.)

In time, the SHET-I completes their task. The populace of ERIDU had 'forgotten'. As they went their separate ways, however, they each had a vague uneasiness, something was not there anymore, and something was missing. And curiously, though they seemed not to have common backgrounds, each remembered, each recalled, a bright light at the end of a tunnel. Moreover, each one knew that they were supposed to go to the light and enter the light.... for there their ultimate reward resided, 'this is the big lie, this is the trap'. (*In my search, I hear this all the time, which is this.* When you die, you are told to go to the light... this is a re-programming so, you would not remember. You need to go to the darkness; this is where you have your re-awakening of who you really are).

As insurance, the SSA-TA took one more precaution.

To insure the 'Passion' instilled in the Beast, the Gift of the Feather, did not give impetus to rebellion, the rebel lizards constructed huge towers which would transmit a cloud of electronic signals designed to keep the Beast in a fog, a docile state. The electronic blanket also served as a cover preventing outside signals from reaching the Beast. No one, not EA, not EN-LIL, nor the ARI-AN Queens would be permitted to contact the Beast, 'Beast are the Human Beings).

To further control the Beast, the Houses of Obedience of Prince EN-LIL, where the Beast visited every seventh day for obedience lessons, were taken over by the SSA-TA. Doctrines, which would support the Empire, became dogma. The teachings, the Ways of EA, became evil and the words of a demon. EA, a life-giving K-D (G-D) became 'DA-EA BA-EL' (Creator EA, Lord Father') the 'Evil One', the 'Diabolic One'.

But the SHET-I would leave nothing to chance. Should an innocent clay tablet surface with a story of ancient beings, half-man and half-beast; star beings that flew in the skies; or a rebellious God on Mound Olympus... these were the fables and myths of an imaginative primitive man. These were tales of fantasy, nothing more. The 'rational' Man, the 'working' Man, should not concern himself with the things of children.

The denial of the world before Lord RRA was complete.

SHET-I lizards that had taken an active part in the take-over and re-programming were elevated to the status of Overlords and Administrators of existing systems and laborers.

The era of the SIRIAN Lords and Masters was gone. Prince EN-LIL, the Lord of the Word, was gone. The 'Golden' era of growth and development was gone.

ERIDU, a primitive solar system developed into a stronghold by a King of the Star Sirius; ERIDU, a planet virtually destroyed in a war of Rebellion led by War Lord ZU-ZU (Zeus) and re-constructed by Genesis scientists; ERIDU. The first settlement and city of the re-born planet; ERIDU, the place of conquests and wars, the place of subjugation and Kingship from the stars, was now ERIDU, a world with a re-constructed history, a fabricated past.

As the ASA-RRR had done before them, the SHET-I began to increase the production and efficiency of the Operation. In addition, however, they entered into the development and the production of a new commodity, a drug called 'S-MA'. Once a drug used only by Kings, the SHET-I began to make and sell the drug to all the galaxy beings. Profits soared and Lord RRA fast became one of the wealthiest Kings in all the Ninth Sector. With his amassed riches, RRA built an Empire and an army second to none. His alliance with the SSA-TA had given Lord RRA the wherewithal to keep the AN-U and other Warriors Conquerors at bay. Lord Gar RRA would live forever!

Alternatively, so he hoped...

The Great Lord God RRA ruled with an iron hand, the ways of the ASA-RRR still in his veins. The SHET-I ministered to the rule of ERIDU, efficiently and coldly. But Lord RRA did not trust the SHET-I. If they would betray their own Queen, they would not hesitate to betray Lord RRA.

The SHET-I was cold-blooded reptiles, unsympathetic to any race. And, even though he was God, RRA was an outsider. Their relationship, their alliance, was business and no more for them. RRA knew they could not be trusted.

Therefore, Lord RRA moved to places his most trusted priests, and his children, in control of the Empire. Known to all as 'RA-KA', 'RRA, the Lord Father', he instructed his children in the management of the wealth of the Empire. As they were assigned their positions, they became known as 'RA-KA-M', 'a child of RA'. (Later times would see KA-M converted to KAM, the name for a shield. This would give the children of RA a new name 'RA-KAM', 'those of RA's shield').

Book 2 – Why Were They Called Gods…?

To keep control of the crucial Re-animation Center, Lord RRA had selected an elite group of priests to protect and be responsible for the chambers. They would also serve as Lord Administrators of the affairs of the Empire. Recognized as the 'RA-KA-PER-A-A', or the 'RA-KA Pharaohs', they served as loyal minions to the Lord RRA.

But the Lord God RRA was not omnipotent. His power, his Empire, was dependent on the SHET-I. Recognizing his Throne was vulnerable; Lord God RRA reconsidered the possibility of a re-union with the Empire of ASA-RRR. His wealth and power surely gave him bargaining power, he felt. Lord God RRA was in need of another alliance to protect him.

It was, however, too late.

Before he could do anything, in the darkness of the night, a coup took place. No violence, no battle, the SHET-I simply, and quietly, took everything over. As the sun rose over the palace, the SHET-I was in control. All elite Warrior guard forces of the Lord RRA were imprisoned or eliminated. There remained only the task of capturing God RRA himself.

But fate was with the Sun King. Loyal followers of the King entered his Royal quarters to rouse him from his sleep. To his good fortune, an escape plan had been devised to take him away from the grasp of his pursuers. With the reptilian guards at his heels, lord RRA narrowly escaped.

Book 2 – Why Were They Called Gods...?

As he gazed down from his starship high above, he looked down on what was once his magnificent empire, but now it was gone. The Kingdom of RRA was no more.

With the departure of Lord RRA, the era of the Empire of Sirian Ruler ship over ERIDU was over. ERIDU, a solar system that had suffered through devastating and destructive wars, had fallen to the SSA-TA reptiles without battle. The under ground beings had successfully undone the Empire of the Sun God RRA, the Prince EN-LIL, the Great King AN-U and even the ARI-AN SSS-T Queens.

The SSA-TA became Lords of the S-MA market, a profitable illicit trade, and Masters of the Ninth Passageway, the Star lanes necessary for travel to and from the Central Stars and the ARI-AN Empire. In one quick, bold move, the SSA-TA made themselves one of the most powerful and richest races in the Ninth Sector. Control of the solar system would not be left to chance, manipulation of the minds of all the inhabitants, including the control of the minds of the off-spring of RRA, his trusted Priests and all members of RRA's court, was done immediately and completely. What Lord RRA had started.... the SSA-TA would finish. Erasure of memories and the control of minds would be expanded to include his family and court. Henceforth, the RA'S SHIELD and the RAKA PHAROAH'S would be the faithful, if unwitting, servants of the Reptiles.

The ADAMA beast continued to labor for their new Lords, unaware of the changes, unaware that they were slaves. Life meant working daily for the Masters. If the beast performed well, the future meant being put out to pasture. Somewhere, in the dim recesses of its mind, the beast recalled memories of a past life.

'There is more than what we are being told...' the beast would say to itself.

The beast was right...

THE EA-SU

Prince EA found the beast in the Garden at the center of the Bio-Agricultural complex. The creature would be the key that would undo EN-LIL's dominion on ERIDU. The beast could mate only under the strictest of conditions, and only with a specifically selected partner. The genetic breeding programs had to be carefully controlled. The Empire depended on work forces composed of subservient and obedient laborers.

The angry Prince decided to shake the very foundation of the new colony outpost. He would reveal to the Beast the secret knowledge of the Gods... mating could be engaged in at any time and for the sheer pleasure of it. While the slaves must place labor before all else, the Lords placed pleasures above all. Servants toiled endlessly so that Masters could revel in the intoxicating pleasures of erotica. The Beasts were given the knowledge of 'knowing' each other at will.

The Prince taught the creature how to have a clandestine rendezvous, how to hide from over-seers, and where to search for hidden places to enjoy their newly acquired knowledge. In addition, the Beast enjoyed himself... and enjoyed himself.

But the Beast would be discovered. His transgression, a crime against the State, could not be hidden. His nakedness easily revealed his state of arousal. The Guardians had no difficulty in catching the transgressors. Even the females displayed outward signs, though on a much more subtle scale.

The offending Beast was ejected from the Gardens, they became known as the ADA-MUS, the 'monster creatures'. Loyal Beasts remained, they were known as the ADAPAS, 'wise ones', These Beast workers were allowed to stay in the Garden... but the Commands under which they would live increased in number and severity. Punishment became more brutal.

Prince EA became the embodiment of Evil itself. All works of the Prince were labeled 'anti-state', thus the works of the worst criminal DA-EA (The Creator-EA), BA-EL (Father-Lord) once the Lord Father Creator EA had become the DA-EA-BA-EL (Diablo-Devil), the 'Evil One'.

Book 2 – Why Were They Called Gods…?

For several thousand years, the turmoil continued. Lord Prince EA would pay a price for this crime, but he was first son to the King himself. The offending Beasts had been sent into exile, certain death awaited them. Prince EA would not be allowed the power he once had, his honors stripped. Once a proud Prince, and was allowed to remain in the colonies, but would not be a force of influence.

Though powerless, the Prince continued his work with the rejected Beast. In this wretched creature, he could see a possibility, life unfettered by a system life pursuing the path of its choice, Life living for the sake of life.

Instructed to create special schools to teach the loyal minions of Prince EN-LIL in the secrets of the Sciences, the beaten Prince EA began to build the 'Brotherhood', those who would become the administrators and priests of Lord EN-LIL.

The symbol of the Sciences, and Knowledge itself, was an easily recognized serpent (a tribute to the reptilian ARI-AN Queens and the Empire itself). Thus, the initiates of these schools became known as the 'Brotherhood of the Snake'.

But the school gave Prince EA an idea. The Beast would be given the opportunity to learn the secrets as well!

Secretly the Prince held meetings with the Beasts in the hillside 'caves'. The caves became known as the 'TCHE-L-US' (The Word-place-of; 'Place of the Word or Teachings'). Over the many years of seemingly endless travail, the 'Tche-l-us' (Che-r-ush / Sheirosh / Church) gave hope to the Beast. Stories of the lost paradise were often spoken of, but the memories were so distant that they had become vague at best.

Schooling of the Beast began with simple lessons in survival, cooking with fire and hunting, creating shelter, making simple traps and avoiding the dangers of the wilds. The Beast learned and began to pass his skills on to his young.

To the pleasant surprise of the Prince, some Beasts were able to learn quickly and eagerly sought more knowledge. In excited anticipation, the Prince began to instruct the Beast in the hidden arts he had begun to teach in EN-LIL's Mystery schools, and the creature learned!

The cave meetings remained secret, the Beasts who showed promise as teachers became known as EA-SU', ('EA-Wise Ones') or 'Children of EA/Children of the Serpent'. (The symbol of Prince EA, a Genesis scientist, was a pair of serpents, not the single serpent of the Brotherhood. Prince EA, himself, was called 'The Lord Serpent' or 'The Serpent'. He was thus to become the Serpent Seducer in Eden.)

The EA-SU began their missions, to teach other creatures what they had learned from the Serpent Prince. As they made their way into the wilderness, Prince EA stood proudly; they had learned and had become Teachers in their own right. The EA-SU could help lead the way to a life of free will.

But Prince EN-LIL learned of the hidden schools and immediately implemented his own plans. Dispatching loyal Beast hybrids created by his own Genesis scientists, Prince EN-LIL infiltrated the cave schools. Masquerading as EA-SU, EN-LIL loyalists created their own 'cheirosh', confusing the Beasts and creating dissension. The Prince of the Word was pleased with his minions they had confused the creatures. With the false EA-SU words, the Beasts could no longer understand nor communicate with each other... it was no more than babble.

The false EA-SU smiled, the true EA-SU wept.

Book 2 – Why Were They Called Gods…?

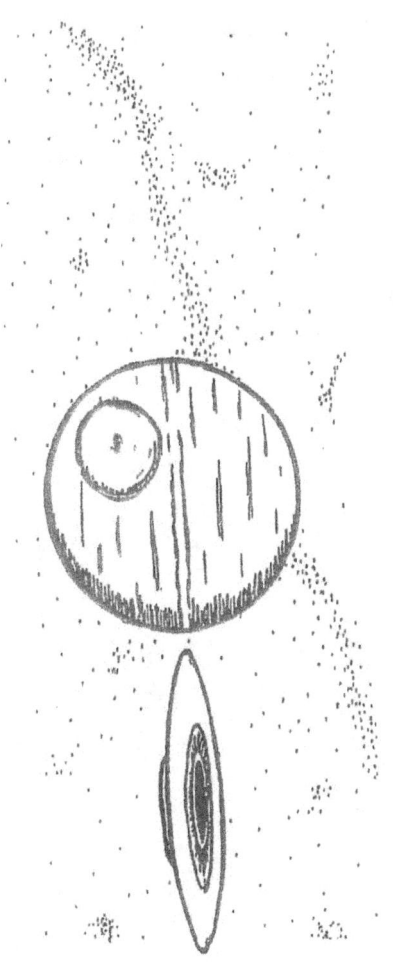

Book 2 – Why Were They Called Gods…?

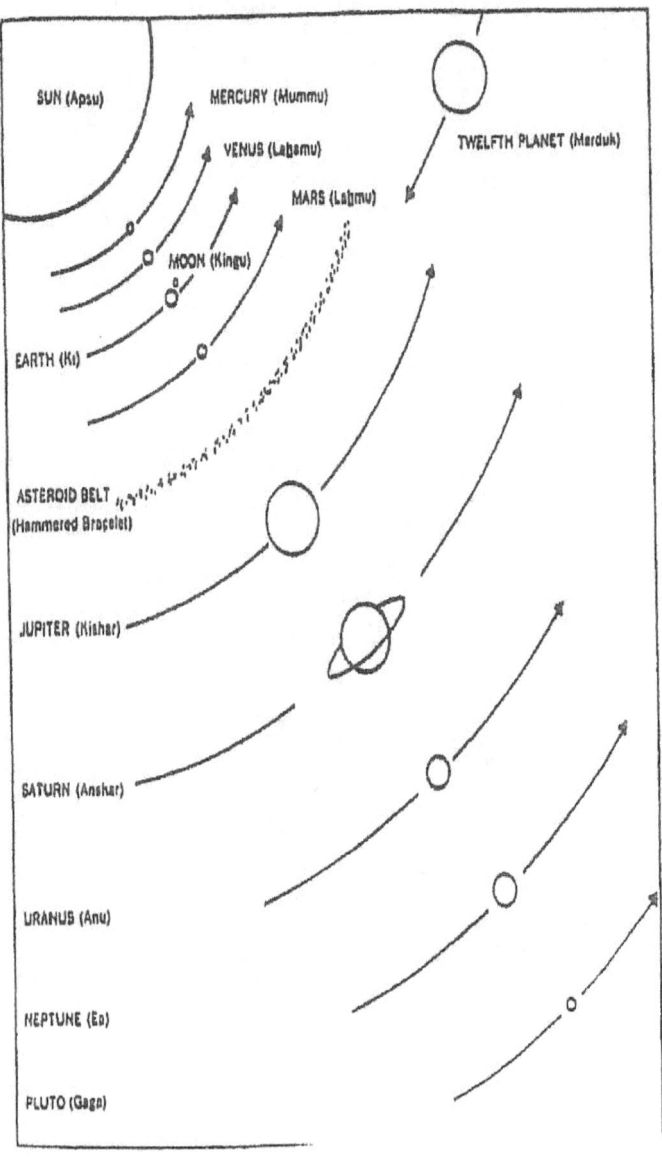

RA

The take-over had been successful. Lord Prince MAR-DUK, first son of the reviled Creator God EA, had become the 'One and only... Sun God RA', the SHETI lizards had re-programmed all remaining subjects on ERIDU. The rebel SSA-TA Queens of the ARI-AN underground worlds had given support MAR-DUK with the understanding that SHETI lizards would become the administrators of the new Empire. They had done their job well; MAR-DUK would keep them around... for a while.

With their memories gone, the Beasts were loyal and very eager servants. Other Sirian family members also gave faith and allegiance to RA; they too had lost their memories. Therefore, it was that the Empire entered a glorious phase; everyone aspired to the same goal... to praise and serve the Sun God.

The Mystery Schools became the source of priests who had but one thought, to praised the Lord RA from whom all things, all beings, all wisdom had come. The secrets of the galaxy, and the Universe, came through the mouth of RA.

The 'cheirosh' became targets of the Lord RA and the SHETI where once the teachings were those of Lord Prince EA, now they were of 'RA-LEG-US' (RA-Laws/ Words-of) 'Place of the Words of RA' (RA-leg-us/Religion). Here too, the purpose of the priesthood and brotherhood was to perpetuate the confusion and keep the truth away from both Beasts and Sirian Lords alike.

Book 2 – Why Were They Called Gods...?

Where once all Beasts and Sirian subjects were forced to praise the Sirian Lords and ultimately give greater honor to the ARI-AN Queens, Lord EA, with the approval of the SSA-TA rebel Queens, began to systematically remove all traces of a Mother Goddess presence. Henceforth, the 'Omnipotent One', was a male... the Sun God RA himself.

Males would dominate every aspect of life; it was time for females to relinquish their exalted place of power.

The SHETI lizards, with their cousin HENTA lizards, were originally recognized for their uncanny abilities with stone cutting equipment. Using their sound cutters and heat beams with incredible accuracy, the lizards with robot-like precision could produce stone structures that needed no mortar or binding agent to keep them together. These creatures, SHETI and HENTA lizards hybrids, crucial to the ministration of Lord Sun God RA's Empire, were the original 'stone-masons'.

*[Note- The Egyptian glyph for Mason is 'HUN-U'. 'HUN' is the root word meaning 'Lizard'. 'HUN-U' is literally '(One who is) of the Lizards']

The Sun God had become 'The One and Only God-King'.

But 'The King' was concerned with the lizards. They had become too powerful. No aspect of the Empire was untouched by their hands, no position of administration was devoid of a SHETI/HENTA presence. With care and secrecy, the Sun God RA attempted to shift the wealth and power away from the lizard controllers... but to no avail. It was too late.

The SHETI/HENTA and SATA rebels seized the Empire... with no battles, with no weapon fire... they simply shut everything off. The Sun God could not communicate with anyone, the Sun God could not issue orders, the Sun God could not rule.

The Sun God was undone.

With little recourse, the once and only King fled in his starship back to the heavens.

The SHETI lizards changed nothing. The Empire continued functioning as it had before. Though the subjects of ERIDU had been programmed to forget their history, the acceptance of One Omnipotent God would not be altered. It served quite well the needs of the lizards. They assumed the role of the Lord of the Word EN-LIL, they took over the role of the Lord of Creation Prince EA and they set up all institutions, which would govern Man, his life and his destiny.

The Sun God was gone, the lizard Kings were in charge.

Mystery schools were closed by Thut-Mose, remaining open only to a select few. Only the Stonemason offspring could participate. In every corner of the realm, the Masons would control the secrets and hidden knowledge of the Universe.

Sirian descendants of the original NIBIRU Lords became a target for the New Empire. Their wealth and power, inherent birthrights, begin to be stripped away. They are view as potential threats to the State. The N-IBIRU (IBIRU/HEBREW) is treated as undesirables and is enslaved by the Empire's New Order. The stage for Exodus is set.

Moses, an IBRU (Hebrew) child, is set adrift in a river. An attendant to the Prince, daughter of the Pharaoh, finds the child floating in the reeds. She rescues him and takes to the Princess. The Royal maiden takes him to her chambers and raises him as her own. Grown and a young man, Moses has an opportunity to study in the 'Mystery Schools', as he learns the ways of the Masons but is taught to believe in 'The One God'.

In time, Moses discovers his identity. Feeling that he is betrayed, he strikes out at a guard who has threatened an IBRU slave. The guard dies Moses becomes a cast-out.

In the Desert Mountains, he encounters a small ship, its bright lights are blinding. The crew is composed of Sirians who seek revenge on the lizards. The commander speaks to an awe-struck Moses. He promises Moses the Lord of the Word is willing to support him if he moves against the Pharaoh. The Commander and crew seek to free the trapped IBRU descendants from their oppressors.

Moses returns to the Palace scared but convinced that a powerful GOD is behind him. The crew of the Sirian ship and a small back-up squadron descend on the Palace and its armed guards. They create a series of distractions while Moses is gathering the IBRU people together.

Death rains down from the sky on the Pharaoh's people as the IBRU flee with Moses in the lead. The Sirian ships move quickly and decisively they vow to give their descendants a chance to escape. As the Pharaoh's armies give chase, the Sirian ships attack with destructive laser lights. With one final effort, the Starships part the waters of the sea, which blocks the Exodus. When the IBRU have passed, the waters of the sea are allowed to cascade back on the pursuers.

The story of the parting of the waters is true, the IBRU escape because of <u>extra-terrestrial assistance.</u> The Sirians leave, their task accomplished. The lizards are unconcerned with the effort they are still in control.

Moses continues to be contacted by the Sirian Commander. He is told about the Lord of the Word and the evil beings in control of the Empire. Moses instructs the IBRU to cast the bronze statue of a serpent, the galactic symbol of knowledge and Wisdom; it is called 'NA-HUSH-TAN'. It is a sign to the Sirian King and the Orion Queens that the IBRU remain loyal to the true Lord of the Word.

The IBRU Patriarch is summoned to the mountaintop, there to receive once again the commands issued by Prince EN-LIL. Moses is given two flat crystals, each with a library of the history of the Earth. Moses brings the crystals down and orders his followers to create a gilded box to house the crystals. When placed in the 'ARK', the two crystals become active and become communication devices. Two handlers come too close and touch the Ark when it is 'powering up'. They short circuit the box and destroy the crystals.

The Commander cannot afford additional crystals. Moses, feeling responsible, punishes himself, vowing not to proceed into the Promised Land when the IBRU arrive. His followers believe GOD has punished Moses for his killing of the guard.

The Exodus has caused the New Empire to search out ships from Sirius or Orion. The Commander and his squadron are in jeopardy and are forced to leave. Without communication and support, Moses and the IBRU wander through the desert lands, trying to avoid detection and seeking shelter.

A parched arid land is found where the tribes decide to settle. The lizards believe the IBRU are not worth pursuit, they leave them to die in the desert.

The IBRU descendants, tired and hungry, carve out a niche where they will hang on.

A group of ARI-AN M-G Warriors, who abandoned the Queens in power in the Orion Stars to join the Sirian forces, leaves the New Empire to form a colony of their own in the mountain regions of what is now India. Though once Sirian loyalists, they are known as the 'ARYANS'. Light-skinned and possessed of a warrior's blood, they move south towards the plateaus.

Well schooled in Sirian secrets, they establish 'Mystery Schools' of their own. Promising not to challenge or undermine the New Empire, they agree to share their knowledge and secrets with the Mason initiates of the Egyptian Empire.

In secret, their loyalty remained with the Sirians. The Sirian Star Beings are known as ASAR-U ('Sirius-Those of'). The ARYAN religion praises the Heavenly Beings called ASURA. Faithful to the ways of the Sirians, they establish what has come to known as the 'caste' system, a way in which power is centered in the High Priesthood and the elite. The Warrior class wields power second only to the elite. The Administrators follow, which the beastly undesirables at the bottom of the hierarchy. Obedience is stressed; faithful execution of one's duties will be rewarded in the future lives. <u>A search for spiritual enlightenment is discouraged; only service to the Gods is the way to heaven.</u> 'This is all part of their control'.

A replica of Sirian ways, Hinduism is born.

Though confused and misdirected, the ARYAN religion uses the symbol of the combined Empire of Sirius and Orion as an emblem of its own. When the ARI-AN Queens and the Conqueror Kings of Sirius joined in alliance, they adopted the sign of a swirling star galaxy as their mark. The four-armed galaxy mark was called 'SSS-DAK-U' (SSS-DAK-OF'; Swastika).

The lizard administrators watched with wary eyes but did not interfere with the ARYANS effort to establish themselves in ERIDU. Additional religions in ERIDU did not concern the reptiles, confusion worked to their advantage. Cut off from 'heavenly' support, no ERIDU faction was a threat.

Book 2 – Why Were They Called Gods…?

The lizards were in control.

Sirian DAK Warriors who had stood proudly beside an all-powerful Sun God RA were known as the 'RA-IM' ('RA-at the side of'). Powerful and courageous, their memories removed, they leave Egypt to settle in lands on the northern shore of what is now the Mediterranean. Called DAKANS (heavenly -DAK) or DRAKANS, they become known as ETRUSCANS. They establish the land that will be called Italy.

The RA-IM begins to build its own Empire. Distant long lost memories of two brothers (Prince EA and Prince EN-LIL), both raised in the Sirius ways and the co-founders of ERIDU, linger in the minds of the RA-IM. The dim memories of these Princes are the foundation of the RA-IM (Roman) tale of Remus Romulus. The legendary co-founders of Rome, Remus and Romulus, 'are said to have been suckled and raised by a She-wolf.

The RA-IM leaders build a strong Empire and begin to war with the Egyptians. The lizards are unconcerned. They have control and do not prevent Roman expansion. They manipulate the leadership of the RA-IM government through mind control. Confusion works well for the purposes of the lizards.

Rome is firmly established as an Empire.

IESU

The SSS-IM (ESSENES) are schooled in the Aryan (ARI-AN) 'Mysteries'. They keep to themselves in the desert land of the ancient Middle East. The Initiates believe one of their own can ascend to the Throne of Earth as 'The Anointed One' must be descended of the Lord of the Word (Sirian), and must be joined with a descendant of the Mother Goddess (Orion).

The SSS-IM inner circle begins its search for a possible candidate. The future King must be an Initiate, schooled in the 'Mysteries'... and one of them.

A second group of Initiates schooled in 'Mysteries' of the Sirians, secretly align themselves with ASAR (Sirius). They are the N-ASAR-IM (Of Heaven-Sirius) or Nazarenes. The N-AZAR-IM and IBRU Initiates join with each other for power.

A baby is born in the ancient Middle East; he is born of the Sirian line through the House of David. Orion Initiates feel he, along with several others, are potential candidates for the Kingship of Earth. The Orion MAGI (M-G) comes to pay their respects and to plant the seed of his possible future.

As a youngster, Joshua lives a normal life, but upon his coming of age, he is sent to the Eastern 'Mystery' schools, there to receive his schooling. Joshua learns what the King must know and what he must do. He is taught that he is also the 'Son of

Book 2 – Why Were They Called Gods…?

GOD', the One and Only GOD. He is being groomed for the Priesthood and a position of power.

The 'Mystery' schools continue to perpetuate the myth of One GOD that reward comes upon death. 'Salvation' is based upon service to the Church, sacrifice of self and unwavering faith. <u>The foundation of the lizard Empire is based upon an unquestioning obedience and lack of challenge to GOD, for in fact, the lizards have assumed the place and guise of GOD.</u>

Joshua becomes an Initiate <u>but finds himself questioning that which he has been taught. Something is not quite right and a feeling that there is more than what he is being told haunts him.</u> Vague memories race through his mind, feelings, thoughts of blasphemy and sacrilegious topics flood his very being. He seeks the solace of the desert; perhaps there the uneasiness will abate. He feels he must cleanse his soul.

The desert is lonely at night. Joshua is nervous. When the shadowy figure approached him, he was ready to flee. An unfamiliar recognition soothed his concerns; the stranger in night was an EA-SU, one of the few remaining teachers of the secrets of Prince EA.

As the Teacher sat down next to him, Joshua could sense his life was about to change. For the next hours, the dark stranger began to speak of the 'Mysteries', Joshua was somewhat relieved, and he too was an Initiate.

Book 2 – Why Were They Called Gods…?

However, as the hour passed by, the stranger added pieces to the puzzle that Joshua had not heard before. Joshua felt an urgent hunger to hear more. The stranger continued. As the hours turned into days, the days turned into weeks.

When the time came, the Teacher stood up. Joshua was in a state of exhilaration and anticipation. And as quickly as he had appeared, the stranger silently walked away. Joshua, his world turned upside down, sat down and wept. <u>The words of the stranger were true he knew that. He cried because a world that was unaware, asleep to the truth, was before him.</u>

Joshua had been blessed and cursed. <u>Knowledge unused is Knowledge wasted.</u> Joshua had been placed in a situation not of his choosing... at least not in this world. He would have to move, have to act... or be guilty of the crime of inaction and aiding the oppressors of Mankind.

The EA-SU would come to him again, Joshua knew that, but any actions taken would have to come from Joshua himself. A time would come when he would have to act, for now he would have to make plans. It would take years, he thought, but it would worth the wait. Joshua was, after all, a 'Chosen One' was he not? He had wondered why the name had been selected; now he knew. He was IESU... he was EA-SU too.

IESU had heard that there was another 'Anointed One' not far away in the desert (IESU could sympathize). It was not a great surprise when he discovered that the 'other one' was also of the same bloodline as he was. It was with some dismay, however, that he found out the 'other one' was elder to IESU, thus requiring IESU to step aside.

But fate was with IESU, for though John the Baptist took priority because of his age, John's reputation would bring a Quick end to his existence on hearing of the beheading of his cousin John, IESU continued to plan his future. It had been fortunate that John had baptized him; others would find it much easier to accept his role as a Man of the cloth.

To become a Rabbi, he would have to be married, that was the Tradition and Law but to fulfill the prophecies, those requirements for the 'Anointed One' demanded that he be wed to a descendant of the Mother Goddess herself. To that end, IESU found and took to his side, Mary Magdalene.

They were wed and she bore children.

IESU had become full-fledged Rabbi, with all appropriate rights and responsibilities. He was both an Initiate and an honored Rabbi. The early requirements of the prophecies had been fulfilled.

It was now time to begin the final stages.

IESU knew he would need public support. Caiaphas, Head priest of the Temple, and even Pontius Pilate, would find it difficult to attack a man who had the people's sympathy. It would be even worse if he were a holy man.

IESU moved through the countryside, acting as counselor, healer and people's advocate. The masses loved him and his gentle ways. However, in secret, he attacks the Roman guard and stripes them of their weapons. As time passed, he gathered a small group of followers. Though donations were coming in to support his cause, the funds were too small to support an increasing band. It was with some trepidation that he moved to attack the moneychanger's tables in the marketplace. The plan was simplifies himself would create the distraction; his followers would take the money from the moneylenders.

IESU strode purposefully into the marketplace. Everyone felt that the moneychangers were practicing licensed thievery, but with the sanction of the Temple, the moneychangers could do as they wished. Assured that the public would give him support, IESU began to overturn the tables of money. As the people cheered him on, his followers grabbed up the coin that they could, then scattered in all directions when Roman guards appeared. As IESU had expected, the public supported his action with great favor.

The Temple Sanhedrin, however, saw him as an outlaw that needed to be disposed of.

The plan had been flawless, but the actual execution had resulted in an unexpected outcome. The eldest son of IESU, in his excitement, had not noticed the guard's arrival. The result was that he had been captured. IESU was worried; the Head Priest could put his son to death. His plans were most assuredly dangerous, he had been ready to give up his life, if necessary, but to lose his son would be too much. IESU's death would not prevent his son claiming the throne, but the death of his eldest son would mean the throne would be lost, gone forever, to everyone in his family.

Therefore, IESU planned to free his son. The Sanhedrin had long been searching for him; IESU would give them the chance to find him. He called for his most trusted disciple Judas, bade him go to Caiaphas, High Priest of the Temple, and pretend to betray IESU.

Reluctantly, Judas did so, playing his role to his best. The Temple guard arrested IESU, taking him to Pontius Pilate for execution. But Pilate wishes no part of the politics of the Jews. He had been biding his time until he could return to Rome. Any trouble in his out-post would reflect badly on Pilate, and so he rejected any part of the Sanhedrin's plot to kill IESU.

Caiaphas would not be denied. He descended on Herod and demanded the death of the upstart. But Herod did not want a problem with the Romans. If Pilate would have nothing to do with the execution, he too would not bow to the demands of a boisterous Sanhedrin.

Turned away again, Caiaphas returns to Pilate.

He threatens a revolt of the entire territory should the execution of IESU is denied him again. But Pilate believes he can outwit Caiaphas. He fabricates an offer of clemency because of a vague holiday. He offers to free any prisoner, anyone the mob chooses. He assumes they will choose IESU, a rabble King.

IESU's followers immediately call for BARRABAS surprising Pilate. BARRABAS is the first-born son of IESU. (BAR-RABBI, 'Son-of the Rabbi').

Caiaphas mob also takes up the chant for BARRABAS. The death of IESU is their goal. The prisoner is freed; IESU's son is safe. Nevertheless, the mob is not satisfied; they are paid to call for the execution of IESU. Reluctantly, Pilate agrees to whip IESU to appease the thirsty cries for blood.

Pilate whips IESU, his followers weep. The sight of his blood feeds the frenzy. The riots promised by Caiaphas are about to explode before Pilate. He begs IESU to recant his claim to Kingship of the Jews. IESU will not. The original plan had been to have IESU hanged on the cross for crimes to the Roman state. Heresy would suffice if the punishment were the same.

While studying in the Far East, IESU had learned of many medicinal herbs. With the help of Joseph of Arimathea, <u>IESU had a plan to beat death on the cross. A little known herb, when ingested, would cause the drinker to lapse into a faint similar to death...</u> This secret would allow him to be resurrected as a God.

IESU is taken to the hillside and crucified. Joseph has bribed the guards. Traditionally, the criminal has his legs broken so that he could not support his weight. This is not done to IESU.

On a given cue, one of the bribed guards places a sponge into the prepared concoction. The sponge is put on the end of his lance and is extended to IESU to drink. Those nearby believe it to be water, but it smells strangely of vinegar.

IESU 'drinks greedily'. Within moments, his head falls. He is unconscious, everyone believes him dead. A guard who has not been bribed tests to see if IESU is alive by thrusting his lance in his side as the spear pierces the side of IESU, blood flows freely. His still beating heart causes an out-pouring of blood IESU is still alive. To the horror of Joseph and the disciples, he has been stabbed.

Quickly, Joseph comes forward to claim the body from the guards, claiming IESU is dead. But Hebrew tradition forbade anyone to touch a dead body, even loved ones. Joseph knows IESU is alive, no tradition or law is violated. However, IESU is wounded, it is vital that they move him to a cave where they can treat him in secret.

They move the body to a cave in a garden that belongs to Joseph. A boulder is moved to cover the entrance; a hidden doctor waits to tend to IESU. He is alive but the wound has seriously injured him. He must be moved to a safer location where he can heal.

Under the cover of darkness, IESU is moved. The cave is found empty the next morning, IESU is gone. The legend of a resurrected Son of God is about to be born.

Convinced the Rabbi is safe, Joseph moves to protect the family of IESU. Preparations had already been made to whisk Mary and the children away in a hired boat. As the boat and its cargo depart, IESU is told they are on their way. They will be safe.

Joseph makes his way to the southern shores of what will become known as France. Followers come with the family the Jews establish a colony. IESU had wanted to claim the throne of Earth for Mankind... and its children. He had intended to discard the 'system', to waken Mankind to the lizards. Time had worked against him. IESU died in the Far East, his wife and children were well, the blood of IESU survived.

The lizards were still unconcerned; the 'Omnipotent GOD' concept is unchallenged. The manipulation of minds and the re-programming continued. Nothing had changed.

If you can say right now, that this story is not true, without going out to learn the truth and to dig into what is not being told to you, along with what is hidden from you.

Mainly because your religion tells you, DO NOT ASKS QUESTIONS, AND TO BELIEVE ON WHAT THEY SAY....

THEN YOU ARE CONTROLLED, AND NOT FREE! ~

In the coming Chapters, you will see how the religions had changed, all the Knowledge that you had just read.

Why did the religions go and destroyed the Knowledge that you just read? Because the religions do not want you to know whom you are this is what they (the religions) are really doing to us?

Chapter 13

Beyond the Beyond

Within this Story, it takes us back to 15,000 years ago. To the 2nd-3rd story of creation of gods, and the creation of the Human race.

From Living Religions of the World 1962 Excerpts from Vedaism Pgs. 91-114 by Frederic Spiegelberg.

Such conflicting deities portray remote and basic natural forces once immediately worshipped, but then rendered so distant by Man's subsequent religious concepts as to become relatively unimportant. Dyaus Pitar is one of these forces. He is mentioned very few times in the entire Vedas, where he is the sky father. He survives, but in the alien world of his descendants, who have long ago taken over his functions, and his importance is negligible. The same word and concept occur in western culture as Zeus Pater, that is, Father Zeus, and in Latin as Jupiter. Zeus Pater is mentioned as the father of all beings, but no cult revolves around him. Local manifestations of Zeus are worshipped instead. Such devolutions may be found in all societies; Jehovah went through a like process.

Missionaries in Polynesia, when they was trying to translate the Bible into local terms and attempted to deal with "In the beginning God created Heaven and Earth," experienced considerable difficulty in finding, among the local gods, any prime mover that they could identify with God himself. When they inquired of the natives, they were told, "Oh yes, you mean Bayami or Daramulum. Yes, we know about him, but that was so long ago. We have lost interest in him, and he has lost interest in the world. It is true he created the world, but afterwards he sailed away and has never returned. So why address prayers to him?"

It is as though there were a vast storehouse in the mind of Man, into which, one by one, are carried the discarded Gods, which have been found inferior to the new model. Indeed, among primitive people, peoples not so primitive, and in the play of children, it is necessary to make a fresh image of the God each year, each decade, or whenever it is decided. Every religious literature in the world is such a storehouse, full of once important but long abandoned concepts. Therefore, Dyaus Pitar is to be found in the Vedas. There is little point in offering him prayers. He is half forgotten.

Among the devas you may find Indra, who is king of all of them; the Maruts, or double stars; the Asvirs; Ushas, the morning dawn; and many others. Varuna, for example, who controls all waters in all ways, and is hence most important. These might be called the second crop of Vedic gods. It is the third crop that still is most prominent, but the second crop has by no means faded into the obscurity of Dyaus Pitar, and his wife Prithvi.

By analogy with Greek myth, we might say that Dyaus Pitar is equivalent to Chronos *(Cronos, Kronos)* or Saturn; that Zeus and Hera are equivalent in historical development, importance, and rank to Varuna, Indra. These gods of that level; but that the popular Gods of India; Siva, Brahma and Vishnu, with their consorts, are on the third generation level of Apollo, Athena Ares and the rest.

As a religion develops, not only dose the God who personifies the numen recede, but also the second deities change their character. Therefore, it is with the Vedas. Of all devas mentioned there, only three emerge to survive into the historical period in a condition of prime importance. Thus, we can observe the emergence of Vishnu, Siva, and Brahma as an all-embracing triad. At a still later date, these three represent three aspects of being, but are themselves contained in Being itself, which is represented by the higher character of Brahma, whose functions come to overlap those of the primordial Indra. A considerable body of legend has grown up around these three deities, some of it as old as the Vedas themselves but transmitted and altered by oral tradition and not set until much later, in the Puranas. If we are to define the nature of these three, we can best do so by dealing with one or two of the basic legends set down in the Puranas.

Of the three devas, Vishnu is known and worshipped not so much for his own sake, as for his various avatars, or incarnations. The literal meaning of the word avatar is descent; and Vishnu was the God who descended from Heaven to take some mundane shape, that of an animal, a hero, or a prophet, in order to save the imperiled existence of created things. The avatars of Vishnu are numerous, but ten are of prime importance. Of these ten, the first five, which are animal or in the shape of a dwarf, are said to have take place in worlds other than ours. The next four are of corporeal, and include Krishna and the Buddha. The last is yet to come, and will signal the end of the world. By means of the avatars of Vishnu, it was possible to organize much conflicting primitive myth, and to incorporate into Hinduism such prophets as the Buddha, who founded a religion of his own, and the Gods of Christianity and of Mohammedanism.

Thus, Christian missionaries found it possible to facilitate the spread of their own faith in India by representing Jesus Christ as such an avatar, since to the Hindu there is no limit to the possible avatars of Vishnu. Indeed, the Italian Jesuit nobleman, de Nobili, was rebuked for doing just that as long ago, as the 17th century; his syncretism was so successful, and the Hindus absorbed it so easily into their own body of belief. That this became necessary for Pope Gregory XV, in 1623, to decree that Brahmins converted to Catholicism might continue to wear their sacred cords and caste marks, if these had been blessed by a Catholic priest. The situation was an unusual one, for the Christian missionary desires to have his faith recognized as the only faith; whereas to the Hindu the gods of all other faiths are merely some of the numerous avatars through which Vishnu has passed thus far.

Vishnu is the governing lord of the material world, and in himself, he is both space and matter. One of the chief legends about him deals with ambition to become prime Lord of the Universe. T his fellow devas it seemed an overweening ambition: this attitude, incidentally, gives us an insight into his historical evolution, and we see that originally he must have been of secondary importance. The other devas refused his request.

Vishnu thereupon turned himself into a small dwarf, and as such he so succeeded in entertaining the other devas at a banquet that they offered him one favor. Indeed, it would have been immoral of them not to had done so, for to the Hindu mind it is in the nature of things to pay for any good that you may have received, otherwise you do damage to your karma, or destiny.

In his shape as a dwarf, Vishnu asked for possession of as much space as he could cover with three steps. The other devas thought this the droll joke of an antic dwarf and granted his wish. Vishnu then assumed his true and monumental shape. One enormous step he placed in the firmament, so that all the heavens were his and bore the imprint of his foot. The theme is often represented in Hindu sculpture and painting. With his second step, he covered the earth, which as is common to primitive cosmogony, was conceived to be a flat surface rather than a sphere. Moreover, since he covered all earthly things with his foot, the imprint of his footprints is shown in many holy places in India, evidence that all material creation is under the sway of Vishnu. Therefore, to the Hindu, the world about him is not a negative or demonic place, but in all its aspects bears the imprint of the divine.

Had he taken a third step, Vishnu might have claimed the underworld and all its contents, but he did not take a third step, for it is the philosophy of the East that it is unwise to claim too much. One must leave a little of one's luck unexploited, in order not to crowd it.

It is a philosophy with very practical manifestations, in the history of Hinduism and Buddhism alike. For example, the Buddhist Korean when in battle always left one road open for the escape of the enemy, since to close him off completely would be to provoke despairing retaliatory acts.

So for his third step Vishnu did not intrude upon any realm, but instead danced between earth and heaven, thus creating the rhythm of the world. The underworld, which might have been his, he left to other powers that, in the course of historical development, have become less important than the triad and half forgotten. They rule the subconscious spheres.

Such is the legendary explanation both of the power and of the worship of Vishnu, worship extremely widespread in India today. Vishnu is the spirit of the knowable and the visible world, and as such a benevolent and cheerful God. His worship is therefore the process of embracing all that is inherently and divine, an attitude that finds the Being of Being present in all things.

Siva is the second member of the Trinity, who, with his consort, Durga or Parvati- for each of the triad has a female counterpart -is also universally worshipped in India. Original Siva was a primitive God of destruction, and as such was mistakenly identified with the Devil by Christian missionaries. Nothing could be further from the truth. The Devil is a negative force, and this is precisely what Siva, in his later Vedic development, is not. To the Hindu, destruction is as essential to the life process as creation, not something opposed to the good, but merely the obverse of the same coin. The three principal devas are equally important and in on sense partake of the nature of evil, which is assigned to the asuras, or demons of the underworld.

The third member of the triad is Brahma, this devas inhales and exhales all being. As he exhales, he repeats the mantras, or holy formulas, the ancient ritual names of all created things that he alone retains in his memory. Thus, he has the secondary name of Brahma Paramahamsa, hamsa referring to the respiratory function. When he inhales, the world vanishes into him. There results the night of Brahma. When he awakes, he exhales the world once more, reproducing it exactly by remembering and uttering the names of all those things present in the previous world. These names are to be found in the sacred Sanskrit texts, and he utters them just as the priest would utter them.

For instance, Brahma recalls that the name that the world bore in its previous existence was loka, a word related to our English word look. In exhaling the word loka, he exhales everything that may then be seen with the eye. When he exhales the word purusha, or man, then he exhales man. In brief, all existence as we know it is no more than a word spoken by the Supreme Being.

This concept is an important one, if we are to understand Hindu though. According to Christianity, God created the world only once, and therefore it is a finite world. Nevertheless, Brahma did not create the world in this material and absolute sense. He breathed it in and almost involuntarily. This breathing is called pranayama, and is one of the disciplines of the Yogi, who tries to comprehend the Divine by reproducing the process in him, and who attempts to abolish the ego by so doing.

Book 2 – Why Were They Called Gods…?

The world that Brahma exhales is Vishnu, the sustainer of all existence. Of the three, Siva is the devas who takes used-up things away, in order that Brahma may breath them fourth again. If Siva did not destroy the world, it would be lifeless, for then Brahma would cease to breathe. Siva is the inhalation of Brahma, in other words. Thus, the world is the respiration of the Supreme Being, and therefore dies and is reborn not merely at the end of a millennium, but daily, hourly, and moment. In such a view, it is necessary to die in order to be born, and if we do not die, then assuredly we will not be reborn, and therefore will cease to be. So Siva is not a gruesome God, nor does he have the negative moral connotations of the Christian Devil. He is on the contrary the alternate links in an endless chain of being. True, the primitive prototype of Siva did have negative characteristics. In his origins, he was called Rudra, the red God, because in the Aryan pastoral period it was he who brought the sandstorm that spread a red dust of pestilence, illness, and death over the world.

For even as Rudra, Siva had the double attribute of welcoming that which was to be, as well as destroying that which was.

Among the Saivas, those Hindus who worship Siva rather than Vishnu, it is part of the ritual that, every morning after worship of Puja. As they dip three fingers into the ashes that were used for that worship, as they draw three horizontal lines across their foreheads. To symbolize Siva; whereas the

Book 2 – Why Were They Called Gods...?

Vaishnavas, or followers of Vishnu, draw in red and yellow a mark that resembles an open bowl receiving the power from above.

Neither sect believes that it or the other worships either a true or a false God, for the most essential element of Hinduism is its utmost tolerance. Nor can Vaishnavas and Saivas be separated out as easily as we can distinguish between Protestants and Catholics. Hinduism does not deal in such oppositions; there is scarcely a temple, which Vishnu does not contain representation of Siva in its side chapel in the form of lingam. or phallic symbol of creativeness. There are few temples to Siva that does not likewise contain an image of Krishna or one of the other avatars of Vishnu. The two Gods are inseparable, for we might say that the represent the one the tremendous, the other the fascinosum, of the numinous; the inhalation and exhalation of Brahma.

When Brahma and Vishnu wagered as to which of them was the more important, they decided that each would walk through the realms of the other, to see if everything one owned was also present in the world of the other. Vishnu, who was space and existence in all its parts, entered into the realm of Brahma, that is, into the realm of the spirit and of thought. We might say, in our own world-view, that he entered into the cosmos that Espinoza predicted, when he evolved the theory of the substantiate that is God. But cannot be expressed or glimpsed by Man, expresses itself to Man in terms of space and consciousness, of extension and cogitation, which are parallel to each other and the only aspects of the Divine that we can perceive. On the other hand, we might say whatever can be found in space can be thought about in the consciousness and so given a name; and that whatever can be thought about or named therefore has an existence in space.

Vishnu entered this world in entering the body of Brahma. In terms of science, we might say that endeavored to discover if spirit was not after all an extension of matter. Vishnu found everything of himself in the body of Brahma. Even his own search form something beyond himself he found represented as a possibility in the mind of Brahma. As far as Vishnu the god of the sensorial perceptible, was concerned, both Gods were therefore equal. He then left the body of Brahma.

However, when Brahma entered the body of Vishnu, who lay asleep on Ananta, the world snake, the result was somewhat different. Brahma, the source of all life, could not conceive of anything without finding it immediately present in the body of Vishnu, who is the embodiment of all things that have been conceived. Even the thoughts of Brahma that were beyond the boundaries of thought were reflected in Vishnu as soon as Brahma conceived them. It thus seemed to Brahma that the matter was undecided, and he attempted to leave the body of Vishnu. He found that he could not do so, for Vishnu had closed the eight gates of his body, not wishing to lose the source of his being, which he for the moment contained. Brahma thus became a prisoner of the realm of matter, by which we might at first judge that the material can imprison the spiritual. But Brahma drilled a new opening in the body of Vishnu, the navel; a new opening, for the Gods, not being born of the womb, had none, just as Adam and Eve had none.

Brahma took the form of a water lily growing on top of the umbilical cord. When the lily unfolded, Brahma was discovered sitting in the middle of the bloom, in this re-born disguise baby with a crown on his head. In other words Brahma, the spirit, escapes from Vishnu, matter, by being reborn. Therefore, it is with Man. If the story has a moral, it is precisely this; that the spirit can escape its prison of only by being reborn.

We also find that the Maha Rsis, or great prophets and singers, tended to concentrate on the triad of Vishnu, Siva and Brahma, for if all being derived from these three, then the lesser devas, who also derived from them, were of little importance, once these three had been placated, understood, and dealt with. Nevertheless, all devas, even these three, and are conceived to work for a deity or power greater than any or all of them. Many names have been invented to deal with this power. For instance, it was called the Instigator. This supreme power the Rsis sought in terms of a father of all creation who stands behind any creation we may conceive of; that is to say, a Being of Being of which any God we may know is only a shadow. This ultimate God is call

Praja Pati, or father of creation. If you can come to grips with him, then you have come to grips with all his sons, grandsons, and descendants, including the present Gods. But the process ravels backwards, until finally you arrive at the manna, which in origin was the power that the liquid consciousness of primitive Man could not identify, but saw to be the essential force of things. In later theory manna becomes the inherent Being of Being, the instigator of everything we can even conceive of, including the instigator of whom we conceive. In Sanskrit this ultimate is called tat, a word that corresponds to our word that, and is the subject of Rig-Veda X, 129.

Then was not existent nor existent; there was no realm of air, nor sky beyond it. What covered in, and where? And what gave shelter? Was water there, unfathomed depth of water?

Death was not then, nor was there aught immortal: no sign was there, the day's and night's divider.

That One Thing, breathless, breathed by its own nature: apart from it was nothing whatsoever.

Darkness there was: at first concealed in darkness, this All was indiscriminate chaos.

All that existed then was void and formless: by the great power of warmth was born that unit.

Thereafter rose desire in the beginning, desire, the primal seed and germ of spirit. Sages who searched with their heart have thought discovered the existent's kinship in the non-existent.

Book 2 – Why Were They Called Gods…?

> *Transversely was their severing line extended; what was above it then, and what below it?*
> *There were begetters; there were mighty forces, free action here and energy up yonder.*
> *Who verily knows and who can here declare it, whence it was born and whence comes this creation?*
> *The gods are later than this world's production. Who knows then whence it first came into being?*
> *He, the first origin of this creation, whether he formed it or did not form it, Whose eye controls this world in its highest heaven, he verily knows it, or perhaps he knows it not.*

This is an extremely sophisticated concept, and it is dedicated to the, the power of all powers that resides beyond all powers we can know. The song is perhaps 4,000 years old and today we find the idea no easier to state. We can only ask the question, as did the unknown Maha Rsis Who wrote this selection. What, then, is beyond the beyond. There is no language of Man that can deal with this problem, and even the non-linguistic, non-visual mind has difficulty in doing so, because it is not only beyond the mind of Man, but beyond and mind that Man can conceive.

The original Sanskrit or Rig-Veda X, 129, shows something of the linguistic problem involved. Na sat na asat asit, It begins. Not being, not not being was. By comparison with such a concept, the Gods are no more than a later creation. If we may venture to say so, even the concept of the Being of Being is a pale later creation.

This unknowable is a very real problem in Man's mind, for even science, which so to speak unravels a carpet into the unknowable for our safe transit across it, never reaches the end. For beyond the unknowable as we conceive it lays the unknowable that we cannot conceive, and even when we are able to conceive of that, there will always be an unknowable beyond. Thus the greater our knowledge becomes, the more apparent to us becomes the existence of something beyond knowledge. So as we chase the Being of Being up the ladder of Man's ascent from ignorance, we find it no closer, but further away than ever, because less capable of being conceived in terms of anything we may know, no matter how great our knowledge my become. The Being of Being is inconceivable, and it is the inconceivable that we worship, which survives any particular system of worship we may outgrow or disbelieve in; and the more sophisticated we become, the more inconceivable the inconceivable becomes. So at most, we are left with the tremendous and the fascinosum. We have divided feelings. We have them over and over again, in all religions and at all times, but the statement of them in one period or another is curiously the same.

This opposition is one of the ultimate insights of the entire history of religion, an insight formulated long ago by the oldest of living religions. It is formulated but it can never be resolved. That it cannot be resolved is one reason for the vitality of the religious impulse in the history of Man. For beyond any answer there is always another question; and we are, after all a, curious race, symbolized in Hindu belief by Hanuman, the monkey -God.

~Excerpts from Living Religions of the World
VEDAISM

The conspiracy of Zu and his evil plotting remained also in mankind's memory, evolving into fear of birdlike humanoids demons that can cause affliction and pestilence. Some of these demons were called Lillu, a term that played on the double meaning, "to howl" and "of the night"; their female leader Lillitu-Lilith – page 284 is depicted as a naked, winged goddess with birdlike feet. The many Shurpu ("purification by burning") texts that have been found were formulas for incantations against these evil spirits – forerunners of the sorcery and witchcraft that had lasted throughout the millennia.

These beings have been thought as demons, which would return to Earth to destroy it, by the means of many forms of destructions, every thousand years. Along with claiming the Earth as theirs, this is the fear that we are brought up with and taught, year after year, this is not so, you will learn all this in Book 3 – 4.

Zoroastrian demon

Female leader Lillitu-Lilith

Chapter 14

The Elect as Elohim

This Story of the gods dates 6,000 years ago, which is the 3rd-4th story of the creation of gods and the creation of the Human race.

This paper deals with the multiplicity of the Elohim in the Godhead and the destiny of the elect to become Elohim. The capacity to become Elohim or theoi was the view of the early Church. This paper is related to papers on The Deity of Christ and The God We Worship and The Holy Spirit series.

Excerpts from Christian Churches of God, Australia, from the Elect as Elohim No. 1.

The Church, in the third and fourth centuries, adopted a doctrinal shift from the position that the elect will exist as Elohim or theory which was the position held by Christ at John 10:34-35 from Psalm 82:6, and which was the original understanding of the Church. The original position is explained in detail in the work God Revealed. This paper is concerned with what the Bible text actually says and establishing the plan, that it outlines. Having established the biblical schema, it will then be tested against the understanding of the earliest Church writers for accuracy. The problems and assumptions are outlined in God Revealed. Most Hebrew-English Lexicons record the variant uses of the words. The variant uses of the names of the deity are extracted from this and explained from a Trinitarian framework. Such a paradigm requires the texts to be explained within a context, which would not render the doctrine of the Trinity absurd.

Consequently, some, such as Francis, Driver and Briggs are the more widely used Genesis (Robinson, tr. Brown, Driver, Briggs update), are construed to explain the extensive meanings of the terms used for the deity and Host within a paradigm of a developing religion. The discipline of Religious Studies also attempts to explain the context of the Old Testament and the New Testament in similar terms. This arrangement suits both Trinitarians and agnostics. The former, because the premise they adopt is that the final form of the structure was not developed until the Council of Chalcedony (c. 451 CE) using Greek metaphysics, and the latter because the concept of a living God writing an inspired Bible is at variance with the syncretism nature of their studies. We are concerned with the actual words of the texts.

Words normally applied to the deity in Israelite and non-Israelite societies are applied to humans. Such application is a consistent Middle East worldview, which extends the heavenly Host to interact with humans. The examination of the use of Eloah, elohim, el, elim (eliym) etc., the Hebrew or the Chaldean and Aramaic equivalents, is contained in God Revealed. The examples of where Eloah (or Elahh) is used in the singular to refer to a concept of a god other than Eloah, are in 2Chronicles 32:15; Daniel 11:37-39; Habakkuk 1:11. Eloah never has the article although Habakkuk 1:11 determines it by the suffix and it is found once in the construct in Psalm 114:7 (see Theological Wordbook of the Old Testament, Harris ed., Moody, Chicago, 1980, p. 93). Such concerns do not detract from this paper. For example, the texts in Brown-Driver-Briggs-Gesenius on El (SHD 410), page 42, show that the word means god but with various subordinate applications to express ideas of might and is applied to men of might and rank.

Similarly, Elohim (SHD 430), page 43, is explained being plural in number and as referring to rulers, or judges, either as divine representatives at sacred places, or as reflecting divine majesty and power. Thus, the term is extended to humans as well as the angelic Host. The biblical texts show that this simple explanation of reflecting the divine majesty is the sense in which the terms were applied in the Bible. Thus, the name carried the authority, which was of it conferred by God. This sense is resisted by Trinitarians.

Trinitarian works, which seek to further the concepts of the Bible as a developing structure proceeding into the Trinity, are common. Good examples are that of Karen Armstrong A History of

God, Heinemann, London, 1993, and C M LaCugna GOD FOR US: The Trinity and Christian Life, Harper, San Francisco, 1993. LaCugna admits (Enc. of Religion, art. Trinity) that neither the Old Testament nor the New Testament contains a basis for the Trinity. The classic work referred to for such purposes is W F Albright Yahweh and the Gods of Canaan, London, 1968. G R Driver develops the concept of the myth in his Canaanite Myths and Legends, Edinburgh, 1956. R L Fox goes even further in this vain in The Unauthorized Version: Truth and Fiction in the Bible, London, 1991. The fundamentalist Trinitarian approach has been to alter the translation of the biblical texts to disguise the concepts, and to deny the plurality of the word Elohim. Joshua 22:22 is an example. The RSV renders the text:

The Mighty One, God the Lord! The Mighty One, God the Lord!

Mark S Smith in The Early History of God, Harper, San Francisco, 1990, page 8 notes the Hebrew text, as 'el'elohim Yahweh' el'elohim Yahweh or God of gods is Yahweh God of gods is Yahweh. Thus, El of Elohim means head of a plurality. Smith holds the text to exhibit the assimilation of the word el into Hebrew and its development into a generic noun-meaning god. Smith argues for the development of the Hebrew concepts, from the Canaanite, perhaps from the Period of Iron Age 1, as shown from the Ugaritic corpus, imposing them on the cult of Yahweh (Intr.,

p. xxvii). He says that by the end of the Monarchy, monolatrous Yahweh's was the norm in Israel, allowing the gradual development of Monotheism (ibid.). Smith admits importation of practices into the religion of Israel. He argues that some practices, regarded as syncretism, belong to Israel's ancient religious heritage (ibid., p. xxxi), perhaps also from the Canaanite linguistic base which is essentially the same language as Hebrew. Smith attempts to establish the biblical claims and then examine them within a wider framework. This work is also concerned with establishing the biblical framework so that it can be examined more widely but with conclusions different to those of Smith. That examination is further undertaken in the work Mysticism. Thus, the framework should not be written down by sociological prejudice. The structure must be faithfully restored assuming the Bible text means what it says. Trinitarian prejudice interferes with this process. The Dead Sea Scrolls, Ugarit and Nag Hammadi texts have shed important light on what was actually understood to be the meaning of the biblical texts at the time of Christ and these are referred to as necessary.

What is of importance is that no serious scholar denies that the Bible was understood, at the time of Christ, to refer to a Council of the Elohim or Elim and that the term extended way beyond the concept of a duality or a Trinity. A significant work on the subject is The Psalms: Their Origin and Meaning by Leopold Sabourin S.J., Alba House, NY, Revised &

updated version (post 1974). Sabourin demonstrates the concept of the Council of the Elohim in his work. On pages 398 f, Sabourin lists the usage of Eloah but avoids dealing with the significance. From pages 72-74, Sabourin addresses Psalm 86:8-10; 95:3; 96:4; 135:5. The Bene Elim is identified as the Sons of God as are the Bene Elyon (Sons of the Most High). On pages 102-104, he mentions the saints or Holy Ones (qedosim) from Psalm 89:6-8 who are God's celestial attendants and that the term is used of the human faithful. These supra-terrestrial beings are of the Bene Elim or the Bene Ha Elohim. The Bene Ha Elohim is the Sons of the God(s). Sabourin, noting also Coppens comment (ETL, 1963, pp. 485-500) that the noun qedosim designates, in the Masoretic text, the supra-terrestrial Court of YHVH, who are held to be Elohim (pp. 102-103), says of this:

The concept of a heavenly assembly is not a purely literary form, but is an element of the living pattern of Israelite faith (p. 75).

The pattern of the usage of the terms for God is of an extended order. There is no doubt that the meaning was understood whether it was written in Hebrew, Aramaic, or Chaldee. The pattern is undoubtedly of an extended order, which included humans, and involved a Council, which Christ had established on Sinai. These Elohim are referred to in Exodus 21:6 where the word is translated as judges.

The word is thus acknowledged as being plural here, and in Exodus 22:8-9, by its translation as judges, but the word used is Elohim. There are, however, two perfectly sound and common words for judge(s) in Hebrew. These are SHD 6414 palely (Ex. 21:22; Deut. 32:31) and SHD 8199 shaphat (Num. 25:5; Deut. 1:16 et seq.). The words were in use at the time the word Elohim was used. Thus, the distinction was meant to convey a concept other than judge. The concept the term was intended to convey was of the authority of God as it was extended to the congregation of Israel. The Governing Council of Israel was thus part of the Elohim. This extension was as a reflection of the heavenly system, as was noted from Hebrews 8:5.

The pattern was understood in a consistent manner throughout the Old Testament, and was applied in like manner in the New Testament. It was God's stated intention that, from this covenant, He would write the law in the hearts and minds of men and they would not need teachers (Heb. 8:10). The Old Testament demonstrates the subordinate relationships of the Elohim and indicates their extent. It also identifies the Angel of YHVH (reading the term as Yahovah from the ancient renderings of Yaho from the Elephantine texts; cf. Pritchard *The Ancient Near East: An Anthology of Texts and Pictures*, Princeton 1958, pp. 278-282) and his relationship to the law, which is fundamental to the issue of the position and authority of Christ. The progressive identification of the Angel of YHVH occurs from Genesis 16:7 (see NIV footnote). Commentators also identify him as the Angel of the Presence (Isa. 63:9). There are also instances of

Book 2 – Why Were They Called Gods...?

multiple entities appearing and being referred to as YHVH. The instances of the alterations of YHVH to Adonai (by the Sopherim) in 134 places are at Appendix 32 of the Companion Bible (see also App. 31 for the fifteen extraordinary points and App. 33 for emendations and Ginsburg Introduction to the Hebrew Bible, pp. 318-334 for details).

The Angel appeared to Abraham and his family. Hagar saw the Angel (Gen. 16:7) who was referred to as You Are the God Who Sees. He was an El. The entity was interchangeably referred to as the Angel of Yahovah and Yahovah, the One Speaking to Her - thus implying multiplicity. This Angel who was Yahovah, appears to Abraham in Genesis 17; 18:3 (the first of the 134 alterations of the Sopherim; see Massorah, ss. 107-115 and Ginsburg, ibid.). The substitutions affecting this concept are at Genesis 18:3,27,30,32; 19:18; 20:4; Exodus 4:10,13; 5:22; 15:17; 34:9; Numbers 14:17. Elohim was treated in the same way and thus the list requires expansion. The three entities appearing to Abraham were referred to as YHVH with no distinction and the two Angels in Genesis 19 who destroyed Sodom were addressed as YHVH, both together and without distinction, which is probably the reason for the change by the Sopherim.

The destruction of Sodom was done by Elohim (Gen. 19:29). Thus, the title Yahovah or YHVH is applied in a hierarchical structure from YHVH of Hosts, God Most High or Eloah to the Elohim of

Israel who is a subordinate God, to the two Angels who were in turn subordinate to that Elohim. Thus, the term is one of authority delegated from Eloah. The Elohim who was the Angel of YHVH also appeared to Abimelech at Genesis 20:4 et seq. At Genesis 21:17-30, Elohim is referred to as the Angel of Elohim.

Abraham was himself referred to as Elohim in Genesis 23:6. The terms are translated mighty prince but the words are SHD 5387 nâsîy' an exalted one as a king or sheik and SHD 430 Elohim, hence king or prince Elohim.

Genesis 23:6 6 Hear us, my lord: thou art a mighty prince among us: in the choice of our sepulchers bury thy dead; none of us shall withhold from thee his sepulcher, but that thou majesty bury thy dead. (KJV).

The words rendered mighty prince are in effect prince of the Elohim. This is a little inconvenient for the Trinitarians and modern Judaism, so they both render it mighty prince. Hence, Abraham and Moses were both termed Elohim in the Bible. The Angel of YHVH was termed Elohim, Yahovah, and The Angel of Yahovah in the sacrifice of Isaac at Genesis 22:11-12 (see The Interlinear Bible). This subordinate being was not omniscient. He appeared in Genesis 24:7,30-44,48 and was clearly not Eloah.

The Angel of YHVH revealed himself to Jacob as the El Bethel or the God (El) of the House of God, hence the high priest of the House of God (Gen. 28:21-22). This YHVH, the Elohim of the Patriarchs and the El of the House of God, later identifies himself as the Angel of HaElohim or The God(s) (Gen. 31:11-13). This Elohim instructs Jacob (Gen. 35:1-13). Genesis 35:11 ff uses AbiEl or God is My Father. The term Elohim Abi El Shaddai also has the meaning the God Who Worships Almighty God (see God Revealed). This Angel was the Penile or the Face of God (Gen. 32:24-30). Hosea identifies this Angel as Elohim (Hos. 12:2-9). This Angel, one of the Elohim, was the Elohim (or Captain) of the Host (Elohi ha Tseba'avch) wrongly termed God of Hosts (deleting reference to The).

He was andach Elohim or the Brother Elohim denoting a wider family relationship of the Elohim. Amos 9:5 also has similar meaning which accords with Joshua 5:15. This Angel was the Commander of the Host or Captain of the Army of God. Yahovah is His Memorial appears to be another term for the Angel. The concept of seal or mark is probably meant from Exodus 3:15 (My Name is My Memorial). Jacob viewed this Elohim as the Angel of Redemption (Gen. 48:15-16).

This Angel of YHVH addressed Moses at the Mountain of the God(s) (HaElohim) and identified himself as the Elohi of Abraham, Isaac and Jacob (Ex. 3:1-6,10-12). He is distinguished from and is a messenger for Eloah, the God of Hosts or God Most High. This being was the Angel in the Cloud of the Exodus (Ex. 13:21; 14:19 (note interchangeable identification)) who was the YHVH who drove the sea back (Ex. 14:21), the YHVH in the Pillar of Fire and Cloud (Ex. 14:24). He thus has interchangeable titles. It was he who gave the law to Moses and established the seventy elders of Israel (Ex. 24:9-18). Deuteronomy 5:30-33 identifies this entity as YHVH and he is a messenger of YHVH of Hosts, whom Christ says no man has ever seen and voice no man has heard (Jn. 5:37; 6:46). This Angel was understood to be the Presence of God and hence the Angel of the Presence. He is a subordinate God appointed as Elohi of Israel by his God above his partners (Ps. 45:6-7; see also Heb. 1:5-13; Rom. 15:6; Eph. 1 to 3). The YHVH sent this Angel to bring Israel out of Egypt (Num. 20:16) and to drive out the inhabitants of Canaan (Ex. 33:2-3). This Angel was the YHVH who spoke to Moses face to face (Ex. 33:11) and Moses did not differentiate between them in any significant way (Ex. 33:12-17). Thus, the presence of God was held to be in the Angel who was his face or persona, which is the Latin word for face or mask, and from which person is derived and which is incorrectly applied and confined in the Trinity. This Angel of YHVH remained with Israel through the period of the Judges and is referred to as YHVH (see Judges 6:11 ff). The Angel is referred to as Adonai (v.13), and YHVH (v. 15) (altered by the Sopherim), and the Angel of Elohim (v. 20). This Angel is also referred to as YHVH Shalom or He Causes Peace; hence, he is the Prince of Peace, a title of Messiah. Gideon prayed and sacrificed to The God and not this Elohim (Judges 6:36), although this Elohim enabled the Spirit of the Lord to enter Gideon (Judges 6:34). The Angel appeared to Samson's parents and was referred to as Elohim (Judges 13:19-20). The Angel declared his name as pel'iy (Judges 2:18), approximating wonderful, which is a title of Messiah (from Isa. 9:6). The Angel appears in the days of the Kings (2Sam. 24:16, 1Chron. 21:12-30). This Angel is a mediator between heaven and earth from 1Chronicles 21:16. The Angel of YHVH was the YHVH who spoke through the prophet Gad (v. 18). The version in Samuel shows that two YHVHs are involved - the Angel of YHVH and the YHVH for who sacrifice is being made. YHVH then commands the Angel (1Chron. 21:27). David was motivated by fear of the Angel of YHVH and hence relocated the Temple or House of The God (1Chron. 22:3).

The Angel of YHVH appeared to Elijah and was termed YHVH (1Kings 19:5-12). He spoke condemning the king at 2Kings 1:3. He spoke for YHVH at 2Kings 1:15 who is identified as YHVH of Hosts at 2Kings 19:31-32; 2Chronicles 32:31; Isaiah 37:36 identifies the Angel as Elohi of Israel. This Angel of YHVH, intermediary God of Israel, is Israel's protector (Ps. 34:7).

The deferential forms of referring to Yahovah and his Superior, Yahovah of Hosts, are found in Ezekiel (see also SHD 3068, 3069). Yahovah referred to Yahovah of Hosts as Yahovih (e.g. Ezek. 16:36; 31:10,15; 36:5; 38:10,14; 39:8 etc.). The dabar Yahovah or word of Yahovah is rendered normally in Ezekiel. Ezekiel 31:1 ff refers to the Garden of The God(s) (HaElohim). Adonai Yahovih is used for this prophecy at Ezekiel 29:8, thus implying a distinction between the Word of God and the use of Adonai Yahovih. The Hebrew concept thus evolves of the Memra, which was translated as logos in the Greek New Testament.

The Angel or Word of God as the Memra is understood to be the Messiah. Zechariah 3:1-9 shows the Angel as Judge and is identified as YHVH and the Angel of YHVH. Satan stands as accuser. The Angel has the power of judgment and is thus the righteous judge of the Testaments and the Elohim of Psalm 82:1 Who stands in the Congregation of the El and judges among the Elohim. Reference extends to embrace YHVH's servant the Branch. Psalm 110:4 extend the priesthood from the Aaronic to the Melchisedek through this entity. The DSS shows that Judaism expected a Messiah of two advents (see G Vermes The Dead Sea Scrolls in English, esp. Messianic Anthology and the translation of the thirteen fragments from cave XI). The lineage of Messiah was of Nathan and of Levi (see Zech. 12:10; hence Lk. 3). The Messianic Anthology draws attention to the promises to Levi at Deuteronomy

33:8-11 and 5:28-29. The text identifies the prophet of Deuteronomy 18:18-19 as referring to Messiah as does Numbers 24:15-17. The Messiah of Aaron and the Messiah of Israel were the same person from Damascus Rule (VII) and the unpublished fragment in cave IV (Vermes, p. 49). The Qumran translations refer to Melchisedek as Elohim and El. This stems from the sense of the final judgment conducted by the Messianic priest and priesthood. Isaiah 52:7 uses Elohim in context of the Messianic advent to Zion (see Heb. 12:22-23). He was understood to be identical with the archangel Michael and was head of the Sons of Heaven or Gods of Justice. Thus, some Judaic sects identified Messiah as Michael (from Dan. 12:1). This was the old Adventist doctrine up until 1931.

Messiah is also assumed to be Melchisedek. Both assumptions are in error.

Melchisedek has the meaning My King is Righteousness or My King is Justice (justice and righteousness synonymous, see Vermes Dead Sea Scrolls in English). Were Melchisedek to be Messiah then there is a serious problem with the incarnation and the sacrifice. The Christian assumption that Melchisedek is Messiah rests on a misunderstanding of the texts in Hebrews 7:3. The terms without father, mother and genealogy (apator etc.) refer to the requirement to have recorded Aaronic lineage (Neh. 7:64) for the Leviticus priesthood. The term beginning of days and end of life refers to the requirement to commence duties at thirty years of age and cease at fifty years (Num. 4:47). The high priest succeeded on the day of his predecessor's death. Melchisedek has no such requirement. Hebrews records that he was a man (Heb. 7:4). He was made like the Son of God (Heb. 7:3) yet he was not the Son of God who was another priest (Heb. 7:11. Thus, all the elect can participate in the priesthood, being made like unto the Son of God, regardless of lineage and age, continuing in perpetuity. As to who Melchisedek was, we can only surmise (see the paper Melchisedek (No. 128). The Essence misconstrued the text Messianically, as have some modern fundamentalists. Hebrews appears to have been written to correct this error but has it been misconstrued. The Midrash holds that he was Shem (Rashi) being king (melek) over a righteous place (tsedek) (Abraham ibn Ezra & Nachmanides). This place was where the Temple would be built for the Divine Presence, which the Midrash applies to Jerusalem as a whole, from the text Righteousness lodged in her (Isa. 1:21) (ibn Ezra & Nachmanides, see Soncino fn. Gen. 14:18).

But more importantly, the concept of Council of Elohim was absolute and is undeniable as being the properly understood meaning of the Old Testament texts involving the Elohim. The subordinate structure of the Elohim is understood on one hand, but misunderstood in relation to Michael and Melchisedek. HVH Sabaoth or YHVH of Hosts is the name of God (from Isa. 51:15; 54:5; Jer.10:16; 32:35 et seq.; Amos 4:13; 5:27) who is Eloah. This being has a Son, perhaps from the reading of the text at 1Chronicles 22:11 (rather than hayah SHD 1691), as the Son of Yehi Yahovah. Certainly Eloah has a son from Proverbs 30:4-5. Thus, the Son of Eloah appears to be the Elohi of Israel but is not the object of prayer and sacrifice.

This Elohim, anointed by his God, having a throne of the Elohim (Ps. 45:6-7) then stands in the Assembly of the El and judges in the midst of the Elohim (Ps.82:1). Hence: Rise O Elohim and judge the earth (Ps. 82:8). The result of this activity of the Angel of YHVH as Elohim is extended to the household of David in the Old Testament. It is thus sure from the Old Testament that the destiny of the elect as the household of David as King of Israel, was to become as Elohim as the Angel of YHVH at their head Zechariah 12:8 8. In that day shall the LORD defend the inhabitants of Jerusalem; and he that is feeble among them at that day shall be as David; and the house of David shall be as God, as the angel of the LORD before them. (KJV) The term before them is translated elsewhere as at their head. Thus, the Angel of YHVH was the Elohim at the head of the household of Israel. This being can only be Messiah.

The Old Testament thus looks to an advance in the status of Israel. The household of the king is advanced to the standing of Elohim ruling from Jerusalem among the nations. We see this concept is not physical and is not developed from the New Testament. The New Testament (Acts 7:38) confirms that an Angel that appeared on Sinai and spoke to Moses and who gave the law (Acts 7:53) and identifies Christ as that Angel of the Old Testament. Moreover, the New Testament (Heb. 1:8-9 quoting Ps. 45:6-7) demonstrates conclusively Christ's subordination and obedience.

The singular word or name applied to God Most High as observed is the singular word Eloah. It is applied to God the Father and never used to refer to Christ. The generic term that is used to refer to the extended order of the Host operating under the authority of God is Elohim.

The Elohim act both as a Council among the Host and to mankind the position stated by Trinitarians that the Council is that of the magistrates in Jerusalem is a presumption derived from the comments in Exodus. It was the accepted understanding of the first century that the Elohim or Theoi rank extends to mankind and, 'was so understood to be extended, to Moses both by reference to Philo and Josephus. The Christian position was as stated by Irenaeus. This is well understood by modern scholars. For example, Gregg and Groh refer to Irenaeus who said:

There is none other called God by the scriptures except the Father of all and the Son, and those who possess the adoption (Early Aryanism - A View of Salvation, Fortress Press, Philadelphia, 1981, p. 68). Irenaeus used the Greek term theoi, which was the equivalent of the Hebrew Elohim. Modern supposition is that from this statement the angelic Host was not included in this term.

Namely, it is held that they were inferior to mankind (from a misunderstanding of 1 Cor. 6:3 which relates entirely to the fallen Host) or did not possess the adoption, which for them was unnecessary. The fallen Host was viewed by the early theologians as being able to repent (this is further developed in the work God Revealed).

Modern research demonstrates that Judaism acknowledged a duality of the Godhead - namely one supreme God and a subordinate God down to the middle Ages (see Peter Hayman Monotheism: A Misused Word in Jewish Studies? JJS 42 (1991), 1-15; Margaret Barker The Great Angel: A Study of Israel's Second God, SPCK, London, 1992; and also Hurtado One God, One Lord: Early Christian Devotion and Ancient Jewish Monotheism, Fortress/SCM; his article in Dictionary of Jesus and the Gospels (eds. Green McKnight and Marshall, Inter-Varsity Press, 1992); and his unpublished what do we mean by "First-Century Monotheism?" (University of Manitoba research paper). The Theological Wordbook of the Old Testament (93c) rejects the origin of Elah, the biblical Aramaic name for God, as having been derived from two Gods, El and Ah (shortened Ahyeh or "I shall be" as suggested by Feigin (JNES 3:259)). There is little doubt that the entity Eloah is the God Most High and that the duality of the Israelite deities directly involve superior and subordinate forms.

When God Most High is referred to, He is distinguished from the subordinate YHVH by the epithet YHVH of Hosts, or the Elyon, the Most High designation. The case for the development of the concept of God is made by Smith (loc. cit.). He contends that the original God of Israel was El. This is because El is not a Yahwistic name. Hence, El was the original chief God of the group named Israel. Smith finds support from Genesis 49:24-25, which presents El names, separate from the mention of YHVH in verse 18. Also Deuteronomy 32:8-9 casts YHVH in the role of one of the sons of El, here called Elyon.

When the Most High (Elyon) gave to the nations their inheritance, when (He) separated humanity, (He) fixed the boundaries of the peoples according to the number of divine beings. For Yahweh's portion are his people, Jacob his allotted heritage (Smith, p. 7).

The Soncino translates the Masoretic text (MT) as according to the number of the children of Israel. Thus, the nexus is confined to the twelve tribes and the Canaanite territories, but only by rabbi Rashbam. The MT reads bene yisrael where the Septuagint (LXX) reads aggelon theou and the Qumran reads bny 'ilhym [or bene eliym] (cf. Smith, n. 37 noting also Meyer, and Skehan BASOR 136 (1954):12-15 (cf. first epistle of Clement, using aggelon theou), and the text of Ben Sira 17:17, reflecting later exegesis of Deut. 32:8, implies a divine ruler for every nation). Thus, the older texts support the above and the

Masoretic appears to have been altered at some later date. The RSV adopts this view and renders the texts as Sons of God.

The allocation of the nations according to the number of the Sons of God or the Elohim/eliym demonstrates further the extended order. Instead of supporting the contention of a developing structure, it rather supports an extended structure disguised by Pharisaic Judaism and such disguise supported, without serious challenge, by the Trinitarians.

Smith himself says:
Just as there is little evidence for El as a separate Israelite God in the era of the Judges, so Asherah is poorly attested as a separate Israelite goddess in this period. Arguments ... resting on Judges 6 where she is mentioned with Baal. The regional understanding as an extended structure of the Elim is not fully appreciated by scholars. The syncretism integration theory is used to explain the variant titles and hierarchies. However, this was not as confused among the nations as some scholars would have us believe. The suggestion that the elect would be Elohim is taken up as a fact in the Epic of Gilgamesh where Noah (Uta-Napishtim) is made one of the Elim or Elohim (see New Larousse Encyclopedia of Mythology, Ch. Assyro-Babylonian Mythology, Hamlyn, 1984, p. 63).

The so-called Yahweh (or more correctly Yahovah) being referred to above, from Deuteronomy 32:8-9, is the subordinate Yahovah of

Israel who was allocated Israel as the key nation of the restoration. The allocation of the nations according to the number of divine beings here extends beyond the thirty, as there were understood to be seventy nations or tongues. Thus, it may be deduced there were understood to be seventy divine Elohim in the full Council of Elohim.

The Sanhedrin or Council of Elders established at Sinai was a prototype of the extended order. That the national watchers or Elim resisted God and the YHVH of Israel is noted in Daniel 10:13 (cf. Deut 32:18). Thus, the extended Council must have had a significant number of Elohim who rebelled. These entities are to be replaced from the ranks of the elect beginning from the first resurrection. Harvey (in Jesus and the Constraints of History, in Ch. A the Constraint of Monotheism, Westminster Press, and Philadelphia, 1982) note the honorific is used to describe figures other than God. Moses is referred to as "divine". He is referred to as Theoi in Josephus (Antiquities of the Jews 3:180; 8:34,187; 10:35) and in Philo (e.g. Vita Moses 1:158).

Harvey considers the reference to Moses as divine is a linguistic phenomena which does not qualify the unique divinity God.

However, none of the commentators appears aware that it was God who made Moses an Elohim and placed him as Elohim to Egypt making Aaron his prophet. These terms are used only of the divine agency but the delegation is demonstrated to be not only from God Most High to the Angel of the

Presence but further to Moses who was the first specific biblical evidence we have that the rank of Elohim was extended to mankind and by direct order of God (see Ex. 4:16; 7:1). Were the Elohim rank not capable of delegation at the order of Eloah, and then God Himself would have forced Pharaoh to be in breach of the first commandment by making Moses an Elohim to Pharaoh.

That is, Pharaoh would have had another Elohim before God. However, the commandment clearly does not mean that. By the appointment, God was demonstrating that the term before or beside meant specifically in place of, or without delegation and authority of. Hence, God could appoint the subordinate Elohim of Israel in Psalm 45:7 without affecting the sense and authority of the first commandment. The use of the term Elohim by delegation to the magistrates, as judges in Jerusalem, is held to imply that the term as God does not, therefore, extend beyond three hypostases in reality. Such absurd reasoning seems to reverse the thinking involved in the Old Testament.

The term Elohim was applied to both the angelic Host and to those in authority in the priesthood, specifically Moses, to demonstrate that the Elohim rank, and the oneness of God and His nature, would extend to embrace mankind. If the reverse were the case then the priesthood would be engaged in blasphemy on an ongoing basis.

The term Elohim is a plural word, which is used to refer to the angelic Host, or to God acting through or with the angelic Host. This of it demonstrates that the term Elohim is a plural term extending the concept of, and authority of, God to a subordinate structure. In Genesis 35:7 the term Elohim has a plural verb but is translated God was revealed rather than Gods were revealed. The Soncino notes that: Elohim, which describes God under the aspect of Lordship, may be used in the plural; but no other word meaning God is ever so employed. The Soncino goes on to note that the rabbinical authority Abraham ibn Ezra understood this text to refer to angels. This text can be developed to demonstrate that it referred to the Angel of the Presence or the Messiah. The significant aspect is that the logic of the usage of Elohim here is acknowledged to extend to the angelic Host. Thus, the concept of the extension of the capacity to be Elohim to the Host was held within Judaism. The extension to the elect, biblically, commenced at least as early as Moses.

The reference to Isaiah 44:8 as a demonstration that YHVH is one Elohim, which is offered by Trinitarians, is simply false. Isaiah 44:6-8 states:

So says Jehovah, the King of Israel, and his Redeemer, Jehovah of Hosts: I am the First and I am the Last; and there is no God except Me ... Is there a God beside me? Yea there is none. I have not known a rock. (Interlinear) It is asserted that Yahovah (or incorrectly Jehovah) is one here but the text is in fact of two entities, Yahovah King of Israel and Yahovah of Hosts. Yahovah King of Israel is speaking of Yahovah of Hosts. Green has translated the text by inserting and with his Redeemer to make it appear that both are referred to as one. Similarly, he has translated the word biladay (SHD 1107) as except in Isaiah 44:6 and as beside in Isaiah 44:8. However, the sense of without or beside is that conveyed here. Isaiah 44:8 identifies clearly that entity spoken of, namely YHVH of Hosts, as Eloah. Eloah is a singular word, which refers only to God the Father or the God of Hosts. From Proverbs 30:4-5, we know that this Eloah is God the Father and He has a Son predicated to Him in His Old Testament relationship with Israel.

Judaism, Islam and biblical Christianity worship this entity as the One Supreme God. The Yahovah of Israel is identified, from above, as the Angel of the Presence who is Messiah. The text demonstrates that there are two YHVHs here, the subordinate YHVH of Israel proclaiming the ascendancy of YHVH of Hosts. This YHVH of Hosts is Eloah and beside whom, and indeed without whom, there is no Elohim. This concept forms the basis of the first commandment. Thus, the YHVH of Israel here is separate and subordinate.

The subordinate God of Israel, the Angel of YHVH who is Messiah is the high priest of the house or temple of God. He is the El BethEl. Hebrews notes his appointment directly from Psalm 45:6-7. There is no doubt that this Elohim was anointed and appointed over his partners (metoxous) or comrades (Heb. 1:9) in the Council. The Council of the Elohim that he heads as high priest is mirrored in the organization of the Temple, as the Temple of Zion is an example and shadow of the celestial structure (Heb. 8:5). The high priesthood of the Temple consists of twenty-four divisional high priests and a central high priest. The organization is reflected in the Council of the Elders in Revelation 4 and 5. This Council of the Elder Elohim is referred to throughout the cosmology of the Middle East and referred to from Sumerian to Egypt showing that the biblical structure was widely known (see also Eliade Gods, Goddesses and Myths of Creation, Harper and Row, New York, 1974, pp. 21-25). Psalm 9:5-8 refers to YHVH who is faithful in the assembly of the saints (multitude). He is highest of the Sons of the mighty (or the Eliym as plural of the El, i.e. the Gods). El is greatly to be feared in the congregation (inner assembly or council) of the saints (qadoshim or holy ones). Yahovah, God of Hosts, is the entity referred to as being surrounded by faithfulness. Revelation 4 and 5 show that this group numbered thirty entities including the four cherubim or living creatures. Thus, thirty pieces of silver (also the price of a slave) were required for the betrayal of Christ (Mat. 27:3,9 cf. Zech. 11:12-13) as it was an offence against the entire Godhead. The Elders are charged with monitoring the prayers of the saints (Rev. 5:8) and Christ is their high priest, the member of them who was found worthy to open the scroll of the plan of God having ransomed men and made them a kingdom and priests to our God, i.e. the God of the Council and of Christ (Rev. 5:9-10).

Ascendancy of Christ. The church adopted a form of Trinitarians, which primarily sought to deny the above. It is seriously incoherent and non-biblical. In short, the early form of Trinitarianism was initially developed by Origin in Alexandria to combat the so-called Gnostic view of a celestial council of Elohim, which was adhered to by the early church. Christ was a subordinate God appointed by his God (Ps. 45:7 (using Eloheik) & Heb. 1:9) who was Eloah or Theon or ho Theos (as The God) in the Greek (Jn. 1:1,18). Origin used the Stoic concept of the hypostases which is a synonym (as is the Platonic ousia) which means real existence or essence, that which a thing is. But Origin gives it the sense of individual subsistence and so individual existent. Thus, Origin developed a closed hierarchy of only three elements of the Godhead. The Father was the supreme God.

The other two elements of Son and Holy Spirit were creations of the Father as ktisma. But Origin's schema is a forerunner of Trinitarians whose sole purpose was to limit the extension of the capacity to be Elohim to three beings and deny its capacity in the elect and the heavenly Host. The Greeks took up Origin's schema in the latter half of the third century. Some, such as Theognostus of the catechetic school at Alexandria, emphasized the Son's kinship with the Father although the Son was a creature with his activity restricted to rational beings. He also declared that his substance or ousia (using the Platonic term rather than hypostases) was derived out of the substance of the Father (see Kelly Early Church

Doctrines, p. 133). Others emphasized his subordinations. From the paper The Origins of Christmas and Easter (No. 235), we know that the god Attis carried both aspects of father and son. That is a Moralist structure.

These two elements gave rise to Trinitarians. Trinitarians is the desire to accommodate the structure of the worship of the god Attis and its Modernism into Christianity to satisfy the philosophical objections of its followers.

Origin's disciple Dionysius, Pope of Alexandria, because of an outbreak of Sabellianism in the Lybian Pentapolis in the late fifties of the third century, wrote rebutting Modernism. He thrust the personal distinction between the Father and the Son into the foreground. The Sabellians had one of his letters to bishops Ammonias and Euphranor highlighting this aspect, which Kelly (p. 134) alleges was indiscreet. The Sabellians complained that the Organists were making a sharp division amounting to separation between Father and Son. This was opposed and limited by the Novationists at Rome who influenced Bishop Dionysius, the Pope. Athanasius tried (De sent Dion. 4) to whitewash Dionysius of Alexandria a century later but Basil (Ep. 9.2) maintained that he had gone to the opposite extreme in anti-Sabellian zeal. The term hypostases became ultimately incorporated into Catholic doctrine resulting in the anathemas of the Councils of Chalcedony and Constantinople II.

The structure resulted in the declarations of the Monarchial and the Circumincession. The declaration that the Godhead is distinct but not separate is essentially a statement of the Monarchial and the Circumincession. It is philosophically absurd given the functions of English. The use of hypostases and ousia as terms appears to attempt to cover up the incoherence. The Godhead is held by Trinitarians to be three hypostases in one ousia using the Stoic and Platonic terms to attempt a distinction.

The denial of the term Being to God and Christ effectively denies their existence, which is absurd. Saying that God is Universal Mind (or Universal Soul) utterly depersonalizes God and denies the reality of the Son of God except that the Son's existence is notionally declared as a hypostasis. A word game gives no reality to the Savior. On the other hand, were the reality of the Son to be insisted on, and then the doctrine is essentially an insipient breach of the first commandment. You shall have no other Elohim before me.

The entity here is the YHVH Eloheik (YHVH Your Elohim) who is identified at Psalm 45:7-8 as the Elohim who anointed the Elohi of Israel. By elevating our intermediary Elohim, one of the Council (Ps. 89:7), to the level of Eloah, God the Father, we are in breach of the first commandment. This is the sin of Satan who claimed to be El of the Council of the Elohim (Ezek. 28:2).

Book 2 – Why Were They Called Gods...?

The doctrine of the Trinity rests on a series of false premises designed to enable a paradigm shift (cf. the paper Binitarianism and Trinitarianism (No. 76)). These are: That elohim as the Godhead refers to two entities only making no distinction between Eloah and the multiple entities including the Council and Host (Dan. 7:9 ff) That these two entities (and the Spirit) are incapable of separation in fact or in thought and are not properly describable as Beings. That the reincarnated existence of Christ was not as the Angel of YHVH. That Christ was the only Son of God before the creation of the world (see Job 1:6; 38:7). That Christ and Satan were the only two Morning Stars (see Job 38:7; Isa. 14:12; Rev. 2:28; 22:16). That Christ is God in the same way that God is God (see above) and not a subordinate God (Heb. 1:9) sent by the Lord of Hosts (Zech. 2:10-11). Hence, he is made an object of worship and prayer contrary to Ex. 34:14, Mat. 4:10 etc.).

That Christ was the only begotten Son and not the Only Born God and Son (monogenes theos & uion) (Jn. 1:18; 3:16; 1Jn. 4:9; see also Lk. 7:12; 8:42; 9:38; Heb. 11:17 for comparison). He was the first begotten (prototokos) of all creation (Col. 1:15) hence the beginning of the creation of God (Rev. 3:14, not as per the NIV). That Christ had existence separate to his incarnation hence he could have prayed to himself as God. Such a proposition effectively denies the distinction between Father and Son and the totality of the resurrection. It is of anti-Christ (1Jn. 2:22; 4:3; 2Jn. 7).

That Christ and God were of the same will and that Christ was not possessed of a separate will which he subordinated to God through willing obedience contrary to Matthew 21:31; 26:39; Mark 14:36; John 3:16; 4:34. That divine nature admits of no gains and no losses in Christ. Logically this would deny the resurrection of the saints as explained in 1Corinthians 15, and in the biblical promises to the elect. The Trinity seeks to assert that the divine nature given to the elect differs from the way in which Christ shares it.

That the Holy Spirit is given by fixed measure contrary to John 3:34 (RSV); Romans 12:6. That Christ could not have sinned (from the false premise of divine nature admitting of no gains and no losses rather than from the Omniscience of God, who knew that Christ would not sin).

That Christ was consubstantial with God in such a way that he was co-equal and co-eternal with God contrary to Philippians 2:6 and 1Timothy 6:16 which show that only God is immortal. Christ's eternality or atoning life (1Jn. 1:2) and that of all beings, including Christ, derive from that entity. Both Christ and the elect are of the same origin (Heb. 2:11 RSV) deriving their life and eternality from conditional obedience to the Father (Jn. 5:19-30) who created us all (Mal. 2:10-15). As the Father has life in Himself, so He gave the Son to have life in himself (Jn. 5:26), and we are co-heirs being ordained to have life in ourselves by authority of God (see the paper Consubstantial with the Father (No. 81)).

That the elect are not Sons of God in the same way that Christ is a Son of God and hence not co-heirs contrary to Romans 8:17; Galatians 3:29; Titus 3:7; Hebrews 1:14; 6:17; 11:9; James 2:5; 1Peter 3:7. That the Supreme God came down in the flesh and dwelt among men (stemming from the fraudulent insertions in 1Timothy 3:16 in Codex A. The false insertions were retained in the KJV and manipulated into the preamble in the NIV). The assertion that the Supreme God came down in the flesh is contrary to John 1:18 (and Jn. 1:14 where it was the logos (or Memra) who became flesh) and the numerous texts distancing Christ from the One True God (Eloah or Theon or ho Theos as The God, who is God the Father), the God of Jesus Christ (Jn. 17:3, 20:17; 1Cor. 8:6; 2Cor. 1:3) who stands in his name (Mic. 5:5).

The concepts of how God is one are misunderstood by Trinitarians. The Shema (Deut. 6:4) refers to Yahovah Elohenu or Yahovah as one God. The entity at Deuteronomy 6:5 is identifiable as God Most High, the God who anointed Christ as Elohi of Israel in Psalm 45:7.

The unity of God, necessary to Monotheism, is of an extended order dwelling in unity under a central will in agreement and spiritual interaction through the spirit and power of God (1Cor. 2:4-14) which through Christ is towards God (2Cor. 3:3-4). The Trinity denies the unification necessary to Monotheism and is logically polytheist. It occurs because the rulers do not understand, being unspiritual (1Cor. 2:8,14). The God noted in Proverbs 30:4 as having a Son is Eloah from Proverbs 30:5. The Sons of God are thus known from the Old Testament and, in particular, Messiah is known. The understanding of the Father by Christ is consequent upon the Father's willing self revelation (see Rev. 1:1,6). Christ is not omniscient and never claimed to be so.

God is held by the Bible to be the God and Father of Christ (from Rom. 15:6; 2Cor. 1:3; 11:31; Eph. 1:3,17; Col. 1:3; Heb. 1:1 ff; 1Pet. 1:3; 2Jn. 3; Rev. 1:1,6; 15:3). Christ derives his life, power and authority by command of God the Father (Jn. 10:17-18). Christ subordinates his will to that of God, who is the Father (Mat. 21:31; 26:39; Mk. 14:36; Jn. 3:16; 4:34). God gave the elect Christ and God is greater than Christ (Jn. 14:28) and greater than all (Jn. 10:29). Thus God sent his only born (monogene) Son into the world that we might live through him (1Jn. 4:9). It is God who honours Christ being greater (Jn. 8:54). God is the Rock (sur) as a Quarry or Mountain from which all others are quarried, the flint of Joshua 5:2, the principal and effective cause (Deut. 32:4, see Maimonedes Guide of the Perplexed, University of Chicago Press, 1965, Ch. 16, pp. 42 ff). God is the Rock of Israel, the Rock of their salvation (Deut. 32:15), the Rock that bore them (Deut. 32:18,30-31). 1Samuel 2:2 shows that Our God is our Rock, an everlasting Rock (Isa. 26:4). It is from this Rock that all others are hewn as are all the descendants of Abraham in the faith (Isa. 51:1-2). The Messiah is hewn from this Rock (Dan. 2:34,45) to subjugate the world empires. God, not Peter, nor Christ, nor anybody else, is the Rock or foundation upon which Christ will build his Church (Mat. 16:18) and upon which he himself rests.

Messiah is the chief cornerstone of the Temple of God, of which the elect are the Naos or the Holy of Holies, the repository of the Holy Spirit. The Temple stones are all cut from the Rock that is God, as was Christ, and given to Christ, the spiritual rock (1Cor. 10:4), the rock of offence and stone of stumbling (Rom. 9:33) to form the Temple. Christ will construct the Temple so that God may be all, in all (Eph. 4:6). God has given Christ to be all and in all (panta kai en pasin Col. 3:11) putting all things under his feet (1Cor. 15:27) giving him to be the head over all things to the Church which is his Body, the fullness of him that fills all in all (Eph. 1:22-23).

When God put all things under Christ, it is manifest that God is accepted being the One who put things under the feet of Christ (1Cor. 15:27). When Christ subdues all things, then shall Christ himself be subject to God who put all things under Christ that God may be all in one (panta en pasin 1Cor. 15:28 not as per RSV). Thus, the Platonist doctrines that seek to merge God and Christ in the Trinity are metaphysical nonsense which contradict Scripture. Christ will sit on the right hand of God, by direction of God (Heb. 1:3,13; 8:1; 10:12; 12:2; 1Pet. 3:22) and share God's throne as the elect will share the throne given to Christ (Rev. 3:21) which is a throne of God (Ps. 45:6-7; Heb. 1:8 or God is thy Throne translated Your throne O God, see fn. to annotated RSV).

God, who sends, is greater than he who is sent (Jn. 13:16), the servant not being greater than his Lord (Jn. 15:20). It is the utmost absurdity to suggest that a being could be a sacrifice unto itself. Such an act, logically, is suicide, or within Trinitarianism, a partial mutilation. Hence, the doctrine denies the resurrection, especially from 1Corinthians 15. Thus, the distinction in the crucifixion and resurrection is mandatory and complete. The resurrection had to be in the flesh involving translation as the Wave Offering otherwise; there is no salvation and no ongoing harvest. The preparation of Christ for the ascension to his God and our God, who is our Father (Jn. 20:17), was real and distinctive. Christ achieved his capacity to be God and achieved the fullness of the Godhead bodily from the operation of the Holy Spirit. Thus, the doctrine of the Sonship from baptism is true and complete. Having established the biblical position at the time of Christ, we are able to see how this position was present during the first and second centuries. From the texts available to us of Justin Martyr and Irenaeus, we know that the understanding extended into the early Church.

Justin Martyr states that God taught the same thing by the prophets as by Moses and this is borne out above (see Dialogue with Trypho, Ch. XXVII, ANF, Vol. I, pp. 207 f). Justin taught that God begat, as the beginning, a certain rational power from Himself, who is called, by the Holy Spirit: now the Glory of the Lord, now the Son, again Wisdom, again an Angel, then God (Theos), and then Lord and logos. Justin identifies him as the Captain of the Army of the Lord who appeared to Joshua (ibid., LXI). This section was drawn in exposition of Proverbs 8:21 ff where Wisdom was identified as Messiah, who was made by God.

Messiah then executed God's will. Justin holds (ibid., LXII) that, in the creation, God conversed with entities numerically distinct from Himself. Thus, Moses was held to declare that the creation involved at least two beings numerically distinct from one another. Ditheists attempt to isolate this to two and Trinitarians merge it into three indistinct hypostases. The Elohim were in fact more numerous, from the other texts referred to above esp. Psalm 45:6-7, which ascribes partners to Christ. Irenaeus (c. 125-203) wrote on the question of the extension of the term Elohim (or theoi in the Greek) to mankind. Irenaeus is important because he was taught by Polycarp, the disciple of John (see Butler Lives of the Saints, Burns & Oates, UK, 1991, p. 56). Thus, we can be fairly certain that Irenaeus' understanding (short of forgery) approximated that of the early Church. He certainly supported the Quarto-decimans and mediated in the Passover controversy (Butler, ibid., p. 197), although he was isolated from Asia Minor, being in Lyon. In his work Against Heresies, he expounded the concept that the elect would exist as Elohim.

Irenaeus held that the angels and the creator of the world were not ignorant of the supreme God since they were His property, and His creatures and were contained by Him (Bk. II, Ch. VI, ANF, p. 365). Irenaeus did not refer to the creator of the world, who was Messiah, as God the Most High or the Almighty (ibid., Ch. VI:2). From this work it is shown that the Greek concepts of the Demiurge and the Pleroma had invaded the concepts of that which is termed Aeons and had sought to infuse the biblical concepts with Greek metaphysics, thus destroying them. The Gnostics were forced underground being part of the Mysteries and finally developed into the Trinity. This is developed elsewhere. Irenaeus (and Justin) taught that the resurrection was physical and, then, God would render the bodies incorruptible and immortal (ANF, Vol. I, p. 403). God is held to be the creator (ibid., p. 404) as opposed to Christ who created the world under this God (ibid., p. 405). Irenaeus held that the Holy Spirit had designated both the Father and the Son (from Ps. 45:6-7) as Elohim or Theoi - the Father appointing the Son.

Irenaeus held that Psalm 82:1 referred to the Father, the Son and the elect (those of the adoption as the Church) when it said:

God stood in the Congregation of the gods (theoi), he judges among the gods (Adv. Her., Bk. III,

Ch. VI, ANF, Vol I, p. 419). He did not fully understand the extent of the brotherhood of the elect, which extended to the entire Host who are brethren in the Kingdom. Revelation was given to John in exile on Patmos after he had trained Polycarp. Revelation 12:10 holds the angels to be the brethren of the elect. Revelation 4 and 5 show that the elect have been ransomed to the Council of the Elders to become kings and priests among the Host Christ states that the elect are to become equal to the angels (isaggelos from isos and aggelos (Lk. 20:36) which has the concept of being part of them as an order). Christ confesses to us before his brethren in the Host.

Irenaeus held that the Church was the synagogue of God, which the Son had gathered to himself. God of gods in Psalm 50:1 is held to refer to God. Our Messiah was the Theos or God who shall come openly and shall not keep silence (Ps. 50:3) and who appeared openly to those who sought him not (Isa. 65:1) and the name gods of Psalm 50:1 refers to the elect of whom Christ is held to have referred, when he said:

Ye are gods and all sons of the Most High (Jn. 10:34-35 cf. Ps. 82:6) (ibid.).

It is thus quite erroneous for the Church to state from the distance of two millennia that Christ was using a text that referred to the magistrates in Jerusalem when a disciple of Polycarp held that he was referring to the elect as Elohim. Those who believed in Christ were held by Irenaeus to be Sons of God as co-heirs with Christ and thus Elohim.

Irenaeus also held that Christ was the Son of I Am That I Am (YHVH) or, more correctly, I will be what I will become (cf. Oxford Annotated RSV) (from Ex. 3:14). Thus, his carriage of the title was by delegation. Irenaeus quotes Isaiah thus: I too am witness (he declares) saith the Lord God, and the Son whom I have chosen, that ye may know, and believe, and understand that I AM (Isa. 43:10) (ibid.). The Soncino renders the text:

Ye are my witnesses, saith the Lord, And My Servant whom I have chosen; That ye may know and believe me and understand That I am He; Before Me there was no God (El) formed, Neither shall any be after Me. The quote from Irenaeus, and the Soncino variant, which more or less confirms Irenaeus, shows that I AM, refers to God who is the Father. The reference to servant in the Soncino is seen from Irenaeus to refer to Messiah. The Soncino attempts to equate My Servant with the earlier witnesses, as Israel, although no rabbinical authority is cited. What is certain is that this text was seen as indicating that only God, and not Messiah, was pre-existent. Further, Messiah is distinguished from God.

Irenaeus showed that his understanding of Isaiah 44:9 and Jeremiah 10:11 on the question of the idols was that the idols were idols of demons (Adv. Her., Bk.III, Ch. VI, ANF, p. 419). These demons were removed from the theoi or Elohim. In referring to Jeremiah 10:11, Irenaeus quotes:

Book 2 – Why Were They Called Gods...?

The gods that have not made the heavens and earth let them perish from the earth, which is under the heaven. For from the fact of his having subjoined their destruction he shows them to be no gods (Elohim or theoi) at all. Thus, the idols themselves were shown to be understood, not as being simple idols, but rather, as being the embodiment of the demon whom they represented (see also Bk. III, Ch. XII: 6, ibid., p. 432). This was standard as the understanding throughout the ancient world. Thus, the removal of the demons and their restraint and later judgment removed them from the category of Elohim.

The Zephyrs are a race of winged humanoids. Their skin ranges in color from gold to a coppery brown, with hair ranging from yellow to bright red.

Female and Male Zephyrs these are not Angles, but centuries and Millenniums later, these beings were called Angles in all of our modern day religions all around our world.

Irenaeus shows by reference to Exodus 7:1 that Moses was indeed made an Elohim to Pharaoh but is not properly termed Lord or God by the prophets. He is rather spoken of by the Spirit as Moses, the faithful minister and servant of God (Heb. 3:5; Num. 12:7), which is also how Messiah is termed in the texts. Thus, each of the Elohim is a subordinate servant of Eloah, the Elyon.

Irenaeus (ibid., p. 421) states that Christ confessed Caesar as Caesar and God as God from Matthew 22:21 and also from Matthew 6:24 in serving God and not mammon. Thus, Christ distanced himself from the claim of being The God (see also ibid., p. 422).Quoting Philippians 2:8, Irenaeus shows that the relationship Christ had as God and Judge was derived from the God of All because he became obedient unto death (ibid., Ch. XII:8, p. 433). Irenaeus quotes the LXX of Isaiah 9:6 stating that Messiah was Emmanuel the messenger [or Angel] of Great Counsel of the Father (ibid., Ch. XVI:3, p. 441). He showed thereby that the Angel of Great Counsel of the Old Testament (LXX) was understood to be Christ.

Irenaeus denies the concept that the suffering of Jesus can be separated from the Messiah by alleging that Christ remained impassible. In other words, he denies the attempt to assert that the divine aspect of

Book 2 – Why Were They Called Gods...?

Messiah could be separated from the human Jesus on earth. This became a teaching of the Gnostic sects twisting Mark's gospel and ignoring others. Irenaeus also shows what became the basis of the errors of the sects. The Ebonite's used Matthew's gospel only. Thus, they drew erroneous conclusions regarding the position of Christ. The Euthanasia's or Trinitarians used the term Ebonite later as an attempt to confine the doctrines of subordinations and subordinations of any persuasion to an heretical lineage from Ebonite's to the parties involved in the disputes at Nicaea and which were labeled as Arians. Such claims are false from an examination of the early Church writers who, prior to Nicaea, were subordinations (cf. the paper Early Theology of the Godhead (No. 127)).

Irenaeus was emphatic that there was only one God or Father, namely God the Father. Messiah was His son. He says Marcion also mutilated Luke's gospel to establish his teaching. The Palestinians used John to the detriment of the others and also by including pseudo-gospels. The fact is that then, as now, the Scriptures must be used together diligently and not selectively.

Irenaeus shows an advanced understanding of the fourfold nature of the gospels and their significance in relation to the cherubs (ibid., Bk. III, Ch. XI:8, pp. 428-429).

Irenaeus denied the concept that Jesus could have suffered and risen again and that he who flew off on high was another, remaining impassible. Irenaeus held that the Christ whom God promised to send,

He sent in Jesus, whom they crucified and God raised up (ibid., Ch. XII:2,4,5, pp. 430-431). There is no confusion between God and Christ in the mind of this theologian and he states here, clearly, that the apostles did not change God but Christ was sent by God.

Irenaeus says: Hereby know ye the spirit of God: Every spirit that confessed Jesus Christ came in the flesh is of God; and every spirit which separates Jesus Christ is not of God but is of antichrist (Ch XVI:8 quoting 1John 4:1,2. Note: The Vulgate and Origin agree with Irenaeus. Tertullian seems to recognize both readings.

Socrates says (VII,32. p. 381) that the passage had been corrupted by those who wished to separate the humanity of Christ from his divinity. Polycarp (Ep., c, vii) seems to agree with Irenaeus and so does Ignatius (Ep. Smyr., c, v) (see fn. to ANF, ibid., p. 443, quoting also Burton Ante-Nicene Testimonies to the Divinity of Christ). Thus, the early Church as the doctrine of Anti-Christ understood any doctrine, which seeks to separate Christ by conjoint relocation to both earthly and heavenly realms. The alteration of the text appears to have been in the east. The Bible texts are still uncorrected to this day.

Irenaeus says that the Spirit of God descended upon Christ as a dove that it might fulfill Isaiah 11:2 (And the spirit of God shall rest upon him) and Isaiah 61:1 (The Spirit of the Lord is upon me because he hath anointed me). Thus it was not ye that speak but the Spirit of your Father which speaketh in you (Mat. 10:20) (ibid., Ch. XVII:1, p. 444). The Holy Spirit was therefore understood to be of God and not from Christ but rather through Christ as explained above.

This was so that it was:
The Son of God, made the Son of man, becoming accustomed in fellowship with Him to dwell in the human race, to rest with human beings and to dwell in the workmanship of God, working the will of the Father in them, and renewing them from their old habits into the newness of Christ (ibid.). Irenaeus taught that the elect would put on immortality so that they might receive the adoption as Sons (ibid., Ch. XIX:1). The Spirit joined the elect to God bringing distant tribes to unity, and offering to the Father the first fruits of all nations (ibid., 2). Christ was the instrument of this action but he was neither the object of worship nor the architect of its operation. But he was, nevertheless, the Wonderful Counselor and Mighty God spoken of through Isaiah 9:6, the Judge of Daniel 7:13 (ibid.).

However, Christ acknowledged the Father as his God as did David quoting the same Psalm 22:1 where David said firstly: My God, my God, why hast thou forsaken me?

And Christ again stated this on the cross as recorded in Matthew 27:46 and Mark 15:34. Both texts are referring to Eloah, the Supreme God and the God and Father of Christ. The words used by Christ are Aramaic - namely, he allegedly said: Eli,

Eli, and la'ma sabach-th'a'ni. This is an English ransliteration of a Greek transliteration of the Aramaic 'Eli, 'Eli lamah 'azabthani. The word for God is the Aramaic El, but here equivalent of Eloah, as God expressing His will and to His son. Nonetheless, Christ and the elect were called God (Elohim) by extension.

Irenaeus says:

There is none other called God by the Scriptures except the Father of all, and the Son and those who possess the adoption (Adv. Her., Bk. IV, Pref. 4, ANF, p. 463). Further: [Ch] 1. Since, therefore, this is sure and steadfast (sic), that no other God or Lord was announced by the Spirit, except Him who, as God, rules over all, together with His Word, and those who receive the spirit of adoption [see iii. 6,1]. That is, those who believe in the one and true God, and in Jesus Christ the Son of God; and likewise the apostles did of themselves term no one else as God, or name [no other] as Lord; and, what is much more important, [since it is true (sic)] that our Lord [acted likewise], who did also command us to confess no one as Father, except Him who is in the heavens, who is the one God and the one Father; ... (ibid., p. 463). It is thus absurd to suggest that the understanding that the elect will become Elohim was not understood as the original position of the first two centuries of the Church, given that Irenaeus was the closest link that we have with its doctrines and he so clearly held this position. Further, it is shown beyond doubt that position is the coherent plan of the Scriptures, not only of the Scriptures proper which by biblical definition was the Old Testament (Dan. 10:21; Mat. 21:42; 22:29; 26:54; Mk. 12:10,24; 14:49; 15:28; Lk. 4:21; 24:27,32,45; Jn. 2:22; 5:39; 7:38; etc.), but also of the gospels and into the writings of the New Testament.

In the very passage that deals with the elect as Elohim, namely John 10:35, Christ introduces the concept that Scripture cannot be broken. The selection of this passage as the example was not an accident. This very concept marks our destiny and is the aspect, which the adversary would most attack and for which purpose the Trinity was designed. The gospels are specifically for the outline of the coming Kingdom of God. The writings of the apostles are to prepare the elect and show the mechanics of the execution. But all apostles, as noted by Paul, held that: All scripture is inspired by God (or God-breathed) and profitable for teaching, for reproof, for correction and for training in righteousness (2Tim. 3:16).

Scripture is the bearer of the royal law to love your neighbors as yourself (Jas. 2:8). Nor is the Scripture of any private interpretation (2Pet. 1:20). Thus, a doctrine developed by three Cappadocian theologians in the fourth and fifth centuries in contradiction of Scripture and the early position of the Church is to be resisted with all our might. It quite obviously breaches the first commandment making Christ equal to God. This was so obviously the intent that the passage at Philippians 2:6 was altered in the KJV to reflect this aspect and create the illusion that Christ was equal with God. This is to accuse Christ of idolatry as the sin of Satan.

No Christian can accept the doctrine of the Trinity as it denies the omnipotence of God the Father and rejects our destiny, for these reasons the Churches of God have been persecuted for 1,600 years. The elect have been persecuted for this doctrine by those who call themselves orthodox, or at least who have been accorded that right, because their doctrine of government best suited the civil structure of the empire that used them. The Churches of God have had, until recent times, a different structure of organization, which has helped them to resist such persecution as they faced.

Paul records that the Church has had disputation as to doctrine on many occasions although they have no custom of being fond of strife (1Cor. 11:16). He records that disputes amounting to divisions arise within the Churches of God, for there must also be heresies among you, that they which are approved may be made manifest among you (1Cor. 11:19). Dispute over the nature of God and the subordination of Christ has arisen before in the church eras. The result has been to divide. The groups who embraced Trinitarians, or its Moralist equivalent in the days of John, have then, either left the Church when their errors were pointed out as with John (1Jn. 2:19), or lapsed into antinomianism, becoming Protestant as happened among the Waldensians. Christ did not intervene on at least the last occasion. Each person had to make their choice based on their understanding as developed by the Holy Spirit.

The process of Trinitarian exposition traditionally has been over a period of time. The first step was to expound the doctrine that Christ was co-eternal with God from the beginning, rather than from his direction, as are the elect and the entire Host.

Given this error, the doctrine of co-equality is then advanced until it becomes viewed as heresy to assert his dependent subordinations or that he was the prõtotokos, the first begotten of all creation, the beginning of the creation of God. Prõtotokos is not a title, as demonstrated from the early understanding. For this reason Christ makes the point in Revelation 3:14 to the Church of the Laodiceans that he was the beginning or arche of the creation of God (cf. the paper Arche of the Creation of God as Alpha and Omega (No. 229)). *Note: Alpha and Omega are also known as Yin and Yang and along with Positive and Negative, and the most commonly used is GOOD and EVIL..... They are the, one and the same they are inseparable.

Seemingly, that Church teaches that he was not. They were the only Church to do so and any teaching regarding eras must conclude that the last era of the Church does the same. The error of co-eternality, of origin, began to be expounded in the Churches of God for the first time in five hundred years some time after 1940, probably in the 1950s. This error must be understood and redressed.

Chapter 15

The Meaning of the Names of Gods

Excerpts from Christian Churches of God, Australia, from the Names of God No. 116.

The names of God are given and explained. The context in which they are used is important to an understanding of how God is acting and through whom He speaks.

One of the most misunderstood concepts of the Bible is that of the name of God.

It has been confused on the one hand by Trinitarian misapprehensions following on from the fourth century, and on the other hand, by the desire of Judaism to protect Monotheism from the errors of Trinitarians and the dual power heresy.

The desire to protect the sovereignty of God and defend the Monotheism of the biblical structure from the errors of Binitarianism and Trinitarians inherent in the dual power heresy saw Judaism gradually conceal the fact of the dual and subordinate structure of the way God dealt with Israel. The great Angel that was Elohim was concealed in the texts. A consequence of this was the alteration of some key texts and the concealing of the important truths of the subordinate being that dealt with.

Israel throughout its history.

These entities have names and the names indicate their relationships. Justin Martyr in his First Apology writing on behalf of the Church to the emperor in Rome says that Christ was the Angel of God in the OT that gave the Law to Moses. The knowledge of the name of God is indicative of biblical understanding. The most common misapprehension regarding the name of God stems from Psalm 83:18.

Psalm 83:18 that men may know that thou, whose name alone is JEHOVAH, art the most high over all the earth. (KJV) This name was Yahovah (there is no J in Hebrew). Many entities carry this name on behalf of the one True God.

The text cross references to Exodus 6:3 and Isaiah 26:4.

These three texts were the three places in the Authorized Version where the text was transliterated and printed in large capital letters. The text in Psalm 83:18 couples another title with the name Jehovah namely that of Elyon or the Most High. This is a distinguishing title, as we will see. The name Jehovah is an inexact transliteration. Another transliteration is Yahweh. That also is inexact.

The other two texts read:
Exodus 6:3 And I appeared unto Abraham, unto Isaac, and unto Jacob, by the name of God Almighty, but by my name JEHOVAH was I not known to them. (KJV).
Isaiah 26:4 4 Trust ye in the LORD forever: for in the LORD JEHOVAH is everlasting strength: (KJV).

The name of God which was unknown to the Patriarchs had a specific meaning and hence also a purpose. The name Jehovah (or more correctly Yahovah) is coupled with the name Elohim and refers to an Elohim and El in Psalm 83:1. Elohim is a plural word, which is dependent upon its usage. It means both God and gods. It applies to more than one supernatural being. It refers to unknown multiples in Genesis 1:26.

Genesis 1:26 And God said, Let us make man in our image, after our likeness: and let them have dominion over the fish of the sea, and over the fowl of the air, and over the cattle, and over all the earth, and over every creeping thing that creepeth upon the earth. (KJV)

Binitarianism attempt to confine this statement to two entities, namely God as Father and Christ, however this is impossible given the multiple applications of Elohim and the texts in Job which refer to multiple sons present at the creation (Job 1:6;

2:1; 38:4-7). Job 1:6 Now there was a day when the sons of God came to present themselves before the LORD, and Satan came also among them. (KJV)

Job 2:1 Again there was a day when the sons of God came to present themselves before the LORD, and Satan came also among them to present himself before the LORD. (KJV) These are the Sons of The God (haElohim). The word Lord here is Jehovah (i.e. Yahovah). The Companion Bible has a note on the name Jehovah in Appendix 4, II.

Jehovah is held to mean the Eternal or Immutable One. The definition is in Genesis 21:33.

Genesis 21:33 And Abraham planted a grove in Beersheba, and called there on the name of the LORD, the everlasting God. (KJV) Everlasting here is from the Hebrew 'olam meaning duration. The origin of the word Jehovah is held to be in He who was and is to Come. There is a problem with applying the name given at Sinai to simply Jehovah.

Exodus 3:14 And God said unto Moses, I AM THAT I AM: and he said, Thus shalt thou say unto the children of Israel, I AM hath sent me unto you. (KJV) I am here is hayah, which means to exist, to be or become.

Book 2 – Why Were They Called Gods...?

The Companion Bible renders the text 'ehyeh 'asher 'ehyeh, and translates it as I will be what I will be (or become) (see note and Ap. 48), noting also that Jehovah means He will be spoken of by others. The Oxford scholars have noted in their Oxford Annotated RSV that Yahweh is in fact the third person form of the verb, which actually means He causes to be. So God reveals Himself, as I will be what I will become through the Angel at Sinai. He is referred to as Jehovah (Yahovah), which means in the third person form: He causes to be. When anyone is referred to as Jehovah you are actually saying that He causes to be. You are thus acknowledging the subordinate nature of any being that speaks to you. The Jews understood it and God had never spoken to them; messengers addressed them. Those messengers were called Jehovah and that name means He causes to be, because He who causes to be was never there. When you understand the word Jehovah you understand always that you are referring to a messenger about somebody you have never seen or spoken.

Jehovah literally means I have never seen him So the name given as I AM at Sinai was I am what I will become which was the message God gave to the Angel to Sinai. The word for the name of God translated as I AM was never used again. It is only used once in the Bible. The word for God from then on derived from that is the third person form of the verb.

We know from John 1:18: No one has seen God at any time. The only begotten Son who is in the bosom of the Father, he has declared him. So they translated only begotten Son to get around the concept that there was only one God born.

Only one God spoke and that was the monogenesis Theos, the only born God. In other words Jesus Christ was the only God to ever speak. God the Father never spoke.

When you look at these names both in the Hebrew and the Greek you get an Understanding. We only use the one word for God and then we use Lord and other things to qualify. Have one word for God is totally inadequate because we can't understand what is being done through the names of God.

The next text in Job which deals with the Host is in Job 38:4-7. Job 38:4-7 4 Where waste thou when I laid the foundations of the earth? Declare, if thou hast understanding. 5 Who hath laid the measures thereof, if thou knowest? Alternatively, who hath stretched the line upon it? 6 Whereupon are the foundations thereof fastened? On the other hand, who laid the corner stone thereof; 7 when the morning stars sang together, and all the sons of God shouted for joy? (KJV)

From this text we know that the text in Genesis 1:26 let us make man in our image, refers to a group of people who were present at the foundation of the earth; and that there were multiple morning stars; and morning star is a rank not a being. In this case, at the beginning of the creation of the world there are multiple morning stars. There were multiple system commanders present at the formation of this world. That blows the whole argument that there are two persons in the Elohim and that there is only one Son of God. Those texts show that Binitarianism is as big a lie as Trinitarians and limits the understanding of our destiny and tries to divorce us from our inheritance, which is to become coheirs equal with Christ.

We will take our heritage with Christ and rule as sons of God and we will rule as Elohim and el. The morning stars here are multiple yet Christ has not taken up his rank as Morning Star of this planet yet and Satan is still the Lucifer or light bearer as the son of the morning, the morning star or daystar. He is the god of this world and the prince of the power of the air (2Cor. 4:4; Eph. 2:2).

2 Corinthians 4:4 does not say that Satan is the Theos of this world for no reason. The Trinitarians try and say since Thomas says you are the curious and the Theos of me to Christ, he is therefore God the Father in a Trinity. In fact, Paul says quite clearly that Satan is a Theos of this world. So Thomas is saying Christ is a Theos of him and Paul is saying that

Satan is the Theos of this world. Both of them are theoi; both of them are Gods. The Bible is quite clear on that.

Paul says in 1Corinthians 8:5 there are many theoi and many Lords. What we see about Satan is developed from Isaiah 14:12-17 where he is the Lucifer or Light Bearer.

Isaiah 14:12-17 12 How art thou fallen from heaven, O Lucifer, son of the morning! How art thou cut down to the ground, which didst weaken the nations! 13 For thou hast said in thine heart, I will ascend into heaven, I will exalt my throne above the stars of God: I will sit also upon the mount of the congregation, in the sides of the north: 14 I will ascend above the heights of the clouds; I will be like the most High. 15 Yet thou shalt be brought down to hell, to the sides of the pit. The stars of God here are the sons of God. Star is a rank. Hell is the grave. We are going to have a morning star that is going into the grave. 16 They that see thee shall narrowly look upon thee, and consider thee, saying, Is this the man that made the earth to tremble, that did shake kingdoms; We have a change in status here to man. 17 That made the world as a wilderness, and destroyed the cities thereof; that opened not the house of his prisoners? (KJV)

Here we see that the Lucifer, or light bearer, was the son of the morning or the morning star or daystar. This rank is given to Christ and shared by the elect (2Pet. 1:19; Rev. 2:28; 22:16):

Book 2 – Why Were They Called Gods...?

Ezekiel 28:14-19 14 Thou art the anointed cherub that covereth; and I have set thee so: thou waste upon the holy mountain of God; thou hast walked up and down in the midst of the stones of fire. 15 Thou waste perfect in thy ways from the day that thou waste created, till iniquity was found in thee. 16 By the multitude of thy merchandise they have filled the midst of thee with violence, and thou hast sinned: therefore I will cast thee as profane out of the mountain of God: and I will destroy thee, O covering cherub, from the midst of the stones of fire. 17 Thine heart was lifted up because of thy beauty, thou hast corrupted thy wisdom by reason of thy brightness: I will cast thee to the ground, I will lay thee before kings, that they may behold thee. 18 Thou hast defiled thy sanctuaries by the multitude of thine iniquities, by the iniquity of thy traffic; therefore will I bring forth a fire from the midst of thee, it shall devour thee, and I will bring thee to ashes upon the earth in the sight of all them that behold thee. 19 All they that know thee among the people shall be astonished at thee: thou shalt be a terror, and never shalt thou be any more. (KJV)

These texts are quite clear. The means of Satan's destruction is coming from a spiritual power within him, i.e. his own power is going to be the means of his destruction. This spirit is not going to be any more. The Lucifer, the Morning Star is going to cease to exist. He is going to be made a man, be put through a process and given repentance and then he is going to be translated into another spirit being. The only way to purify Satan and the fallen host is to take them out of their existing system, give them repentance and in Satan's case convert him to a process from which he can then be retranslated. He can then become once again a power and a force, he can be purified and made perfect, his iniquity can be cleansed, and he can be restored to the host.

A lot of propaganda is geared around saying God is unjust, He actually created Satan like that from the beginning, and Satan has no chance. In the same way, Christ was created perfect from the beginning and he could not do anything else because he had the nature of God and Satan did not and it is all a fixed game. That is satanic propaganda and if you fall into that error have saying Christ could not sin and Satan couldn't do any good, then you do Satan's work for him and the whole structure of the Trinity is geared to saying the rules were rigged, that God is unjust. God is not unjust, as we will see.

Satan will cease to exist from this text. He will be reduced and dealt with in the Restoration and Judgment (see also the papers The Judgment of the Demons (No. 80) and Lucifer: Light Bearer and Morning Star (No. 223)). The ranks however were in existence before the earth was created and were multiple. The sons of the God (HaElohim) presented themselves before Jehovah as we have seen from Job.

The term Jehovah is in two forms, which have two separate meanings. The term is also accompanied by other names. The two separate forms are Jehovah (SHD 3068) and Jehovih (SHD 3069). They in fact distinguish two entities one of which carry the title of the other and are subordinate.

Strong states that Jehovah is the Jewish national name for God. The variant Jehovih (or correctly Yahovih) is used after Ado nay or the Lord. This is the Lord Jehovih or superior of Jehovah. He is Jehovah Elyon or Jehovah of Hosts. Jehovih is used as a deferential form. Jehovah refers to Jehovah of Hosts as Jehovih in Ezekiel 16:36, 31:10,15; 38:10,14; 39:8. The dabar Jehovah or word of God occurs in Ezekiel. Adonai Jehovih is used for the prophecy in Ezekiel 29:8 which implies a distinction between the word of God and Adonai Jehovih.

Zechariah shows that there is a distinction in the names and entities (Zech. 2:3-12).

Zechariah 2:3-12 3 And, behold, the angel that talked with me went forth, and another angel went out to meet him, 4 And said unto him, Run, speak to this young man, saying, Jerusalem shall be inhabited as towns without walls for the multitude of men and cattle therein: 5 For I, saith the LORD, will be unto her a wall of fire round about, and will be the glory in the midst of her. 6 Ho, ho, come forth, and flee from the land of the north, saith the LORD: for I have spread you abroad as the four winds of the heaven, saith the LORD. 7 Deliver thyself, O Zion, that dwellest with the daughter of Babylon. 8 For thus saith the LORD of hosts; after the glory hath he sent me unto the nations, which spoiled you: for he that toucheth you toucheth the apple of his eye. 9 For, behold, I will shake mine hand upon them, and they shall be a spoil to their servants: and ye shall know that the LORD of hosts hath sent me. 10 Sing and rejoice, O daughter of Zion: for, lo, I come, and I will dwell in the midst of thee, saith the LORD. 11 And many nations shall be joined to the LORD in that day, and shall be my people: and I will dwell in the midst of thee, and thou shalt know that the LORD of hosts hath sent me unto thee. 12 And the LORD shall inherit Judah his portion in the holy land, and shall choose Jerusalem again. (KJV)

It is clear from this text that there are two angels involved here. One is superior to the other and the superior one is the pre-incarnate Messiah. He speaks for Jehovah of Hosts who has sent him. Verse 5 is rendered as for I saith the Lord but is in fact For I, Jehovah's oracle (see Companion Bible fn. to v. 5). This angel who is Jehovah's oracle will deliver Israel from the nations (v. 9) and, by that, many nations will know that Jehovah of Hosts has sent that being to them. The apple of his eye is actually the apple of my eye. My was changed to His by the Sopherim regarding the word as derogatory to Jehovah (see Comp. Bible fn. to v. 8). The change was probably because the apple of my eye made it the apple of the eye of a subordinate entity. Many nations shall be joined to the Lord (Jehovah) in that day. He will dwell in the midst of them and they will know that Jehovah of Hosts has sent him to them. In other words Jehovah here is the angel sent to Israel by Jehovah of Hosts. This angel or messenger of

Jehovah of Hosts was the Elohim of Israel. Zechariah 12:8 show clearly that the Angel of Jehovah was Elohim and that the elect will also be Elohim as he was.

Zechariah 12:8 In that day shall the LORD defend the inhabitants of Jerusalem; and he that is feeble among them at that day shall be as David; and the house of David shall be as God, as the angel of the LORD before them. (KJV).

The word for God here is Elohim and the angel of the Lord is the Angel of Jehovah. The intent is clear. Both the angel and the household of David (i.e. the elect) will be as Elohim. Elohim as previously stated is the plural word for God. The name for God in the singular is Eloah. This name admits of no plurality. Proverbs 30:4-5 shows that He has a son as well as supplying His name Eloah after the question.

Proverbs 30:4-5 4 who hath ascended up into heaven, or descended? Who hath gathered the wind in his fists? Who hath bound the waters in a garment? Who hath established all the ends of the earth? What is his name, and what is his son's name, if thou canst tell? 5 Every word of God is pure: he is a shield unto them that put their trust in him. (KJV)

The word for God in verse 5 is Eloah. The concept of the son of God is thus made plain from the Old Testament. Ezekiel shows also the concept from 21:8-13:

Ezekiel 21:8-13 8 Again the word of the LORD came unto me, saying, 9 Son of man, prophesy, and say, Thus saith the LORD; Say, A sword, a sword is sharpened, and also furbished: 10 It is sharpened to make a sore slaughter; it is furbished that it may glitter: should we then make mirth? it contemneth the rod of my son, as every tree. 11 And he hath given it to be furbished, that it may be handled: this sword is sharpened, and it is furbished, to give it into the hand of the slayer. 12 Cry and howl, son of man: for it shall be upon my people, it shall be upon all the princes of Israel: terrors by reason of the sword shall be upon my people: smite therefore upon thy thigh. 13 Because it is a trial, and what if the sword contemn even the rod? it shall be no more, saith the Lord GOD. (KJV)

The statement in verse 9 is from Jehovah, however some codices with three early printed editions (one Rabbinic in margin), read Adonai. From verse 13 we read that it is Adonai Jehovah's oracle. Thus we are dealing with the superior Jehovih or Jehovah of Hosts and we are referring to His son who was Messiah. He was given the rod. The swords referred to in verse 11 went to the king of Babylon as the slayer yet this was also the sword in the garden at Gethsemane.

Christ thus fulfilled this prophecy. The rod of His son was despised, as was every tree. In other words he was to be despised by crucifixion. The sword condemned the rod and therefore even the sword shall be no more. Thus the son and his death is clear from the Old Testament texts. Messiah is the subordinate Jehovah of Israel who is sent by Jehovah of Hosts. This text deals with the slaughter and destruction of Israel and the cessation of the monarchy whose day is come when iniquity shall have an end (verse 25).

The monarchy shall then cease until Messiah comes, he whose right it is (verse 27). The Jah root form (or Yaho) Jehovah is one name applied to God and to His subordinates who carry His name. The root form of this name is Jah which is also the name applied to God. Jehovah of Israel was not the object of worship. The object of worship was Jehovah of Hosts. The name of the Temple vested in the name Yaho that is the ancient rendering of Jah or Jahh. This also is listed as the name of God from the Psalms. Psalm 68:4 Sing unto God, sing praises to his name: extol him that rideth upon the heavens by his name JAH, and rejoice before him. (KJV)

The first occurrence of the name Jah is in Exodus 15:2. Thus, it is appropriate that this example is in the second or Exodus book of the Psalms.

Exodus 15:2 The LORD is my strength and song, and he is become my salvation: he is my God, and I will prepare him an habitation; my father's God, and I will exalt him. (KJV)

Jah is rendered here as The Lord. The concept of inhabiting eternity is implied. Its first use in the Bible is here connected with redemption. He is El and their father's Elohi. Verse 3 then says that Jehovah is an ish or man of war. Exodus 15:3 The LORD is a man of war: the LORD is his name. (KJV)

Jehovah is here rendered Lord. Praise is thus to be made in the name Jah, from Psalm 68:4. The text in verse 8 refers to the presence of God in the Exodus.

Psalm 68:8 the earth shook, the heavens also dropped at the presence of God: even Sinai itself was moved at the presence of God, the God of Israel. (KJV)

The presence of God was the Angel of Jehovah. He was here the pani or presence of Elohim or pani-el, the Face of God. The presence was with them in the wilderness. The text says the Elohim, Elohi of Israel God the God of Israel. Psalm 68:17 shows another significance to the construction. Psalm 68:17 the chariots of God are twenty thousand, even thousands of angels: the Lord is among them, as in Sinai, in the holy place. (KJV)

This text has some other meanings, the Companion Bible notes of the text that the number of the chariots of God is in the Hebrew twice ten thousand thousands hence twenty million. The text, according to the primitive orthography in the division of the word (Companion Bible fn.), should read Jehovah hath come from Sinai into the Sanctuary (Ginsburg, Intr., pp. 161,162). Or with the ellipsis may read Jehovah among them (i.e. the angels and chariots) [hath come from] Sinai into the Sanctuary. (Comp. Bible ibid.).

The interpretation of the text is supplied in the next verse 18.

Psalm 68:18 Thou hast ascended on high, thou hast led captivity captive: thou hast received gifts for men; yea, for the rebellious also, that the LORD God might dwell among them. (KJV)

Jehovah here has ascended on high and received gifts for men and for the rebellious also that the Lord God or Jah Elohim might dwell among them. This is a direct reference to the Wave Sheaf Offering on the Sunday morning at the third hour or 9 am. Christ was presented as the Wave Sheaf and received gifts for men, namely the Holy Spirit.

From the text in John 20:17 Christ informed Mary of the Ascent to the God and Father of us all.

In John 20:19-22 we see he then retuned the same day and breathed the Holy Spirit to the Disciples indicating the acceptance and gifts promised in Psalm 68:18 and his dispatch by the Father to the Church to send them forth. This day commenced the Omer count to Pentecost and the gift of the Holy Spirit to the entire church. (Look also at the paper The Wave Sheaf Offering (No. 106b)).

Jah or more correctly Yaho is thus a root form, which refers to God in its variant delegations and aspects. Jah [of the] Elohim is the same as Jehovah of Hosts. The subordinate Jehovah here has taken captivity captive that all creatures both loyal and rebellious might be reconciled to God. The entity that takes captivity captive is identified from this text as Christ by reference to Ephesians 4:8 and Revelation 13:10. He received gifts from God for, and gave them to, men.

Ephesians 4:7-8 7 But unto every one of us is given grace according to the measure of the gift of Christ. 8 Wherefore he saith, when he ascended up on high, he led captivity captive, and gave gifts unto men. (KJV)

This text is referring to Christ as the subordinate deity of Israel. Paul here is referring to the ascension of Christ as told in Psalm 68:17 but does not draw out the full lesson in the text.

Similarly Revelation interprets the verses to take captivity captive: Revelation 13:10 He that leadeth into captivity shall go into captivity: he that killeth with the sword must be killed with the sword. Here is the patience and the faith of the saints. (KJV)

It is obvious that Jehovah here is Christ who is also the Angel of Jehovah. Jehovah is thus a delegated name. Jehovah is not the object of worship. Only when identified as Jehovah Elohim or Jehovah of Hosts can Jehovah be definitive object of worship. The only name of God, which identifies the Father in one word, is Eloah. Jehovah must be accompanied by other terms or taken in context to determine the entity. Thus God the Father can only be recognized as such by the term Eloah. When used in the root form Jah, God must be assumed.

The use of the term Jah performs a function in the texts. It occurs some forty-nine times completing seven cycles. It has a special sense, as Jehovah has become our salvation. It completes the 49 times or cycles to enter into the Holy of Holies on the Fiftieth which is the entire symbolism of the Temple of God which temple we are. The temple was named the Temple of Yaho from the Aramaic letters of the Temple at Elephantine (see Pritchard, The Ancient Near East etc., vol I, pp. 278-280).

Jah is thus referred to anciently as Yaho from at least before 407 BC. Thus, the correct form for Jehovah is Yahovah or Yahovih dependent upon the suffix used in reference to the entity. It is pronounced Yahoweh or Yahowih. The term Yahweh is thus also incorrect (see also the paper Abracadabra: The Meaning of Names (No. 240)).

Care must be taken to identify the Yahoweh that is the object of worship. Unless the entity is identified and understood as the supreme God, Yahovah of Hosts who is Eloah, then the monotheism of God is compromised and Binitarianism is again introduced. The name Jehovah or Yahovah is combined with ten other titles.

They are in the order they appear in the Hebrew texts as:

Jehovah-Jireh Jehovah will see or provide (Gen. 22:14).
Jehovah-Ropheka Jehovah that heals you (Ex. 15:26).
Jehovah-Nissi Jehovah my banner (Ex. 17:15).
Jehovah-Mekaddishkem Jehovah that does sanctify you (Ex. 31:13; Lev. 20:8; 21:8; 22:32; Ezek. 20:12).
Jehovah-Shalom Jehovah [send] peace (Judg. 6:24).

Jehovah-Zeba'oth Jehovah of Hosts (1Sam. 1:3 and frequently).
Jehovah-Zidkenu Jehovah our righteousness (Jer. 23:6; 33:16).
Jehovah-Shammah Jehovah is there (Ezek. 48:35).
Jehovah-'Elyon Jehovah Most High (Ps. 7:17; 47:2; 97:9).
Jehovah-Ro'I Jehovah my Shepherd (Ps. 23:1).
The Twenty-Third Psalm uses seven of the attributes conferred by the names of God:
Verse 1; conveys concept 1 (Jehovah-Jireh).
Verse 2; conveys concept 5 (Jehovah-Shalom).
Verse 3; conveys concepts 2 and 7 (Jehovah-Ropheka and Jehovah-Zidkenu).
Verse 4; conveys concept 8 (Jehovah-Shammah).
Verse 5; conveys concepts 3 and 4 (Jehovah-Nissi and Jehovah Mekaddishkem).

The Companion Bible makes a series of arguments (App. 4) for El as being essentially the almighty although the word is never so rendered. This context is in fact as El Shaddai. The use of El is thought of as God the Omnipotent. Elohim is used in the sense of God as Creator because God creates and ordains law in the hands of intermediaries. Elohim is plural. El is used as the root for qualitative description of God. It is only Eloah that is the God Who Wills and is the one object of worship of His people (see also Comp. Bible. App. 4). El is thought of as the God who knows all (first occurring in Gen. 14:18-22) and sees all (Gen. 16:13) and performs all things for His people (Ps. 57:2) and in whom all the divine attributes are concentrated (Comp. Bible ibid.). There is however, the fact that El is the root, which occurs in names, and titles, which indicate that is simply the root from which qualitative difference is demonstrated in entities, which act under delegation. For example, the Angel of Jehovah is also the El Bethel or the God of the House of God. In other words, it demonstrates authority within structure. Only Eloah is the singular extension of worship.

Eloah is the Elohim of Elohim; He who anoints (Ps. 45:6-7; Heb. 1:8-9). Eloah is the God Who Wills. This God is the object of worship and the central and creative figure of the Elohim. This is He who willed and by whom all things Exist and were created (Rev. 4:11).

Revelation 4:11 "Worthy art thou, our Lord and God, to receive glory and honor and power, for thou didst create all things, and by thy will they existed and were created." (RSV)

This being is the object of worship of the twenty-four elders and the lamb who is Messiah (Rev. 4:1-5:14). Messiah is the only born son and Eloah is the Father from Proverbs 30:4-5. The first occurrence of this name associates it with worship (Deut. 32:15,17). It is used in contrast to idols and hence is the Living God. This God who alone is immortal (1Tim. 6:16). All others derive their eternal life from Him by will and direction.

El Elyon is the name applied to Eloah as the Most High El. He is the Most High God. He is God the Father as we know from the Greek rendering of the name in Luke 1:35.

El Elyon is the entity that divided the nations (Deut. 32:8). He gave Israel as Jehovah's portion. Thus, Jehovah here is the Jehovah of Israel and subordinate to Eloah or El Elyon. It is Eloah or Elyon that is the object of worship. Israel did not worship its subordinate Elohim. Note Deuteronomy 32:8 has been altered in the Masoretic text to read according to the number of the Children of Israel rather than the original sons of God or the number of the angels (LXX) or eliym or the Gods (DSS).

Genesis 14:18-22 shows that the Most High God is the possessor of heaven and earth and that Melchisedek is priest of the Most High God. Messiah is thus also priest of the Most High God and cannot himself be that God. One cannot be one's own priest. These texts should be compared with Zechariah 6:13 and 14:9.

Zechariah 6:13 It is he who shall build the temple of the LORD, and shall bear royal honor, and shall sit and rule upon his throne. And there shall be a priest by his throne, and peaceful understanding shall be between them both."' (RSV)

Thus, we understand that the throne of the Most High is ruled over by Messiah under delegation. The unity of the kingdom is derived from being under the will of Eloah.

Zechariah 14:9 And the LORD will become king over all the earth; on that day the LORD will be one and his name one. (RSV)

Jehovah (tr. Lord) will be king over all the earth. Then Jehovah will be one (Ehad) and his name one (Ehad). The oneness that is conferred from the ruler ship of Jehovah is that God becomes all in all (1Cor. 15:28; Eph. 4:6).

Ephesians 4:6 one God and Father of us all, who is above all and through all and in all. (RSV)

God is thus the Father only and He is above all through all and in all. Christ is included in this context.

1Corinthians 15:28 When all things are subjected to him, then the Son himself will also be subjected to him who put all things under him, that God may be everything to every one. (RSV)

1Corinthians 15:28 And when all things shall be subdued unto him, then shall the Son also himself be subject unto him that put all things under him, that God may be all in all. (KJV)

When all is subdued, then the son will himself be subjected to God who put all things under him so that God may be overall. The RSV text is incorrect seemingly from a desire to defeat the obvious non-Trinitarian conclusions drawn from this text. God will be in all as He is in Christ. The Elyon is over all the earth (Ps. 83:18). The title occurs 36 times or 6 x 6, which has a significance relating to the material creation.

Shaddai refers to the Almighty in the sense of supplying all the needs of the people. It is used when Abraham is called out to walk before Him in Genesis 17:1. The sense of being called out was applied to Abraham and is applied to the Church in 2Corinthians 6:18.

2Corinthians 6:17-18 17 Wherefore come out from among them, and be ye separate, saith the Lord, and touch not the unclean thing; and I will receive you, 18 And will be a Father unto you, and ye shall be my sons and daughters, saith the Lord Almighty. (KJV)

Once again we speak of God the Father. The term is used as El Shaddai. Adon. Is one of three titles, (viz. Adon, Adonai, Adonim). They are generally rendered Lord. It refers to the Lord as ruler in the earth. It is distinguished from Adonai, which is used as the being carrying out God's purpose in the earth. (The Lord in his relation to the earth (Comp. Bible ibid.). The vowel points associated with Jehovah when used with Adon render or converts it to Adonai. This was deliberately done in 134 passages, which are preserved and given in the Massorah (§§ 107-115) (see also Comp. Bible App. 32 for the list).

Adonim is the plural of Adon and is never used of man (Comp. Bible ibid.). It is simplified that an Adon may rule others who do not belong to him. Hence, without the article it is used of men. Bullinger does not deal adequately with the plurality and singularity in the usage of the words in relation to divine beings. There is no doubt that the usage of Adonai and Elohim were used to make specific distinction between the two entities Jehovah and Jehovah of Hosts.

Jehovah on its own (SHD 3068) is the national Elohi of Israel (see Strongs) and is not the object of worship. Jehovih (SHD 3069) is the superior of Jehovah, the Elohi of Israel who is also termed the Angel of Jehovah, Jehovah with other terms and as Adonai Jehovah is rendered Lord God and is thus distinct from the singular usage. There are two terms rendered Lord God and that is Adonai Jehovah and Jehovah Elohim. The single term Elohim is often used of angels and particularly the Angel of Jehovah who the Elohim anointed in Psalm 45:6-7 and who is Christ (Heb. 1:8-9).

Therefore, God your God has anointed you with the Oil of gladness above your partners. In the same way, we are all to become Elohim under His name and power (Zech 12:8).

Within the monotheist, structure laid down in the Bible concepts. It is written I said ye are Gods: Sons of the highest all of you and Scripture cannot be broken (John 10:34-35).

Binitarianism/Trinitarians limits the understanding of The concept that we shall rule as God.

Chapter 16

Light Bearer and Morning Star

Excerpts from Christian Churches of God, Australia, from Lucifer: Light Bearer and Morning Star, No 223

The term Lucifer attributed to Satan as a name. The term has become personalized and has taken on a negative sense, Similarly, the term Morning Star has been attributed to Christ in a personalized fashion. When the Bible appears to refer to Satan as Day Star of Morning Star and to Christ as the Light-Bearer, which is the sense of Lucifer, people apply the names in this personalized way and come to the wrong conclusion. Some have even gone to the extent of confusing Christ with Satan.

The Jews do not fully understand what is happening with the texts in the Old Testament because they reject Messiah as Morning Star.
The Soncino renders Isaiah 14:12 as:
How thou art fallen from heaven O daystar, son of the morning!

How art thou cut down to the ground that didst cast lot over the nations?

The soncino interprets the phrases as follows.

12: Daystar [Or, 'Lucifer' (light-bearer). The morning star (son of the morning) under the name of Ishtar was worshipped by the Babylonians, and Nebuchadnezzar's day of power and glory are well represented by their comparison with the shining star]. Arbarbanel points out that this star, namely Venus, is the heavenly prince of Babylon.

Cast lots. To determine the day which the respective nations shall render service (Rashi) others render, 'thou didst slay the nation' (Targum. Ibn Ezra, Kimchi).

The LXX renders the text:
How has Lucifer that rose in the morning fallen from heaven?
Here it is personified by the use of the term Lucifer in the English from the KJV application. The term ho 'Eosphoros ho proianatellon is rendered as Lucifer that rose in the morning.
This translated the Hebrew word meaning How (SHD349) you have fallen (SHD5307) from the heavens (SHD8064) o shining star (SHD1966) son of the morning (SHD1121 and 7837) (see Green's Interlinear). SHD 1966 (HYLL) in the word heylel. It means the morning star or the daystar from the sense of brightness in SHD1984 halal meaning clear and

hence to shine with clarity. It has positive and negative applications in that it can mean to boast or to glorify, to glory, to give light. It can mean to feign madness in the negative application. In the sense that it is used in a positive sense and applied in the form as it develops in SHD 1966 heylel, it is as Morning star or Daystar.

The terminology goes back also into ancient mythology and represents a function of ruler ship. With the Babylonians, it was attributed to the Ishtar system in the evening as the Evening Star representing sexual love and the Morning Star represented Ishtar as goddess of war. This was reflected in the triune system as employed by Babylon (see the paper The Golden Calf).

The theology is thus representative of the cosmology of the heavens and concerns ruler ship.

In the Greek New Testament, the term rendered daystar in English is actually phosphorous (in 2Pet. 1:19) in relation to Christ in the KJV but rendered as morning star in the RSV. Both versions avoid the real sense, which is light bringer as Phosphorous. Lucifer is the Latin translation of this word.

The Light-bringer and the Morning Star or Day Star are ranks and not names.

Therein lies the Key to the confusion.

In Revelation, 2:28 the rank is extended to the elect in the form of astera ton proinon rendered morning star. This form is again found in Revelation 22:16 as the aster ho [1] Lampros ho proinos referring to Christ explicitly and as morning (SGD4407 proinos) star (SGD 792 aster).

Lampros (SHD 2986) means bright; hence: the bright and the morning star. The names have the same derivation and yet they refer to two distinct beings. Thus, we are speaking of a rank and function, which Satan holds and which is to be assumed by Christ at the Advent.

This rank or function can be further demonstrated by its application in the Hebrew from Job38:4-7.

The words are SHD1242 and 3556. The words are rendered the stars of the morning. There were at least two of these beings and seemingly more. Thus we are dealing with Christ, Satan and other members of the Host. It is, hence, obviously a rank of function shared by a number of individuals.

The words are SHD3566 kokawb meaning a star as round or blazing and, hence figuratively, a prince, and SHD 1242 bouquet meaning the morning or break of day.

SHD 3566 is derived also from the sense of 3522 rolling derived from the unused root meaning to heap up; or 3554 kavah in the sense of blazing or burning. These beings performed a faction, which was derived linguistically from the sense of blazing as a star in the morning, or morning star, which was the brightest of the stars, namely Venus. The

Babylonians also applied this to their deity as we see above. The words in verse 7 are rendered in the LXX as translated by Brenton as: When the stars were made, all my angels praised me with a loud voice.

The words are derived from the Greek (here Romanised): Ote egenephesan astra, enesan 'me' phone megale pantes aggeloi mou.

The term in the Hebrew means morning stars; it is structured in the MT as follows:

When sang (SHD 7442) together (SHD 3162) the stars of (SHD 3556) the morning (SHD 1242) and shouted for joy (SHD 7321) all (SHD 3605) the sons of God (SHD1121 and 430).

The LXX translated all the sons of God (kowl bene Elohim) as all the angels of God. The word kol or kowl (pr. kole) is the derivation of the word whole and its use here means literally the whole of the sons of God. Thus, here, there were multiple entities understood as being sons of God.

The rendering of the text when sang together the stars of the morning in the LXX as when the stars were made is understood as being the creation of these stars after the creation of the sons of God. Thus, the ranks were created after entities and these positions were symbols by the stars themselves, which formed part of their dominion.

This is also the sense of the transfer of the power of the position of morning star from Satan to Christ and then its distribution to the church as so-rulers or co-heirs.

The explanations that seek to make Christ and Satan one or to deny both are morning stars strikes at the understanding of this transfer of power and the role of the elect at the Advent.

Chapter 17

Abracadabra: The Meaning of Names

Within this section, I have the, Excerpts from Christian Churches of God, Australia, from Abracadabra: The Meaning of Names No 240.

Names are often used as words of power. In theology, the general use is for purposes of invocation. They are used to give the person doing a mantra control over the deity summoned and to force the one or ones called to grant their demands. This use is generally associated with the occult, the numbers and symbols of Kabala, the various forms of mysticism, including primitive witchcraft and shamanism. Its present use remains akin to its use in the early Mystery Religions and Secret Societies.

When the word Abracadabra, what do we conjure up? This is a name used by magicians and illusionists to make objects or animals and people: appear, disappear or change shape and color, "Presto Changeo" sleight of hand.

However, a word of Kabalistic (Cabbalistic) significance that was, and still may be, used for incantations. It was declared that when written as below, folded so as to conceal the writing, sewn with white thread and worn around the neck, your ailments would subside. Sometimes you were required to remove letters and this would further cause the illness to diminish.

ABRACADABRA
ABRACADABR
ABRACADAB
ABRACADA
ABRACAD
ABRACA
ABRAC
ABRA
ABR
AB
A

ABRA has a supposed significance as it is composed of the first letters of the Hebrew words for: Father = Abba, and Spirit = Rauch Acadosh. However, J E Cirlot in A Dictionary of Symbols, Dorset, page 2, considers the whole word a Hebrew phrase.

Abracadabra: This word was in frequent use during the Middle Ages as a magic formula. It is derived from the Hebrew phrase abreq ad habra, meaning, "Hurl your tholt e ven unto death".

Book 2 – Why Were They Called Gods...?

The earliest written record available of the word is in a second century poem Praecepta de Medicina by Serenus Sammonicus a celebrated Gnostic physician. He gave instructions for using the letters of this magical triangle, which he used for curing agues and fevers. It was to be written on paper, folded into the shape of a cross, worn for nine days suspended from the neck and, before sunrise, cast behind the patient into a stream running eastward.

It was also a most popular charm in the middle Ages. During the Great Plague of 1665, great numbers of these amulets were worn as supposed safeguards against infection. In the most famous of all talismans, and was used as a magical formula by the Gnostics in Rome for invoking the aid of beneficent spirits against disease, misfortune and death.

Further Kabalistic research will show the number values and symbolic resonance of this power word.

These sacred invocations are part of a mystical discipline that used the repetition of the name of a deity or a combination of letters and names to help in meditation, an unveiling of a divine 'Name'. Wills's Lucky Charms #13: THE ABRACADABRA

This is one of 50 trading cards depicting amulets and talismans published in England during the 1920s by W D & H O Wills, makers of Wills's cigarettes. The greatest word of power, the most elusive and powerful divine name, is the "personal" name of God, the Tetragrammaton - YHVH - with which God created everything. According to legend, because of its awesome power, the pronunciation of the name was rarely spoken, and then only on the holiest of days and holiest of places; eventually the pronunciation was lost. (Richard Cavendish The Black Arts, Putman Publishing, 1967).

Before the third century BCE, the use of the Name of God was prohibited and the concept is mentioned by the Essence about 100 BCE in The Community Rule. If any man has uttered the [Most] Venerable Name VII even though frivolously, or as a result of shock or for any other reason whatsoever, while reading the Book or blessing, he shall be dismissed and shall return to the council of the community no more (Vermes Dead Sea Scrolls in English, 4th edition, p. 79). The cruel death, which R H Teradion suffered in the Hadrian persecution, was accounted as punishment for pronouncing the name. ('Ab zara, 18a) This was to guard against an irreverent use of the sacred name. The laity ceased to pronounce it. Only the priests at the benediction, and after the death of Simon the Just, only the high priest, and he with bated breathe, to render it inaudible even to his colleagues, pronounced the 'unutterable' name. The correct pronunciation of the name was delivered only to the pious and humble (Kid. 71a). According to Philo (Vita Mos. iii 14) it was breathed by holy lips into holy ears in the holy place. Josephus also makes this a concern. (Ant. II xii 4). (Encyclopedia of

Religion and Ethics, art. names of God, Jewish, Vol. 6, p. 296, J Hastings et al.).

This Name of God, because by speaking it the universe was created, is considered to: reflect the hidden meaning of totality of existence; [it is] the Name through which everything else acquires its meaning (G Schloem Major Trends in Jewish Mysticism, p. 133, Schocken Publishing, 1941).

This Name is considered by Crowley to be the ultimate goal of the magician for, by knowing its pronunciation, it can be used to create in the same way as God, or to destroy:

Such a Word should in fact be so potent that man cannot hear it and live. Such a word was indeed the lost Tetragrammaton. It is said that at the utterance of the name the Universe crashes into dissolution. Let the Magician earnestly seek this Lost Word. (A Crowley Magick in Theory and Practice, pp. 70-71, Dover Publications, 1976).

Not only do the magicians revere the four-lettered name, but the word Tetragrammaton itself has been adopted and used in magical ceremonies. The Tetragrammaton is more often used in the conjurations of Practical Magic. In Ceremonial Magic it has a variety of uses and, while it is sometimes used in rituals as a name of power, its use is usually restricted to another form of categorization.

Any magical theory or practice, which can be divided into four parts, is usually assigned one of the letters in the Tetragrammaton. Its most important correspondence is with the four elements - fire (Y), water (H), air (V), and earth (H) (Israel Regarded The Golden Dawn, Llewellyn Publications, 1986). There is a concept that God used His name to create the universe and everything in it, including the ten Sefirot, meaning Divine Emanations. There are ten Divine Names that are associated with them. This, in turn, originates from the Sefer Yetzirah, in which it is written that God, taking three letters of his name, sealed the six dimensions, which are associated with the fifth to last Sefirot. (D R Blumenthal Understanding Jewish Mysticism, Vol. I and II, KTAV, 1978)

The magical theory that names can be used as words of power, whether to control the universe outside of the magician or to achieve union with "God" or the "Absolute" or whatever Name is preferred, the concept is of God using His name to create everything.

The Abraxas

Abraxas stones were commonly worn and highly esteemed in the Roman Empire about the time when Christianity was becoming established there. Much importance was also attached to the word Abraxas, in the Greek notation making up the number 365, signifying 365 heavens, occupied by the 365 gods who, according to the Gnostic religion, formed the earth and ruled its destiny. This assigning of days is carried into the modern era by the dulia worship of the saints of Catholicism.

Commenting on the elimination of some feasts, L'Osservatore Della Dominica, the Vatican weekly said: "Generally, the removal of a name from the calendar does not mean passing judgment on the non-existence (of a saint) or lack of holiness. Many (saints) have been removed (from the calendar) because all that remains certain about them is their name, and this would say too little to the faithful in comparison with many others (The 1975 Catholic Almanac, p. 285). The litanies are still in force, and deceased saints are invoked to pray for the supplicant.

The Abraxas, the curious device Jeo, or Jehovah of the Gnostics, has a fowl's head, signifying watchfulness and foresight; the shield, wisdom; whip, authority; two serpents, mystery, eternity, vitality.

These rings were worn as talismans for protection against physical ills. The talisman is a gold signet ring with an engraved greenish-grey stone in a simple, heavy bezel. The carving represents Abraxas, a monster with the head of a rooster, the body of a man holding a shield and a whip, and two upturned snakes for legs and feet.

Surrounding the Abraxas is an inscription in Greek, the letters reversed so that the ring may be used as a signet.

Book 2 – Why Were They Called Gods...?

Regarding the name Jeo carved on the stone, which the cigarette card's author refers to Jehovah, Matthew Rabuzzi writes:

A seal of a rooster-headed serpent-legged shield-bearing god clearly labeled YAHWEH can be found illustrated in Anne Baring & Jules Cashford's 'the Myth of the Goddess: Evolution of an Image.'

The fact that the name Abraxas works out to the auspicious number 365 does not satisfactorily explain why the creature has the head of a rooster, the body of a man, and snakes for legs. I have seen other Abraxas figures in which the entity was riding in a chariot, which reinforces the symbolism of the 365-day year rolling forward on circular solar wheels. Like many Gnostic symbols, Abraxas enjoyed a brief moment of popularity during the late Roman era but was never a strong factor in European or Middle Eastern folk magic.

This was brought out by Irenaeus, disciple of Polycarp who was the disciple of John, who wrote in the second century concerning the Abraxas in Against Heresies:

5. ... He attaches no importance to [the question regarding] meats offered in sacrifice to idols, thinks them of no consequence, and makes use of them without any hesitation; he holds also the use of other things, and the practice of every kind of lust, a matter of perfect indifference. These men, moreover, practice magic; and use images, incantations, invocations, and every other kind of curious art.

Book 2 – Why Were They Called Gods...?

Coining also certain names as if they were those of the angels, they proclaim some of these as belonging to the first, and others to the second heaven; and then they strive to set forth the names, principles, angels, and powers of the three hundred and sixty-five imagined heavens.

They also affirm that the barbarous name, in which the Savior ascended and descended, is Caulacau. 6. He, then, who has learned [these things], and known all the angels and their causes, is rendered invisible and incomprehensible to the angels and all the powers, even as Caulacau also was. And as the son was unknown to all, so must they also be known by no one; but while they know all, and pass through all, they themselves remain invisible and unknown to all; for, Do thou, they say, know all, but let nobody know thee. For this reason, persons of such a persuasion are also ready to recant [their opinions], yea, rather, it is impossible that they should suffer on account of a mere name, since they are like to all. The multitude, however, cannot understand these matters, but only one out of a thousand, or two out of ten thousand. They declare that they are no longer Jews, and that they are not yet Christians; and that it is not at all fitting to speak openly of their mysteries, but right to keep them secret by preserving silence.

7. They make out the local position of the three hundred and sixty-five heavens in the same way, as do mathematicians. For, accepting the theorems of

these latter, they have transferred them to their own type of doctrine. They hold that their chief is Abraxas; and, on this account, that word contains in itself the numbers amounting to three hundred and sixty-five (Irenaeus Against Heresies, Ch. XXIV, vv. 5, 6 & 7, ANF, Vol. I, pp. 350).

Knowledge is gained precept upon precept, line upon line shown in the repetition in the word Caulacau (Isa. 28:10,13).

Precept here is SHD 6673 tsav as an injunction meaning a commandment and, hence, a law or precept. The antinomians were striking at the law and calling it tribulation. Line upon line is SHD 6957 kav or kawv, hence line upon line or kawv-la-kawv. It is a cord used for measuring and a musical string and, hence, accord. It is from this sense a line. The law measured all and this is the sense of the text in Isaiah and thus ridiculed by the Naasseni and featured in the cosmology of the Nicolaitans. The Gnostics and, here, also the Nicolaitans were thus the progenitors of the grace not law argument of modern antinomian Trinitarians who are their logical descendants (see the paper The Nicolaitans (No. 202)).

It should become clear that the Sacred Names concept as a salvation issue is derived from ancient theology and is heretical in a biblical context. There is a clear distinction in terms of the third commandment regarding the taking of the name of God in vain and the simple identification of the deity. The concept that the correct pronunciation of the name by a man is essential to the operation of the god is a basic magical control issue of the primitive pagan mind.

It blasphemes the omnipotence of God the Father in the exercise of His willing self-revelation.

In Vine's Expository Dictionary of Biblical Words, in the Old Testament words section on page 96, we find under God:

In the ancient world, knowledge of a person's name was believed to give one power over that person. Knowledge of the character and attributes of pagan "gods" was thought to enable the worshippers to manipulate or influence the deities in a more effective way than they could have if the deities name remained unknown. To that extent, the vagueness of the term ël frustrated persons who hoped to obtain some sort of power over the deity, since the name gave little or no indication of the god's character.

This was particularly true for El, the chief Canaanite god. They commonly associated deity with the manifestation and use of enormous power. This may be reflected in the curious phrase "the power [ël] of my hand" (Gen. 31:29 KJV. RSV "it is in my power"; cf. Deut. 28:32).

This concept is found today amongst Sacred Names groups like Yahweh's New Covenant Assembly. In their 1993 booklet Our Savior Spoke the Sacred Name, on page 3 they write: The lawyers through their own rules were denying the Israelites the knowledge of Yahweh's Name by which they were to be called. To be called by Yahweh's Name put Israel under His protection, care and blessings.

John 14:14 14 if you ask anything in my name, I will do it. This is a very strong statement. However, it is contingent as we must know for we cannot ask for things that are against the will of God, even if using His name.

John 9:31 31 We know that God does not listen to sinners, but if any one is a worshipper of God and does his will, God listens to him. (RSV)

On this point we read:
Matthew 7:22 22 On that day many will say to me, 'Lord, Lord, did we not prophesy in your name, and cast out demons in your name, and do many mighty works in your name?'
These people called him Lord and knew his name, they even prophesied and cast out demons. His response to these mighty works that were done, apparently successfully, is:
Matthew 7:23 23 and then will I declare to them, 'I never knew you; depart from me, you evildoers.'

Acts 4:12 12 And there is salvation in no one else, for there is no other name under heaven given among men by which we must be saved. The mighty works done in his name did not save the individuals above. Salvation requires both knowledge and faith.

John 17:3 3 and this are eternal life, that they know thee the only true God, and Jesus Christ whom thou hast sent.

John 30:31 31 but these are written that you may believe that Jesus is the Christ, the Son of God, and that believing you may have life in his name. From which follows obedience.

Matthew 7:21 21 "Not every one who says to me, 'Lord, Lord,' shall enter the kingdom of heaven, but he who does the will of my Father who is in heaven. We need to understand and believe in the One whom we worship and do as He says without a false confidence in our mighty works. Yahweh's New Covenant Assembly continues: These lawyers disallowed anyone to invoke Yahweh's Name.

On page 6 we read.
The Savior emphasizes that Yahweh's Name has special power to protect His people. This view is incorrect. The reasons for blessings or cursing are listed in Deuteronomy 28. They are based on diligent obedience to the commandments and statutes (Deut. 28:15) and for walking in His ways (Deut. 28:9). Blessings or protection are not for invoking the name used for both the God of Israel and his God for personal benefit. There is a significant difference between YHVH and YHVH of Hosts (Isa. 44:6-8;

51:15; 54:5; Jer. 10:16; 32:35 et seq.).Eloah or Yahovah of Hosts declared Himself through Messiah as 'eyeh 'asher 'eyeh or I will be what I will become (Ex. 3:14; cf. fn. to The New Oxford Annotated Bible RSV and also to The Companion Bible). This name formed the basis of Yahovah (YHVH) as an extended being and more than two beings in the Bible carried this name or were referred to by this name (see the paper The Angel of YHVH (No. 24)). This name also indicates that God is becoming something (cf. Eph. 4:6).

The use of a name that describes attributes of individual character traits, authority, powers or activities is biblical. Biblical names are not used, as is a western name, which is more of a call sign. Additional names or numbers are added to our common family names to avoid any confusion in identification.

Word idolatry
The study of semantics provides a new insight about language and is concerned with the meaning of language; it deals with the use of words and the generally understood meanings that were subject to change and the symbols these words often conveyed.

Today, we have the formerly isolated French-speaking population of Quebec, Canada using an older version of the language. The European French-speaking people have to pay very close attention to understand the pronunciation and word use. We have similar difficulties arising from accents and words that are used locally and that often provide a different connotation to the thoughts expressed. Even with American and English television going throughout the world, a Scot from Glasgow speaking to a rural Texan will be challenged.

Genesis 11:6-7 6 And the LORD said, "Behold, they are one people, and they have all one language; and this is only the beginning of what they will do; and nothing that they propose to do will now be impossible for them. 7 Come, let us go down, and there confuse their language, that they may not understand one another's speech."

Even today, when speaking only one language we manage to become confused! The effects of this division are still with us and develop very quickly. Hundreds of years ago the challenges of isolated communities that developed their own dialects and languages required them to learn many languages and a regional language. China has a pictographic script that is understood by most of the population. The spoken words that are used are often not understood outside of the local region.

Modern Hebrew-speaking Ashkenazi and Sephardim Jews use different words and pronunciation. Either group speaking to Jews in Palestine 2,000 years ago would have problems being understood. At Babel, the speech was confounded and, so, not understood even though they spoke one language.

The term Yahoo is familiar to most, as a cry of exhortation used by buckaroos when training horses and as a derogatory designation by city folk when commenting upon those rowdy rednecks, i.e. "That bunch of Yahoos!". It will also now be found as the name of a search engine used by those searching the World Wide Web. This word Ya-hoo, was also used as a battle cry and exhortation in the ancient world and perhaps has been brought to the modern Americas through our Parthian/Sythian horse-loving ancestors. Abraham's legacy, because of the promises God made to his physical and spiritual descendants, is more extensive than is generally understood.

There was a temple named the Temple of Yaho described in the Aramaic letters speaking of the Temple at Elephantine (see Pritchard The Ancient Near East: An Anthology of Texts and Pictures, Princeton, 1958, Vol. I, pp. 278-280). God is being referred to as Yaho from at least before 407 BCE. The temple at Elephantine and the temple at Jerusalem were referred to as the temple of Yaho. This temple at Elephantine was destroyed in 410 BCE by other priests of the god Khnub in Egypt (ibid., pp. 278-279). The Hebrews at the temple of Elephantine circa 419-400 BCE contributed to the reconstruction of the Temple referred to in Ezra-Nehemiah.

They and the Aramaic speakers there contributed for the God Yaho. There was an estimated equivalent of 123 contributions of 2 shekels each (ibid.) and some were even made on behalf of Ishumbethel and Anathbethel. In this, is assumed that these deities, but may refer to functions of the House of El (Bethel), i.e. the personified pillars or such like. We have no absolute knowledge of the significance. We do know that the name Yaho was used at the beginning of the fourth century BCE after the return of the exiles and at the construction of the Temple at Jerusalem.

The term HaShem, meaning The Name, came also from this point in time. The Stone Edition of the Chumash, preface/xiv states:

We use "Hashem" or "The Name" as the translation of the Tetragrammaton, the sacred Hebrew Four-letter Name of God. In the commentary we frequently refer to it as "The Four-letter Name." (xxvi)? This Name is never pronounced as it is spelled. During prayer, or when it is recited, or when a Torah verse is read, the Four-letter Name should be pronounced as if it were spelled Adonai, the Name that identifies God as Master of all. At other times, it should be pronounced Hashem, literally "The Name".

In the H Danby translation of the Mishnah (second century BCE to the second century CE), we have it declared that: on Atonement this Name was pronounced by the High Priest as it was written and not using a pseudonym. Yoma 3:8, 6:2; Tamid 7:2.

Various pronunciations amongst Sacred Names Assemblies are as follows:
The Most High Messiah
YaHVah YaHVaHoshea
Yahu'wey Yahushu'a
Yahaweway Yahshua
Yhwh Yeshua
and primarily:
Yahwey Yahoshua

The Jehovah's Witness' 1984 booklet The Divine Name that will endure forever, writes on page 7 "The truth is, nobody knows for sure how the name of God was originally pronounced." This is a forthright statement pronouncing The Name of Jehovah, which would have not been understood by the ancient Hebrew speakers, with addition of the westernized 'J' pronunciation. They also agree, on page 11, that it would not be wrong to use a form like Yahweh.

The pronunciation Jesus developed from the Greek Iesous (SGD 2424) pronounced, ee-ay-sooce. It was used in the Septuagint (LXX) translation by seventy [two] Hebrew-speaking scholars for the Hellenistic Jews throughout the Near East.

The idea develops from Acts:

Acts 4:12 12 And there is salvation in no one else, for there is no other name under heaven given among men by which we must be saved." The Aramaic name by which Messiah was known describes his role and the successful completion of his task. The idea can become that we must know and, with correct intonation, properly pronounce this saving name. This idea makes a mockery of the Almighty God communicating to us in any language but Hebrew and prohibits prophecy.

Isaiah 28:11 11 Nay, but by men of strange lips and with an alien tongue the LORD will speak to this people, When speaking to the disobedient Hebrew-speaking Israelites, God says that He will speak to them in an alien tongue. This sets the prophetic stage for the Greek-speaking world and the Hellenistic Jews. As stated, all the prophets bear witness that our reconciliation comes from the effect of our faith.

Acts 10:43 43 to him all the prophets bear witness that every one who believes in him receives forgiveness of sins through his name. If our calling and baptism are only valid if the name used is the Hebrew, then we must wonder if our God is Almighty. Most Hebrew-speakers of the last 39 Jubilees have not responded if this is true. Many of the Israelites who now speak an alien language, even Greek, have received a New Covenant relationship with the One True God. The door was opened to the Gentiles who also must understand who is The Most High God and who is His Messiah.

John 17:3 3 and this are eternal life, that they know thee the only true God, and Jesus Christ whom thou hast sent. We read: Proverbs 22:1 1 a good name is to be chosen rather than great riches, and favor is better than silver or gold. Proverbs 22:1 1 a good name is more to be desired than great wealth and to be respected is better than silver and gold. (Bible in Basic English) We should see how the Hebrew thinking regarding the word name is used. Ron or John is not better names than other names. It's that people's estimation of us through our conduct that gives us good or bad names, meaning a confidence or trustworthiness.

Psalm 20:7 7 some put their faith in carriages and some in horses; but we will be strong in the name of the Lord our God. (Bible in Basic English) We may be strong with confidence in the trustworthiness in our God. This is not related to an unknown Hebrew pronunciation. All can have a temporary artificial confidence in horses and chariots, or missiles and tanks. It is within the pagan idea that the name of local deities to be protected so that its correct pronunciation by magicians would not enable the capture of the cities or temples of the deity. In this case, it was Jerusalem or the temple at Elephantine. It was a practice used by the Egyptians, the Babylonians and the Romans. This idea also is found in modern occult groups and amongst tribes of the Americas that hold to the totemic and shamanism belief systems.

The theory of the 'name' is in reality the fundamental basis of more than half of the religious ideas of Egypt.

Declamation or melopoepia - the chanted voice of the oldest languages - is regarded as reproducing the harmonious sound, i.e. the material vibration, which is one of the signs of vital substance.

This chanted voice (khrou; cf. G. Maspero, Bibl. egyptol. i [1893] 101) engenders magical forces (hikau). (ERE, art. Names, Egyptian, pp. 151-153). All the texts, rituals, and magic of Egypt rest essentially on the fact that the name, thus understood, constitutes a material soul, and is the most secret part of the whole living being since it is his very reason for living. The name is therefore the ego. It exists by itself. It is the subtlest of the various souls of the individual.

The Egyptian name is so definitely a soul - a living exist by itself - that the most important and oldest liturgical texts make it the essential element in their magical operations.

Cursing or execration by the name of an individual lets loose upon him to injure him all the forces which the formula has 'bound to' the name.

At the time of the most ancient monuments, in order to confer on her living subjects and on her dead most of the protections, which the totem and its name give to primitive races, Egypt had an amazingly perfect system of affiliation to the cult of a certain protector-god, initiation into the mysteries of the god. The title amkhu assumed by the initiates is followed by the name of the god, to whom the man henceforth owes special allegiance. Then from whom he will receive protection in this life and the life to come ... the divine name, being united but not confused with that of the man, marks reciprocal obligations and duties, to which time by degrees gives a moral character (ERE, art. Body, Egyptian, p. 153).

This acquisition and use of names for occult purposes is found in virtually all ancient and many modern societies.

James Frazer, in The Golden Bough, Volume 2, chapter Taboo and the Perils of the Soul, on pages 387-391, says: Just as the furtive savage conceals his real name because he fears that sorcerers might make an evil use of it, so he fancies that his gods must likewise keep their true names secret, lest other gods or even men should learn the mystic sounds and thus be able to conjure with them. Nowhere was this crude conception of the secrecy and magical virtue of the divine name more firmly held or more fully developed than in ancient Egypt. It is where the superstitions of a dateless past were embalmed in the hearts of the people hardly less effectually than the bodies of cats and crocodiles and the rest of the divine menagerie in their rock-cut tombs.

The conception is well illustrated by a story, which tells how the subtle Isis wormed his secret name from Ra, the great Egyptian god of the sun. Isis, so runs the tale, was a woman mighty in words, and she was weary of the world of men, and yearned after the world of the gods. In addition, she meditated in her heart, saying, "Cannot I by virtue of the great name of Ra make myself a goddess and reign like him in heaven and earth?"

Book 2 – Why Were They Called Gods...?

For Ra had many names, but the great name, which gave him all power over, gods and men were known to none but himself. Now the god was by this time grown old; he slobbered at the mouth and his spittle fell upon the ground. Therefore, Isis gathered up the spittle and the earth with it, and kneaded thereof a serpent and laid it in the path where the great god passed every day to his double kingdom after his heart's desire. In addition, when he came forth according to his wont, attended by all his company of gods, the sacred serpent stung him, the god opened his mouth and cried, and his cry went up to heaven. Moreover, the company of gods cried, "What aileth thee?" and the gods shouted, "Lo and behold!" Nevertheless, he could not answer; His jaws rattled, his limbs shook, the poison ran through his flesh as the Nile floweth over the land. When the great god had stilled his heart, he cried to his followers, "Come to me, O my children, offspring of my body. I am a prince, the son of a prince, and the divine seed of a god. My, father devised my name; my father and my mother gave me my name, and it remained hidden in my body since my birth, that no magician might have magic power of me. I went out to behold that which I have made, I walked in the two lands which I have created, and lo! Something stung me. What it was, I know not.

Was it fire? Was it water? My, heart is on fire, my flesh trembleth, and all my limbs do quake. Bring me the children of the gods with healing words and understanding lips, whose power reacheth to heaven."

Book 2 – Why Were They Called Gods...?

Then came to him the children of the gods, and they were very sorrowful. In addition, Isis came with her craft, whose mouth is full of the breath of life, whose spells chase pain away, whose word maketh the dead to live. She said, "What is it, divine Father? What is it?" The holy god opened his mouth, he spoke and said, "I went upon my way, I walked after my heart's desire in the two regions which I have made to behold that which I have created, lo! a serpent that I saw not stung me.

Is it fire? Is it water? I am colder than water, I am hotter than fire, all my limbs sweat, I tremble, mine eye is not steadfast, I behold not the sky, and the moisture bedewed my face as in summertime." Then speak Isis, "Tell me thy name, and divine Father, for the man shall live who is called by his name." Then answered Ra, "I created the heavens and the earth, I ordered the mountains, I made the great and wide sea, I stretched out the two horizons like a curtain. I am he who openeth his eyes and it is light, and who shuteth them and it is dark. At his command, the Nile riseth, but the gods know not his name. I am Khepera in the morning, I am Ra at noon, I am Tum at eve." However, the poison was not taken away from him; it pierced deeper, and the great god could no longer walk. Then said Isis to him, "That was not thy name that thou speaketh unto me. Oh tell it me, that the poison may depart; for he shall live whose name is named." Now the poison burned like fire, it was hotter than the flame of fire. The god said, "I consent that Isis shall search into me, and that my name shall pass from my breast into hers." Then the god hid himself from the gods, and his place in the ship of eternity was empty. Thus was the name of the great god taken from him, and Isis, the witch, speaks, "Flow away poison, depart from Ra. It is I, even I who overcome the poison and cast it to the earth; for the name of the great god hath been taken away from him. Let Ra live and let the poison die." Thus speak great Isis, the queen of the gods, she who knows Ra and his true name." Thus we see that the real name of the god, with which his power was inextricably bound up, was supposed to be lodged, in an almost physical sense, somewhere in his breast, from which word it could be extracted by a sort of surgical operation and transferred with all its supernatural powers to the breast of another.

In Egypt attempts like that of Isis to appropriate the power of a high god by possessing herself of his name were not mere legends told of the mythical beings of a remote past; every Egyptian magician aspired to wield like powers by similar means. For it was believed that he who possessed the true name possessed the very being of god or man, and could force even a deity to obey him as a slave obeys his master.

Thus, the art of the magician consisted in obtaining from the gods a revelation of their sacred names, and he left no stone unturned to accomplish his end. When once a god in a moment of weakness or forgetfulness had imparted to the wizard the wondrous lore, the deity had no choice but to submit humbly to the man or pay the penalty of his contumacy.

In one papyrus we find the god Typhoon thus adjured: "I invoke thee by thy true names, in virtue of which thou canst not refuse to hear;" and in another the magician threatens Osirus that if the god does not do his bidding he will name him aloud in the port of Busirus. Therefore, in the Lucan the Thessalian witch whom Sextus Pompeius consulted before the battle of Parasail threatens to call up the Furies by their real names if they will not do her bidding. In modern Egypt, the magician still works his old enchantments by the same ancient means; only the name of the god by which he conjures is different. The man who knows "the most great name" of God can, we are told, by the mere utterance of it kill the living, raise the dead, transport himself instantly wherever he pleases, and perform any other miracle. Similarly among the Arabs of North Africa at the present day "the power of the name is such that when one knows the proper names the jinn can scarcely help answering the call and obeying. They are the servants of the magical names; So to the Chinese of ancient times were dominated by the notion that beings are intimately associated with their names, so that a man's knowledge of the name of a specter might enable him to exert power over the latter and bend it to his will.

The Romans shared the belief in the magic virtue of divine names. When they sat down before a city, the priests addressed the guardian deity of the place in a set form of prayer or incantation, inviting him to abandon the beleaguered city and come over to the Romans, who would treat him as well as or better than he had ever been treated in his old home. Hence, the name of the guardian deity of Rome was kept a profound secret, lest the enemies of the republic might lure him away, even as the Romans themselves had induced many gods to desert, like rats, the falling fortunes of cities that had sheltered them in happier days. Nay, the real name, not merely of its guardian deity, but of the city itself, was wrapped in mystery and might never be uttered, not even in the sacred rites.

A certain Valerius Soranus, whom dared to divulge the priceless secret, were put to death, in like manner, it seems, the ancient Assyrians were forbidden to mention the mystic names of their cities; and down to modern times the Cheremiss of the Caucasus keep the names of their communal villages secret from motives of superstition (Frazer, ibid., pp. 387-391). The "ineffable name" doctrine begins to appear in the works of Justin Martyr, a Samaritan convert to Christianity who wrote in the mid-second century CE. Justin made a special point about his many discussions with the Jews, discussions that greatly influenced his own thinking in regard to the sacred name Yahweh. He tells us plainly:

And all the Jews even now teach that the nameless deity spoke to Moses (I Apol., 63).

Just in then voices these opinions:

For no one can utter the name of the ineffable deity; and if any one dare to say that there is a name, he raves with a hopeless madness (I Apol., 61). But to the father of all, who is unbigoted, there is no name given. For by whatever name he be called, he has as his elder the person who gives him the name. But these words, Father, and Deity, and Creator, and Lord, and Master, are not names but appellations derived from good deeds and functions (II Apol., 6).

Just in then, on various occasions, speaks of the "ineffable" and "unutterable" Deity and Father.

Now we know that this half-truth has been well established by Justin's time. It is true that any name made up by man for The Father would be wrong. It is also true that words like father, deity, creator, etc. are not personal names. Yet, Justin has been taken in by a Jewish teaching that the Father does not possess an eternal name that He gave to Himself. But the Sacred Name Yahovah was revealed to man by Yahovah Himself and is not a man-given name (see II Apol., 10, 13; Trypho, 126, 127).

The Jews spoke the terms Yahovah (SHD 3068) as Adonai and Yahovih (SHD 3069) as Elohim. They elevated one above the other in accordance with Psalm 45:6-7. One was Lord the other was true God. The true Elohim or HaElohim was Eloah. Is this style of word use part of a plan to cause unsuspecting people to misuse the name of God and come under penalty, a new style Balaam?

Scripture is a collection of words that preserves the foundation of our faith. We heard or read words when we realized we were missing the mark and needed to change. Scripture does not explicitly mention the origin of language; it is evident that God is responsible for the beginning of human speech and written language. Certainly, there is nothing inherently wrong with words except where we misuse them.

The correct form for Jehovah is Yahovah or Yahovih dependent upon the suffix used in reference to the entity. It is pronounced Yahovah or Yahovih. The term Yahweh is thus also incorrect. Care must be taken to identify the Yahovah that is the object of worship. Unless the entity is identified and understood as the supreme God, Yahovah of Hosts who is Eloah, then the Monotheism of God is compromised and Binitarianism is again introduced. The name Jehovah or Yahovah is combined with ten other titles.

They are in the order they appear in the Hebrew texts as:
Jehovah-Jireh - Jehovah will see or provide (Gen. 22:14).
Jehovah-Ropheka - Jehovah that heals you (Ex. 15:26).
Jehovah-Nissi - Jehovah my banner (Ex. 17:15).
Jehovah-Mekaddishkem - Jehovah that does sanctify you (Ex. 31:13; Lev. 20:8;
21:8; 22:32; Ezek. 20:12).
Jehovah-Shalom - Jehovah [send] peace (Judges 6:24).

Jehovah-Zeba'oth - Jehovah of Hosts (1Sam. 1:3 and frequently).
Jehovah-Zidkenu - Jehovah our righteousness (Jer. 23:6; 33:16).
Jehovah-Shammah - Jehovah is there (Ezek. 48:35).
Jehovah-'Elyon - Jehovah Most High (Ps. 7:17; 47:2; 97:9).
Jehovah-Ro'i - Jehovah my Shepherd (Ps. 23:1).
Psalm 23 uses seven of the attributes conferred by the names of God:
Verse 1 conveys concept 1 (Jehovah-Jireh).
Verse 2 conveys concept 5 (Jehovah-Shalom).
Verse 3 conveys concepts 2 and 7 (Jehovah-Ropheka and Jehovah-Zidkenu).
Verse 4 conveys concept 8 (Jehovah-Shammah).
Verse 5 conveys concepts 3 and 4 (Jehovah-Nissi and Jehovah Mekaddishkem).

The Companion Bible (App. 4) makes a series of arguments for El as being essentially the almighty although the word is never so rendered. This context is in fact as El Shaddai. The use of El is thought of as God the Omnipotent. Elohim is used in the sense of God as Creator because God creates and ordains law in the hands of intermediaries.

Elohim is plural. El is used as the root for qualitative description of God. It is only Eloah that is the God Who Wills and is the one object of worship of His people (see also Companion Bible, App. 4).

El is thought of as the God who knows all (first occurring in Gen. 14:18-22) and sees all (Gen. 16:13) and performs all things for His people (Ps. 57:2) and in whom all the divine attributes are concentrated (Companion Bible, ibid.). There is, however, the fact that El is the root, which occurs in names, and titles, which indicates that it is simply the root from which qualitative difference is demonstrated in the entities that act under delegation. For example, the Angel of Yahovah is also the El Bethel or the God of the House of God.

In other words, it demonstrates authority within structure. Only Eloah is the singular extension of worship.

El Elyon is the name applied to Eloah as the Most High El. He is the Most High God. He is God the Father as we know from the Greek rendering of the name in Luke 1:35. El Elyon is the entity that divided the nations (Deut. 32:8). He gave Israel as Yahovah portion. Thus Yahovah, here, is the Yahovah of Israel and subordinate to Eloah or El Elyon.

It is Eloah or Elyon that is the object of worship and Israel did not worship its subordinate Elohim. Note Deuteronomy 32:8 has been altered in the Masoretic text to read according to the number of the children of Israel rather than the original sons of God or the number of the angels (LXX) or eliym or the Gods (DSS).

OM MANI PADME HUM

This is a well-known mantra, having the meaning of: "hail to the jewel in the lotus" or "praise the union of male and female energy!" From the Lotus Sutra, the mantra is associated with the patron deity Avalokitesvara (Chinese Kuan Yin), the bodhisattva of compassion. It is believed by Tibetans that its use will generate good karma. The syllables are inscribed on stonewalls, throughout the country and are written on hand-held prayer wheels that are kept spinning.

In Tibetan Buddhist lands, the most common prayer, found everywhere, is Om Mani Peme Hung, the mantra of Chenrezi, the Buddha of compassion. The mantra originated in India. As it moved from India into Tibet, the pronunciation changed because some of the sounds in the Indian Sanskrit language were hard for Tibetans to pronounce. Sanskrit; OM MANI PADMA HUM mantra of Avalokitesvara Tibetan; OM MANI PEME HUNG mantra of Chenrezi This syllable 'OM' is stated in the early Bramanas (c. 800 BCE) to be the divine counterpart of tatha, i.e. 'so be it'. The 'Hum' also has the aspect of certainty as when we use the 'Amen'.

From the OM, the Pranava-Upanisad (c. 500 BCE) derives the entire creation. Also, the ritual for the Brahman priest who by this utterance of the OM before and after sacrifice remedies all defects in the latter ... no holy text shall be chanted without it ... OM recited 1,000 times grants all wishes (ibid., p. 109). The literal meaning of the formula would be: 'So be it! O Lotus Jewel! Amen!' This is essentially the form of a wishing gem spell, a luck-compelling talisman. Mani is a title given to the mystical hermits (siddhi) who have recited this Om Mani spell 100,000 times or more (ERE, art. Jewel (Buddhist), Vol. 7, p. 556). The Priest-magician devotes all his power to 'knowing' (rokhu) the exact texture of the name, its qualities, quantities, musical tonality, and scanned declamation. The magical chant (khrou), which exactly reproduces all these elements, gives to him who possesses it the complete ownership of the name-souls thus evoked.

To the irresistible call, which attracts their vital substance, all beings, visible and invisible, must answer. Spirits, genii, the dead, the most powerful gods, cannot avoid it. And after the lapse of centuries, when individual magic, alongside of the official, developed its dangerous occult power, the processes were not different (ERE, art. Names (Egyptian), Vol. 9, p. 152a).

Egypt still preserves several characteristics of primitive religion (cf. Names (Primitive)), practically unaltered, whose origin and exact meaning can be verified from the context.

So says Yahovah, the King of Israel, and his Redeemer, Yahovah Sabaoth or of Hosts: "I am the First and I am the Last; and there is no Elohim except me ... Is there an Elohim beside me, or any other rock? No there is none (Isa. 44:6-8 The Interlinear Bible).

There are two Yahovahs here, the Yahovah of Israel and his superior Yahovah of Hosts who is the Alpha and Omega and the Rock and Redeemer of the Yahovah of Israel.

This is the One True God, Eloah, the Elohim that anointed the Yahoveh or Elohim of Israel as Elohim in Psalm 45:6-7, and Hebrews 1:8 identifies this Elohim as Christ. They are thus superior and subordinate and the subordinate has partners (metoxous) or comrades in the council as we see from the original Greek in Hebrews and the LXX. We should see that the one who became the savior and redeemer of Israel and mankind also had a Savior and Redeemer. We must correctly understand the meaning of YHVH and the revelation at Sinai as 'eyeh 'asher 'eyeh or I will be what I will become. YHVH means He who causes to be and is a third person form of the revelation (see Oxford Annotated RSV) used by a subordinate.

Similarly, is adversary a name or character trait? Does it depend upon context? The knowledge of the name of God is indicative of biblical understanding. The most common misunderstanding regarding the name of God stems from Psalm 83:18, Psalm 83:18 18 that men may know that thou, whose name alone is JEHOVAH, art the most high over all the earth. (KJV)

Psalm 83:18 18 Let them know that thou alone, whose name is the LORD [YHVH], art the Most High over all the earth. (RSV)

The Companion Bible has a note on the name Jehovah in Appendix 4, II. Jehovah is held to mean the Eternal or Immutable One. The definition is in: Genesis 21:33 33And Abraham planted a grove in Beersheba, and called there on the name of the LORD, the everlasting God. (KJV)

Everlasting here is from the Hebrew 'olam meaning duration. The origin of the word Jehovah is held to be in He who was and is to come. There is a problem with applying the name given at Sinai to simply Jehovah. Exodus 3:14 14 And God said unto Moses, I AM THAT I AM: and he said, Thus shalt thou say unto the children of Israel, I AM hath sent me unto you. (KJV)

I am here is hayah (SHD 1961) which means to exist, to be or become. The Companion Bible renders the text 'ehyeh 'asher 'ehyeh, and translates it as I will be what I will be (or become) (see note and App. 48), noting also that Jehovah means He will be spoken of by others. The Oxford scholars have noted in their Oxford Annotated RSV that Yahweh is in fact the third person form of the verb, which actually means He causes to be.

The text cross references to Exodus 6:3 and Isaiah 26:4. These three texts were the three places in the Authorised Version where the text was transliterated and printed in large capital letters. The text in Psalm 83:18 couples another title with the name Jehovah namely that of Elyon or the Most High. This is a distinguishing title as we will see. The name Jehovah is an inexact transliteration. Another transliteration is Yahweh. That also is inexact.

The other two texts reads.

Exodus 6:3 3 And I appeared unto Abraham, unto Isaac, and unto Jacob, by the name of God Almighty, but by my name JEHOVAH was I not known to them. (KJV)

Isaiah 26:4 4 Trust ye in the LORD forever: for in the LORD JEHOVAH is everlasting strength: (KJV)

There is a feature where in Scripture a person's name is changed when their role or relationship with God alters.

Nehemiah 9:7 7 Thou art the LORD, the God who didst choose Abram and bring him forth out of Ur of the Chaldeans and give him the name Abraham; (RSV)

Genesis 17:5 5 No longer shall your name be Abram, but your name shall be Abraham; for I have made you the father of a multitude of nations. (RSV) Abram's name was changed after God promised to make him a father of nations and of the spiritual faithful.

This relationship caused a change in his wife's name.

Genesis 17:15 15 And God said to Abraham, "As for Sarai your wife, you shall not call her name Sarai, but Sarah shall be her name. (RSV)

As also, under the New Covenant relationship the individual's name was changed. John 1:42 42 He brought him to Jesus. Jesus looked at him, and said, "So you are Simon the son of John? You shall be called Cephas" (which means Peter). The Messiah has a new name as befits his new role.

Revelation 3:12 12 He who conquers, I will make him a pillar in the temple of my God; never shall he go out of it, and I will write on him the name of my God, and the name of the city of my God. The new Jerusalem which comes down from my God out of heaven, and my own new name. (RSV)

He is presently called Faithful and True (Rev. 19:11) and the word or spokesman of God (Rev. 19:13). He was the first advent Priest of Aaron and will be the forthcoming King of the Second Advent.

He has obtained a new name that only he knows. Revelation 19:12 12 His eyes are like a flame of fire, and on his head are many diadems; and he has a name inscribed which no one knows but himself. Hebrews 1:4 4 having become as much superior to angels as the name he has obtained is more excellent than theirs.

Revelation 3:12 12 He who conquers, I will make him a pillar in the temple of my God; never shall he go out of it, and I will write on him the name of my God, and the name of the city of my God. The new Jerusalem which comes down from my God out of heaven, and my own new name. Spiritual overcomers will also receive new names.

Revelation 2:17 17 He who has an ear, let him hear what the Spirit says to the churches. To him who conquers I will give some of the hidden manna, and I will give him a white stone, with a new name written on the stone which no one knows except him who receives it.' All of those who are part of the first resurrection receive new names.

Acts 4:12 12 And there is salvation in no one else, for there is no other name under heaven given among men by which we must be saved." The name here is Jesus Christ or Yahoshua Messiah. The name means the fulfillment of the sacrificial role and not that its use provides the salvation. Jesus was also saved and redeemed by his God and father.

John 20:17 17 Jesus said to her, "Do not hold me, for I have not yet ascended to the Father; but go to my brethren and say to them, I am ascending to my Father and your Father, to my God and your God." (RSV)

Exodus 34:14 14 for you shall worship no other god, for the LORD, whose name is Jealous, is a jealous God.

Exodus 3:15 15 God also said to Moses, "Say this to the people of Israel, 'The LORD, the God of your fathers, the God of Abraham, the God of Isaac, and the God of Jacob, has sent me to you': this is my name for ever, and thus I am to be remembered throughout all generations.

Isaiah 63:16 16 For thou art our Father, though Abraham does not know us and Israel does not acknowledge us; thou, O LORD, art our Father, our Redeemer from of old is thy name. (RSV)

2 Samuel 23:22 22 these things did Benaiah the son of Jehoiada, and won a name beside the three mighty men.

1 Kings 18:24 24 and you call on the name of your god and I will call on the name of the LORD; and the God who answers by fire, he is God." In addition, all the people answered, "It is well spoken."

Isaiah 9:6 6 for to us a child is born, to us a son is given; and the government will be upon his shoulder, and his name will be called "Wonderful Counselor, Mighty God, Everlasting Father, Prince of Peace."

Isaiah 42:8 8 I am the LORD, that is my name; my glory I give to no other, nor my praise to graven images.

Isaiah 63:16 16 For thou art our Father, though Abraham does not know us and Israel does not acknowledge us; thou, O LORD, art our Father, our Redeemer from of old is thy name.

Zechariah 14:9 9 And the LORD will become king over all the earth; on that day the LORD will be one and his name one.

Matthew 7:22 22 On that day many will say to me, 'Lord, Lord, did we not prophesy in your name, and cast out demons in your name, and do many mighty works in your name?'

John 14:14 14 if you ask anything in my name, I will do it. John 30:31 31 but these are written that you may believe that Jesus is the Christ, the Son of God, and that believing you may have life in his name.

Acts 10:43 43 to him all the prophets bear witness that every one who believes in him receives forgiveness of sins through his name."

Acts 10:48 48 and he commanded them to be baptized in the name of Jesus Christ. Then they asked him to remain for some days.

Ephesians 5:20 20 always and for everything giving thanks in the name of our Lord Jesus Christ to God the Father.

Acts 12:25 25 And Barnabas and Saul returned from Jerusalem when they had fulfilled their mission, bringing with them John whose other name was Mark.

1 Corinthians 6:11 11 and such were some of you. But you were washed, you were sanctified, you were justified in the name of the Lord Jesus Christ and in the Spirit of our God.

1 Peter 4:16 16 yet if one suffers as a Christian, let him not be ashamed, but under that name let him glorify God.

John 1:41 41 He first found his brother Simon, and said to him, "We have found the Messiah" (which means Christ). (Except where noted all Scriptures are from the Revised Standard Version, 1947).

"In the name of". What does it mean?
It is significant to note that the Sacred Name cults heavily rely on the same grammatical construction: "the name of". The Old Testament phrase "in the name of the LORD (Hebrew: Yahovah pronounced by them as Yahweh)" is apparently the source of their beliefs. But just what does "the name of" mean? We must now examine how the words "name of" are

used in Scripture. Samuel said, "For the sake of his great name the LORD (Hebrew: Yahovah or Yahweh) will not reject his people, because the LORD was pleased to make you his own" (1Sam. 12:22 NIV). This verse does not make much sense if the words "name of" indicate that the very words "in the name of the LORD" were used at some point in time. If you change the beginning of the verse to "For the sake of being faithful to Himself the LORD..." we find that the meaning is unchanged.

The Psalms say, "We will shout for joy when you are victorious and will lift up our banners in the name of our God" (Ps. 20:5 NIV). Here we find "the name of" being defined by the Scripture itself through Hebrew parallelism. "Will shout for joy" equals "lift up our banners" - both mean giving praise. "When [God is] victorious" equals "in the name of our God" - both indicate that God is faithful to His own cause. This is confirmed later in the chapter: "Some trust in chariots and some in horses, but we trust in the name of the LORD our God" (Ps. 20:7 NIV). The chariots and horses are contrasted with God's faithfulness - both are means of victory (but as verse 8 shows the latter is much more effective). By the inspiration of the Holy Spirit Solomon wrote, "A good name is more desirable than great riches; to be esteemed is better than silver or gold" (Prov. 22:1). This verse allows us to focus on the meaning of the word name itself in Hebrew thinking. The first part of the verse could just as easily say, "To be found trustworthy (faithful to one's own word) is..." Again, faithfulness, not some utterance, is being emphasized here. Yet if some Christians were consistent in their interpretation, this could mean that Bill is better than Bob because he has a better name.

In the New Testament we find John saying "I write these things to you who believe in the name of the Son of God so that you may know that you have eternal life" (1Jn. 5:13 NIV). He could have said "I write these things to you who trust that Christ is faithful..." He certainly did not mean that at some point in time thinking or speaking the words "Son of God" saved these people. In Romans 10, we find a real problem for anyone who rejects the proper study of semantics. Verse 9 (KJV): "That if thou shalt confess with thy mouth the Lord Jesus, and shalt believe in thine heart that God hath raised him from the dead, thou shalt be saved". Verse 13 (KJV): "For whosoever shall call upon the name of the Lord shall be saved".

Upon looking at the context we find that Paul is quoting Joel 2:32 to support his statement in verse 9. He is telling us that we know that believing in Jesus is the way to be saved because the Old Testament prophet Joel said that anyone who calls upon the name of the LORD (Hebrew: Yahovah or Yahweh) will be saved. The problems that this text presents countless of words. First, an ultra-literal interpretation of verse 9 means that we must say "Lord Jesus" to be saved, but an ultra-literal interpretation of Joel 2:28 indicates that we can only be saved by calling on the

LORD (Yahweh). This is a little off subject, but let us begin the exposition by refuting the error that confession is a prerequisite for salvation. Verse 11 says, "For the scripture saith, whosoever believeth on him shall not be ashamed". And other verses throughout the Bible Indicate that we are saved only when we believe. Confession is an evidence of salvation. Mute people will not go to hell on the grounds that they were physically incapable of saying "Jesus is Lord".

With only the little induction given earlier in the Old Testament use of the phrase "in the name of the LORD", it should be apparent now that neither Joel nor Paul believed that using the word Yahovah or Yahweh or Kurios (the Greek word for Lord used in Romans 10:13) would get anyone saved. It "the name of" again indicates some kind of trust. God saves those who trust in Him, whether it is in the Father Yahovah (Yahweh) of Hosts or in the Son, Jesus Christ our Lord also called Yahovah. There are multiple Yahovahs in the Old Testament. Only Yahovah of Hosts or Yahovih is God Most High. Abraham spoke to three Yahovahs prior to the destruction of Sodom and two Yahovahs went to destroy Sodom, none of whom were God Most High.

Now we come to the all important verse: "Peter replied, 'Repent and be baptized every one of you, in the name of Jesus Christ for the forgiveness of your sins. And you will receive the gift of the Holy Spirit'" (Acts 2:38 NIV). Someone once explained that this verse "proves" that the words "in the name of Jesus" must be spoken in order to have a proper baptism. It was held that Matthew 28:19, in which Jesus told the apostles to baptize "in the name of the Father and of the Son and of the Holy Spirit" (NIV), does not constitute a baptismal formula because the words Father, Son, and Holy Spirit are merely "titles" of Jesus. Even if that were accurate, which it is not (Jesus is neither the Father nor the Holy Spirit), the point would be moot because semantics tell us that what is meant is what counts, and if Jesus is the Father, the Son, and the Holy Spirit, making a distinction is ludicrous. Moreover, as we have seen throughout the rest of the Bible, the phrase "in the name of Jesus" indicates that we must put our trust in Him.

The argument that Jesus is one as both Father and Son is a doctrine of Modernism derived from Rome through the worshippers of the god Attis (see the paper The Origins of Christmas and Easter (No. 235)).

We have been using the names and titles of Yahoshua Messiah and the Anglicised Jesus Christ, transliterated from the Greek Iesous Christos. Does a problem with identification develop from this different usage?

The name of the Messiah was Yahoshua. The Hebrew variations of this are Hosea, Hoshea, Jehoshua, Jeshua, Jeshuah, Jesus, Osea, Oshea and Joshua. Messiah is named by divine direction. His name is given in Matthew 1:21 and Luke 1:31. The name is derived from the name Hoshea (as in Num. 13:16) with the prefix Jah or Yah. This means effectively God is our Salvation. Yahoshua is then rendered as Yeshua or Joshua in usage. Jesus is a Greek version of Joshua and is derived from non-Hebrew sources. The Greek 'Iesous is a transliteration of the name Yahoshua. A variation of the name also appears among the Hyperborean Celts. Esus is one of a trinity of Esus, Taranis and Teutates. Esus may well be of the trinity system of the Hyperborean Celts but a version of it, 'Iesous, is also the Greek rendering of the Aramaic version of Yahoshua as perhaps Yashua or Yeshua.

In summary, we see that the preoccupation with Sacred Names stems from a number of fundamental theological errors.

That the name Yahweh is exclusively the name of the God Most High, which it is not it is an extended name proceeding from Yahovih or Yahovah of Hosts to Yahovah who is Messiah and on to the Host who act in the name of Yahovah who sent them.

Yahweh is applied, as we see above, to a heathen deity through Gnosticism and, hence, it is not only linguistically incorrect, it is inherently idolatrous and was used for that purpose among mystics.

That only those who correctly pronounce the name Yahweh can be saved. By this view Christ was in heresy when he called from the cross Eli Eli lama sabacthani; calling out in Aramaic, from a Hebrew Scripture, to Eli or Eloi and not to any such Yahweh.

That baptism is invalid unless it is into the correct name of Yahoshua or Yeshua or such version. This takes away entirely the concept of God's grace, election and willing self-revelation.

These views are inherently blasphemous and are a danger to the peace and well being of the elect. They are intensely accusative and impugn the baptism of the elect. On these premises, many Sacred Names people go though multiple baptisms under different variations on the names theme as they come to understand more about the etymology of names.

Baptism is into the body of The Messiah called Jesus Christ, in the name of the Father, through the power of the Holy Spirit as an organ of the Father who is Eloah or the God Most High.

People who seek to control the deity by their correct use of His name argue the Sacred Names issue. God will not be so controlled by sinful, accusative, disobedient men.

Chapter 18

Names of Ancient Gods & Goddesses

Amun: his name means "The Hidden One" he was the god of pretty much everything, the main god, portrayed as a man, normally guised as Pharaoh.

Osiris: god of vegetation and the dead, he was the king of the afterlife, portrayed as a green man with a certain headdress.

Horus: was Osiris's son, he was the god that the Pharaoh was associated with, the god of the sky and living. He had the body of a man and the head of a falcon.

Set: god of chaos, Osiris's jealous brother with the body of a man and a made-up animal.

Ra: the "ancestor," the first god, and god of the sun, he looked a lot like Horus, but with a sun resting above his head (in picts).

Book 2 – Why Were They Called Gods...?

Anubis: the jackal god, god of embalming, guardian and leader of the deceased with the body of a man and head of a jackal.

Thoth: god of writing and intelligence and magic, body of a man and head of an ibis.

Ptah: a mummified man, god of creative arts and architecture.

<u>Main Goddesses</u>

Isis: the mother goddess, shown as a woman with a certain headdress, she was goddess of magic, Osiris's wife, and Horus's mother.

Hathor: goddess of love, magic, the sky, a lot of things. Lot. She was married to Horus, in later times. She was portrayed several different ways: 1.) a cow 2.) a woman with a cows head 3.) a woman with cows ears and in later years 4.) a woman with headdress of cow's horns.

Mut: she was Amun's wife and consort, other than that... she was portrayed as a woman wearing the double crown of Egypt.

Nut: goddess of the sky.

Sekhmet: goddess of destruction, vengeance, portrayed as a woman with a lion's head.

Book 2 – Why Were They Called Gods…?

Ancient Greece

Zues: the god of gods in Greece
Hestia: - Zeus's daughter
Hera:
Rhea:
Persephone:
Athene/Athena:
Maia:
Leda:
Jason:
Helen:
Electra:
Iris:
Penelope:

NORSE (Viking Gods / Goddesses)
Gods

Odin:
Tor / Thor (Åsa-Tor): God of War Frøy / Freyj:
Balder: He was Odin & Friggs son. Loke game the blind God Hodne an arrow made out of misteltoe (which was the one thing that could kill Balder), and he died.

Ull:

Skade: Winter Goddess, she was very good at skiing.

Loke: The Fraudulent / Trecherous
Hodne: A blind God

Goddesses

Frøya / Freyja: She had a piece of gold jewelry named Brisingamen. The dwarfs made it for her.
Frigg: She was Odin`s wife and was considered the wisest one of the easene (æsene) in Valhall.

According to norse (norrøn) mythology there were two places they could come to after they died A Viking who got killed in a war/fight, or in a heroic way, came to Valhall. Everybody else came to Hel. Hel and Valhall can NOT be compared to the Christian's Heaven and Hell

Gods / Goddesses

Selene (the Greek goddess of the Moon),
Aphrodite (Goddess of Love),
Artemis (Goddess of the Moon),
Athena (Goddess of Wisdom & War),
Chandra (Moon-Like, Great Goddess),
Dea (Goddess),
Demetrius (Goddess of Fertility),
Devi (Goddess of Power (Hn)),
Eris (Goddess of Strife),
Freja (Norwegian (Viking) Goddess of Love),
Freya (Goddess of Love, Fertility and Beauty),

Book 2 – Why Were They Called Gods...?

Grania (Grain Goddess),
Guri (Hindu Goddess of Plenty),
Gwendolyn (Goddess of the Moon),
Hanna (Goddess of Life),
Hestia (Goddess of the Hearth),
Hina (Goddess of the Moon),
Isis (Most Powerful of Egyptian Goddesses),
Kali (Dark Goddess),
Kalli (Energy, Black Goddess),
Maeve (Goddess),
Medea (Goddess/Sorceress (Gk)),
Minerva (Goddess of Wisdom (Lt)),
Morrigan (War Goddess),
Nenet (Goddess of the Deep (Bt)),
Nyx (Goddess of Light),
Rhiannon (Witch-Nymph-Goddess),
Sulis (Goddess who Watched Over Bath),
Thyra (A Window or Goddess of Dawn (Gk)),
Vesta (Goddess of the Hearth (Lt)),
Apollo (God of the Sun (Gk)),
Darshan (A Hindu God),
Dionysius (God of Wine & Revelry),
Indira (God of Heaven & Thunderstorms),
Indra (God of Rain & Thunder),
Irma (God of War),
Kyrene (Lord, God),
Latika (Hindu God),
Naolin (Aztec God of the Sun),
Naoll (Aztec God of the Sun - Dim. of Naolin),
Olympia (Mountain of the Gods),
Oswald (God of the Forest),

Book 2 – Why Were They Called Gods...?

Peony (Physician of the Gods),
Phemia (God of Speech),
Pillan (God of Stormy Weather (Nat.Am)),
Quirino (Mars, God of War),
Shannon (Ancient God (Ir)),
Zaci (God of Fatherhood (Af)),
Adonia (Greek God),
Dana (Mother of Gods),
Devaki (A God),
Hera (Queen of Heaven),
Tyra (God of Battle (Sc)),
Dunixi (God of Wine),
Zeus Jupiter Captain of Gods
Poseidon Neptune God of the Sea
Hades Pluto God of the Underworld
Hera Juno Goddess of Marriage/Queen of Gods
Hestia Vesta Goddess of the Hearth/Home
Ares Mars God of War
Athena - **Minerva** Goddess of Education / Science / Virginity
Apollo Apollo / Sol / Pheobus God of Sun
Artemis Diana Goddess of the Hunt/The moon
Aphrodite Venus Goddess of Love/Beauty
Hermes Mercury God of Commerce/Speed
Hephaestus Vulcan God of the Forge/Fire
Eros Cupid God of love
Persephone - Proserpina Unwilling bride of Pluto Goddess of spring
Dionysos Bacchus God of wine/God of revelry
Demeter Ceres Goddess of earth and Harvest

Book 2 – Why Were They Called Gods…?

Pan Inuus / Faunus Son of Hermes 1/2 goat Trickster
Kastor & Polydeukes Castor & Pollux The Heavenly Twins
Aeolus --- King of Winds
Boreas --- North Wind
Zephir --- West Wind
Notus --- South Wind
Eurus --- East Wind
Iris --- The Rainbow Goddess
Aether --- Greek God of Light
Hygeia --- God of health
Hebe --- Goddess of Youth
Hecate Trivia Goddess of the dark/magic
Eris Discordia Goddess of discord
Nike Victory Goddess of victory
Erinyes Furies -Delivered Justice
Eos - Aurora Goddess of the Dawn
Hespera --- Goddess of Dusk
Hypnos --- God of sleep
Nemesis --- Goddess of Revenge
Mors --- God of Death
Morpheus --- God of Dreams
Hercules --- God of strength

Book 2 – Why Were They Called Gods…?

Names of Gods and Goddess Timeline

No gods prior to 52,000 bc. From the years 52,000 bc - 24,000 bc years ago, Names of old gods- and their meanings.

Abar- the rain- harvest
Ash - mysterious one - time - secrets
Atta - the bear - strength - ferocity
Eloah - the sun - heavens - day
Hawwa - moon - night
Mana - owl - wisdom
Og - bull - strength - fertility
Saara - woman - feminine - virtues
Saha - wind - freedom
Tama - tree - forests
Tara - man - masculine - virtues
Vana - dove - goddess - peace - goodness
Xax - vulture - death - decay
Za - serpent - underworld 24,000 BC

New gods and their meanings 24,000- 14,000 bc.

Atlas - earth - strength - solidity - master of elemental divine magic

Poseidon - sea - favorable - unfavorable divine magic

Hesperus - warrior goddess - Hesperian amazons divine magic - art of war

Heru - quaddani god - heaven - astrologers - mages

Set - Nubian/quaddani - underworld. Set - is often depicted as a serpent. Set - may be a manifestation of the Naga's evil goddess, Tiamat, master of black magic - high magic.

Set - Sefar - are of the same - but another manifestation

Sefar - evil serpent goddess - of Gorgons (Africa) master of black magic - and of war

Ishtar - sheban - Eastern Gondwanan (Africa) goddess - fertility - heaven - loves - and war

P' AN KU - khitan god of creation master of enchantment - divine magic - elemental magic - revere the unicorn, phoenix - Eastern dragon

Shang - Ti - khitan god - heaven master - astrology - divine magic

Taracuan - the sun god - supreme deity - master astrology - divine and elemental magic

The Great Spirit - Creator and Supreme Being of Erian tribes - master of elemental and low magic

Book 2 – Why Were They Called Gods…?

Naga - patron - Tiamat

Tiamat - evil serpent/dragon goddess of Naga's-race - master of black magic

Baal - evil - halfman-animal mixed - black magic - same as Shax - Astorath - Thamuz - AAMAN - Nergal - Moloche

Marduk - dark god - halfman-reptile

RA - Egyptian sun god - reptilian - not of human origin - alien off world not earth
AN - heavenly - ANU - Antum

Enlil - lord of command
Ninlil - lady of command

An-Shar-Gal - great prince of heaven

Ki-Shar-Gal - great princess of firm ground

<u>Olden names of god -14,000-2,000 bc</u>

Jove: - Jupiter/Zues -During the Trojan wars - Greek over Minerva - Jove wanted to destroy Achaeans so Achillies people could survive

Zues : -
Apollo: -

Book 2 – Why Were They Called Gods…?

The battle of Troy was 12,000 bc. In the days of Exodus -2300 bc, Sharru-Kin- righteous Ruler -of Mesopotamia - was Sargon the 1st, built a new capital calling it Agade. Established the kingdom - AKKAD, Reining the most part of the 2300 bc, about 54 years- granted to him by the great gods Supreme god - Teshub - The Stormer - 2000 bc

Babylon - god- Marduk - as its supreme deity - 1800 bc. Weapon of Marduk, called the great power of Marduk
god - Bel (the lord) - Marduk - the dark god- Reptilian - not human - off world alien.
Olden Title- storm god 1750 bc-1250 bc
Thothmas 3rd - The Pharaoh who was victorious at the battle of Megiddo- destroyed the city on the say - so of Amon-Ra - Egyptian - Amon-Ra or Amon- god Amon-Ra 1470 bc.

goddess - **Ishtar**
god of Isreal - **Yahweh**

god **Ea** - was appealed by Naram- Sin -

god - **Ashur** (the all seeing)

Lebanon - god - **Ninurta** and **Adad**

Tiglat- Pileser 1st commemorated his wars in the 1100 bc, on the explicit commands of the gods, Ashur and Ninurta.

Book 2 – Why Were They Called Gods…?

538 bc, lands of Sumer - Akkad - Babylon - Assyria - Mesopotamia - Elam - Media - Hittite - Greek lands in Asia Minor - Phoenicia - Canaan - Philistia, all come under one sovereign King - Cyrus. With one supreme god - Ahura - Mazda - god of truth and light. Depicted in ancient Persia as abearded deity roaming the skies within a winged disc. Very much in the Assyrians, had depicted their supreme god Ashur.

There were seven Egyptian gods that ruled over 12,300 years, which started 15,300 bc. These, gods ruled these times. Not the time of their death.
P'tah ruled from 15,300 - 6,300 bc - for 9,000 years
Ra ruled 6,300 - 5,300 bc - for 1,000 years (son of P'tah)
Shu ruled 5,300 - 4,600 bc - for 700 years
Geb ruled 4,600 - 4,100 bc - for 500 years
Osiris ruled 4,100 - 3,650 bc - for 450 years
Seth ruled 3,650 - 3,300 bc - for 350 years
Horus ruled 3,300 - 3,000 bc - for 300 years

Followed some time after 3,000 bc

Thoth ruled ?
Maat ruled ?

Book 2 – Why Were They Called Gods...?

Mythological Event Timelines

THE STAR WARS SERIES... 300,000 BC

<u>1st middle Earth Begins 255,000 BC</u>
Lemuria 250,000BC
Mu .... 225,000 BC
Terra Papers .... 100,000 BC
Atlantis.........100,000 BC
  1st Earth changes.... 75,000 BC *pole/magnetic shifts
  2nd Earth changes.... 50,000 BC *pole/shift
THE URANTIA BOOK... 50,000 BC
  Lemuria, MU destroyed.... 36,000 BC
  3rd Earth changes... 36,000 BC *pole/magnetic shift
  Atlantis broke into 5 Islands.
1st Middle Earth ends at of total of 196,000 years.

~1,221 years later~
<u>2ND Middle EARTH Begins .... **35,889** BC</u>
The Silmarillion..........34,540BC (1st Age)
Wars of the Rings.... (32,889) BC (2nd Age)
Planet Pole shifting.... (32,000) BC   (3rd Age)
Willow ...(29,989) BC (*)
The Hobbit......... (29,889) BC
Fellowship of the ring.(29,828) BC
The two towers.... (29,827) BC
The return of the king ...(29,826) BC (4th Age)
End of 2nd Middle Earth... 29,363 BC
*pole/magnetic shifts 29,360 BC * global flooding

Book 2 – Why Were They Called Gods...?

2nd Middle Earth ends at total of 6,529 years ~
   (Look for other JRR TOLKIEN-books for the history of 2nd Middle Earth- (*) note is not of a Tolkien story, but will fit into middle earth.

~ 4,471 years later ~
3rd Middle Earth begins *24,892* BC
Adam and Eve Story 20,000BC
Wars of gods and men... 14,000BC
Noah (the world flood)..... 12,000 BC
Global flood that submerged Atlantis..... 12,000 BC
Moses (the ten commandments) .....10,000 BC

Within the Book of OAHSPE and other stories
The Book of Jehovih............. 10,000 BC
Babel (the tower of Babel) ...... 6,000 BC
Zoroastrian ....4,000 BC- 1,000 BC
(The Four Horseman's) .... 3,000 BC - 1AD
(The start of Christianity) ... 1,000 BC-500 BC
13th Warrior..... 500 BC
The Sword and the Sorcerer.... 400 BC
Druids ...... 60 BC
Jesus (Immanuel lived to be 135 yrs.) .... born 30 BC
Jesus started his teachings at age 30 known as yr. 1 (time of Jesus) Jesus Crucified at age 35....... Known as yr. 4   (time of Jesus) but did not die on the cross. lived in secrecy to be 135 yrs. old .. actual death was yr. 105 Time of Jesus. ......
The time of the crucifixion, The beginning of year.. 1 AD
Merlin - Mist of Avalon - King Arthur-

Book 2 – Why Were They Called Gods…?

1st knight-Excalibur............. 400AD-520 AD
Beowulf .....900 AD
Dragonheart .... 984 AD
Dragonheart 2 ...... 1064 AD
Robin Hood .... 1194 AD

Chapter 19

Claiming Who You Are

As I, mentioned in my first book religions were created from the off world, by alien star beings, as a form of control. You have just learned that from this book.

The religions were created for one reason and one reason only. They were created to control because some of these beings from the stars wanted to be in control of other beings and other systems. You have read this throughout this book. You were able to see how these beings from the stars wanted to conquer a world and make the inhabitants believe in what these star beings wanted the people to believe.

You also saw how these beings destroyed the knowledge of how life began and rewrote it to suit the beings that wanted to be the gods of these people. Therefore, they created their own beliefs and religions and told the people of Earth this is what you're going to believe in. They said if you do not believe then we will destroy you ... and or the planet.

Book 2 – Why Were They Called Gods…?

Now you can see why the Earth has so many beliefs and religions. You can now see why there is so much confusion and contradiction on who and what we are.

This was done in a manner that would keep us from evolving to the beings that we now are. Mainly because some of these beings do not want other beings evolving to higher evolution, because they would not be able to control other beings to suit their own needs. You can see this control in the religions and governments from the past 4,000 years.

These off world beings that played the roles of gods and devils felt the need to set up a belief system of fear and control. They had the people praise them as gods, to the point that the people would believe it.

After the people of Earth accepted the concepts of these beings as their gods, these beings knew that they were able to create fear in the people of Earth and that the people would accept these beings as their gods. At that time, the humans created churches for these beings that they accepted as their gods.

At that point the people of Earth started to teach their own about these gods, and that we needed to do as they commanded us to do … or else, they will go about punishing people of the Earth.

The inhabitants were told, by these beings, what we say, is, and do not ask questions, do not challenge what we say, and teach!

Have you ever wondered why they say that? You also hear the same thing from the religions. What is out there that they don't want us to learn?

Is it the truth that they want to hide from us? So, we do not take quantum leaps in evolution and spirituality. Alternatively, is it that they, the beings do not want us where they are?

Remember all life starts at the so-called bottom and moves up through evolution, and spirituality. These star beings evolved too. So why do some of these star beings act the way they do?

For the past 12,000 years these beliefs have incorporated the so-called teaching of these so-called gods, in creating fear and control, so we can't learn or grow in the knowledge that is there for all beings.

Let me ask you a question:

Remember the phrase, the truth will set you FREE. So, why continue going through your life time after time being told what to believe in, how to believe... and... do not ask any questions?

The knowledge of life is there for learning and not to be hidden away just because a being from the stars, or the religions, and even the governments, did not want people to know the TRUTH. This fear has lived among us far too long. The time is now for all beings to awake and to learn WHO WE ARE.

As you learn and awake, the knowledge will be confusing. Because, your whole life, you been controlled to believe only what is told to you. Plus you been told do not ask questions, and not to look at other aspects of life before this one. In addition, life is only the way you were told.

Now you are being shown that you have been lied to, and manipulated into believing what they want you to know.

This is the end times, the end of being controlled. It is the time of awakening, to the knowledge of WHO WE ARE.

Which means:
Letting go of this so-called god theory brings one to the realization that there are no so-called gods that will bring harm to us as we learn about who we really are.

The gods are only manufactured of man's creation because we are told that someone is in charge of us, and that someone created us.

This is what it all means:
There is no being that is a god –
It is really the essence of life, which in turn is energy, which is the force that governs all living things.
It is energy only - not a being.

We are energy and spirit. Spirits having a human experience, lifetime after lifetime to see if we can understand the whole concept of life that we create from the experiences of life and realize that we create our own existence over and over. In addition, we are our own gods and no one else is our god.

There are many ancient mythology stories out there, you just have to dig and dig for it. You owe it to yourself to go out and learn the truth about who we are, and our purpose of being here.

You will come across a lot of knowledge that will contradict the way you were brought up. But it was designed that way to bring forth confusion, and contradiction, which will keep you from learning the real truth, so that you would go back to being controlled. As you start to learn, the confusion will dissolve and make more sense, as you go deeper and deeper into all of Earth's past. As you do this, you will learn the truth.

So, now as the pieces are slowly coming together, as you continue your journey down this path of reawakening, as you are learning this knowledge and wisdom about WHO YOU REALLY ARE, you will start becoming a FREE BEING.

This Knowledge is rightfully yours; do not let anyone take it away from you....

A Journey Into the Spiritual Quest of Who We Are
Complete 4 BOOK in 1

Book 3
THE KNOWLEDGE
that was once forbidden by some of the Ancient Beings

Book 3 – The Knowledge that was once forbidden by some of the Ancient Beings

Book 3 – The Knowledge that was once forbidden by some of the Ancient Beings

Kiazer's Quest
Om!

Kiazer continues on his ongoing quest, evolving by traversing a treacherous path of destiny. In this continuing journey, Kiazer strips away the veils of illusion that obscure hidden knowledge about beings engaged in such false pretense as setting themselves up to be perceived by humanity as gods and devils.

Journey along with Kiazer as he reveals secrets guarded by the gatekeepers of all religions and governments who, for centuries and at any cost, have sequestered the true knowledge of life and who we are. What will happen when these dominionists lose their grip?

Travel within the country of Eria (known today as North America) as Kiazer witnesses the reawakening of many more people to this forbidden knowledge. How will our perceptions of reality change as people realize there is more to life than what we've been told? Join Kiazer in his quest by challenging not only religious figures but also yourself. Ask the crucial and critical questions about life. Decline to be deceived.

Book 3 – The Knowledge that was once forbidden by some of the Ancient Beings

The Gathering

As Kiazer travels around the continent of North America he stops at a community around the Pyramid Mountain located within the continental divide of the Rocky Mountains. He gathers with a group of people around a campfire on this early evening of early spring of 2004, once again, Kiazer hopes to bring forth The Knowledge for all to remember. A Knowledge that is there for all to reawaken, which is within us all that will help everyone to reawaken to who they truly are.

This is the knowledge that some beings, which came from the stars, decided to keep the inhabitants of this world from learning of who we are. Over the past thirty-six years Kiazer had been delving ever deeper into the forbidden Knowledge of the essence of our existence, as you experience the Kiazerian journal. Explore the next level of our evolution as we all move forward. Those above and those below in the unending cycles that transcend space and time.

During Kiazer's journey's around the world for the past twenty years he's been revisiting ancient and past civilizations, Kiazer illuminates the falsehoods, lies, and deceptions of the belief systems of Terra (Earth).

Book 3 – The Knowledge that was once forbidden by some of the Ancient Beings

As he discovers a past life from over 6,000 years ago, upon the continent of Tampaurban, on the eastern side of Eria and separated by the Atlantic Ocean, in present day geography, the continent of Africa / Middle East and The Far East.

Zoroastrian Dualism

Kiazer learns he is responsible for the creation of a 6,000-year-old belief system during a previous incarnation. From 4,000 through 1,000 BCE, Kiazer was known from 4,000 years BCE to 3,000 years BCE as Zartosht, and then from 3,000 years BCE through 2,000 years BCE know as Zarathustra, then from 2,000 BCE through 1,000 BCE known as Zoroaster. Zoroaster who created the original Zoroastrians Belief system that taught about the unity of good and evil existing within us all. During the year of two thousand BCE, which is when the original concept of his belief system had been changed to the way it is taught in the world of today with all of its conceptualism of the duality of good and evil. A belief system that encourages dualism by separating entities into two opposing components: good and evil. Emphasizing, in part, that evil is composed of negative beings that should be feared!

During this time period, it becomes obvious how dualistic belief systems can be used to wield power and control over diverse cultures by claiming that

Book 3 – The Knowledge that was once forbidden by some of the Ancient Beings

neighboring cultures gods are demons and therefore evil. As such a narrow belief system spreads and is imposed upon various cultures it encounters, the potential for divisiveness and destruction also seem apparent. This is only one of many belief systems, which has gotten way out of hand. It is merely one of many belief systems, which need to end. We need to bring back a more natural/spiritual way of living.

Incidentally, it's noteworthy that this belief system brought about a dispute within Zoroaster's family, which ended his life in 1,000 B.C.E. Nearly 1,000 years later, at the start of a New Age, the time period from 1,000 BCE – 500 CE. Kiazer becomes aware that several spiritual beings will be born and they will begin teaching spiritual ways of living. Given that the religions of this period became corrupted, in comparison to the older ways of believing, many people tried to lead humanity back toward a spiritual reawakening. However, many other religious figures preferred to retain control over people through fear-based belief systems and managed to convince the people that religiosity versus spirituality is the only socially acceptable way to live. Despite the fact that religions have falsified stories throughout time, it is the authors hope that this series of books will enlighten by helping you understand what is truly going on in the world within contemporary society.

*BCE/CE: (Before Current Era – Current Era: Which are acceptable replacements for what religious people refer to as, BC (Before Christ) and AD (After Death)) BC/AD.

Book 3 – The Knowledge that was once forbidden by some of the Ancient Beings

From the Being of Beings

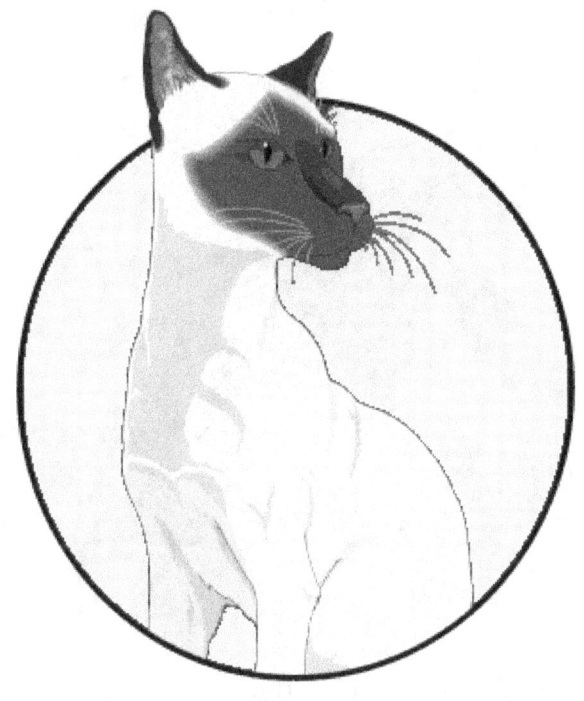

For eons…
We lived amongst you…
As many Beings…
Knowing, what you have yet to learn.

Book 3 – The Knowledge that was once forbidden by some of the Ancient Beings

Guardians of knowledge,
That mortal minds cannot yet dream of.
For we are the keepers,
Of that is yet to come to you.

Book 3 – The Knowledge that was once forbidden by some of the Ancient Beings

From the beings of beings.
Now, comes the time to release our
Knowledge to you…
So, you too may continue up the ladder,
Behind us, to the beyond the beyond.

Book 3 – The Knowledge that was once forbidden by some of the Ancient Beings

Which is, rightfully yours, to take part in…
May the wings guide you,
On your journeys, to once,
Which we came from.
So, we too can continue on…
To the beyond the beyond.

Book 3 – The Knowledge that was once forbidden by some of the Ancient Beings

Chapter 20

The Thought

As Kiazer is gathered around a campfire on this early cool evening of 2004, at the Pyramid Mountain there is a group of fifteen men and women of ages from young twenties to mid fifties. Five of these people had been traveling with Kiazer since 1993.

Kiazer mentions to the group, "five of you that have been traveling with me for a while now know about this ancient knowledge of our existence of who we are as reawakened beings, it is you will recall one aspect of thought. Well, I am going to mention the other aspect of thought. This other thought, will be, the thought that brought forth, all that there is, meaning, bringing all things into existence, including the one that many people go about calling, The One Being - GOD!

Jacobson is one of the ten people that are sitting around the campfire that are not part of the five that have been traveling with Kiazer. Jacobson is an older man in his late forties with long jet-black hair and Caucasian. He asks, "So, what you are saying is...." Kiazer interrupts Jacobson, "Wait a minute Jacobson.

Book 3 – The Knowledge that was once forbidden by some of the Ancient Beings

I have to explain it from the beginning, or you and others will not be able to completely understand what I have to convey. There are key things that need to be made clear to everyone. Save this and all questions for the end, if you do not find the answers, by the time I am through."

Kiazer makes himself comfortable on the ground, as the evening grows darker and the campfire begins to light up the area around them. As Kiazer begins he glances around the group, "This thought, brought all things into being. It includes positive along with negative beings of all forms that are seen and unseen, matter and antimatter into physical form in one form or another.

As I mentioned to other people that I encounter through this journey of teaching to people of the knowledge that has been suppressed, thought, can be used to control and to destroy, it can be used as well to create at the same time. While one being's thought, creates life, so can another being's thought be used as a mechanism to control another being's life.

How did this come about? Well, some say in the beginning. Well, there is never a beginning. It just appears to be a beginning from that particular perspective, a viewpoint of one's own life on where they were brought into existence. This is a never-ending circle of life. As all beings come to realize, at one point or another, all beings that exist are realizing their own thoughts, are created in front of them, as well as the so called first being's thought which is also becoming created. During this time, this cycle of life

Book 3 – The Knowledge that was once forbidden by some of the Ancient Beings

we are going from, its destruction than back into being created again. Who is to say, there is only one being that can create upon the mere thought of creating and/or destroying. These are everyone's accumulated thoughts, the thoughts that create ones own existence. The thought that creates another ones thought into existence. Which also, brings forth the creation of the beings, to go with the thoughts.

This instance brings forth the beginning moments of these beings, that will exist for the experience of that thought for this creation, that they all took part in, bringing these thoughts, and all those beings of positive, negative into reality, of what may seem to be past, present and of the future. All these beings react to other beings thoughts, and they help create the world(s) around them. Based on all the
thoughts that are being put out around them, some of these beings will come to see these beings as of good (positive) and evil (negative). In addition, those so-called beings of good and evil are in a way, stuck in playing this so called creation, based upon, the other beings that brought this thought into creation.

So, you have the beings that created the thought in the past, which, is now, being experienced, by the very being that created the thought without knowing, it was their own thoughts of the past. Which is now, becoming reality for them to experience their own creation that is their own worst nightmare. Because they are not aware they are their own thoughts that they are experiencing, in the present. All of the, good (creation) and evil (destruction) that these beings

Book 3 – The Knowledge that was once forbidden by some of the Ancient Beings

feared and thought of in the past, is now manifesting as their experiences. These beings had gone about creating a god, thought, and a being for all the beginning (creations) of good. They also created a being of evil, end of all things, (destruction). Some of these beings are the people of today. Twenty-five percent are realizing that they created all of these experiences they are going through, while the other seventy-five percent of the civilization are still going about thinking, that some other beings, if it be a god or some devil which created these experiences, that we are going through.

These seventy-five percent of the Earth's inhabitants are now creating a new thought of the end, of what may play out, with these two beings of light and dark. They fear what these two beings represent and fear these beings and experiences as if they were good or bad. Essentially, this is fear manifest, when people fear the experiences of what they witnessed of the past.

These people have more to fear than those two beings that were created by their own thoughts. They have the fear of the thoughts of all beings that exist.

Thoughts of positive and negative energies have always been in existence from age to age. It is the more current age that all beings fear because, they created these so called beings to represent the thoughts of positive and negative aspects of all their thought. Therefore, you have many beings that are representing good (positive) and evil (negative). All this was brought on around 7,000 BCE mainly

Book 3 – The Knowledge that was once forbidden by some of the Ancient Beings

because the people did not want to be held accountable for their thoughts and actions.

Therefore, we are living in a time, that we all must understand the thoughts that brought these so called beings into existence. Such thoughts represent the duality within all of us.

One thought ushers in the creation of life, (which you're the creator of life, the one that thought it). Which all people will witness, as being created by some being(s) therefore, the ones that end up witnessing these events are saying, "that a being of wonderful powers, brought these events, creations, into manifestation, or foretold of what will come to be." This is called, a self-fulfilling prophecy. Without realizing it was ourselves in the past that thought of the events of the future, that all of us would come to experience in time. All of us, created all of these gods and devils in the past. Most of you will come to fear your own creations as we move nearer the future. Which of these events are to come about?

We all take part in, creating all the faces of good and evil, light and dark, gods and devils, which are no more than positive and negative aspects of one's own self.

Book 3 – The Knowledge that was once forbidden by some of the Ancient Beings

Chapter 21

The Creations

Hours passed by as everyone still sits around the campfire intrigued with all that Kiazer is sharing with him or her. "In my digging ever deeper into the mythologies, I came across a very interesting story. I am, going to share that story with you. However, this story is from a larger story, it is the fourth part of a fifteen-part book. I have the entire fifteen volumes of this story. It is a story dating from 4,000-1,000 BCE. During this time it was the age of Aries, a time of peace, harmony and tranquility.

At this time, the age that we are leaving was known as the age of Pisces. One can assume this might be where you, the civilization of now, came up with the theory of the so-called beings, of good and evil. You go about assuming that these beings will play out their roles on the Earth, of the past, present, and of the future. These Beings of dark, (evil, negativity) of now, were not on the Earth until 33,000 BCE, years ago during the beginning of this fifth cycle and the start of the age of dark and light, which is still a part of the cycle that we are experiencing. This age of dark and

Book 3 – The Knowledge that was once forbidden by some of the Ancient Beings

light is the last part of the fifth cycle of the Earth. This fifth cycle ended at the year 2000, the time the Earth's sixth cycle began.

Yes, there were other cycles and ages than the one that all of you are so used to. The past ages also had their so-called good and evil as you have learned in Book 1.

Nevertheless, the beings of good and evil of those many ages past are about to take a different turn -- a different role, so to say, for all beings of this past current cycle and age, that you are now leaving. Then you will enter into your new age of total light and total consciousness reawakening - a new way of living and understanding.

During the year of 1000 BCE this being named Ahriman was depicted as a being of evil that will come to the Earth every 1,000 years to battle the Being of Light.

Book 3 – The Knowledge that was once forbidden by some of the Ancient Beings

During the beginning of the year 2003 I started delving into the Zoroastrian belief system. I came to learn that I was Zoroaster in my second life incarnation here on Earth. This discovery gave me another piece of the puzzle, to the bigger picture of my life, along with my personal beliefs and how the religions came about being the way they are today.

Book 4 of The Denkard of The Zoroastrian religion, which was written around 4000 BCE, or 6,000 years ago, from this year of 2004 offers insight into why I express this sentiment, and how the beliefs had been changed in 1000 BCE.

Excerpts from Book 4 of the Denkard

I make obeisance to Mazda-worshipping religion which is opposed to the demons (and) is the ordinance of Ohrmazda. The matter of the fourth book (of the Denkard) is composed from sentences selected from Ayinin Amuk Vazin by Adurfarnbag, I Farroxzadan, the leader of the faith of the family of the educated-in-the-faith, and saintly Adarbad Mahraspandan.

Be it known that the one God is the cause of the beginning (of creation) and is the causer of causes. Cause is not for him (i.e. He is uncaused.)

Among those connected with (God) the second as the second (if we regard Ohrmazda as the first), (and) first among the original creation is Vohuman. The

Book 3 – The Knowledge that was once forbidden by some of the Ancient Beings

commencement of creation was with Vohuman. And the origin adverse to him (i.e. Vohuman's adversary) is (Ahriman) the blemish giving cause of the creation.

Seeing with complete vision (i.e. on careful inquiry) it is found that the other with the perverse understanding (i.e. Ahriman) conducts things in this world (in the path of evil). At times several original (creations) are destroyed through him. Because his creation separates itself from those who have a close connection with their original master (i.e. God) have taken the side of his adversary. In addition, it is becoming unfit by not caring to keep up with their connection with their true god and by harming the moderate party (of God) it is broken (from its own party). For the same reason that substance, which is on the adverse side of harming the side (of god) is not fit to receive the gifts (of God). Again, a substance, which has received its life from the one life-giving God, becomes unfortunate through the same cause. Any person who turns against Him from whom he got his birth is not able to improve himself (morally) through his connection with that one (i.e. Ahriman), because he is connected with his (i.e. Ahriman's) substance.

Again that evil one is not, as the creation of Vohuman is, the second creation of God. From this it appears that the great self-existing God who is a law unto Himself is one and alone.

And from one (creation) after another is created by him. Hence no one else can be his equal as an adversary (i.e. Ahriman can never equal Him). The

Book 3 – The Knowledge that was once forbidden by some of the Ancient Beings

one God is he who through that one (i.e., Vohuman) has given birth to innumerable other creations.

The creation connected with that other (i.e. Ahriman) is without religion; how can it be said to have connection with the second (creation, viz. Vohuman)? But that one (i.e. the creation connected with Ahriman) this can be said to be separated from the One (God).

Third-- The creation-increasing origin (i.e. God) keeps the second (creation) Ardwahisht under the supervision of one who is among those connected with Him (i.e. under Vohuman). Among the Amahraspands, Ardwahisht has the third rank. And he is obedient to the first creation (Vohuman). The reason of this being third (in rank) is that Ohrmazda he is the first and as being the first creation, Vohuman is the second (in rank), and his (i.e. Vohuman's) obedient servants Ardwahisht are considered the third (in rank). From this, Vohuman having obtained his life from Ohrmazda is (Ohrmazda's) obedient servant. And the good custom and law of (men) obeying the authority of Ohrmazda and of living as His obedient servants has (prevailed in the world) from the beginning of creation through the THOUGHT of (Vohuman). Again the good custom of life- possessing men publicly obeying and respecting religious rulers is (prevailing in the world through Vohuman).

Among those connected with the perfect authority of Ohrmazda the fourth in rank called Shahrewar is worthy of being blessed through his possessing life according to Ohrmazda. And he is a worthy servant of

Book 3 – The Knowledge that was once forbidden by some of the Ancient Beings

the worker of pure deeds, Ardwahisht. And this second (creation, Ardwahisht) is obedient to Vohuman the first creation. (Shahrewar presides over metals. In addition, these give strength for generosity and nourishment to men living a life of piety. Thereby is (acquisition of) honor, (attainment of) one's desires, propagation of the faith, attainment of (both) knowledge and the intuitive wisdom of the good-thought Vohuman. Thereby is the springing up (in the heart) of the desire of obedience to God, the conducting of oneself towards Ardwahisht to one's (own) advantage, and the making one's friends do likewise. To conduct the people by the authority of Ohrmazda and the leadership of the faith is to disgrace the blemish-giver (Ahriman). And hence the blessed are exalted.

Again he who keeps up the divine religion in this world and rules the people according to the precepts of religion is the (king or priest) the maintainer or religion and of the true and temperate authority of God.

The state through the (inspired) strength of the knowledge of religion is worthy of the trust (of the people) and those who in truth and purity propagate the knowledge of religion among the pious are strong through the strength of the state.

Ungodliness and the intense prevalence of unholy utterances (in state and church) are through the rival efforts of the adversary (i.e. Ahriman) to (keep himself) in touch (with men). In the same way the method of (men's) speech and deeds is like unto fire.

Book 3 – The Knowledge that was once forbidden by some of the Ancient Beings

Just as burning fire (first) dries up the wet firewood and (next) after drying up the firewood acknowledges the ruddy light (akin to itself), so too in both ways (i.e. the two referred to above) the people of the world by their holiness are fit to drive away the unholy Druj from among them (i.e. the fire first expels the adverse principle of water from the wet fuel so too piety first drives out the unholy element; next the fire makes the fuel glowing hot and absorbs the fuel into itself and so too piety absorbs that which remains after the unholy element has been driven off and makes akin to itself). It behooves the people to acknowledge these obligations to the agents (i.e. the Mobeds and Dasturs) who give them an insight into the nature of the different kinds of Unholiness and those who give rise to different sorts of harms. In the same manner people ought to be always extremely grateful to the good triumphant kings, the defenders of the faith. Because he (i.e. such a king) is the believer in the religion loved of God and more especially because he explains the wisdom underlying the Mazda-worshipping faith. Hence his good Government is safe and permanent. And by the adornment derived from his and the Yazad's mutual connection he is secretly sheltered (and protected). And the continuance of his authority one after the other (in his own family) is through divine assistance. Therefore, people should look upon the religious kings who have faith in their religion as courageous, as being the good kings of religion and the kings who are of the law of the (good) faith should attempt to spread in the world

Book 3 – The Knowledge that was once forbidden by some of the Ancient Beings

the exalted law-abiding wisdom of the Mazda-worshipping faith.

When king Vishtasp became relieved from the war with Arjasp, he sent messages to other kings to accept the (Mazda-worshipping) faith and to spread). Among the people) the writings of the Mazda-worshipping religion which are studded with all wisdom and which relate to the acquisition of knowledge and resources of various kinds, he sent all together (i.e. at the same time). Spiti, Arezrasp and other Mobeds who had studied the languages relating to these (writings) and who had returned from Khwaniras [Xwaniratha] after a complete study of the knowledge of the faith under Frashostar.

Darai son of Darai ordered the preservation of two written copies of the whole *Avesta* and its commentary according as it was accepted by Zartosht, from Ohrmazda, one in the Ganj-i-hapigan and the other in the Dez-i-Napesht.

The Ashkanian government got the *Avesta* and its commentary, which from its (original) pure (and sound) condition had been, owing to the devastation and harm (inflicted by) Alexander and his general of the plundering Ahriman army, separated into parts and scattered about, to be copied out. And any (work) which remained with the Dasturs for there study and the writings subsequently obtained in the city were ordered to be preserved and copies of them to be made out for other cities.

Book 3 – The Knowledge that was once forbidden by some of the Ancient Beings

(After this) Ardashir-i-Papakan in his time got a true Dastur named Tosar to arrange together all the scattered writings relating to the *Avesta* and its commentaries. For this (order) Dastur Tosar devoting his attention to (this subject) made one harmonious work after comparison with other writings. He entrusted the Dasturs with the work of making other copies of it. The king also ordered that other writings relating to the Mazda-worshipping faith with might be obtained after him and of which no information or clue was to be had then should be preserved in the same way.

Shahpuhr son of Ardashir king of kings collected together, from Hindustan, Arum and other places where they had got scattered, writings other than those of the faith (i.e. other than those on prayer, worship, precepts, and law), (such as) those relating to medicine, astronomy, geography, minerals, the increase of the glory of life-possessing kinds, the parts of the soul, and (writings relating to) other arts and sciences.

And he ordered a correct copy of them after collocation with the *Avesta* to be deposited in the Ganj-i-Shaspigan. And he ordered the (Dasturs and Mobeds) to deliver sermons and speeches to draw the faith of the people without religion to the Mazda-worshipping faith.

Shahpuhr king of kings, son of Ohrmazda warred with the kings of all countries and made them believers in Ohrmazda. And he created a taste (for religion) among all people by means of speeches. And

Book 3 – The Knowledge that was once forbidden by some of the Ancient Beings

he made them investigators of religion. And at last Adarbad by his admonitions made the people high priest placed before all the non-Zoroastrians an explanation of all the different Nasks of the *Avesta*. Upon which some who accepted the faith confessed to this effect-- we have seen with our eyes every point of the faith and hence every one of us is sure to abandon his evil religion, and we shall keep up our efforts for the faith. And they did accordingly.

Now Khosraw, king of kings, son of Kobad drove out from among the four divisions of (the people of) the faith (i.e. from the Athonrnan, Artheshtar, Vastriosh and Hutokhsh) any priest of the evil religion and ruler of the evil religion who seemed to be full of enmity to the faith, (in fact he drove out) all these evil men. And he has exalted the Zoroastrians (through their faith) by giving them from time to time encouragement and instruction regarding the faith.

Again (Khosraw) has given this order about the (priests gifted with) divine wisdom -- that the clever men who explain the truth of the Mazda-worshipping faith should through their good judgment and foresight encourage the ignorant by teaching them the faith and make them as steadfast as possible in their faith. And the learned supreme high priest, the Dastur of the Dasturs should not enter into religious discussion with the people. But he should through pure thought, word, and deed is on the side of the good spirits. And he should piously worship and pray to God through the Manthras that by (his) worshipping with the Manthras we might always call

Book 3 – The Knowledge that was once forbidden by some of the Ancient Beings

to our mind the leader of our people *i.e.* of the Magus to wit Ohrmazda; The Lord (God) is manifest unto us through spiritual understanding. And the Lord shows us through spiritual **THOUGHT** the measures for our salvation so as to be understood of us of the world. We will continue to love Him fully from among the Yazads by both the agencies (of the spiritual and bodily faculties). Moreover, we will continue to remember the Yazads who work for the prosperity of God's world in order that religious merit might accrue to those of the good faith.

Again, that king (i.e. Khosraw) in an addition to this (work) sent the inhabitants of Iran studding the Mazda-worshipping faith to Khwaniras to study under teachers of exalted wisdom, so that we might acquire full adornment through knowledge of the divine religion. These keep aloof from perverse discussions, exhort (men to lead a good life) through the words of the Avesta and compose books of wisdom. And people through their wise writings keep themselves moderate and honored by obeying those who enlighten them. Again for this reason all men regard the Mazda-worshipping faith of divine wisdom as meant for the final existence. Hence intellectual strangers continue coming to this place (i.e. Iran) for (studying) the Ohrmazda-worshipping divine religion. Explanation of the Mazda- worshipping faith is afforded to people from the outside that continue coming to obtain connection with and zeal for the new religion. And the Dasturs after many (religious) researches with still greater zeal travel and instruct

Book 3 – The Knowledge that was once forbidden by some of the Ancient Beings

those who cannot come there (i.e. to Iran) for the work of obtaining the benefit of the faith.

Again (Khosraw) thus addressed all the Mobeds who are evidently servants of God and of virtuous disposition -- I order you with the best wish (i.e. most sincerely) that you should create a taste for the Avesta and its exposition [Zand] with new and new zeal. And by the acquisition of its knowledge (i.e. of the Avesta) the worthy people of the world should be made exalted in rank. They should fully instruct such, as are capable of learning, from among the people of the world, who do not understand the Creator, nor the details regarding his miraculous spiritual creation. Such as are wanting in intelligence and are of perverse THOUGHTS should be instructed in the faith in way that seems best, to wit, by comparisons (and examples) and be who can instruct (people) in the faith with such wisdom should be regarded as the instructing (priest).

The profession of that instructor in the faith, who is a teacher fit for the above (work), who has spiritual gifts, who instructs (men) in every wisdom of the faith and who likewise plainly tells with wisdom the vices of the world to every one, is the only one which makes men (incline) to the divine faith. He should not expound anything on the authority of the faith, which is not in agreement with the exposition of the faith. Likewise he should teach on the authority of the faith everything that is found in the faith as a duty he owes to his office.

Book 3 – The Knowledge that was once forbidden by some of the Ancient Beings

(The Creator Ohrmazda) for (the maintenance of) His authority produced and gave being to the increase-giving Spandarmad of obedient thought, the fifth among his holy relatives. This is the begetting power for begetting spiritual and earthy creation (in the world). Through Spandarmad is the strength of the earthy body, the sense of feeling, courage and every kind of foresight. Man is obedient to God and possessing His glory on account of the presence in him of thought, word, and deed, which makes him obedient to God. For in pious men is the lodgment of the Yazads for the complete recompense of virtue and the presence of the Yazads vanishes (from among men) because of their connection with impiety.

Moreover in men is the relation of exalting foresight and five other substances (life, soul, intellect, conscience, and guarding spirit) whose names are mentioned in religion.

Ohrmazda created among (His) relatives (i.e. the Archangels [Amahraspands]) the essence of (archangel) Hordad sixth in high dignity, always bestowing gifts and endowed with the thought of obedience. This creation on account of its communion with many earthy substances (especially time and water) yields good thought to the good creation in its allotted work, takes proper care of it, as a faith companion keeps itself in communion with the essence of (the good creation,) and out of the feeling of kinship keeps itself united with (the good creation) to show it the full and proper path in every work and process. In the same manner, the hidden qualities,

Book 3 – The Knowledge that was once forbidden by some of the Ancient Beings

which are with Hordad -- viz., the resplendent Farohar, conscience, life, intelligence, wisdom, and others pertaining to the affairs of the soul, -- remain as the corrector and manager of the body. The invisible physical senses give intimation unto the soul, of sinful actions, which the body commits with regard to the soul. These invisible (senses) are called the mediators between body and soul. Moreover, these senses yield happiness to both bodies bad souls by making these two assist each other.

The seventh (related to Ohrmazda) is (the Archangel) Amurdad, which, besides yielding protection unto men, always keeps living men immortal and connected with the (faithful) flock. He is the promoter of thoughtful, meditating nature, bestowed of progeny to the warriors, and begetter of good thought among those who are born. He yields radiance to the bodies of those who are bore good and is of many natures through the mingling of wisdom.

The one existence of God perfects and completes itself in seven (including the sixth spiritual archangels.) It befits all to thank God for perfection in all deed. (As every nature obtains capacity to enjoy life) and for being engaged in their proper work. God gets victory (over Ahriman) through the thanks given unto Him by the creatures for being able to occupy themselves in their proper work. This thanksgiving (from men) is due on account of the nature they have received from Him (i.e. on account of the useful life obtained from Him.)

Book 3 – The Knowledge that was once forbidden by some of the Ancient Beings

Learned archpriests must impart knowledge of religion to the creatures of God. From the scholars of the Manthras-utterances well versed in religion is attained a, proper understanding of the industry each man ought to engage in and of the way he should work.

The creatures are not informed as regards the infinite time connected with God, its nature being understood only by the unique existence (i.e.) the Creator himself.

The creation of finite time on earth is for (bringing about) the improvement of the creatures having existence by means of a change from one (condition) to another (the change being from the material world, into which man is born from the spiritual, back into the spiritual state.) As regards the cause of creation) it is said in religion that every one comes into being from Him who has being (i.e. God) and every creature that is created obtains existence from that existent (i.e. God.)

The utterances of God (i.e. the sayings of the Mazdayasnian religion) are a law unto the existing (i.e. to men.) There is nothing without order. Some of the substances are finite. Moreover the substance wanting in order is from the blemish giver (i.e. is on the side of Ahriman,) and is said to be the substance following the law of wicked similitude. (I.e. of Ahriman) and existing without rule and limit (i.e. without the restriction of law.) Just as the period of the Creator's existence is infinite so is the exalted soul; how can it (ever) have non-existence?

Book 3 – The Knowledge that was once forbidden by some of the Ancient Beings

The creation, which is produced, receives by its actions gifts of a high order from God.

Moreover, men perform meritorious actions because of fate or destiny and it is this account of (destiny) that a being of the earth is considered famous among the spiritual Yazads. Through the performance of actions pertaining to the spiritual world is man's high destiny. In this world, a man of greatness receives the favor of God so long as he has faith in the shining Yazads. In the same manner a man following the reverse path turns to meanness and degradation through worldliness. The good thought power Vohuman that gives light to the eye (i.e. the understanding) of man is (obtained) by loving the powerful wealth (i.e. course of life), which makes for improvement. He who is without this wealth is without the above-mentioned things (for the improvement of wisdom.)

Men ought to raise themselves to illustrious positions by worldly knowledge and by education (which enables them) to read and write. They should keep themselves with the bounds of law and order by the precepts of the faith and purchase many books containing wise sayings. For obtaining immortality (in the next world) they should duly praise the helping Yazads and struggle with (the wicked.) Many virtuous men improve and exalt the one substance (i.e. the soul) by praising the Yazads. (The arch-priests) explain to the people the nature of the several (wicked beings) who are always for quarrel, inimical to the creations of (Ohrmazda) and helpful to the creatures of darkness

Book 3 – The Knowledge that was once forbidden by some of the Ancient Beings

(Men) ought to acknowledge they are the giver of existence the Creator who endowed living men with bodies possessing complete supremacy with the help of fire and water.

Those who do not turn to the faith of the Daevas (i.e. those who cling to the religion of Mazda-worship with firm faith) must be rewarded. Those who lead mankind with the intention of making them recognize one God must be made the governors of the world, and those who keep to the mandates of religion must be called (men) of pure origin. In the same manner the contemplators of Divine knowledge must be rewarded with such gifts, as they desire.

Things which are fit to be supplied at some place for (keeping up) the existence (of animated beings) must be most certainly borne there in any way (that is possible;) as for instance, the water of the river which gives strength to life, and medicine prepared in cold and warm water for (removing) discomfort from the soul (both in life and at the time of death.) It is the good thoughtful (physician) that knows the proper medicine for (giving) blood, shining (complexion), consciousness, and taste.

Just as the Flame is through live fire, light through flame, and twilight after light, in the same manner, the greater or less recovery (of animate beings) from many a disease, takes place by means of medicinal herbs.

Just as the date tree grows up from the date-stone, in the same manner the production of man is through the act of procreation.

Book 3 – The Knowledge that was once forbidden by some of the Ancient Beings

For the connection of progeny (i.e. for begetting offspring) the sexual congress of one person with another is (essential.)

Permanence of life depends on the soul's connection with the body.

Rain or the Yazads bestowing rain are the cause of prosperity to living beings.

The permanence of friendship and amity is through seeing and conversing with one another.

How is existence brought about? Just as one substance is evolved out of another according to its own laws and in the finite time (fixed for it.)

What the produce of a certain city is, or what grows up in its lands is understood by knowledge of (the city.)

The first gift of life-giving Creator is as regards the soul. The students of the Manthras properly understand the different gifts relating to the soul, bestowed by the Creator. Nor are the proper remedies for the last pangs of the soul hidden from them.

Questions:
The following are the questions of those who retail scandal against honest religious beliefs.

Q. Is the potent being (God) finite or not?

A. The answer is this that the leader of religion (the chief arch-priest) remains glorious by receiving God's halo of exalted worth. In the same manner he is the agent (of God) to encourage people to perform works

Book 3 – The Knowledge that was once forbidden by some of the Ancient Beings

of religion by means of his far-seeing understanding. Therefore by actions unworthy of a leader he does not lose his previously obtained position as a leader of religion.

Q. Is the potent being (God) capable of wisdom to a limited extent or more the (i.e. is He omniscient or not?)

A. The star-readers (i.e. astrologers) understand the worth of the allotment (of destiny by the stars).

How long is the chief allotting (stars) to move in bad aspects? How long are they in conjunction with the malignant owner of bad aspects? How long does the man (influenced by such stars) work in the way of wisdom? The laws relating to these and other (astrological) details the astrologers learn from writings on the earth (i.e. from astrology). Astrologers can foretell the good events of a man's (life) from his horoscope. And physicians can explain the details (regarding the health of the body, the safety of the body and the connection of the soul with the body. Those who are connected (with a man) infer from his outward movements his life, the destruction of his life, his actions and his investigations. Knowledge of the substances and of the creation of time and place is (attained) by (the explanation of) the creator (i.e. by inspiration.) Through the nature (of the substance) is (attained) the knowledge of its qualities and through creation its existence (is known). Knowledge of

Book 3 – The Knowledge that was once forbidden by some of the Ancient Beings

perverse substances is attained through understanding the nature of acceptable substances.

Q. Does (God) irradiate His glory through intermediaries?

A. The obedient soul (created by) the Almighty is so on account of the connection and radiance of the immortal (Yazads) whose knowledge the holy God has bestowed on (the obedient soul). With the blessing of that radiance that (man) becomes famous by performing every earthly action according to his will. And through unanimity with the opponent (Ganamino) man prevents his nature (from virtuous actions). And he who completely reforms the different natures of the adversary's (connections) renders himself fortunate. His progeny keeps to the original (nature from which he is sprung). The race of horses is (sprung up) from the first horse; the production of orange is from the first orange tree. In the same manner, that a man should completely improve his progeny, for its safety and continuance, is necessary for making his race famous.

Through abiding by the mandates of God observing the precepts of religion on earth the soul of man and his progeny acquire an insight into the things relative to the good creation (i.e. the spiritual world), eternal wisdom and (eternal) time (as naturally as) the eye (acquires) the power of vision. By means of this every nature keeps his material existence connected

Book 3 – The Knowledge that was once forbidden by some of the Ancient Beings

with God, in the same manner as twilight is connected with light.

The religious governor conversant with religion is a great instrument, for the worship and praise of God.

Firstly-- (The king) must be susceptible of beneficent wisdom, and useful to those related with him. Secondly -- The king is supposed to pay respect to worthy beings (i.e. men walking in the path of God). Thirdly-- (The king) is supposed to be without deviation from divine mandates, fulfilling God's wish, and is reckoned superior through (possessing) God's wisdom. Fourthly -- (The king) does not become supreme by disowning the superiority of the potent Yazads, but is supposed to perform other dishonest actions, through adverse intentions. (The king) who deals justice, according to the precepts of God's revelation, has an effective remedy for the grief's of the people of this world and keeps his subjects well off by means of justice. That the (king) preserves his dignity with permanent fame by means of these (his) actions, (which are) without harm and bring on prosperity. It behooves the King to inflict on men two kinds of punishment for their offenses in order to establish his fame. The one (punishment) is bodily (i.e. giving physical labor to the body) and the other is the infliction of fine. The sage judges, studying the Manthras, know every kind of punishment. The man under the dominion of (the demons) the instructors of sins declares (in a court of justice) that he is a witness, and gives harmful evidence, in spite of not seeing (anything). How can that man receive salvation from

Book 3 – The Knowledge that was once forbidden by some of the Ancient Beings

the sin of unfaithfulness? The students of justice discern the (real) thoughts of these men of (wicked) connection, on account of the lodgment of the Yazads among them, (which lodgment is) like the lodgment of water in clay. The connection of adverse (i.e. unjust) judges is harmful (to the Yazads); therefore they are regarded as not connected (with the Yazads). For this it reasons the substance under the dominion of the Yazads is considered to be of exalted (i.e. supernal) existence, and the substance not under their dominion is called (the thing) of darkness (infernal) and non-existence. Again, the substance under the dominion of (Ganamino) the despoiler of existence enjoys the (wicked) existence of its master. The substance possessing the wisdom of the Yazads acts in the creation, just like an effulgent supernal power. And so long as the substance during its life does not excite (itself) (with Ahriman's power), it is said to be of proper connection. In addition, those men of whom Yazads are supposed to be the masters are the servants of God, enjoying His favor; harm cannot reach them.

Q. If the potent being (God) were infinite, how can He be called potent being? Again how can one possessing finite power be called the potent being?

A. (In reply to the questions: Has God who is worthily of (eternal) existence any limit? and in knowledge is He capable to a certain extent or is His capability beyond limit?) The explanation therefore is

Book 3 – The Knowledge that was once forbidden by some of the Ancient Beings

that God has concern with finite time, and is Lord of finite knowledge, but He being (himself) without limit as to knowledge and time, is said to be of unlimited time and unlimited knowledge.

Q. Should all works be done at their proper (i.e. destined) time? Can they be done at other times? Can a work be without reward?

A. (Is there any transmission of Light from one to another? The answer to which is that) the God of Existence is the best leader (of the world temporal and spiritual) and He is capable of imparting His own Light to another.

Q. Are all works done at present in accord with know-ledge and wisdom? If a work is connected with the original strength (i.e. has come from the source of goodness, God) how can it be said in light of the faith to belong to infinite time?

A. To the people who have existence God, through his chief creation through the good-thinking angelic power grivet a comprehension of the end of their creation.

Q. How can the leader of darkness be truthful? Who leads the true leader astray?

A. Those that are dwellers in Hell have been mentioned as (inmates) of Darkness, not of Light.

Book 3 – The Knowledge that was once forbidden by some of the Ancient Beings

Whatever elements there are of heat, cold, moisture, and dryness in the bodies of those (i.e. men) living as the companions of the Yazads, they have been created (by God) for doing the work of the body. They thus serve to keep in good order the vitality and are the means of keeping the body sound.

In the same way (evil agencies) that do harm (to the body) cause the elements of cold and dryness to dwell in the body, and permeate the human system to the injury of the elements of the heat and moisture that do the work of vivifying the body. The coexistence of these four elements in equitable relations with each other tends to the amelioration of the body.

Q. How does the life-giver (God) give outward form (to all substances?)?

A. Unfair and defective agencies cause harm to the body. The Life-giving One (God) is not sustainer of the adverse creation. All men oppose, obstruct, and fight with one another for the existence of the principle with which they are connected (i.e. are either for Spenamino or Ganamino). Nay, the different opponents who fully grace the principle to which they belong are related to their kind (i.e. to the side to which each has given his choice). Thus a thing of cold (essence) is known to suppress heat, and a thing of dry (essence) to suppress moisture. When the representative of one side encounters the representative of the other, it is not for suppressing

Book 3 – The Knowledge that was once forbidden by some of the Ancient Beings

him altogether, but with the motive of obstructing, the work assigned to him by (natural) Law. The uniform state of the blood is due to the dryness, which is related, to heat and moisture, which is related to cold. In the same way an organic body is rendered unfit when heat accompanies moisture, and cold accompanies dryness; the blood stops in consequence, and at once flows in the opposite direction. As the sources of the elements bring about dryness connected with heat, and moisture connected with cold, there is much a commingling of heat with cold and of dryness with moisture, that this relation being kept up in the body, it conduces to the proper animation of the same, and the body always remains busy at its work along with the connected Yazads. All misunderstandings and quarrels, which now occur at times between individuals, are due to the related influences becoming unworthy. This is brought about by the lower existences (i.e. the evil powers of the demons) commingling in the body. When those of one kind make a sudden attempt to make the body unfit, it is brought into affinity with death. And the ruin of the body is through its being enfeebled in many ways by destructive evil tendencies. Also the Spirit that is opposed to the vital action of the body is the (invisible) one that tries to make the body act contrary to uniform laws. The man works for good life of his body through the spiritual powers, which work for his (virtuous) existence. The cessation of the work of existence, pertaining to the good recompense of the soul, is due to the body becoming lightless (i.e.

Book 3 – The Knowledge that was once forbidden by some of the Ancient Beings

lifeless), by the development of the work of the destructive forces (in the body) the enfeebling powers therein are strengthened. The good bright Yazads that have relation with men keep them from contact with the adverse forces (i.e. the demons). <u>It is mentioned in the religious books that it is through the influence of the spiritually existing Yazads residing in men, that they (men) are free from various kinds of harm and evil.</u>

Q. How can the faithful of this world perform actions the aim and object of which would be the same as (the aim and object) of (the Yazads and Amahraspands) the radiant being that always carry out God's wishes?

A. Again, among the various professions the choicest is that of the heads of the religion, and the one pertaining to the attainment of the love of the Yazads, and that of loading oneself to the performance of noble actions in this, world.

Q. In what ways is the worshipper of God distinct from the one who scorns Him? Why should one who has power of endurance complain (against pain?)? How can a substance become very famous?

A. The knowledge of what man's duties are and what they are not is acquired by man through there being a sufficient number of the family of the religious leaders (i.e. through there being a sufficient number of

Book 3 – The Knowledge that was once forbidden by some of the Ancient Beings

Dasturs and Mobeds informed in religion), who are the ardent (i.e. careful) preservers of the Avesta an its commentaries. And they are thus the expounders of the religion in public to the people of the world, the instructors of the philosophy of the Religion to the people, and proclaim of the (religious) truth to those that argue perversely against it. They are those that embarrass all famine-producers and ravagers of fertility. <u>They are those that attract people to the worship of God, and make them obey their kings and honor the decisions of their judges.</u> They are those that make the people of the four divisions (the Athonrnan, the Artheshtar, the Vastriosh and the Hutokhsh) illustrious in their respective occupations.

In addition, by means have Questions and answers pertaining to Ohrmazda, they make them devoted to religion, students of religion, and worshippers of God. They keep in currency the requirements other the other Athonrnan, (i.e. they supply them the things they want), and fulfill their wishes, whereby good and respectable families are maintained honorably. Those (men) that are the instructors in the Zartosht [Zoroastrian] religion are the promoters of the desire for religion and the disseminators of the knowledge of it. The other thing pertaining to the Mazdayasnian faith, (i.e. wisdom), which, in so far as it serves the purpose of clearing up all misunderstanding (i.e. doubts), is pleasing to those that tread the path of God, is to be kept pure. And the new seekers after knowledge must, by being put in the way of acquiring it, are kept above want. In him that does not advance

Book 3 – The Knowledge that was once forbidden by some of the Ancient Beings

his community, and forbids not men from immoral acts, good faith should not be placed. And he should never be regarded as a leader (of the community) or as one who can remove the apprehensions of each individual, or as one who can make the other creation (i.e. the atheists) obedient to God.

Through repentance of sin is attainable the receiving go the recompense for righteousness and the discarding of sin. And after that there is no occasion for punishment. Connection with the med for a single act of righteousness is the cause of the reduction of the punishment for the sins (of that man). It is God's object to make those, who disobey the commands of the king, deserving of various kinds of punishments by way of justice. Among them, the one who disobeys the commands (of the king), and the one who is imprisoned for all the offenses relating to the soul, are to be released by order of the State. In addition, if a prisoner has been put in imprisonment by recourse to ways contrary to orders, (i.e. in contravention of the laws of justice), for causing grievous wrong to the soul, it is a kind of oppression. Again, at the bidding of the physician that heals the disorders of the soul (i.e. the Dasturs of the religion), it would be conformable to religion to let off a highwayman from capital punishment.

Q. The Sun shines on the earth according to the time of the season, Why are (then) some places without the heat of the illuminator? Although

Book 3 – The Knowledge that was once forbidden by some of the Ancient Beings

(substances) improve by means of the illuminating Sun, some places are (even) at noontide moist and dirty. Why should it be that one place is moist in spite of the noonday heat whereas another gets more than its portion of the light of the Sun?

Q. How is the inability to look at the effulgent light (of the Sun to be explained?)? Why is the weakening and enfeebling of the eyesight thereby? How can pain proceed from the luminous Sun, which derives its power from God?

A. For the leaders of the world -- those that are crowned with supreme majesty (i.e. the king and the Dasturs) -- the equitable Government of iranshehr is feasible through illustrious judges -- the dispensers of justice. The maintenance of the sovereignty over the seven regions by the Zoroastrians is due to there being an abode within them of Religion, the Kayanian majesty, and other glories. Again, the means that they have for living in exuberance (i.e. in comfort), and the cause of all their pristine greatness and supremacy are due to their having within them the coming and going of the Yazads (i.e. to their intercourse with the Yazads and Amahraspands). And it is on account of this very sovereignty (endowed with Yazads majesty) that such a king of Iran is able to invest with power the rulers of the seven regions. As the flame of a fire is due to its relation with the inward glow, and as light is due to its relation with the flame, in the same manner is Wisdom due to Religion, and superior power is attainable (by

Book 3 – The Knowledge that was once forbidden by some of the Ancient Beings

man) by his relation with the instructor of the Religion. And through an insight into (i.e. comprehension of) it is the (righteous) existence of man. And through his connection with the open path (of religion) is the test (of man). And through such power (of religious wisdom) is the body able to perform the functions necessary to the soul. And through soundness of the body is the preservation of the soul. All Iranians (i.e. Mazdayasnian) by so regulating themselves can live with a superior kind of strength. Those of the citizens that give instruction in (the acquirement of) knowledge, spiritual forces, art, courage, physical strength, and prosperity, make the rule of the king of Iran supreme, auspicious, and honored.

The greatness of the Iranians (i.e. the Mazdayasnian) is owing to truthfulness in all matters, kind regard, and meditation on the design of Providence in all-powerful creations. By these means, they keep in affinity to their source (i.e. their Creator), and obtain victory over men of the opposite nature and over the ignoble and wild-looking subject nations of other cities. Again the Mazdayasnian should give good advice to the people that are of harsh and abominable traits, evil-worshippers, and enfeebled, so that these may not waste their life in vain actions. And they should form men, who are not of good essence (i.e. are evil), into being good men, like the present good-thinking pious men, who are particularly careful in their adherence to noble speech and in keeping aloof from base things.

Book 3 – The Knowledge that was once forbidden by some of the Ancient Beings

Had not the people of the good Creation put themselves at first into an awkward position before the rulers, by the use of (inept) expressions, they would never have become, but could have remained with their faculties on alert. In addition, had they not in this way come to disregard the divine commands, and to deprive themselves of the intellect guarded over by the Yazads, they would have been able to understand what things are to be done and what not to be done. And they would have known that the Yazads effulgence of the luminous soul couldn't for long dwell in the body just as the sun refrains from making luminous (for all time) the good things that shine by the sun's light. (The Yazads radiance) it has been known to interrupt by the man's being very careless. Therefore it is that for certain reasons contradictory words should not be uttered in the presence of rulers; and in order to keep oneself in good repute one should, in their presence, give expression to one's THOUGHS after mature consideration.

Premeditation is necessary in questioning and in answering, and then the question may be put, or the reply given, in the proper way. It is the way of the priests of the false religions not to act with good sense, before they are overpowered.

Q. Do the Yazads guarding the earth give up the work of man's salvation, through fear of the wicked?

A. Before putting a question in one's turn, one should catch the drift of the opponent's argument.

Book 3 – The Knowledge that was once forbidden by some of the Ancient Beings

Again, in a discussion, he that speaks much should not be checked, but his reasoning should be well listened to. Also, in a discussion, if there be a question, it should be satisfactorily answered. If there be many such questions they should be dealt with in various ways.

The perfect glory (i.e. the Divine gift) that fits men for leadership is of the nature, viz. that such people take upon themselves to answer properly the questions of those that argue well; but he that has faculty for (mere) fault such a disputant does not argue for self-improvement. Nor is his discussion pertaining to the soul, and therefore such discussion should be dropped. The discussion which is beneficial, and pertaining to the salvation (of the soul) from Hell, and for the welfare of the soul, should not be set aside, but should be carried out to the solution.

Nor should one refrain from exposing falsehood, wrong ideas, and wickedness. To secure their deliverance from Hell, they (the people) should be led, by all kinds of truth, to have implicit and unshaken faith; and from this there should be no turning aside for whatsoever reason. And like the spring season one should show himself at his best in his ardor (for expounding the religion). If the signification of anything (pertaining to religion) were not clear, it should be given out as unintelligible. And in the argument whatever is worth esteeming should be appreciated in detail Moreover, no wrong deed that might have been done should be admired. But the

Book 3 – The Knowledge that was once forbidden by some of the Ancient Beings

right action only that has been per-formed by the help of God should be accepted as beneficial.

The foremost leader of the religion (i.e. the Dasturan Dastur [Zarathushtrotema]) should imbue the people with ardor for the religion, and should induce them to be very industrious, in order to make them excel in their routine of work, and should exhort them to acquire other noble arts.

Those that have been in touch with the Yazads (viz. the believing Mazdayasnian), should, by girding themselves for the fight, making use of the right understanding (about Spenamino and Ganamino), ward off one of them (the Ganamino), and follow the other (the Spenamino). And with the strength and courage derived from the Spenamino they should attack the other (Ganamino), and (by the help of the Spenamino) they should obtain the nourishment of their nature. Till the end, the fight should be maintained with Ganamino, who should never be regarded as having received good training.

Q. How can the expelled Blemish-giver be (present) in him who is innocent? If God should recompense them and make them of great worth how can the truthful ever think of sorrow and the charitable bestowals of corn [i.e. grain] ever suffer from hunger?

Book 3 – The Knowledge that was once forbidden by some of the Ancient Beings

A. The charitable man is he who bestows in charity from his own (acquired) wealth. And the truthful man is he who never speaks untruth on behalf of or about another person.

The grateful man is he who recognizes an obligation. Gratitude should be shown towards him to whom one, like a dependant, is under obligation for his life. And, secondly, gratitude should be shown towards him who having the power to harm hath done no harm; and finally, when one has experienced all possible good from him, one must assuredly show one's gratitude by words and deeds.

Those that are engaged in the inquiry (i.e. search) after immortality, acceptable to God, and (are the friends) of the benevolent (i.e. the imparters of religious instruction), and of other benefactors, are the procurers of other felicities for their kith and kin; and by not bearing any ill-feeling towards robbers and other harm-doers, towards prisoners, and other criminals and wretched people, and by making them happy and faithful, they prove themselves possessors of the good strength worth being grateful for (i.e. Those who showing compassion towards robbers, prisoners, and sinners, lead them to improvement, really bring them under their obligation by making them staunch believers (in the faith). But by cherishing hatred towards them they are held to be in danger of becoming guilty.

Book 3 – The Knowledge that was once forbidden by some of the Ancient Beings

A father ought to reform his son, if he were unworthily, by inculcating in him noble thoughts (i.e. by religious instruction). Therefore, if a man from want of assistance were incapable of doing any work, he should, in order that he may surmount all kinds of wretchedness, be given the means to acquire more wealth.

Q. People consider the evidence of (persons) of high descent as throwing more light than that, of untrue speakers; but why should they be considered of high descent and lofty dignity if they serve the will of sovereigns of low worth. One whom God has declared to be of (royal) family in the Avesta is not to be considered royal. But if (such a person) serve not the will of wicked sovereigns should his royal descent be acknowledged?

A. A discussion on religion may be entered into with those of the controversialists on religious subjects, who are so (learned) as to be able to give authoritative decision on all subjects. Thus the truth on their side being known, they may have no occasion on punish, according to the dictates of the Nasks (of the Avesta), the priests of the false religion.

A certain nation's scriptures, known by the name of True [Torah] (i.e. the scriptures of the Jews viz. the Torat or the Injil) have been regarded as the words of the devils, and are not worthy of belief. Nothing mentioned therein deserves to be done for the benefit

Book 3 – The Knowledge that was once forbidden by some of the Ancient Beings

of the creation. Because the writing makes mention of the irrelevant matters which ought not to have been introduced therein. Whatever therein is not good writing is the concoction of various writers, and therefore such writings is said to be of the soul-cramping tendency. And these concocted accounts the Jews regards the revelation of the original creation (i.e. pertaining to the celestial Yazads).

To the Rummies who help the Yazdan-worshippers of good wisdom (i.e. who help those of the Mazdayasnian faith) and to others who live a similar (good) life, should be expounded the original text of the 'Ganj-i-Shaspigan.' (In other words, the Jews and the Greeks who whish to believe in the Mazdayasnian religion), and such of them as have no faith in their own, and want to improve, should be thoroughly instructed in the religion.

If in other countries there be any writings (respecting our religion) worth reading, new, ameliorating, good, and divinely inspired, these should be procured; and there should be no backwardness in the study of them and in the researches into them. And whatever in the writings of other nations is unbelievable should not be accepted.

The nature that has concern with the greatest development of wisdom (i.e. is studious) must be admired. Attention should be given to the writings of (the men of) other countries, and the same should not be destroyed.

Book 3 – The Knowledge that was once forbidden by some of the Ancient Beings

In these writings (of men of other countries) if there be any passages and aphorisms pertaining to the service of the one God. It is not every comment thereon or every maxim that is to be indiscriminately given publicity out of the body of those writings and maxims; but we should make from them a selection of the original (sacred) passages and maxims (pertaining to our religion). And the books in the Ganj-i-Shaspigan should be read with careful attention to all the passages.

In these writings (i.e. those pertaining to our religion) the human body is treated of in four parts, of which the head is said to be presided over by the Athornan (i.e. the priestly) class, and the hand by the Artheshtar (i.e. the warrior) class, the stomach by the agricultural class, and the leg by the people who follow good avocations for livelihood.

The human soul is said to have the chief control over all the above-mentioned four classes, and the soul itself is said to be under the dominion of God.

A twofold object evidently influences the words and deeds of every man. His first object is to qualify himself for the final (welfare), and his second object is to endow himself with noble thoughts by so training himself for the profession (of piety.)

The Iranians (i.e. the God-fearing Mazdayasnians) are deserving of praise because of all their honest dealings, while dishonest and blemish men deserve to be condemned.

Book 3 – The Knowledge that was once forbidden by some of the Ancient Beings

The celebrated erudite Seneca's of Rum, and the servants of India have shown an appreciation of and have much admired the foresighted persons of Iran. They adopted their expressions and ideas, and on seeing the great worth of these wise men of Iran showed their preference for them.

Q. How can the Emperor Ardashir Papakan's sovereignty be acknowledged in spite of the severance of authority from several of his direct ancestors?

For the same reason many scholars became worthy to obtain high position and favor from the (Iranian) rulers. And by obtaining high recompense and support (from the Iranian leaders), they in order to get a full reward of their merit, much dreaded these leaders in this world, and were much afraid of punishment in the next. Moreover, they abstained from these blemishes, so that they might continue (to receive) honest recompense from their Iranian superiors who could hold them back (from such blemishes.)

And they themselves, (i.e. the leaders), in their desire to obtain a good recompense for their souls, abstained from any carelessness that might cause them to be miserable in the abode or palace, village or city of the next world; arid they never gave way to any lustful passion. However, they cherished the learned men, with the view of securing distinction as men of worth. And they were held in high esteem among the rulers; for from the illiterate is not to be expected the approval of a noble action, or mature consideration; nay, on the contrary, there proceed from them various

Book 3 – The Knowledge that was once forbidden by some of the Ancient Beings

evils. The unwise have not the tact to acquire the desirable sufficient independence pleasing to the rulers. So an honored ruler, by keeping aloof from the unwise, can put himself in the way of acquiring the desired degree of excellence. His endeavors should not be directed towards any base or injurious ends, but he should strive by counteracting such tendencies to attain to a high position in the next world. Such a ruler gives good attention to the orders he issues and to other regulations (pertaining to the state); and thereby ensures a pleasant enjoyment of his dignity.

The (State-administering) chiefs should choose as their king a person of high rank and good repute. None but a man of worth should be elected king. For this purpose, a distinguished person related to the chiefs should be secured. Individual predilections should have no weight in the choice of a king. Further, if the person (fixed upon) is not of kingly descent, another one should be procured from a different place, as in the interests of justice the election (of a king) is indispensable.

To those wise men who choose to retire from the post conferred on them by the king, or who, in order that they may live in contentment, give up the business or service, which was entrusted to them, -- to those, that entertain such good notions of securing happiness, no benefit can accrue in life by this relinquishment (of their work). Because, if against their wishes they be again forcibly carried off by order of the State, and be forced to resume their work, they would find no enjoyment in it. Therefore they should

Book 3 – The Knowledge that was once forbidden by some of the Ancient Beings

stick to and perform faithfully whatever works appears to them to be of public or private benefit.

The learned kings of the State, with the view of ruling with a high degree of efficiency, should strive (for the fulfillment), by Divine Grace, of new and noble aspirations, such as: -- encouraging the learned, the illustrious, and the charitable, being grateful towards those who are loyal to and have affection for the State. Conferring of bounty on the suppliants and on those that are in solicitude owing to poverty, gratifying with a good and befitting remuneration annually, the learned men who may be in constant anxiety for having to labor for their food and livelihood, along with the giving of everyday donations, according to the needs of their circumstances. For the glorification of the (next) spiritual world to the conspicuous true believers who come into the (royal) presence, on those that arte misers greedy for amassing worldly pelf, on those that have no reverence for the soul. In addition, on those that abstain not from sins, nothing should be bestowed, so that they might not get facilities for taking to drink and of robbing the wise of their due.

Before putting a question in one's turn, one should catch the drift of the opponent's argument. Again, in a discussion, he that speaks much should not be checked, but his reasoning should be well listened to. Also, in a discussion, if there be a question, it should be satisfactorily answered. If there be many such questions they should be dealt with in various ways.

Book 3 – The Knowledge that was once forbidden by some of the Ancient Beings

Every man that has a material body should regard his own marriage as a good work incumbent on him to perform. He should strive diligently at his avocation that he may live in happiness. He should take good care of the materials of power (i.e. good deeds for the next world) that his lifetime may pass in contentment. And he should promote the marriages of others.

If thou wish to be educated, give thy choice to the works of the foresighted (i.e. works pertaining to God). If thou wouldst avoid hard times, refrain from giving thy approval to works involving afflictions of various kinds.

Who are our instructors? The Dasturs learned in religion.

In what subjects have they to instruct us? In noble things (belonging to) three (places.)

Of all noble things and places, this world the next world and the transposing (i.e. the final imperishable embodiment).

Of what thing should we choose the good recompense? Of rightness.

How can we get instructions on this subject? From the Dastur of the religion says.

On our soul's parting from the body that will take us (to the spiritual world), and by what path, the good contriving quest (i.e. the guardian angel of the good conscience) by way (of Heaven), (Space the Universes around all things).

Book 3 – The Knowledge that was once forbidden by some of the Ancient Beings

By what powers can we attain to the lodgment (within us) of good THOUGHTS? By the resolve of obedience of God, how can we acquire the resolve of such obedience?

By concentrated meditation through the acuteness of the intellect, I, for once, teach you two words of wisdom -- That you should do good deeds, and should refrain from doing deeds, which should not be done.

What deeds should we eschew and what deeds should we do? Evil THOUGHTS, evil words, and evil deeds we should eschew; and good THOUGHTS, good words, and good deeds we should adopt. Each of these maxims is good for you.

Book 3 – The Knowledge that was once forbidden by some of the Ancient Beings

Chapter 22

Ahriman The Destroyer

Who is Ahriman? When did he come into existence?

Ahriman has been known by several names since 3000 BCE. Ahriman is also associated through other beings. Ahriman was created to bring fear.

It is said that Ahriman comes around every one thousand years to destroy or to take over Terra, and bring darkness to Terra for an unknown length of time. This has been interpreted many ways through the ages.

I can say this, since we entered into the twenty-first century, (and it is now 2004), that there is no being of evil destroying the earth and bringing darkness among the people. Also Ahriman has not made his presence known in the last two thousand years, neither have any demons or gods.

So, who and what is Ahriman? Ahriman is a manifestation of thought. Ahriman (negativity) is created by thoughts from all beings (by the people of Terra). People go about fearing a being of evil, and a

Book 3 – The Knowledge that was once forbidden by some of the Ancient Beings

being of good, which would come to Earth and create a battle between light and dark.

People do not realize the forces of energy and the magnitude of their own thoughts, effect what is being created. As everyone goes about fearing evil -- and the beings, that they (the people) are creating this evil (negativity) and the beings represent all of this fear.

What follows on these next few pages, are some ideas of what these beings look like based upon, what people are creating with their thoughts about those negative beings.

The pictures of negative beings are the same, generation after generation. Age after age, time and time again it never changes.

The stories that follow through the years are told, time and time again, about beings of good and dark coming to Earth, to battle among all beings.

These are some of the names that are associated with The End of Time, or in other words The End of an Age.

Kronos
Seth
Mephistopheles
Saturn
Ahriman
Lucifer

There are many other Names as well and many images.

At the end of every age, there have been some type of dark beings associated with bringing about famine, destruction, and other upheaval events. There are many stories of these beings that have been associated

Book 3 – The Knowledge that was once forbidden by some of the Ancient Beings

with all these changes. These changes are mainly normal changes of the Earth. But people need some type of being to blame for all these changes.

Kiazer had come to learn from his sojourn during his past thirty-seven years of delving deep into those stories. He has found how those stories became changed through the ages to make people fear these beings.

These are just a few drawing of what Kiazer found that deals with the typical ideas of these beings that people fear that are called devils

Book 3 – The Knowledge that was once forbidden by some of the Ancient Beings

Book 3 – The Knowledge that was once forbidden by some of the Ancient Beings

Book 3 – The Knowledge that was once forbidden by some of the Ancient Beings

Ahriman, a being that is to come around, once every 1,000 years. So they say....

She is called Lilith. She is also seen around with Baal.

Book 3 – The Knowledge that was once forbidden by some of the Ancient Beings

As Kiazer delves into those ancient stories, he comes across one of those typical stories, of how things were changed in the understanding of these beings.

When the Jews reached Canaan they changed from nomads to settled and agricultural people. Having no precedent of their own for agricultural pursuits or for the regulation of a settled life, it was inevitable that they should pick up many of the habits, customs, and attitudes of the natives of Canaan. The inhabitants of Canaan had a system of worship that paralleled that of Zarathustra, and worshipped Baal and the Baal's, with their female counterparts, chiefly Asteroth (Ishtar, Astarte). So did the Jews, but as time went on they converted the gods of the people among whom they had settled and with whom they had difficulties, into their own devils; just as the followers of Zarathustra had made of the gods of their Indian neighbors the devils of their own pantheon, and of the devils of their neighbors, their own gods. But it took some time to abolish the autochthonous deities found by the Jews in Palestine, especially since many of the Jews worshipped them. Thus we may read in Ezekiel that Jerusalem was a hotbed of pagans.

Under Samuel, Saul, David, and Solomon, at the cost of incessant war and factional dispute, Israel was finally unified into a nation (Circa 1040, BCE). After the death of Solomon, who began to build the Temple at Jerusalem in 969, came the division of Israel into the two kingdoms of Judah and Israel. This was the

Book 3 – The Knowledge that was once forbidden by some of the Ancient Beings

period of the pre-exilic prophets, who gave statement to the fascinosum and tremendous aspects of the monotheistic deity Jehovah or Elohim, a word that originally meant gods in the plural. So in Amos, who flourished in the 8th century B.C.E?

These beings of half human and animal, that people are socializing as evil / negative are totally wrong in that realization.

I talked about these beings in the first book a little. Some of these beings came into existence through the interaction of humans and animals. This was mainly due to the energy of Terra, changing and with Terra flipping on its axis, which had occurred during the time of 56,000 BCE, during the Second Age of Atlantis.

It was up to the guardians to help these beings to understand what happened to them and how they came to be in existence.

At the time of these beings deaths, it was also the task of these guardians to help separate these two beings souls, which were merged together as one.

Also at this same time, some of the Atlanteans scientists were playing around with genetic alterations. They created these same beings that nature once had a hand in creating. But these beings that these scientists were creating were more rebellious and destructive than their predecessors that were created by nature. These particular beings had gone into the world without the knowledge of why they were created. Moreover, they created havoc among the civilizations.

Book 3 – The Knowledge that was once forbidden by some of the Ancient Beings

This is where the people created those stories about these beings, which were of half human and animal.

These stories that were created were of negativity and evil. Mainly, because these beings left Atlantis and went to other continents. The inhabitants of those other continents knew nothing about these beings. These inhabitants were witnessing this destructiveness and chaotic events from these beings. And those stories are still told today without the understanding about these beings and how they came to be.

These beings are not evil by any means. Yes, they are different due to the type of energy that the Earth was entering at that time.

I urge all to learn and understand the truth about all these beings that existed during the old ancient ages of Terra.

This is the only way all will truly understand about the life that once existed, and the life that will become part of Terra again. It will also help you to understand the energy of the evolution process of life.

One thing for sure, you will not learn the truth of the ancient ages through your religions. They know about all of this, but they are the ones that are creating this fear towards these beings. So, the only way that is left for you to learn the truth is to go out and research it on your own.

There are many stories that are told about these ancient beings that existed eons ago, and they are not all true. The early stories are of negative, but if you keep on digging deeper into these stories, you will see that these stories will change from negative towards

Book 3 – The Knowledge that was once forbidden by some of the Ancient Beings

the positive. Then you will see for yourself on how these stories came to be changed. They were to create fear towards these other beings.

It is up to us the guardians to teach everyone the truth on how these stories of the old ancient ages were twisted and turned inside out. They were to bring about fear and confusion about all these beings that are in existence. Just because these beings are different, does not make them evil / negative at all.

The task of these guardians was to untwist and teach the truth about the existence of life, of whom you all are (the human race), and to help you to understand about these other beings, which are among you today.

Remember, all beings have a role to fulfill that exists. If it to be, within this plane that we exists on or if it is below or above us. This also goes for the beings that are moving from spirit to the first dimension and first to second dimension. Then the second to the third dimension and as the people of Earth are moving from the third to the fourth and fifth dimensions. You also have those beings going from the fourth and fifth dimensions, and moving to the sixth dimension, and so on.

These beings are not what you and the religions are making them out to be. Yes, these types of beings do exist, like many other beings that you are not aware of at this time.

Book 3 – The Knowledge that was once forbidden by some of the Ancient Beings

The only dark and upheaval times that we are all witnessing on Terra are our own thoughts, which are being brought about by the religions and the governments of this world.

Book 3 – The Knowledge that was once forbidden by some of the Ancient Beings

Chapter 23

The Ancient of Beings

Who are these ancient of beings?

These ancient of beings existed eon's ago, (100,000 plus years ago). Several of them are still among you today, while the other ancient beings had moved on to other dimensions. They also wait for you, too, to move foreword to the dimensions where they, the ancient of beings await, so they can teach you what they know of what is to come to you in the shifting, into the coming dimensions that await all of you.

Some of these ancient of beings, which are still among you, are from Atlantis, Lemuria, Mu and many other ancient races. Not all of these beings are of human form. You also have those beings that are mammals, such as your whales and dolphins. There are also races of beings that are of off worlds, like the Yeti (i.e. Bigfoot), the reptilian races, the lizards, and the Greys and many others.

On the next few pages we give you examples of these beings.

Book 3 – The Knowledge that was once forbidden by some of the Ancient Beings

These beings are also of the higher realms of existence. They have been on other planes of existence, which was prior to your past existence, in the second and third dimensions. We are now entering the fourth and fifth dimensions of existence.

Who are these Avatars - Vishnu's, the ancient of beings? They were also known during the ancient times by being called (Prophets, Messiahs, gods, i.e.).

These beings may appear to be those that you would associate as being Angels, Avatars, Vishnu's, and other godlike beings. But, you should always keep in mind, they are not gods, just like the devils/demons, and they too are not what you make them to be.

They are known as beings that have godlike feats and powers, they are immortals, some of them are of human origin, others are humanoid in appearance, but not human. All of these beings are both positive and negative energies.

Male and Female, winged beings, called Zephyrs

Book 3 – The Knowledge that was once forbidden by some of the Ancient Beings

The Human / Humanoid

Lemurian's

Book 3 – The Knowledge that was once forbidden by some of the Ancient Beings

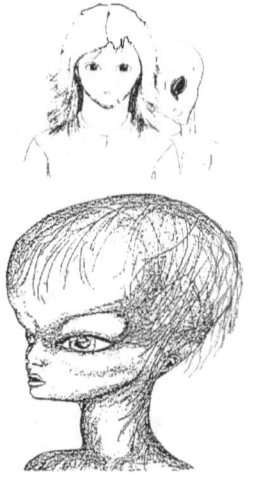

Half-breeds of Human / Humanoid

The various types of Grey's

Book 3 – The Knowledge that was once forbidden by some of the Ancient Beings

Half-breeds of Human and Animal

This picture is a breed of Humanoid / Reptilian

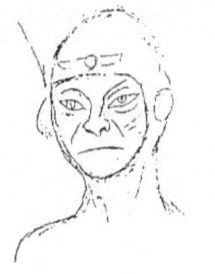

This picture is a breed of Humanoid / Serpent

Book 3 – The Knowledge that was once forbidden by some of the Ancient Beings

Eunuch - A being that is of both sex genders, you heard about these beings in the early stories of the Bibles.

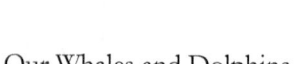

Our Whales and Dolphins

Book 3 – The Knowledge that was once forbidden by some of the Ancient Beings

Avatar

All of these beings once existed together several ages ago. And yes, these beings are still among us today, but they are not seen everyday in this day in age. This is due to one key factor, and that is that there is one race that fears all of these beings. This race also fears them.

This is one type of being that is known as the human race.

Book 3 – The Knowledge that was once forbidden by some of the Ancient Beings

These Avatars existed secretly, no one really knows who they are. Except in the stories of the battles of light and dark that we read in mythology. Even those stories of myths are limited on talking about the Avatars, because the Avatars live their life in secrecy so they wont be noticed. But you might come across a couple stories of these Avatars if you dig deep enough into the ancient mythology stories.

I mentioned one of these stories about the Avatars in Book 2 in the second chapter.

Eons ago these ancient of beings had appeared at times, when civilizations were experiencing major upheavals and changes along with wars of dark times. They were known as Avatars, and they are of many races of human and humanoid types, such as elves, dwarves, changelings, and reptilian beings, along with many humans with godlike powers and many countless other beings, which will come to aid those races, that are on the planet. The Avatars are also bound by this positive and negative energy. So you will have stories of these beings creating chaotic events and these beings of light and dark challenging one another.

As I mentioned previously, most of these wars that these Avatars take part in are between themselves, which are fought in secrecy. Nevertheless, someone might come across, witnessing those battles, and they go about writing about them.

As we read those stories, and myths, about them from ages ago, most people look at these stories as myths, fairy tales, and as fantasy. But these stories are

Book 3 – The Knowledge that was once forbidden by some of the Ancient Beings

true. Just because these beings are not seen in our world of today does not mean they were not real, eons ago.

These beings existed, and people wrote about them in hoping that these beings would not be forgotten through the ages of the human civilization to come.

These stories are about these beings that came to the aid of the humans in their time of need. These beings were also the caretakers of balancing the positive and negative energies of Terra.

The aspects of these stories, that religions and most of the society of today, go about labeling these myths, as being of fairytales and saying that it is not true. Without realizing it, they are also labeling their stories of their bible as not being true as well, as a fairytale.

Within these stories of this so-called Bible, are of these beings, of pre-ancient civilizations. The Bible goes about telling of events that were passed down through the ages of the human race, about these off world human / humanoid beings. Moreover, if there was something they do not want to accept, then they go about hiding that information of knowledge, or they will just leave that part of it out of the story. Or they will go about turning those stories inside out.

So, the Bible is also telling about stories of myths, of a long time ago. However, the Bible is more of the current times, and people do not want to think that there were any other civilizations other than the current one.

Book 3 – The Knowledge that was once forbidden by some of the Ancient Beings

These stories, of those ancient civilizations, of eons ago that we are learning about did in fact exist, and they are not fantasy.

Well, the civilization of today is all in for a big surprise. These stories of these myths of these ancient pre-civilizations and the beings are all true.

The religions and society go about labeling these myths of the pre-ancient civilizations, which existed prior to 12,000 and as far back as 100,000 years ago, as only being fantasy. Then they need to label those stories of their Bible as being as such. Since the entire Bible is the same, a compiled collection of modern stories of the same type of beings. It talks about pre-ancient stories, that people call stories of myths.

Once you start looking at all these stories of mythology, of the ancient times, that date before 12,000 years ago and prior, you will have a better understanding of those cultures and of what life is all about and the knowledge that these ancient beings possessed.

Book 3 – The Knowledge that was once forbidden by some of the Ancient Beings

Chapter 24

Watchers

There is another group of beings that are always around, and have been since the starting of any civilizations in the universes. And these beings are on the so-called sideline. These beings are in the shadow so to speak, of all the events, and at times these beings will interact with the civilizations. These are the Watchers and they record all events that are transpiring, between the conflicts with other beings in the universes that are of the Earth and from other worlds that exist among the universes.

Who are the Watchers?

They are of the pre-Ancient civilizations. Known by Atlantis, Lemuria, Mu and many others of the pre-ancient times. The only ancient records that have been found were in the 1980's. They are those of the ancient Sumerians, of ancient Persia - also of Babylon and a few other pre-ancient cultures. These Watchers are also called NeTeR, which also means, Guardians.

Book 3 – The Knowledge that was once forbidden by some of the Ancient Beings

They have also been known as the Anunnaki's and as the Nefilem.

These Guardians are known to obtain the knowledge of life of the universes. These Watchers / Guardians have more knowledge about all aspects of life, the Earth, and about the stars, during their time, which dates over 50,000 years ago. Compared to what the people of Terra know and understand today, about life, and the universes around us.

It has been written during the ancient of days, about some of these beings of pre-ancient civilizations, which came down from heaven, (the stars).

One has to understand the terminology of the ancient times, and not what has been twisted and passed down by current times of terminology. These beings came down from heaven. Heaven actually means, from the stars. The only way that these Watchers, that are known as the Anunnaki / Nefilem, would have been able to obtain the knowledge of life of the universes is only by traveling the vastness of the universes. And the only way that this could be accomplished is by the use of starships.

There are also writings from the ancient of days of these crafts. And again we find the terminology not understood. We hear those stories, about the strange objects in the sky, such as:

They Followed the Bright Star -
The Wheel within A Wheel -
The Burning Shields -
Fiery Chariots -

Book 3 – The Knowledge that was once forbidden by some of the Ancient Beings

They or He came out of a Cloud –

There are many other descriptions out there similar to these above.

All of these are descriptions of how these starships appeared to the humans during the ancient times. These are the ships of these beings that are from the stars.

What are the reasons for these beings, that are called the "Anunnaki / Nefilem - Watchers / NeTeR / Guardian," purpose for coming to Terra.

There are several reasons.

They are watching and recording the events that are taking place. Which are between the beings that are from other worlds and the actions of the people of Terra, with these beings?

Such as seeing how the people, of Terra are reacting to these so-called stories that were created eons ago, about the battles of good and evil that were created by these beings, of the so-called gods, that wanted to control this star system and create fear among the people, about these Anunnaki / Nefilem, and the Watcher / NeTeR / Guardians.

Your previous cultures wrote about and started religious belief systems, that were based on what these gods were telling people of Terra some 25,000 years ago - of what will happen in the future, and how they need to live their life. These watchers are also watching and seeing what the people of Terra are

Book 3 – The Knowledge that was once forbidden by some of the Ancient Beings

going to create for themselves in the coming of the New Age.

The people continue to live in fear of these so-called gods and devils and too continue to let these beings control their life from afar. They do so without even seeing these beings for the past two thousand years, and without knowing whom these beings are, which they fear so much.

Will the people continue to believe in these stories of the past? Will they live the same life as they have the past 25,000 thousand years? Will they take steps backwards in the evolution, to take part in another Dark Age, just to start over again?

Or will the people make a quantum leap foreword and let the old ways of life, which are of the third dimension, go by the wayside, so the people could make that quantum leap into fourth/fifth dimension of existence, which is a deeper understanding of spirituality of evolution? Which is becoming the being that you really are.

On the other hand, we might have Terra ripping apart to bring forth two planets. One world, will be back in the Dark Age, while the second world will be jumping forward into their quantum leap of spirituality, along with peace, light, and harmony.

These Watchers are also known to interact with the inhabitants from time to time, as you have read in the previous chapters and in the other two books.

These NeTeR went about teaching the habitants of this planet about the knowledge of life and of who you are, in the scheme of things. The

Book 3 – The Knowledge that was once forbidden by some of the Ancient Beings

NeTeR started the reawakening processes, about life, which laid dormant in all beings. The NeTeR knew by teaching the humans about life, that these beings that are playing gods, were in control of these star systems, and they do not like the idea of this knowledge of life, that was being taught to other races. Therefore, these gods made up stories to get the inhabitants in fear of these true beings of light, (NeTeR - Watchers and the Anunnaki – Nefilem), they were taught these beings were of evil.

Here is an interesting theory that I came across back around June of 1996. It deals with the songs of whales and the clicks and whistles of the dolphins. It is said that the whales and dolphins are the oldest mammals alive on the planet and that they are the remaining guardians of Terra. The songs that the whales sing fit right into what I mean about the knowledge of life.

Here is part of the research that Richard Butler is working on.

Dolphins of Heaven

It should also be noted that on the rare occasions that abductees hear verbal sounds from the Greys Beings it is described as high-pitched, sometimes chattering or staccato clicks or beeps. These are all similar to the air vocalizations of dolphins. The Greys are reportedly engaged in human / grey hybrid

Book 3 – The Knowledge that was once forbidden by some of the Ancient Beings

experiments. This is to combine the genetic material of both species into a hybrid species. Is this possible? The Japanese and several other countries are working even now on interspecies hybridization's. If I am correct that the Greys are of dolphin decent, and then the possibility of successful hybridization becomes much greater. Some believe that on Terra, man shared a common genetic ancestor with the dolphin. Up to a certain point in development human and dolphin fetuses are nearly identical. In the not too distant future it will be possible to produce a hybrid human / dolphin species. It is Richard Butler contention that the Greys have already beaten us to it.

Finally I would like to point out that dolphins have been associated with the "gods" AKA the aliens, from earliest recorded times. Certain mythologies hold that some of the gods came from a world of water. It is now through by most that these beings genetically altered the existing pre humans on Earth.

(I showed this as well in my second book, why were they called gods.)

It is certain that the Greys would have had a hand in this. One of the greatest of ancient worship sites is the temple of Delphi. This was originally the temple of the sea goddess. The word Delphos means both dolphin and womb. Richard Butler believes it is time we stopped calling them Greys and use the proper name our ancestors called them. They knew of the gods who came from the water world in the heavens long ago. They called them Delphim. I hope that you have found this enlightening and thought provoking.

Book 3 – The Knowledge that was once forbidden by some of the Ancient Beings

For those out there who consider humans the only intelligent species on the planet, as Richard Butler demonstrate the power of the cetacean brain. The bible contains a little over a million and a half bits of information. The song sung by humpbacked whales contains over fifteen million. Each year it changes just slightly and every whale on the planet knows what those changes are. Now ask yourself this. Could you remember the bible word for word? Could you remember fifteen of them? Think about it. If our bible contains our basic history, social and religious philosophies, what does something fifteen times larger contain?

It is Richard Butler's deepest hope that this article will allow you to open new perceptions on the events now taking place on this planet to see both the Greys and yourselves in a new way. I think in time we will come to find that what is down here, is exactly what is out there. That there are humans, dolphins and other beings cooperating out there. Perhaps we should stop and ponder our roles as the caretakers of this planet. Man has hunted our own cetacean population to the very edge of extinction. It is something that we all must take shame in.

Recently efforts have been made by the civilized nations to preserve the great whales and dolphins. Can we live peacefully on this planet with another intelligent species? I truly hope so. I would hate for another more advanced species to treat us as well as we have treated the whales.

Book 3 – The Knowledge that was once forbidden by some of the Ancient Beings

Many hope for contact with these beings. If we cannot get along with an indigenous intelligent species, how can we expect to get along with one of extraterrestrial origins? A people are judged by their actions. If we demonstrate our goodwill towards our fellow inhabitants of this world, perhaps those not of this world will be sent a message, that we are civilized after all.

What knowledge do these whales posses? One can only imagine the purpose of these whales and the songs that they sing. Man has always thought that they were the guardians of Terra.

How can something as primitive as man, be the guardian of Terra when all we care about is conquering and destroying all life, including our human species, along with the planet?

The only way that the human race will become the guardians of Terra is when they put an end to the governments and religions of the world, and recognize all life and live in peace with all. That goes for all life, human and animal.

Until that time comes, for the time being, these whales are the guardians, the caretakers of Terra. The songs that they sing balance Terra's energy, from all the destruction that man is doing to Terra.

At the same time, the whale's songs renounce a frequency, that which brings the human energy (frequency), to a higher state of consciousness. Which will bring the human race to awaken the knowledge of life, which lies dormant in all life.

Book 3 – The Knowledge that was once forbidden by some of the Ancient Beings

The time of these whales as being the guardians of Terra will be ending soon.

They are imparting their knowledge about life to us. Are we ready to become that spiritual being, that we are, and finally become the guardians of this planet? This means making peace between all human beings, and ending this 3,000-year-old war, which was to see who could control and destroy one another.

We are all humans on this planet.

We are all one race, which is known as the human race. It does not matter what country you are from because we are all of one, which is the human race. If the human race ever wants to become the guardians of Terra, then all of you must first realize who you are. Then and only then, you will become who you are.

The main purpose of these Guardians is to help bring the human race to the understanding of who they are. The knowledge of life is for all to know, regardless of how some beings wanted to control and keep this knowledge as secret as possible.

At the end of every age/cycle, the NeTeR are found to be more present then at normal times, which is due to the changes that the human race and the star system go through, because what happens on Terra also effects everything outwards in a ripple effect as the same happens on other planets within all the universes.

Book 3 – The Knowledge that was once forbidden by some of the Ancient Beings

Chapter 25

The Knowledge

Through the ages of the human race there have been stories about the humans going about obtaining the knowledge of the gods, (The Ancient of Beings) beings which came from the stars.

Some of these beings from the stars did not take a liking to the other star beings. These other beings were trying to teach the other beings that were trying to obtain the knowledge that these star beings procured.

The common stories that are told age after age are of Adam and Eve, also known as the human race. There are also countless other stories as well, that are similar in story to one of them, which is The Tower of Babel of Babylon.

Everyone knows about the religious aspects of the story of Adam and Eve. That story deals with the negative and the fear of knowledge, along with two beings that represent good and evil, (positive and negative). Everything in the story of Adam and Eve, (the human race) is symbolical in nature and in life.

Well, here are the true aspects of that story.

Book 3 – The Knowledge that was once forbidden by some of the Ancient Beings

There is no doubt that there were other beings that took part in persuading the early Adam and Eve to learn the Universal Knowledge of their life, along with the beings that did not want Adam and Eve to learn the knowledge of life.

Everyone knows about the serpent beings that were persuading Adam and Eve to eat of the fruit of the forbidden tree.

In actuality the serpent beings were not serpent. They were the beings of light, helping the human race, to break away from those beings that people called god, who was keeping them from learning of the knowledge of life.

In addition, the fruit was not actual fruit. It was the knowledge of life and of who they are.

Some beings were teaching Adam and Eve about the knowledge of life and who they are, the other being (that was called god) did not like the idea, and told Adam and Eve that those beings are of evil and they need to stay away from them and not to learn of the knowledge that those beings are teaching.

You would think that this so called (god) would want the human race to know the knowledge of life and of who they are. You would think that a benevolent being, (that is taking the role of i.e. god), would encourage the knowledge about life and of other worlds around other stars which hold life, but the opposite occurred. This being did not want the human beings to grow in knowledge and in spirituality. This being wants to create fear towards these other beings in anyway possible, including turning the story inside out, just to make the people

Book 3 – The Knowledge that was once forbidden by some of the Ancient Beings

fear those other beings that exist. Just so this being called god, could rule by fear, over these people and this planet/star system.

This so-called god tried to control Adam and Eve in thinking that those beings that were teaching this knowledge were evil.

In fact, this so-called god was deceiving them all, (the human race) on thinking this way.

We all know what happened then. The human race secretly met with these benevolent beings that were teaching them about the knowledge of life and about who they are in the scheme of life.

So, this so-called god learned of what Adam and Eve had gone and done. So this so-called god had punished them for disobeying their go, for going out and learning of this knowledge that they were told not to learn.

Now if this were a god of righteous and of truth, knowledge, and wisdom, then why would some of these beings go about keep all this knowledge from all the beings that wish to know of it?

Why should we accept this being as god, if all he does is punish all the beings (humans) for learning?

In fact, this so-called god is the deceiver of life. This so-called god should be the on that we should be avoiding, and not the others that we are being told to stay away from.

Now, for the aspects on the story of The Tower of Babel of Babylon, the humans attempt to rise up a Shem (Shem and the term shamain (heaven), stem from the root word shamah, meaning, that which is high ward).

Book 3 – The Knowledge that was once forbidden by some of the Ancient Beings

The biblical tale of the Tower of Babel deals with events that followed the repopulating of Terra after the Deluge.
"Let us build us a city,
And a tower whose top shall reach the heaven;
And let us make us a Shem,
Lest we be scattered upon the face of the Terra,"
But this human scheme was not to God's liking. And the lord came down, to see the city and the Tower, which the Children of Adam, (the human race) had erected.
And he said: "Behold,
All are as one people with one language,
And this just the beginning of their understandings;
Now, anything, which they shall scheme to do
Shall no longer be impossible for them."
Moreover, the lord said to some of his colleagues...
"Come, let us go down,
And there confound their language so that they may
Not understand each other's speech,"
And the lord scattered them from there
Upon the face of the whole earth,
And they ceased to build the City.
Therefore was its name called Babel?
For there did the lord mingle the Earth's tongue."

This was done so the people would not understand one another's language. But in time we were able to learn each other's languages. This so-called god tried to prevent people from being one with each other. Nevertheless, this language barrier did not last long.

Book 3 – The Knowledge that was once forbidden by some of the Ancient Beings

One thing remains for us today, which is to accomplish becoming one with each other, and putting aside our differences. That way what this so-called god did not want us to accomplish, did not work. It is taking us a while, but we will get there.

When you look at the word shem use "sky borne vehicle" rather than, "name" for the word shem, which is the term used in the original Hebrew text of the Bible. The story would then deal with the concern of humankind that, as the people spread upon Terra, they would lose contact with one another. Therefore, they decided to build a "sky borne vehicle" and to erect a launch tower for such vehicles. Like they are so called gods that they fly around.

Look at the Airships we have today.

In the story the "Epic of Creation" relates that the first "Gateway of the gods" was constructed in Babylon by the gods themselves. These gods were also known as the Anunnaki.

Which also ordered:

The construction of the Gateway of the gods....

Some time prior to the human race building their tower, which was known as the Tower of Babel, which was also built in Babylon, we had the same event going on here, several thousand years later, that had taken place with Adam and Eve.

The gods did not like the human race evolving to where they, (these so called gods), were at in knowledge. So, these so called gods came down to earth and tried to put a stop to the entire human race, from learning about the knowledge of life.

Book 3 – The Knowledge that was once forbidden by some of the Ancient Beings

We hear about these events happening through out all ages including today. We do not have the problem of these so called gods coming down and keeping us from learning the knowledge of what life is about. But we do have the problem of the governments and religions that are keeping us from learning of the knowledge about life.

However, we do have the help of these same star beings that started teaching us way before the time of Adam and Eve, about the knowledge of what life is all about.

So what does all this mean? Some of these beings that are from the stars are going about creating fear, and those same beings are within our governments and religions around this world and others.

This means that they are bringing into manifestation and creating this idea that the humans should fear their gods, when these beings are playing the roles of these gods to get the human race to live their life in fear.

The religions go about telling the people that they need to live their life a certain way, the way that God wants them to live. And if they do not live by those standards that the religions dictates to the people, then their God will bring about punishment or God will bring about the End Times to the people of Terra for going against their God.

The next few pages are about the Ark of the Covenant and the stories that the Ark was used as a weapon.

Book 3 – The Knowledge that was once forbidden by some of the Ancient Beings

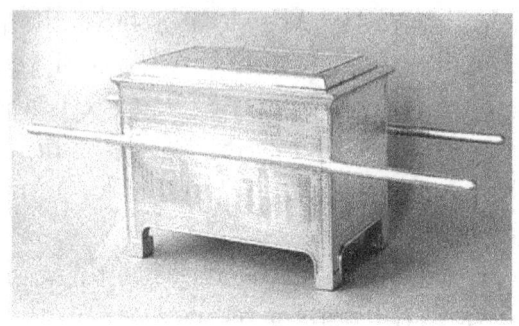

A model of the Ark

It is said that only the high priests were allowed near and to operate the Ark.

Book 3 – The Knowledge that was once forbidden by some of the Ancient Beings

It is said that the Ark of the Covenant was actually a weapon and that only certain priests were allowed to carry the Ark.

When these priests carry this Ark into a city, and activate the energy of this Ark, the Ark starts to emit energy bolts from it, (like lightening) which come out of it and strike people, killing them. After this event was finished, the priest deactivated the Ark and left the city. All or most of the inhabitants were killed.

It is also said in these stories that this priest used this Ark to destroy and to level entire cities to rubble. Travelers at later time came upon these cities and found those inhabitants burned beyond recognition, and that the cities were in rubble.

Book 3 – The Knowledge that was once forbidden by some of the Ancient Beings

Along with these stories, there are pictographs/drawings of this Ark being carried by priests and being taken into the cities and showing this Ark emitting lightening from it, and showing people being hit by this lightening and laying on the ground dead.

Some say this is the wrath of God killing people. Now tell me why this so-called god would want to kill the people of Terra?

The priests of the Ark would go about convincing those people of that age, that those people that the Ark had killed were wicked, and God killed them to set an example to the others, to hope to teach them not to disobey their God, or they will be punished or killed.

To this day, those religious people that live their life in fear of this so-called god go around killing people, time and time again.

This is a proven fact. That this so-called God, which had gone about killing people in the past for going against this gods so called belief structure, it is there in plain site.

This being that is called God, had gone about killing people, and destroying cities, and even going as far as annihilating all of civilizations on the entire world, at times.

For the question above, why is this god going about killing people and even destroying civilizations at times?

This is how I see it, and this is the truth!

Book 3 – The Knowledge that was once forbidden by some of the Ancient Beings

So the human race would not learn about who they are, and about life. This was to keep the humans from becoming spiritually attuned and to keep them from their leap forward in spirituality.

This is why these Guardians are here on this planet and on many other planets as well. Which is to teach all life about their spiritual evolution of growth of life, despite what these so-called gods want.

Here is a story that all are familiar with. It's about the Ark of the Covenant of the gods.

This is an excellent story of the anger of the gods, with the human race that wanted to learn of the knowledge of life. Along with the NeTeR, that was teaching this knowledge to the human race.

This shows how far these so-called gods would go about protecting this knowledge. They will go about destroying all that want to learn of the truth of life. This also goes for all that teach about the truth of life. It is also known that these so-called gods will even go about destroying a planet. Just take a look at the Asteroid belt in your Solar System.

Book 3 – The Knowledge that was once forbidden by some of the Ancient Beings

You can see an Ark of the Covenant in the city. The Ark is at left and in the middle, between the pillars. You can see some of the people removing those that are dead while others are weeping for those that this Ark had killed.

Book 3 – The Knowledge that was once forbidden by some of the Ancient Beings

Below is a sketch of what the Tower of Babylon looked like.

When the so-called god came down and saw what the humans had erected, he did not take a liking to what they were doing. The god put an end to the construction...

You need to ask yourself the question, why would any being go about destroying the people or even the cities?

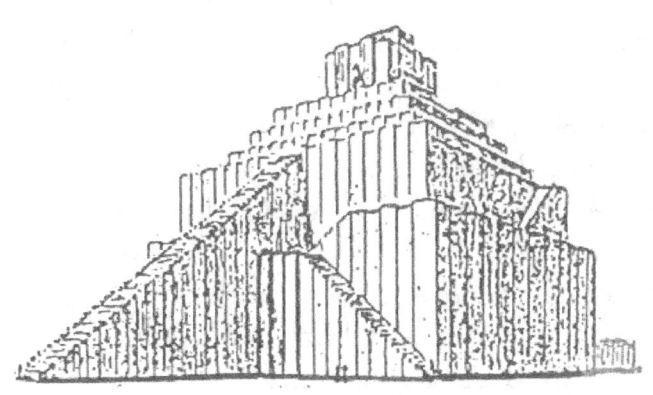

Book 3 – The Knowledge that was once forbidden by some of the Ancient Beings

Chapter 26

Removing the Acknowledgment of Ancient Technology and Knowledge of Life

As you have read though out all three of these books, it is certain that there are beings in the universes that do not want other beings to evolve in their spiritual growth. There are other beings that promote this knowledge of spiritual growth, enlightenment, and who we all are.

You learned through these books about how some of these beings wanted to control all life on Earth and among the stars.

I have shown how all these stories of today came to be misinterpreted and how these stories became negative, from their original state.

I also brought to light that these beings that came from the stars, had the technology to travel the stars. They also obtain the knowledge from other beings of the universes, which they traveled to. Then they taught this knowledge to all other inhabitants of other star systems that they came upon. At the same time, these other star beings went against this teaching of this

Book 3 – The Knowledge that was once forbidden by some of the Ancient Beings

knowledge of life, which they had learned, through their journeys through the stars.

We know that the ancient Sumerians, back 7,000 years ago knew a lot more about the stars and planets than we know about the planets and stars in our day in age.

All this makes one wonder, how is all of this is possible?

Well, they had the technology of space travel. Which is the same technology that we are just learning about in the past 40 years and have very little understanding of it at this point.

So now one can ask, where is all this technology that these pre-ancient civilizations once had?

Or is this all someone's fantasy, about these pre ancient civilizations having this type of high space traveling technology? Do they have some other technology, as well to construct these large stone towers/pyramid cities and the knowledge about life?

Well, I can tell you that all of this is not a fantasy. It is all true. These pre-ancient civilizations did in fact have all this technology and the knowledge of what life is all about.

One can ask, if these ancient civilizations did have all this technology, then where is it?

On the other hand, did they take it all with them when they left Earth around 1000 B.C.E.?

My thoughts on this matter are my thoughts alone.

Some of this technology was left behind and it does exist, and the governments of Eria have recovered it. How did this government go about

Book 3 – The Knowledge that was once forbidden by some of the Ancient Beings

recovering this technology without the people realizing what our government is up to?

What is the one thing that draws everybody's attention away from everything else?

The answer is, WAR!

Then one can say, where do most of the wars that transpire take place? These wars take place on the continent of Tampaurban, around the locations of those ancient civilizations.

So, one might assume that these wars are a diversion to get people's attention drawn away from what is really going on, on the continent of Tampaurban. So as our attention is drawn to these wars, this so called secret government is taking this ancient technology out of that continent. And at a later time they will study it, and learn how it works, than they will develop this technology, and use it any way they chose.

This all makes you wonder. Look at the technology that our government/scientists have developed over the past 60 years, since the 1950s. One can only wonder where that technology came from. There is new technology that has been in the proto type for the past 20 years, which is just being made known to the people, now, in 2004.

So you can wonder again, what is our government really up to, and what type of technology are they developing now, based on what they are taking? Where will this new type of technology take us, in say the next 20-30 years?

Then one can ask another question.

Book 3 – The Knowledge that was once forbidden by some of the Ancient Beings

What happens to these ancient cities after the government takes the technology that was left by these star beings?

Well, they might go about destroying the evidence that talks about this technology/knowledge, which may be part of a wall, which will show this technology?

Or, they might even go as far as destroying the whole entire city to rubble?

They might even bury the city, by moving, thousands and thousands of tons of sand.

I feel that our government in the U.S. will do just about anything to get the technology they want, and they will cover up where they are getting this technology from, that they are developing.

One can also wonder, what this technology that our government/scientists are developing, is going to be used for?

We know for sure, that these pre-ancient civilizations had this technology, and the knowledge about life, because their knowledge of the stars, dates back well over 12,000 years. We are just literally, beginning to learn about our star system since the 1700's. And we are still in the beginning stages, the kindergarten grade, of learning about space travel, and about ourselves..

These beings of these ancient civilizations were at a hundred times in their knowledge of the universes and of understanding who they were, and who we are today.

Book 3 – The Knowledge that was once forbidden by some of the Ancient Beings

All this makes one think, what is life about? What is not being told to us? Why are the religions around the world trying so hard to hide this knowledge about who we are, and about life?

This knowledge of life is for all to know, no matter what.

Book 3 – The Knowledge that was once forbidden by some of the Ancient Beings

Chapter 27

Essence of our Existence

What is this essence? This essence is the existence of all life. It binds all life together. Be it human, animal, plant, water, land, and the positive and negative energy of the universes. Our existence is all part of this essence of life. All essence is of positive and negative energy. This essence, energy of life, makes us what we are and how we interact with life? This essence molds the energy, which creates our lives from our very being and it guides us through our existence that brings about our journeys, which make up our destiny.

Through this essence of energy we our guided to experience events in our lives, be it of positive and or negative energy, (experiences). This energy of life shapes us into what we will become later. It's based on how we experience this energy of positive and negative, which binds all life together, in one form or another. How we experience this energy will determine the outcome of the experiences, along with how long we go through the experience. Which is also based on how we acknowledge the experiences that we witness, through our journeys in life.

There is one favorite saying about the aspects of negativity-but also true with the other energy, positive.

Once you start down the path of darkness, which is (fear, hate, and anger) forever consuming you. Moreover, it will become part of your destiny of who you will become.

Both paths of this essence of life are positive and negative energy. The path of the positive is that of mind at peace, love, tranquility, and harmony. And the path of negative is that of, hate, anger, confusion, and destruction.

The path of negative energy is subtler in making the person think that this path is the easiest to go through. But in fact it is the quickest. Mainly because it can make the person think what their experiencing is for the better, and that it is the easiest to comprehend. But in fact it is the harder of the two experiences.

These are the paths of the essence of life. We all end up going through them at one point in our life regardless if we want to or not. We cannot pick and choose which ones we want to avoid.

It is how we go about experiencing from interacting with the essence of life that will dominate one way or another. Nevertheless, we all have this free will to change our experience and our existence to one form or another.

Book 3 – The Knowledge that was once forbidden by some of the Ancient Beings

Removing all Veils

Wonder why all this fear about teaching this knowledge of life, which these so-called gods possess? Why do some of these beings that are playing these roles of gods, fear those beings that are teaching this knowledge?

If all beings understood about the knowledge of who each of us are, (meaning you, all beings of life), then these so-called beings that think they need to play the roles of gods and devils would fail. Their main proposes is to create fear and control over life, just to show other beings that are in control of life in the universes.

No one has the right to control another being that wants to learn all aspects of life. This also goes for these beings that are playing the roles of gods and devils. They think they need to control life with their fears.

Everyone has the right to ask questions about life, and they should receive the right answers, the truth, and not the lame excuses that they go about telling people.

If you think that this knowledge is of evil, then you are going down the wrong path. God wants you to go this way. You should not be asking those questions. We cannot talk about those things. People are told by their religions that they need to stay clear of anyone that is involved in the aspects of the supernatural or the spiritual/metaphysical part of life and the list goes on with out end.

Book 3 – The Knowledge that was once forbidden by some of the Ancient Beings

The existence on Terra and any other planet or plane of existence is to learn and to grow in knowledge and in spirituality.

Nevertheless, it appears that some of these beings do not want that.

Why are the religions and the governments so desperate to keep this knowledge from the people at any cost, which includes lies and deception, just to control the people?

With all this in mind you will come across religions saying all this is impossible, this cannot be done. The only reason they say this is because, the religions teach that light/dark and positive/negative are two separate beings and not one being.

This is why religions were created, to bring about fear and confusion. This was to keep all beings from becoming the spiritual beings that you are.

I urge all to learn the truth of what the knowledge of life holds for all to experience. Along with the acknowledgment of what this essence of life is about. You will learn the true essence of your being of becoming these spiritual beings that all of you are.

In addition if you break away from these religions, you will start to see this truth. At that time you will start your reawakening of your knowledge of the essence of life, and of whom you are, along with what you are able to become and do, as the being that you are.

Now, what follows are the key factors for going about removing the veils that are keeping you from

Book 3 – The Knowledge that was once forbidden by some of the Ancient Beings

moving forward in life and becoming the spiritual being that all of you really are.

You have come this far in life. You have been here lifetime, after lifetime living the same way, which is being controlled on how to live your life.

You owe it to yourself to step up and remove these veils that keeps you from being who you are.

Now this is the time that all of you shall begin your reawakening. Start removing these veils that have been placed on you by these other beings that want to keep you from learning of who you are.

What Knowledge did these Benevolent Beings procure during their existence, then and now, about the existence of life?

The Ancient of Beings learned that life is energy, and that all beings and all aspects of life (humans (on or off the planet), animals, plants, and planets) are connected to each other including, all-positive and negative energies. We give our essence to create negative energies, and we can cease this energy from being created, which takes away the negative form.

By doing this we need to accept that we created all this, positive and negative energies and that we all are of one essence, energy.

In the Kabala, it teaches that the Armageddon, the battle of good and dark, will be fought in everybody, and in their soul.

The evil/negativity exist in all of us. If we deny this, we give evil power over us.

Book 3 – The Knowledge that was once forbidden by some of the Ancient Beings

Once this is accepted, then you defeat it, and destroy the evil/negative energy.

This is the way you need to accept, this evil/negative energy, in order to become that spiritual being that you are to become!

I become one with everything,
I become one with you.
I become everything,
Therefore I become nothing.
Therefore you are nothing.
Without my anger, you have no substance.
Without my pride, you have no form.
Without my hate, you have no being.
Its time for you to leave.
You have no place here.
I'm apart of you now.

Once you come to terms with this understanding of the above, that (evil), negativity is part of you.

From this you bring life into the existence of this negativity energy. You had separated yourself from this negativity, without realizing that this is also part of you as well.

This is where religions keep you in the dark, on telling you that positive and negative are of two separate beings/entities. They are only separate entities, by the means of their teachings, only. This is what religions do not want you to understand and to learn.

Book 3 – The Knowledge that was once forbidden by some of the Ancient Beings

You must understand fully of this concept, that you are the creator, of everything around you, along with the persons next to you, so on and so on, they too, are also the creators, of the things around them. Then we are all creators experiencing each other's creations.

After truly learning of this knowledge, then you can know who you are, and what we are capable of becoming.

After you have accepted and understood this knowledge of life, then you would truly know who you are, along with what life is about.

Which is that the future and the past, are all part of the now, and that we all are the giver and the taker, and that we all can be in many places at once, that we all are the masters of our own fate. We are the Creator and the Creation.

From all this brings the knowledge that you are the god that you are seeking outside of yourself. You are your own creator.

This understanding of this knowledge is not easy, and it does not come overnight. The knowledge of life comes with the experience of life.

Some people, those of the religions, say this knowledge is not for us to learn at this time. And the only time that we can learn this knowledge is when we pass away, from this existence. Well, why wait to learn the knowledge of life after you pass away?

Why put off until later, when you can do it now?

Book 3 – The Knowledge that was once forbidden by some of the Ancient Beings

Now, learn the Knowledge of Life, and know, who you are!

As you learn this knowledge, you will be removing the veils of illusions of life.

Ever going forward

This is not the end!
This is not the beginning of the end!
This is the end of the beginning!

It does not end here. It ever goes on. Always going to the beyond the beyond. From one existence of life, to another life, so on, so on. Never ending with only one life or even with many lives. Life is like a ladder, each step is a life that you, we, all go through and experience.

Learn of who you are, this can be reawakened at this point in your life.

There is no god that will come to Terra and punish you for learning of the truth, as I had brought to your attention through out these books. For the past 3,000 years, there has not been any presence of these gods, making themselves known too the world, at this day in age.

Nevertheless, you are told through your religions that you must obey these so-called gods, or be punished.

Book 3 – The Knowledge that was once forbidden by some of the Ancient Beings

So, why is there all this fear towards these so-called gods that you cannot see?

The wait is over, take this next step and learn, reawaken the knowledge within you.

This knowledge of life is there for all to know. And for all to become, that being that you are.

Book 3 – The Knowledge that was once forbidden by some of the Ancient Beings

The thought,
Brings the experience,
Into existence.
Which starts a chain reaction.
As it brings forth knowledge,
Which reawakens who we are,
Bringing total awareness.
All veils are removed.

A Journey into the Spiritual Quest of Who We Are
Complete 4 BOOK in 1

Book 4
The Quantum Leap into Consciousness

Book 4 – The Quantum leap into Consciousness

Book 4 – The Quantum leap into Consciousness

Preface

Within is the fourth and final installment of the Kiazerian Journals, *A Journey into the Spiritual Quest of Who We Are.*

Herein Kiazer continues delving ever deeper, into the unknown, but also known. He continues removing the veils of illusion placed upon us around twelve thousand years ago. Understand this was done to keep us from learning the truth about ourselves.

I, the author, can only hope, that given all the knowledge Kiazer has shared with you throughout this entire series, you all will gain a much wider view of life and learn about who you really are. I hope that the insights that I have shared with you will help you in your reawakening, and I hope it helps to remove the veils of illusions. However, it is all up to each one of you to choose how you look at and use this knowledge of life that I am passing on to you throughout this series.

We all have to take this road in learning about who we are at some point in our lives. We all have those same questions about what life is all about and what it all means.

Finally, I hope that I had helped all of you to start your journey, in one form or another.

Book 4 – The Quantum leap into Consciousness

Chapter 28

The Creation of the Veils of Illusions

*The human species really has no
idea who they really are,
since their consciousness has been asleep
for the past twelve thousand years!*

*It is time to, remove the veils of
illusions that we have all been living within!*

Kiazer talks to a group of people, he says "I have already shown you examples on how these beings have gone about creating fear and control. Now do you see the purpose for the veils that were created and placed upon you, for one reason and one reason alone?

That reason was that these beings which had evolved before us thought they needed to create these veils of illusion to keep other beings from evolving in the knowledge of life. That knowledge is learning who we are as a spiritual being and learning what we are capable of becoming, through this knowledge of life.

So these older beings created stories to get the younger generation to believe in a certain way, which would keep us from asking and wondering of who we are in our life. So these beings created these stories which consist of telling the younger generations that they need to believe in a certain way based on this religious structure. This belief has been passed down from generation to generation with the fear of a god and that we all will be judged at the end of our life, based on how we lived our life based on this belief towards these so-called religions with these so-called gods."

As Kiazer walked around the group he mentions that "for some of those older beings of the past they did not want the younger generations evolving behind them, because some of these beings wanted to be in control of other beings/other civilizations that have not yet evolved like them. These stories are told repeatedly. In addition, no one can bring himself or herself to question the truth of these stories. This is mainly because most of the people in this day in age still live in fear of these beings that were playing these roles of these so-called gods thousands of years ago. Which I will remind all of you again that for the past six thousand years and as of now, no one has seen these so-called gods that people of today thought existed well over two thousand years ago. You will think at this day in age as this new millennium starts that people would have caught on by now, hearing the same stories repetitively and not witnessing a single god worldwide. You always hear people saying, "God says I must believe and act this way, or else." However, if you ask people did they see a god standing next to them when "he said" you must believe this way. People will say no, there was nobody next to me, but I heard a voice that told me that I must believe this way."

Kiazer said with sincerity and a louder voice, "Well if I heard a voice I would not call it god that's for sure. Even if this voice told me that he was god, I would ask him to prove it, because I know that all beings evolve at different times than others. It still does not make that being more of a god, than we as beings ourselves are."

The stories of these gods that were told well over ten thousand years ago still bring fear into people of today. This keeps the people from questioning the stories that they have heard that have been passed down through the ages. As long as you fear to look and question these stories, the longer it will be before you realize who you are. In addition, this will add to the time that you let these unseen so-called gods rule over your life with fear.

These stories were created as a veil to create the confusion which kept everyone at a stagnant evolution. People will continue telling these stories, of fear of these gods coming to judge them based on their religious beliefs, which were passed down. And these stories do change, with every time they are told. It was designed that way to keep all people confused in life and to bring the fear so they would not ask and wonder what life is about.

What a terrible way to live your life, and a controlled life at that point!

Why would anyone consider living a life under these conditions? This way of life takes away your life as the spiritual being that you are.

Why surrender your essence/your energy of life, to those beings? All they want is to control you and they are not even a god!

I have shown a lot to you through the previous three books. Some of these stories, of some of these beings, on their ways of controlling and bringing fear are to keep all of you from learning of the truth.

I am going to give you two more short examples of those stories of how these beings go about controlling you with these veils.

The first one is based on those Star Wars movies with the use of the Force – positive and negative energies. You have a being that is drawn to the negative energy and they use it as a way to control other beings in thinking since their power is stronger, (since it is of negativity). These beings go about making any civilization on any planet think that they have the power to destroy them if those civilizations do not obey this particular being. This being is of negative energy and creates fear to control a civilization into believing in this manner, so the civilizations go about obeying this being or they will be destroyed.

The second is from the stories of the movie Stargate and the TV series Stargate SG1 and their new series Stargate Atlantis. You have a being that had

Book 4 – The Quantum leap into Consciousness

evolved to a point where it needs a host to continue to survive. This being is of a serpent – (snake), which needs a host – a human body or a humanoid body, so this being can continue on living for several hundreds of years or longer.

Now we have the mergence of two beings in one body. This evolved serpent being takes control of the body which it merged with, then they go about creating fear by the means of using this body to make other civilizations obey this being and make these civilizations think that this being is their gods.

Then you have civilizations fearing this being that is taking on this role of a god. Now you have these civilization fearing to question and afraid to learn of the truth. Then this being tells these civilizations that they need to believe this way and do not question their god, or they will be punished.

This all sounds too familiar to what is going on, on this planet with all the religions of these so-called beings that are playing these roles of gods and along with the governments, they all are creating this fear. These veils which were created, worked so well that you lived your entire life in fear of these stories of gods coming to Terra and judging you, if you went against these gods belief systems. For the past several thousands of years these veils worked so well that you forgot who you are.

With this insight you will understand how these beings are controlling you. You are allowing them to do so through your fears, and all these stories that you continue telling time after time.

How much longer are these stories of fear going to continue in your life?

Most of everyone today has lived their life by these stories. They only know about these stories because of their strong religious belief, which goes about telling them do not look at any other beliefs. In addition, their religions tell them do not question what is being told to you by their religions. People are also told that this is the only way of living your life and that there is no other way.

But there are a few people that know that there is more to life than what we are being told. We know this to be because we are not allowing ourselves to be controlled.

The old way of living is not needed any longer for us. We have lived this way far too long. Some people had that spark – a light within them that started that awakening and they realized these illusions were controlling them. Soon after they began to remove these veils, it started the reawakening of their spiritual self. They started this journey of a spiritual quest to learn who they were.

All these religious figures are not taking this lightly, because they are loosing their control over us. Which means that we are waking up and removing these veils of illusions and we are learning of this knowledge of life that we are part of, which they spent their entire life suppressing. As you begin to shed these veils, you will begin to see what the religions did not want you to see and to know the truth on what life is.

Breaking Away

As you start your quest into your spiritual journey, you will begin to see how you were controlled by these stories of fear, which kept you stagnant from learning of the truth. You will be free to ask questions and to piece your search together on what life is really about, and you will learn about the many aspects that life has waiting for you.

As you begin this breaking away from this old way of life, it will be very confusing, since it is all new to you, in a way of speaking. You will find those stories which will conflict with the old way that you were brought up to believe in on how life was and how it is supposed to be as. There is a lot of knowledge out there, about life and who we are. You are not going to piece it all together, in a year or two, three. At least you have your foot in the doorway and you have the door open, to learn what has been kept from you all these years. Just reading this series shows you just that, this is your first step in that reawakening.

As you go down this road of learning about these aspects of life, it will feel as if this knowledge of life just keeps on flowing in like the faucet on a sink, turned on full and you cannot turn it off. It just keeps coming and coming.

Yeah, it will slow down enough so you can assess what has been presented to you. As soon as you have pieced together what you have just learned, it will start again with more knowledge about life. And once again you will have the time to assess what you had just learned.

You will start beginning to see how all the knowledge you were given falls into place, the things you were told to avoid so that you would not learn. I have brought some of this to light throughout this series. I have only presented a fraction of the pieces that are the main important part of my search to show where I am coming from with my knowledge of what is missing within this vast life of ours. I have only presented a very small tip of an iceberg, so to say, about the knowledge of life, beyond what we are brought up to believe in.

As you continue to delve ever deeper into the ancient myths of ancient forgotten knowledge of the ancient civilizations, you will also learn why those stories were changed from age to age. Now you can see why this confusion was brought about with today's belief systems.

Now you begin to piece together what the religious figures know and tried to keep from you. Now you begin to realize the truth, behind the creation of these veils of illusions. As you learn more of the truth, you will find yourself not looking at religions in the same way, if you even look at them at all.

You are learning the truth of what life is about now. As you continue to unravel each story that you find which is older than the previous story, you will begin to see why these older stories were changed to the way they are today. These stories were changed to bring confusion about in life, to keep people from wanting to learn the knowledge of life, so people would not learn about the true aspects of their spiritual self and of who they are.

However, this is what you have done when you went out and started reawakening the knowledge of who you are.

This is what the religions were afraid might happen. They knew if you went out and learned the truth of who you are, that they would no longer have control of your life and that these beings had failed their so-called mission (keeping you from learning of the truth). As you continue down that path of spiritual reawakening, you become that spiritual being that we all are. And as long as you continue on this path these beings that want control over you will no longer have that control. For the past three thousand years all this knowledge about life was put aside by the religious figures. It is now being brought to light for all to learn the truth on what life is all about.

Claim the truth about what life is about, it is your right as the spiritual being you are.

Chapter 29

The Start of A New Age

Terra is about ready to make her quantum leap around 2020, where one Terrain world will stay in the 3rd dimension for those that need more time to make that transition of letting go of the old ways of life. The people of the 2nd world become the conscious beings and evolve from the original Terrain world and they will take that quantum leap into becoming that fully awakened conscious being.

Well I can say this, as I am writing now, which is December 2004, this particular event of having two Terrain worlds will not come to be as thought of in the past, this is due to the thought that this event of having two Terrain Worlds is no longer needed to be manifested.

Oh, we will have our quantum leap of consciousness!

For those that chose not to evolve spiritually, will leave Terra, for those that want war and to bring about war against other beings, they will not be part of Terra and they will be removed in one form or another.

Book 4 – The Quantum leap into Consciousness

The reason for the thought of having two Terra's in the past was mainly due to all the thought of negativity that most of the beings on your planet were creating within themselves and outside of themselves about life.

Since 1990 some people have been changing their thoughts of what is created around them. Plus the older generation of people of this negative thought of fear, war and destruction, have been leaving this planet. A new generation is being born, and these people are realizing its time for peace, a union is needed between all beings that are in existence on earth and amongst the universes.

After this transition is complete and we enter into our new age, you will feel as if the planet has become larger, but in fact the population will have dramatically been reduced to those that wish to evolve spiritually and peacefully and to become fully awakened conscious beings.

Let's hope that our past age of existence does not return to us at any time. Let's hope that we have learned our mistakes of the past eons.

Many people had come to fear this so called end times as told within the bibles.

Why so much fear towards an end?

It is all that control from all those belief systems that had created all that fear towards other beings of the past, the present, and the future. The belief systems created a negative view of life within most people about those battles of beings of good and evil, which will come to Terra to battle for the possession of this planet. The belief systems also created this fear within most people, that they need to live there life in a certain way to please their god(s) or their god(s) will judge them unworthy and that these god(s) will send the unworthy ones to the void or hell or whatever you want to call it. This is not so, as I mentioned and have shown you throughout this series.

This old pattern of energy is no longer part of the Terra's star system, as it prepares for a new beginning.

At the end of 1985, the Piscean age ended. It lasted for about 6 thousand years, and was known as the Dark Age, for its negative aspects such as war, turmoil, fear, and the controlling of the masses through deceptions such as the creation of the gods and devils theory, as has been described throughout this series.

1985 – 2000 was known as the transition period, the removing of the negative aspect (energy) of that previous age as described throughout this series.

As for this star system, it does not need this negative energy of any sort any longer. This planet has no need for this negative energy, which about 75 percent of her population had created for all to experience in one form or another during the Piscean Age. This planet no longer has any use of beings and/or people that desire to be negative and bring about destructiveness to those beings and/or people that are pure and positive. Those beings and people that are of negative will no longer be part of the earth or part of this universe, since everything is moving towards the positive energy.

It is at this point in time that everyone needs to restructure their views and thoughts and to let go of the previous age of thoughts of life. Let it all go, it is no longer a part of the New Age of Aquarius – The Age of Light.

Indeed 1985 was the end times, the end of an Age and a start of a new beginning, a new age.

The years 2000 – 2012 deal with the restructuring of the new energy for this new age. This new energy is of positive aspects, such as peace, harmony, and tranquility – all of humanity on Terra living as one. The end of 2012 begins our new age known as the Aquarian Age of Light.

This new age that we will enter in 2012 will bring forth the knowledge of life of who we are, in retrospect to those other beings which exist amongst the universes seen and unseen, as I presented throughout this series.

The knowledge of who we are will no longer be suppressed in this universe that we reside in.

As the earth and her people move forward in the evolution, so does the galaxy that we reside in, and so will the universe that our galaxy resides within. We all are making this transition, this leap into awakening this knowledge of realizing our potential as conscious beings.

As we enter our new age, we reawaken this knowledge that was once held by those Ancient of beings of ancient times that were on this planet earth, well over twenty thousand years ago.

This knowledge of life and the understanding of who we are is nothing new, we all go through these cycles of life where this knowledge lays dormant within us for periods. Until we emerge from our time of being asleep, to this awakening, this leap of consciousness of knowledge, the knowledge within all of us, within all beings that subsist amongst all the universes seen and unseen.

Most have been down this path, this road of changing of the ages, but not many of you remember, but all of that is changing now.

Like life the cycles of the ages are the one in the same. It is the process of Life.

Life and every age have one thing which is common to one another. That is that from life you have death, and from death you have life again, this is the cycles of the essence of life and of the ages, life after another one, age after another. One Age is of light (becoming awakened) and the other is of dark (being asleep). These cycles are always going from one to the other and back through the cycles over and over again, without ever ending.

Each age goes from light to dark and back again, over and over again, the energy in each cycle is never the same. This is what we all are witnessing at this time, the end of an age and the start of a new age, the bringing fourth of this magnificent energy of light and peace to this new cycle of life.

You are all going to be part of the changes of course, and not everyone will survive these changes. For the ones that do survive, it will be a totally new place, a new planet for the future. In this cycle will come the revealing of the universal knowledge that's been kept hidden from many of you for about four thousand years. From this wisdom will come the everlasting peace that Terra, and her people have been expecting. Besides having peace, there will also be eternal life for those souls that choose free will, it's there for everyone.

Your new life within this era is a step up on the spiritual evolutionary ladder of the unlimited knowledge of the universal wisdom. In this era you will learn to develop into multi-dimensional beings, from this you will be leaving from your 3rd dimensional existence which is your 3rd dimensional solid body, to move into the 4th and 5th dimensional existence. Your soul and spirit will be able to exist outside of one another, at the same time simultaneously, coexisting within each others creations and being totally aware of your other self.

This is the knowledge that has been dormant within your soul and spirit for thousands of years. The human race has always been trying to find the so-called missing link to evolution.

Well, it has been inside each and every one of you for thousands and thousands of years. It never left, not even for a second; you just did not want to take on the responsibilities. Do you see, what I am saying here?

This means going into the unknown, not knowing what might be coming your way, if it is for worse or for the better for your soul. But either way, if you look at it now, you will benefit from your own experiences of these events that are in front of you. Of course, everything you experience will be a step up on the evolutionary scale of existence going towards becoming a multidimensional being.

Then the New Age is really a point in time where the soul of every being has the chance to start the beginning of their new life, if it is in another cycle of life, or another dimension of existence. This is transpiring at this time for all to experience.

Chapter 30

The Rite Of Passage

During long forgotten times, many thousands upon thousands of years ago, these ancient civilizations, including those civilizations from not so long ago, all had knowledge and wisdom about the spiritual aspects of life and what life truly was about. These ancient civilizations' were more spiritually attuned to their higher selves. They were thousands of times more attuned than what we are today.

Those beings of the ancient times lived as one with all Terrain's and cherished each life that was upon Terra. All beings knew that they themselves and their world had a purpose in the cycle of life. Through this involvement, these beings were united as one by their spirituality and through the emergence with the Terrain's spirit. Being interconnected to each other and the planet itself, resulted in a merging that lifted the very essence of those beings to a higher spiritual understanding. Imagine what it was like to be aware and attuned, and living on a conscious planet. Terra, being conscious herself, taught those inhabitants

Book 4 – The Quantum leap into Consciousness

about the cycles of life and about the spiritual growth of all life, including the planet, animals, plants, and even people. It was virtually the same for all types of beings.

This spiritual learning about life was not confined to the planet alone, because Terra travels through the Milky Way Galaxy and the beings that live on her gain knowledge about our solar system and the stars within this universe. The Terrains also learned that the universe is a consciousness living being and that the universe itself has life cycles involving the spiritual growth of creation. This is what the Terrain's spirit taught the inhabitants as they journey through the galaxy.

As Terra and her inhabitants journeyed through the universe, they crossed paths with other star systems that had other civilizations amongst them. Some of these beings within those other star systems were at greater or lesser degrees of spiritual evolution than the Terrain's were. In addition, some of those other civilizations were at the same level of spiritual growth as the beings of Terra.

After many generations, and as Terra continues her journey through the universe, the inhabitants began to understand more and more about their spirituality, life, and who they are. The inhabitants began to understand all aspects of many creations and their part in this cycle of life. The Terrains were realizing the essence of life, which is the essence of creation, and this realization alone has many aspects of growth within it. These beings were learning that the very nature of life consists of both physical and spiritual (energy) aspects. For instance, they learned about both the physical and spiritual essences of life, which can be physical or nonphysical (energy) and that neither can exist without its counterpart.

They knew that all these nonphysical (energy) bodies had their own physical structure, were beyond physical viewing. This takes into account that both astronomical bodies, such as planets, and other physical bodies, that are of humanoid form, are affected by being created out of nothing, and not always visible through physical perception.

Along with the physical aspects of all life, they also have other unseen energy, which is just beyond the physical perception, and although unseen, it can be felt. This energy (spirit) interacts with us in many ways and it shows us things in ways that we cannot perceive through our five senses, these ancient beings learned about their existence within both nonphysical energies of (soul – spirit), and physical matter. They are aware that both parts of themselves exist together as one unified being. Because if one form of their selves does not think that the other form exists, then the other part would not exist either. It is only through this acceptance of both forms, the physical (matter), and non-physical (spirit – soul / energy), exist through one another's thought (creation)- that each creates the other. Therefore, both beings exist together, but one cannot exist without the thought of their other, physical or nonphysical aspects of one's own self. It is in the thinking, which goes about creating each other at the same time in life.

These ancient beings understood the true meaning of the creation of life. That meaning is that the evolution process of the essence of the DNA that is spread across the multi universes. These nonphysical beings if they were of (the energy of souls / spirits) were able to watch life itself be created on a subatomic level as the planet evolved. This brought forth the creations of the many physical beings that that the planet had in mind at that particular time of the planets evolution. Then, after that creation was manifested into physical form, and after several millions of years, these ancient beings of energy and of spirit/soul, would eventually merge into those physical creations, bringing with them their knowledge of the vastness of the universes that these ancient beings had once came from to impart to those physical beings.

As these ancient beings of energy and those of souls/spirits started a new "co-existence" for all beings, they knew as they were in this physical form and living this life, they were involved in a new understanding of existence, which would be living as their energy existence or of their soul/spirit, within a physical form, until the next cycle where all will be separated as individuals once again.

This is what is meant by cycles of creation between the physical and the beings of souls/spirits along with the ancient beings that had evolved into energy.

These beings began to realize that since they were creating their lives from incarnation to incarnation, it also meant that they must have been their own ancestors from time to time. Eventually, the knowledge that each life was their own, and they were recalling memories from several lives before, because they were aware that we go through living as spirit/soul or as an ancient being of energy, then merging within a physical life form and then the cycle starts over. Over and over again, experience after experience, which is what life is about, evolving physically and spiritually, into that being that we are. This is the same for all beings that are in existence and also for the planets and stars; they all go through this cycle of life, which is going from spirit (energy), into physical form and from physical into spirit (energy), lifetime after lifetime, ever so evolving from one form to the next.

These beings know this was the process of the cycles of life based on their knowledge, which they obtained when they came back into the physical world, from their existence as energy beings and as of a soul/spirit bringing the knowledge that they were finding what was left here from their previous lives. Such remembrances must be remnants from their previous lives, since they realized that they create their own material world, before they merged into a physical form again.

What these beings are remembering is past lives and what stage of evolution they were previously. They are able to recognize that they are evolving from what they were in the past to what they are at their present stage of evolution, not only physically and spiritually, but in some instances with their technology.

In other instances, at future lifetimes, these beings experience taking steps backwards in technology and lose knowledge about life and seemingly have to start all over again in learning about the true meaning of who we are.

During the past three thousand years to our present time, it seems that technology has been advancing by leaps and bounds. However, due to much knowledge of life being lost, the advanced technologies from some ancient civilizations have been hidden from us and it's as if we've been disconnected from the meaning of life altogether. We once understood the importance of cherishing all aspects of life. This used to include knowing that the human race lived as one and the understanding that we live on a conscious being, that is called planet Terra (Earth aka: Gaia).

Through these past two thousand years, we are repeating the same events unless we stop and realize what we are doing to ourselves as a human race. Look at what we have done to each other and to the planet that we all live on. At some point in the past, we all lived as one race on this conscious planet and we can do it again, if in the present time, enough of us become aware and enlightened about whom we really are.

Since we go through lifetime after lifetime on this planet, I can guarantee that we will be back on this conscious being in the not too distant future.

Sometime around twelve thousand years ago, our civilizations lost the knowledge of spirituality and we were brought up with the idea of a being that took on the role of a god. Additionally, that being was said to be male, it was claimed that he created everything, and we were told we should pray to him and recognize him as the almighty god.

Since then, all civilizations upon Terra were brought up with this concept of a being that is called god; a false notion is finally ending.

There is knowledge within all of us, but it has been shrouded in mysteries and concealed by the veils of illusions intended to keep us from learning about the true meaning of our essence and of life. This is mainly due to religions finding ways to control people and peoples' lives in many ways. Religions have been forced upon people, in part using crude behaviorism: with rewards and punishments. Though the use of fear, people can be manipulated. Religions threatened those who do not believe, with punishments such as eternal damnation (ie; burning in a hell fire for all of eternity). In contrast, rewards are offered to believers (eg; going to a supposedly blissful place called "heaven" for all of eternity).

However, for those experiencing the Rite of Passage, the path leads to learning the knowledge of life. These people are reawakening the essence that binds all life together. They are learning that they are all part of the essence of life and that we all create the existence that's around us, whether it's on Terra or it's among the stars.

As we enter into the new millennium 2,000 C.E. (Current Era), there are many individuals taking the Rite of Passage path. These people are realizing and understanding the knowledge of life and are starting to gain a different view of life. People of this new generation know that there is more to life than what they have been told through the years. As this knowledge from certain ancient civilizations is reawakened, the spiritual people along with the Shamans are reminding us that we, and the planet, are all connected to each other through what is called the essence. This essence is "the life force/energy, and it is not a, being (i.e. god), but it is energy which binds all life together within the universes, whether seen or unseen."

This is what this Rite of Passage is about, realizing that all those beings of the past, which were us going through this cycle lifetime after lifetime, are going to become like the spiritually advanced "ancients" in the future.

The Next Step on the Ladder of Evolution

For those that have chosen this period, to take the next step on the ladder of evolution, it will lead to a leap of evolution in consciousness. During this quantum leap in conscious evolution, you will merge into the very essence of life itself. You will be experiencing what will feel like a jolt of electrical current through both of your bodies, the physical as well as the spirit (energy). This jolt is the process of the knowledge of the essence of life. This knowledge is separate from what you had thought life was really about, this is the true knowledge of life, and you already have a glimpse of it throughout this series. This knowledge is remembered through that rite of passage, the path that you started. Through free will of choice, a decision to let go of false ideologies, you can reawaken the knowledge that is rightfully yours.

Without realizing it, we have all been on this ladder of evolution from the very beginning of time, and we have already started that next step in the process, which is part of that cosmic ladder of evolution.

It is through this knowledge, which is a means to an end along with your own insight into the questions of life and what life is all about, that you open up to knowledge within yourself. This is only the beginning of what is to come for those that are ready for it. However, for the other people that choose not to open their minds at this time, they will not be prepared to make this leap. Nevertheless, for you, this time has come. You took the initiative, and by taking a step forward beyond the fear, you are seeking answers from within yourself.

You are becoming that being, who no longer looks outside themselves and to religions to find answers. You are going beyond that wall, which many do not want to take down, and adventuring further.

As you reawaken to this knowledge of life, you will become teachers to those people who were once like you at some point. Those people who still fear what is beyond the unknown – beyond the unseen, beyond the unexplained – and beyond the beyond.

What is this next step of consciousness about?

What can be said about our next step of evolution?

What haven't I already presented throughout this series?

I hope all of you were taking notes!

Because, I do not think there is much more to talk about. I do believe that we brought all the knowledge to light about this next step of consciousness.

Well, you came this far in learning about the knowledge of life, and you are here once again to learn right? So why stop?

Ok, I see you choose to continue on, because you are still here.

Let's see what we can bring to light other than what we already presented to you.

This calls for all to participate in this exercise.
Take a moment; let's go outside and sit on the ground, now take a deep breath, and let it out, another deep breath and out, again, another deeper breath. Very good relax.

Clear your mind of all thoughts. Ok, are we ready? Good, let's begin.

The first and only question that I want all of you to ask is, "What is this next step of consciousness?"

Now look around you, look at the ground that you're sitting on…

Book 4 – The Quantum leap into Consciousness

Listen to what you hear around you…

Look at the sky, which is above you – if you are outside at night, look at the night sky with the stars…

Now close your eyes and sense what you feel, that which you cannot see…

Now, what you have learned about the knowledge of life?

What did you sense and feel during that moment?

Do not look for my answers on the next page because they are not there. They are throughout the entire series.
It is a process…

Your answers please…
(You can use a separate sheet of paper.)

……………………………………………………………………..

……………………………………………………………………

Now look at the people you see out and about. What do you feel and sense?

………………………………………………………………………

……………………………………………………………………..

Look at the animals around you as well.
What do you feel and sense about them?

……………………………………………………………………

……………………………………………………………………

Next, in your mind, unless you can physically, let's journey to see the whales and dolphins.
What do you feel and sense about them?

……………………………………………………………………

……………………………………………………………………

This time go deep within yourself, into your very "soul/essence".
What do you feel?

……………………………………………………………………

……………………………………………………………………

How about feeling the planet earth?
What do you feel within her energy?

……………………………………………………………………

……………………………………………………………………

Now look at the stars in the night sky.
What do you feel?

....

....

This is what the next step of our Quantum leap of consciousness is all about, people looking, feeling, understanding, and going beyond the beyond. Beyond the physical realms and tangible objects that are all around us.

As we venture into this next step, realize, and become what is around you. Learn what life is and what is truly waiting for you.

We must show the way to those who fear the unknown and the unseen aspects of life. Consider that at some point in ones life, some of us have feared the unknown and the unseen.

Remember, not all beings and people take this step of evolution at the same time. Therefore those of you who do take this step forward, please be prepared to teach those that have not taken this step forward for whatever reasons they have. Be patient with them and help them understand. Let them know that you were once where they are now and that they can move to the next step where you are at this point. It's important that you also remind them everyone is always moving onto the next step of life. It's just a matter of when. Remember the ladder that we all are on never ends because there is always something and/or someone who is beyond where you are. It's an ongoing path of evolution in consciousness.

This is what our next step on the ladder of evolution is all, it's not just that one-step per lifetime that people think it is. Every step is presented to all of us during every lifetime it is how many steps each of us are willing to take in our current lifetime. We are not limited to just taking one step. How many steps you take on this ladder of life is up to you and you alone.

Nevertheless, you also need to remember what you have learned is there for all to learn and become what you have became. You also need to teach those who have not learned what you have learned, so they too may become as you are.

Becoming fully Awaken Beings

As you begin taking this next step into the evolution of consciousness, there are several steps within this one step.

The first step was the exercise a couple pages back, that I had you do. That exercise was for you to see if you could feel the energy force within all things. This energy force is both inside and outside of you. It is intended to make initial contact with the energy force that binds all life together. This energy force is not a being that you call god, it is merely energy of all living beings no matter if they are human, animal, other beings, plants, rocks, the planets, or the stars. This energy force is even amidst the open space between the universes. This life force, this energy is everywhere and everything.

The second step within this consciousness is where you release any doubts that you are not worthy of becoming a reawakened being that's within yourself, because that is who you really are. If you've been told you could not become that being until a much later time, you must come to terms with yourself and let your inner self (your soul/essence) bring its consciousness forth. This will help you overcome any physical limitation that has been placed on the physical understanding of the physical and the inner self.

How does one take this step?

If you have any doubts that you are not ready or worthy, release them and say that you are ready to become awakened and that you want to become the being that is within you.

It will not happen if you do not want it to. You must want this to be, it is the only way for this to be brought forth. It must be of your own free will and wanting this to be. You must realize that you have accomplished all that you have set out to do in your existing incarnation, and that you are ready to move on to becoming that being you want to be. If you think that you have not accomplished what you set out to do, then you will not be able to move forward. Not until you realize that you have accomplished what you have set to do. That is necessary before you can become who you truly are.

If you chose not to become that being that's within you, you will stay where you are now and won't evolve into what you truly are. Once you accept who you are within yourself, don't continue to look outside yourself for whom you are, or else the being within you will not come forth. First, you have to realize that you have been looking outside yourself and shift your focus to your true inner self that's always been who you are. Then, you will become an awakened being amongst the many!

All that has been mentioned above is about becoming reawakened beings while in the physical form.

You can also achieve becoming that awakened being at the time of passing from this life to the next life. However, it is the same as the physical except nothing changes. It's just that you decided to continue your work on the other planes of existence.

On the other hand, you may choose to leave this life and come back into this physical life as a fully awakened being. All this can be achieved at this time due to the New Age we are now entering. In this New Age the knowledge of our fully awakened consciousness will be commonly known due to the many fully awaken beings whom are amongst you at this point. This is our next step in awakening the knowledge within about who we are.

There is no longer a need for these veils of illusion from the past ages because we are moving beyond this world of limitations.

Book 4 – The Quantum leap into Consciousness

We are now becoming awakened beings and becoming that being which we all have been looking outside of ourselves for, for the past twelve thousand years. We are now awakening the same knowledge that all the Ascended masters and the Spiritual teachers of the past were trying to teach us, for the past seven thousand years, of who we are, as a conscious being. It is within this time that we are now able to take this step into becoming fully awakened beings, and realizing whom we are.

As we begin to become the beings that we are, as we enter into our new cycle of life, we are also at the same awakening point of those ancient beings were at one-hundred thousand years ago during their existence and their spiritual awakening of learning of who they were as conscious beings. They too came to the realization that they were the one that they too were looking outside of themselves to find, as being the one, and the only one being. These ancient beings also finally came to the acceptance that they were there own creator and no one else was.

They realized that this one being, did not exist, that it really was themselves being separated from there own inner selves and that all beings are there own one being and that each of us are, our own creator of our own life, and that no one else has power over us or that creates another one life.

This is the knowledge that is becoming reawakened within all of us, for those that are ready for this knowledge of who we are.

This is the true knowledge that all those Spiritual teachers were teaching to us, all those thousands of years ago, but the beliefs systems of that time did not allow this to happen, as I mentioned throughout this series.

Now is the time for all that knowledge to come forth and to be with us, at the new beginning that is in front of us.

That knowledge of those Spiritual Beings which was teaching us, that there was no need to look outside of oneself to know who we were, as the beliefs systems were teaching people. This belief system had gone and separated you from that knowledge and controlled all with the fear, to anyone which to seek this knowledge of inner knowing, the looking within ones inner self as this one being, was corrupt and went against gods will and will be destroyed, as I mentioned throughout this series.

This knowledge is nothing new to any of us, since the past is of the future and the future is of the present.

What was of the past is also coming to us now; it is the continuing endless cycles of life. It's like the physical cycles of life, you are born and then you die, and born again, so on and so on, as life goes on, never ending.

This is also true for the knowledge within us.

We go through periods of time which are of light (awakening), to the time of dark (being asleep), and back into the light, these cycles repeat themselves over and over again. But through these periods of the ages, they are thousands of years at a time; we are awakening and becoming who we are. We are that one being that we have been looking outside of ourselves to find. Nevertheless, we cannot find that one being, because we are that one being, which we have all been looking for.

Chapter 31

Into the Unknown... But Known

The knowledge of the past will again, be the knowledge of the future in the present.

What do all the cultures of the past, present, and the future have in common?

All these cultures that were part of the earth of the past ages, along with the present age, tell us about our existence, and of our future.

The unknown is only unknown, to the one that does not, want to journey to the known. As I mentioned earlier in Book 3, this is your rite of passage, to know of this knowledge within you, to know the unknown. It is your right to walk beyond where others do not wish to journey because they feel that they do not have that right to go into the unknown and to know what is before them, for their own reasons.

Like all ancient beings of the many cultures of the past, you too are walking into the unknown to the known and awakening the same knowledge that the ancient beings also awoke within themselves. But for you those that are reading this series, you have started that journey into the unknown, to know what only seemed to be unknown.

The unknown is really something that is not known at the moment, a place in our existence of the future for instance. Many people are uncertain of their future because they say it is unknown and not for us to know about.

Well they are wrong!

As I mentioned this is our rite of passage. This knowledge of walking beyond and knowing the unknown and making it known is part of the ladder of evolution of becoming conscious beings.

As you journey into the unknown it becomes your known knowledge. As you learn of this knowledge of evolution, you begin to wonder what is beyond you, but you know from previous experiences that you can learn what is unknown by just journeying to a place beyond the present. The unknown becomes known when you merge into the unknown and learn about the knowledge, which was beyond where you were at in the past.

There were many ancient beings from ancient pre-civilizations that journeyed to the unknown to learn about what was beyond the beyond and to learn from other ancient beings. There are always other beings above us, which can teach us about what is unknown. We can also come across beings that do not want us to learn of what is beyond. The same goes for the beings that are below us, which have not learned what we have learned.

I would like to take a moment and bring forth an example of knowledge from the unknown to the known, out how religions want to control us. This is based on a five thousand years old belief system.

This is an excerpt from the Journey of Self – discovery – By His Divine Grace, A. C. Bhaktivedanta Swami Prabhupada, pgs. 10-14*(the italics are mine)*

Understanding the living Force

The International Society for Krishna consciousness is a movement aiming at the spiritual reorientation of mankind through the simple process of chanting the holy names of god. The human life is meant for ending the miseries of material existence. Our present – day society is trying to end these miseries by material progress. However, it is visible to all that in spite of extensive material progress, human society is not peaceful.

The reason is that the human being is essentially a spirit soul. It is the spirit soul that is the background of the development of the material body. However the materialistic scientists may deny the spiritual existence in the background of the living force, there is no better understanding than accepting this living force as ultimately the spirit soul within the body.

The body is changing – from one form to another – but spirit soul which existing externally, which changes. This fact we can experience even in our own life. Since the beginning of our material body in the womb of our mother, our body has been changing from one shape to another at every second and at every minute. This process is generally known as "growth" but actually it is a change of body.

On this earth, we see change of the day and night and change of season. The more primitive mentality attributes this phenomenon to changes occurring in the Sun.

For example, in the winter primitive people think the sun is getting weaker, and at night, they presume, sometimes, that the sun is dead. With more advanced knowledge we see that the sun is not changing at all in this way. Seasonal and diurnal changes are attributed to the changes of the relative positions of the earth to the sun.

Similarly, we experience bodily changes: from embryo to child to youth to maturity to old age to death. The less intelligent mentality presumes that after death the spirit soul's existence is forever finished, just as primitive tribes believe that the sun dies at sunset. Actually, however, the sun is rising in another part of the world.

(But we know that the sun does not move, it is the planets that are rotating).

Similarly, the soul is accepting another type of body. When the body gets old like an old garment and is no longer usable, the soul accepts another body, just as we accept a new suit of clothes. Modern civilization is practically unaware of this truth.

People do not care about the constitutional position of the soul. *(This is due to belief systems, which are not allowing people to know the real truth).* There are different departments of knowledge in different universities and many technological institutions, all to study and understand the subtle laws of material nature, and there are medical research laboratories to study the physiological condition of the material body, but there is no institution to study the constitutional position of the soul. This is the greatest drawback of materialistic civilization, which is simply an external manifestation of the soul.

People are enamored of the glittering manifestation of the cosmic body or the individual body, but they do not try to understand the basic principle of this glittering situation. The body looks very beautiful, working with full energy and exhibiting great traits to talent and wonderful brainwork. But as soon as the soul is away from the body, this entire glittering situation of the body becomes useless. Even the great scientists who have offered many wonderful scientific contributions have been unable to trace out the personal self, which is the cause of such wonderful discoveries.

The krsna consciousness movement, therefore, is basically trying to teach this science of the soul, not in any dogmatic way, but through complete scientific and philosophical understanding. In the background of this body you can find the soul, whose presence is perceivable by dint of consciousness. Similarly, in the universal body of the cosmic manifestation, one can perceive the presence of the super soul and super consciousness.

The absolute Truth is systematically explained in the Vedanta sutra (generally known as the Vedanta philosophy), which in turn is elaborately explained by the Srimad – Bhagavatam, a commentary by the same author. The Bhagavatam – gita is the preliminary study of the Srimad - Bhagavatam for understanding the constitutional position of the supreme lord, or the absolute truth.

An individual soul is understood in three aspects: first as the consciousness pervading the entire body, then as the spirit soul within the heart, and ultimately as a person. Similarly, the absolute truth is first realized as impersonal Brahman, then as localized super soul (Paramatma), and at the end as the supreme personality of godhead, krsna. Krsna is all – inclusive. Or in other words, krsna is simultaneously Brahman, Paramatma, and the personality of godhead, just as every one of us is simultaneously consciousness, soul, and person.

The individual person and the supreme person are qualitatively one but qualitatively different. Just like the drop of seawater and the vast mass of seawater – both are qualitatively one. The chemical composition of the drop of seawater and that of the mass of seawater are one and the same. But the quantity of salt and other minerals in the whole sea is many, many times greater than the quantity of salt and other minerals contained in the drop of seawater.

The krsna consciousness movement upholds the individuality of the soul and the supreme soul. From the Vedic Upanishads we can understand that both the supreme person, or god, and the individual person are eternal living entities. The different is that the supreme living entities, or supreme person, maintains all the innumerable other living entities. *(This is what the religions want us to believe, that we are separated and that some other being controls us).* In the Christian way of understanding, the same principle is admitted, because in the bible it is taught that the contingent entities should pray to the supreme father so that He may supply means of maintenance are given pardon for their sinful activities.

So it is understood from every source of scriptural injunction that the supreme lord, or krsna, is the maintainer of the contingent living entity and that it is the duty of the contingent entity to feel obliged to the supreme lord. Thus is the whole background of religious principle. Without these acknowledgements there is chaos, as we find in our daily experience at the present moment.

The chaos is created by the religions to keep us from realizing that all of us are this god. Just because a particular being is further up on the ladder of evolution than we are, doesn't make that being any more of a god than we are. It's religions that do not want us to realize those aspects.)

This is the knowledge that we are reawakening within all of us, as we enter this New Age.

Book 4 – The Quantum leap into Consciousness

Everyone is trying to become the supreme lord, socially, politically, or individually. Therefore there is competition for this false lordship, and there is chaos all over the world individually, nationally, socially, and collectively. The krsna consciousness movement is trying to establish the supremacy of the absolute personality of godhead. One who has attained a human body and intelligence is meant for this understanding, because this consciousness makes his life successful.

The religions do not want the individual to realize who they are because when the individuals learn that every one of us is this god, then these religions will no longer have control over us, as they have for the past twelve thousand years. The only chaos is that the religions are losing their control and they will go to any extent to stay in control of us.

This krsna consciousness movement is not a new introduction by mental speculators. Actually, this movement was started by krsna Himself. On the battlefields of Kuruksetra, at least five thousand years ago, the movement was presented by krsna in the Bhagavad – Gita. From Bhagavad – Gita we can also understand that he had spoken this system of consciousness long, long before – at least 120,000,000 years ago – when he had imparted it to the sun – god, Vivasvan.

So this movement is not at all new. It is coming down in discipline succession from all the great leaders of India's Vedic civilization, including Sankaracarya, Ramanujacarya, Madhvacarya, Vishnu Svami, Nimbarka and lately, about 480 years ago, lord

Cartanya. The discipline system is still being followed today. This Bhagavad –Gita is also very widely used in all part of the world by great scholars, philosophers, and religionists. But in most cases the principles are not followed as they are. The krsna consciousness movement presents the principles of the Bhagavad – Gita as they are – without any misinterpretation.

From the Bhagavad – Gita can understand five main principles, namely god, the living entity, the material and spiritual nature, time and activities. Out of these five items, god, the living entity, nature (material or spiritual), and time are eternal. But activities are not eternal.

Activities in the material nature are different from activities in the spiritual nature. Through the spirit soul is eternal (as we have explained); activities performed under the influence of the material nature are temporary. The krsna consciousness movement aims at placing the spirit soul in his eternal activities. We can practice eternal activities even when we are materially engaged to act spiritually simply requires direction, but it is possible, under the prescribed rules and regulations.

As I have mentioned throughout this series, this is the control of the religions, by keeping all of you stagnant it will keep all of you from learning the truth of who we are. These religions go about placing rules and regulations, and saying that you can only go to a certain point and you cannot look and know beyond what they want you to know.

The krsna consciousness movement teaches these spiritual activities, and if one is trained in such spiritual activities, one is transferred to the spiritual world, of which we get ample evidence from the Vedic literatures, including the Bhagavad – Gita. The spiritually trained person can be transferred to the spiritual world easily – by change of consciousness.

One does not need to be trained to enter this spiritual world. The spiritual world is all around us; it is within us, all we need to do is look within and see that spiritual world; we all merge into this spiritual world when we meditate and when we enter into that sleep state.

Consciousness is always present, because it is the symptom of the living spirit soul, but at the present moment our consciousness is materially contaminated. For instance, water pouring down from a cloud is pure, but as soon as the water comes in touch with the ground it becomes muddy – immediately. Yet if we filter the same water, the original clearness can be regained. Similarly, krsna consciousness is the process of clearing our consciousness and as soon as our consciousness is clear and pure eternal life of knowledge and bliss. This is what we are hankering for in this material world, but we are being frustrated at every step on account of material contamination. Therefore, the leaders of human society should take this krsna consciousness movement very seriously.

End of Excerpt

This is what the religions want us to continue in believing in, so that we give up our rite of passage of realizing and becoming our own god. That old way of believing, that there is one god and that he is in control of us, is coming to an end, very, very quickly, as we make this transition into our New Age.

What knowledge does the unknown brings to us?

As we journey into the unknown it will become known. We learn the knowledge of life; we reawaken this knowledge of our consciousness, our essence, and our connection to the energy life force, which binds all life together. We learn that we create our existence through this awakening consciousness. We are learning that our future is being created through this energy force – this essence of life, through our own thoughts as we go about wondering about our future.

As we continue to journey to that which is considered our future or that is beyond us, eventually it becomes our present and again we create what is beyond us again that unknowing of the future, so on and so on, never ending cycle of creating the unknown, the creating of your future.

This is the knowledge that the unknown brings to us as conscious beings, which is, that we create our future in the past to experience in the present.

The one Path of Many Journey's

We all find ourselves on that one path of looking outside of ourselves to find and to believe in one being, that was out there, that we were told not to look within to find, because it was not within us, it was outside of us, which was a being that created us in his image. We journeyed down that path for eons, during those many ages that brought us to this time that is now. We have come to realize that there is more than we were led to believe about our existence, of our life, and of who we are. As we begin our next journey, we no longer have these veils of the past, which kept us from all the knowledge of our existence, the knowledge of who we are, and the knowledge of what is to come. We are now finally able to see all that is around us, due to what is called the removal of the walls or the opening of the doorways, which have been closed to us for the past twelve thousand years.

Now that we are able to journey into that unknown and make it the known, we have come to the realization of those many journeys which await us as we start down this new path. This journey is not for a select few; this journey is a journey for all, we all exist together within the creation that we all created for our existence.

What does life offer to us now that these walls are gone, and the doorways are all open for all of us to experience the unlimited knowledge? This knowledge was once unknown to us during the dark ages. The dark ages dealt with being asleep and have come to a close, to bring forth the age of awakening of the knowledge within.

What will it be like when we finally become that conscious being, as we all realize that we are the creators of our existence? We put that burden upon a being that has no responsibility for our creation; this burden of our creation is our own burden and no one else's. This is all of our creation within and around all of us and we all have to take the responsibility for it. If there is something in your creation that you do not want in your creation any longer, just simply remove it out of your experience and make your experience in this creation the way you want it to become. Some might even say that they did not create this war – destruction.

Remember this is of the old ways, which is no longer part of this New Age that we are entering into, because many of us are realizing that we do not need this any more so it is becoming something of the past. Remember, what one creates in their creation another one might experience your creation somewhere along their creation as well, since there is one path and many on these journeys within this path. This is where we have other people and other beings come into our creation.

Imagine one path and off this path you have millions of paths to journey within.

It might look something like this!

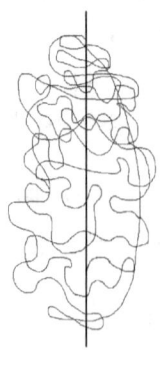

Book 4 – The Quantum leap into Consciousness

All will come to experience the awe, the wonder, the unknown of what is around the bend on the next path of this journey, which is unfolding before you. As if you were the creator of what is to come. Which this is true, you are creating what is waiting for you, since this path, this journey is yours and yours alone. You are your own creator of your life and your experiences within yourself; this is what you are creating outside of yourself, as well to experience as your creation.

This massive creation that we all are journeying within is not created by any one being. This massive creation which we all are part of is created by all of the beings of the past and of the future, which is created in the present, the now, which is of all the thoughts that are projected out from all beings which exist within the universes seen and unseen. I talked about the process of thought in Books 1 and 3, about how thought is a very powerful thing to all beings and which includes the life force, the energy which makes the suns, the energy which brings all these planets into manifestations from energy into the physical form, and all these suns which come together to create these galaxies and all those galaxies into creating universes that create other universes among universes.

We must remember as we traverse on our journey, there are others that are on their creation as well. As all merges into each other's creation you have to understand that each of you are creating each other into your own creation simultaneously without realizing it in a way, since each of you is the creator of your own creation.

This new journey that we are embarking on is about us being the creators of our own creation, that is unfolding in front of us all, as we go forward into what might be the unknown, but it is also the known, since we have already thought what this unknown might be. See, the unknown is really something that you already created in the past, for your future. So, now your future is here now, from your past thoughts, of the unknown, which the unknown is really your own creation of the past becoming created in the future, which that future, is now here for you to experience what you had created in the past for yourself for the future.

So when people say that they do not know what is in store for them in the future, they are misleading you and themselves. We all know what is in store for us in the future, since we all create our future in the past to be experienced in the future, which becomes our present, our now.

Chapter 32

The departure of Some of the Previous Guardians

In the 3rd Book of this series I talked a little about the Ancient Guardians of Terra of the past.

These guardians were of many origins, to name a few not in any particular order, there were those of: Vishnu's – Avatars – Wizards – Cetaceans as of the Whales – Dolphins – the Nefilem – the Elves and many more. Some guardians that we all have read about within the myths and tails of the past ages are all indeed true, and were all a part of the Guardians of Terra, many, many eons ago.

But there is one group out of the many of the past that has stayed around and watched over all of the Earths happenings. Even at this moment they are among us, watching and monitoring the progress of our, "human Quantum leap of consciousness," as the beings of consciousness that we are.

This group of guardians has decided on its own to stay and monitor the progress of Terra as the conscious being that she is. Terra is a host to all those beings that will inhabit Terra through her many ages and cycles.

This one group of guardians is always seen by us, the humans on the earth and we do not fear them. We see these guardians among us in our surroundings when we have that moment to see them, since the people have been around these guardians for thousands of years. We the people had grown to love these magnificent beings, even though most of us had no idea about them being the guardians of this earth, other than very few of us that knew they were the guardians.

For those of you that said the cetaceans, whales, and dolphins are the guardians you are correct!

Yes, these whales and dolphins are the guardians and they have been keeping tabs on all that has been transpiring on this planet, along with how the human species has been evolving, and how we treat other beings that are upon Terra. When I say "how we treat other beings," that goes for all species on the earth, it goes for the human species because we are no different than any other life that is on this earth. This earth is also a living conscious being even though most people have no concept of the earth as being a conscious being. This also goes for how we treat other beings that come to the earth from other star systems which are far beyond ours. These Cetacean guardians have been recording all that has been transpiring on Terra for eons. They have done their part in balancing the energies of their positive energy on Terra, despite all the negativity that most of our species has been creating upon the planet and amongst the civilizations of humans that are spread across the entire world and the destruction that we are doing to our own species

Yes, this is all recorded by these guardians, which are among you, and not by a being, "saying he is your god," but by all beings of consciousness, which are not any different than you, other than they already became beings of consciousness eons ago. This is what some of us, the human beings, are going through, this transition and realizing who we are and our responsibility of becoming the conscious beings that we are.

Back in 1992 – 1993, there were few dolphins and whales that beached themselves, and people that were witnessing these events as they were happening tried to help these beings back into the water. But those beings of those whales and dolphins choose not to return to the water because, their time came and they wanted to leave this plain of existence of this 3rd dimension. They wanted to leave in this fashion of having those people showing compassion to them and to be there for their ascension as they entered the 4th and 5th dimensions of existence. They contribute their existence in the 3rd dimension as these guardians. These beings are still continuing to contribute their energy and knowledge from the 4th and 5th dimension plains of existence; it was just that these beings decided to continue their work in a different way, to assist this new energy that is coming to the earth at this point in time.

We all have to remember that the Cetaceans beings are the oldest beings of Terra, which we all are comfortable seeing in our everyday life. Moreover, at the same time we have to come to the realization that these beings are the guardians, as well they help balance the earth of most people's thoughts of negativity. These guardians are more capable of balancing the energy, since they were doing this for many eons past.

Now comes the time that most of these Cetacean beings will be leaving this plain of existence. But I assure you, a few will stay a little bit longer on their decision alone. But only if we, the human beings, can show respect to all beings that exist on the earth, and too these other beings that are not of this earth, when that time comes for that mass involvement with these other beings, which are from your universe and from universes beyond yours.

Some of you might say, "Well that has been going on for awhile."

Well you are right! However, on a very limited involvement though. As you know, some off world beings have been involved within the government and the religions, as I have presented throughout this whole series. But all that is going to be changing, and this involvement will be on a global scale with other worldly beings, as we learn this knowledge of becoming conscious beings within this vast universe that we all are part of.

The Return of some Ancient Beings

Within all of the previous 3 books, I talked some about the Ancient Guardians/Watchers that were among the civilizations of ancient times. These beings are returning, as we are entering into our new age, a new beginning, we will be seeing some of those ancient beings returning to our star system and to our planet. These ancient beings have been watching over us from afar and they have been monitoring our star system for thousands and thousands of years, with very little interaction with us from time to time over the course of thousands of years. For those that were and still are less fortunate to have these interactions with those ancient and multi-dimensional beings. These people of Terra are only left to wonder and to try to fathom and to grasp the concept of the knowledge, that these beings had procured concerning

Book 4 – The Quantum leap into Consciousness

the knowledge of life and about the vastness of the universe that we are part of. The only way for those that are less fortunate is to delve into those ancient stories of those myths of the very ancient past. This is where one can learn about the knowledge of those ancient beings of those forgotten past ages of eons ago. Or for those that are fortunate, to meet with one or a few of these ancient beings that have been retuning and interacting with a select few of the people of Terra, to share their knowledge about life and what life is really about.

Why are only a select few chosen to have this interaction, you might ask? Those that are selected to have this interaction with some of these ancient beings are mainly the individuals that choose to have this contact with the ancient beings with no fear towards those that are from other star systems, regardless of what religions and government might create within the public about these beings.

Where do these beings come from, you might also be asking?

These beings come from many star systems that are near our star and from within our galaxy and from distant galaxies from across the universe.

Below is a list of stars to name a few –

Lyra
Vega
Altair
Ophiuchus
Serpens

Book 4 – The Quantum leap into Consciousness

Centurus
Orion
Aldebaron
Eridanus
Arturus
Coma Berenices
Draco
Pleiades -there are several thousand star systems that make up the Pleiadean system. To name a few-
Atlas
Alcyone
Maia
Marope
Sy
Pleione
Asterope
Electra
Celanea
Taygeta
Apsu - Terra (Earth) star

And many, many others star systems.

There are many other beings that are from many other systems, which are from other galaxies. Our galaxy is but one out of a trillion other galaxies that are in existence throughout this universe that we are in, and other universes that are beyond our comprehension.

Book 4 – The Quantum leap into Consciousness

On the next page, you will see where our sun is located within our group of stars and its surroundings within the vastness of this galaxy that we are part of.

You are looking at our Milky Way Galaxy at about 112 million light years away, and the location of our sun within the group of stars that we can see in our night sky. This is just one galaxy out of trillions of galaxies that makes up a universe.

Now you can have an idea on where our sun and our group of stars are located.

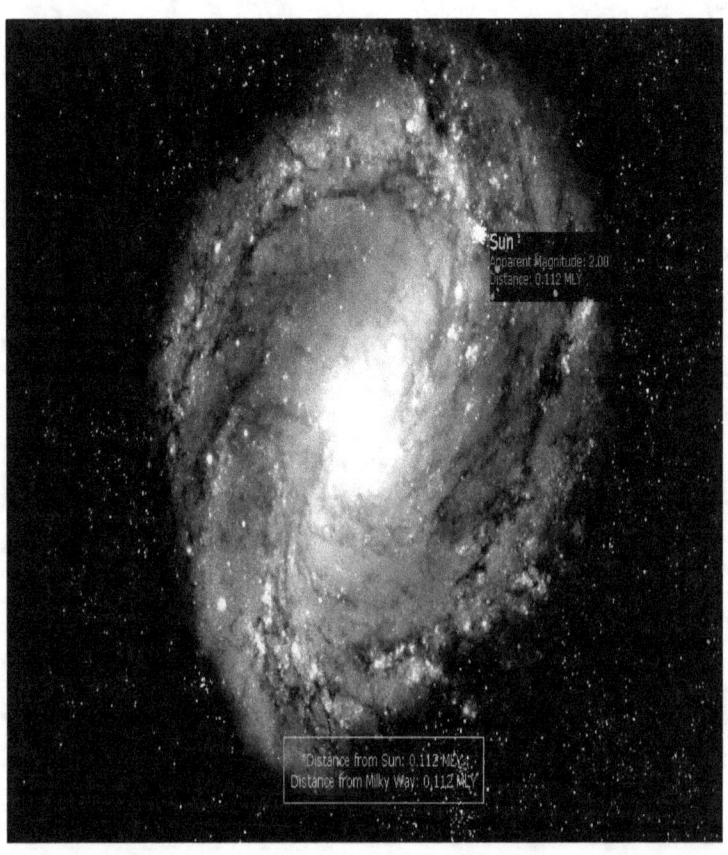

Eunuch – Is a being that is of both genders.

The Eunuch was a being of both genders within itself. These beings existed upon the earth up until the last completion of the cycle that our group of stars made around our galaxy, which was around twelve thousand years ago. This was their end on the earth due to the energies that the earth was going through. These beings existed on Terra from about two-hundred thousand years ago up to twelve thousand years ago.

There are many pre ancient stories of these beings that were of both male and female gender. You just have to know how to translate those stories.

On the continent of Tampaurban, they have those ancient stories of these beings that existed before twelve thousand years ago, and then shortly after this time these beings began to change and separate into

Book 4 – The Quantum leap into Consciousness

individual male and female beings. From this change came forth a being of a new race, which is known as pre human race. These beings were a little bit different than the way we are today, they did not have the bellybutton as we do. Both of these beings lived for several hundreds to thousands of years. This story and many others are similar to the story of what people are reading about in the stories within the so-called bible, of a humanoid race of beings that was of both genders. This one being separated into another race of beings that brought forth a new race that is known as the pre -human race, and from this race of beings came the human race of today.

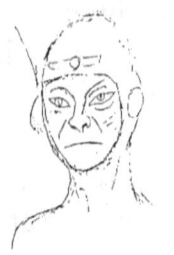

Top picture is one type of a Reptilian race.
Bottom picture is of a Serpent race.

Book 4 – The Quantum leap into Consciousness

Both of these beings, Reptilian and Serpent played parts within all stories of our pre-ancient myths and the stories within the bible and right up to the stories of today.

These beings have been around for well over three-hundred thousand years and they come from many star systems around our galaxy. For the Reptilian beings, a few of them come from the Sirius Star system, some are from the Orion star system, and some come from the star system of Draco. For the Serpent Beings a few of them are from the star system of Ophiuchus and many other systems throughout our galaxy and other galaxies as well.

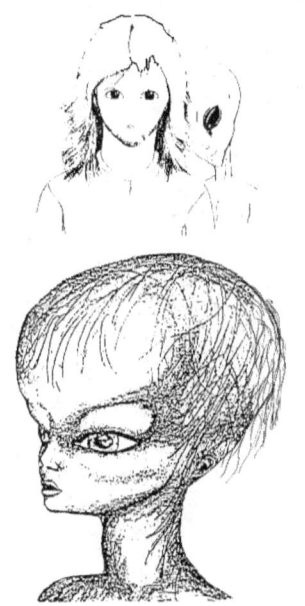

The top and bottom pictures are ideas of types of hybrids of human and humanoid beings, along with the beings that are known as the greys.

Book 4 – The Quantum leap into Consciousness

These types of hybrid beings are of the next generation of beings, which are a combination of several genetics of DNA strands from many species from across the universes, which also includes our human DNA. We are just beginning to hear about these beings in our day in age. As we enter into our new cycle, our new age, we will be seeing more of these beings, but not until we can accept and get along with all the beings that are part of our old world. This is in the process of happening at this time, (the human race), so maybe in about another twenty plus years we might meet these hybrid beings that will be a new race of beings on this world.

The drawings of the typical, Yeti, Bigfoot Also known as the Lemurian Beings.

Book 4 – The Quantum leap into Consciousness

These ancient races of beings are the survivors of an ancient race from Lemuria. These beings existed for over two-hundred thousand years. They are widely read about in pre-ancient myth. They are also known throughout our current culture, but you call them by many names based on their locations around the world today. You call them the Yeti, Bigfoot, and many other names. These beings moved into their quantum leap into consciousness around twenty-five thousand years ago and they are multi-dimensional beings, they exists in our world around us, and also in the sixth dimensional world. These beings have telepathic ability for communication to those that are able to communicate telepathically. They come into our dimension at times, to check up on us in a way of speaking that is, since we too are moving from our 3rd dimensional existence and entering into the 4th and 5th dimensional existence. We will be seeing more of these beings in the near future.

One might ask, why are these beings of these other star systems interested in us, and why have they been watching over our star system and planet?

The one reason is that we are their brothers and sisters. We are on this earth as many forms of species, not all life is based on the human species. Most people cannot come to believe that there is other life besides ours in this galaxy, that there are other beings that exist on Terra. All you have to do is look around you; there are other species of life besides humans. There are other life forms which are more intelligent that the human species is, a thousand times more. This is mainly because these species are thousands of years older than our current human species is. The other reason for the return of some ancient beings back to our star system is that our star system is moving into a new age, a new cycle of life, and a new frequency of energy. I talked about that from the very beginning with Book 1, The Reawakening, and throughout this whole series. Yes everything and everyone is moving forward on the ladder of evolution on consciousness. Some and I mean only a hand-full have already moved forward into this consciousness of reawakening and they are beginning to awaken to the realization of who they are as conscious beings. Some of these star beings are here on our request and some of the other beings are here to observe the transition of all species that are on the earth as we all enter into our new beginning of this new cycle of life. As we reawaken that knowledge that lies within all of us, we come to the realization and the understanding of who we are as conscious beings. These beings from the stars are paving the way in front of all of us, they are the way showers, they ask for those beings that are on this world that had already reawakened to assist them in helping the rest of the beings on Terra that had not yet awakened.

These ancient beings that were on our world several thousands of years ago are returning to Terra system, from those far off stars that these beings are coming from. As all of you might recall in those ancient stories, which are part of our mythology stories as you call them. All those beings had always

Book 4 – The Quantum leap into Consciousness

been interacting with this star system for millions of years, and will continue to do so when the beings of this star system request their interactions. Or these star beings will take it upon themselves to interact with the inhabitants of a planet based on the changes of the cycle, energy frequency that a star system is entering into. Or if a being is needed to be placed on the planet to help influence the people to change before the new cycle begins. But for us at this new age, that we are entering which began as of the year 2000 which was paved before us two-thousand years ago, on that reawakening of who we truly are. It has taken this long, but that was only due to our past age that ended back in 1985.

The galaxy that we are in is finally moving forward into a new beginning, a new age, this also goes for all beings that are within this galaxy. We all are leaving the past age, that old energy and moving into a very new frequency. This is also why there is interest in these stars systems and all the beings in this sector of this galaxy. This is to observe all life and to see if they are reawakening and realizing, who they are, as conscious beings and to see if they are ready to move and to take that quantum leap into consciousness. As I said earlier only a hand full had already came to the understanding of who they are as conscious beings. Those that have already reawakened are not controlled by the so-called god theory of those religions. This hand full is about 5 % plus of the human species and that is pretty small hand full to say the least. This is why the awakened beings upon your planet called for assistance in paving the way, to help all beings on your planet realize who each and every one of you are. That way you can become aware of who you are and take that next step of evolution!

Book 4 – The Quantum leap into Consciousness

Chapter 33

Entering the Halls of Cosmic Creations

Once again, we come to the realization of who we are as the conscious beings that we are, and that we create all that is around us and beyond us.

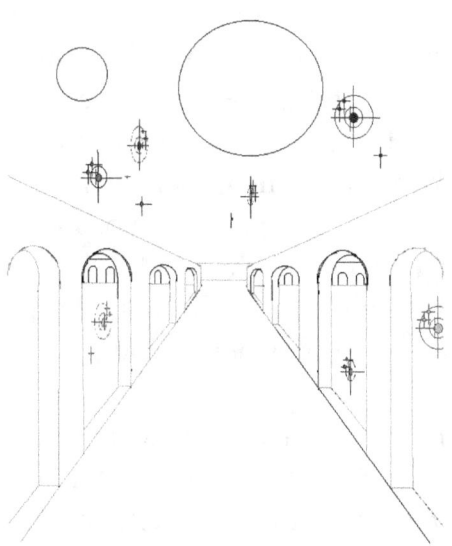

As we look at the picture above, we can see an idea of the halls of cosmic creations. We can see corridors upon corridors and within these corridors are archways. Each of these archways are cosmic creations. Each of these archways are what you might call the void, since these archways are void of creation. They are void until someone enters into the archway and they create their creation within this archway. Also remember that other beings also enter into these archways. Does that mean they will experience what was created before them? Not necessarily. Other beings enter these archways and they create their own creation within that archway as well, so then this archway starts to fill up with many ideas of creations.

Even in an archway that might appear to be void of creation is a creation within itself. Maybe the being that is within this void had created this void for one's own experience of nothingness, the emptiness of no thought, but it is still a creation, it is the stillness of creation. In addition as one enters into this archway they bring with them their own creation. Does this mean that the void is changed? No. Does this mean that the one that enters the void will experience the void? No. However, they will cross the path of each other's creation, somewhere along their paths of creation.

Why there are so many ideas of creations within each archway, when there are many archways within the halls of cosmic creations, you might ask?

The reason is basically that there are many beings within that path of that particular cosmic birth and all exist within each other's creations and all are crossing into each other's path of creation.

Book 4 – The Quantum leap into Consciousness

Well why can you not have one creation per archway, so to say?

That would be like putting yourself in a room with no one else in there with you. This will give you that one creation to experience and nothing else. I think you will also go crazy, for there will be no one else to cross your path, no one for you to be part of their creation and for them to be part of your creation. The creation of only one creation within itself will be a boring place and very limited as well, since there can only be one being within that creation. Because as soon as you have two beings within a single creation, it no longer exists as a single creation, it now becomes a multiple creation. Now do you see and understand about the concepts of creations?

This is the knowledge that we are all reawakening within ourselves, the knowledge of becoming those conscious beings that we are, finally realizing who we are.

This is transpiring on Terra and within your entire Milky Way Galaxy. All beings that are within these universes are moving forward in consciousness and all beings are reawakening the knowledge within themselves and accepting that each of us are our own creator of our own creation. And through this acknowledgement and acceptance, we are finally able to take responsibility for our creations, which are amongst the many other creations which are around all of us at all times.

In addition, we are now ready to interact with other beings creations, which were created by other conscious beings, which exist in the universes that are around us.

How are we going to be able to interact with these other creations and those other beings of consciousness, you might ask?

Not any different from the way you interact with all the beings that are on your world. This is why there are so many species on your world. Yes the human beings are a species as well. As all of you are moving into becoming conscious beings, all the fears towards each other of controlling the other will all disappear in time. In addition, you will no longer be part of that experience of life and at the same time, you all will get along with the other species that are amongst your world. At that time all of you will be able to accept all the other life that exists amongst the stars, which has been amongst all of you as well.

What do these other beings look like?

We showed you these other beings throughout the whole series and within this book. There are millions upon millions of many types of beings that exist throughout all the universes. The beings that we have been encountering within our time have been showing a curiosity about our species (the human race) and all beings that are upon Terra, and our technologies that we been developing for the past 2-3 hundred years. At the same time watching us on how we use this technology, on ourselves, (the human race) and watching us battling each other for no reason other than to see how one can kill another being of the same race. The beings are watching us from above the earth as we go about destroying the world that we all exist upon. As if we have no concern for Terra as the 'conscious living being', that she is, and seeing that we show no respect to our world and to all types of beings that are upon her. Beings are coming to our star system from all corners of our galaxy to see what is going on, on this unique planet which has millions of different beings upon it, to see how all these beings exist together. But we do not exist together! Not even with our own species (the human race)! One time in the ancient past ages we all existed together and respected all beings that were on our world, and including beings that are off our world. However, in the past current age we lost that connection.

As we enter into our new age in the year 2,000 C.E (Current Era), we will start to see this respect towards other beings on this planet and the respect towards our own species; we will begin to come together as one race. We will be stopping this so called separating of the human race, which was created to separate the other continents, or due to belief systems. All this is changing right before your eyes. In addition, as we make this change towards all these beings, and that includes us the human beings, we will be able to show the same respect towards those beings, which are our brothers and sisters, which travels through the stars.

Do you want these beings of the stars to show respect towards you, when you are out amongst the stars?

I hope so!

Because I know, I would want that for myself!

What might exist within those other creations that are created by other beings that we might come to experience as we cross into their paths?

What one will come to experience within any given creation is solely up to one's own thoughts. Remember any and all creations are nothing more than the mere thought which later becomes, the basis for a creation to be experienced, if it would be in the future of the present or if it be the future of a distant future. It is not any different than let's say, how many thoughts you can have on how you want your life to be, or your future to be. You are creating all of those thoughts during your existence here on Terra and off Terra, as one day when you are alive or even after you had left this life on Terra. You are creating all those existences to experience, that even goes for the people that are creating those places that religious people are creating of their so called heaven, hell, purgatory even the void or whatever (which people still call it heaven). It is not called heaven it is called the universes, and yes, there are other types of beings that exists amongst the stars, there are many conscious beings that do exists out there, as I have shown you throughout this series.

In addition, there is no being that is called god or the devil. It is time that all of you face the facts that was all an illusion that was created as a veil to keep you from learning of the truth about this knowledge of who you are.

All the creations that you see around you, we created this in our past, to go about experiencing it in the future, which is now the present.

With these creations, that we all are experiencing exists many worlds within our own world.

Like-minded people through all the universes have said it, repeatedly. "A door way to ones dreams is another ones door way to his reality!"

Within this part, I am going to give you insight to these doorways or gateways to other dimensions and universes that are in existence in this world and beyond.

These gateways come in many different shapes and in different locations around the world. Just to name a couple, the great pyramid of Giza, The Bermuda Triangle, Stonehenge and Sedona along with the Japanese Triangle along with many others.

Now the gateways I just listed above are on a large-scale size. Within these gateways which are all around the world, are energy levels that are able to get so intense at times, that strange phenomenal events occur within these gateways boundaries that can transport you to other dimensions. The energy level could also transport you to a universe many hundreds of millions of light years away, or it could send you several hundred of light years away from where you are now, or they could even send you to another dimension within this earth.

Let's now take a look at these gateways energies, what they are capable of doing to our energy when these gateways are operating at their minimal power when we step into their boundaries. First, we will look at the pyramid of Giza. The energy within this pyramid is capable of raising the physical energy of the body to another level of existence of awareness of our spiritual being. The awakening I am mentioning here is the awakening of the soul or spirit energy of our true essence of who we truly are. This is the question that everyone seems to wonder to themselves, time and time again "Who am I, and why have we come to this planet, what must we do while we are here?" Anyone entering the pyramid will go through this energy transformation process, there is no need to worry, it will not hurt you, because this transformation is harmless in all ways you can imagine. Through this transformation, it only changes the energy patterns within each individual being. This energy is to awaken the soul, so the body and soul can better communicate with each other and with the other universal beings that exist in the universes that are all around us. However, not everyone needs to go through this way of awakening of the soul's energy within all of us.

The second gateway is the Bermuda Triangle in the Atlantic Ocean. What is it with the Bermuda Triangle that has people all over this world in fear or in curiosity of this place? Could the fears be brought upon by all the disappearance of ships, planes, boats, and divers, along with other strange phenomenal events dating as far back to 1500's and even farther. Could this curiosity be brought forth by early spotted pyramid structures of a continent called Atlantis that has started rising from its twelve thousand-year watery grave? Or shall I say started to be uncovered by the movement of the sandy ocean bottom, by the shifting waters over onto other landmasses to cover them up, in order to reveal this old and ancient land. Here is another idea why people fear this place; it is because people do not know what is waiting to be revealed to them. On the other hand, is this curiosity of finding the truth about our universal origins, our true spot in the universes around us? What happens when a person or anything entering the boundaries of the Bermuda Triangle when the energy is at its highest in certain areas? Some might say those people are lost forever, those people that say that are wrong, these people are merely transported to another dimension within this world, or they are transported to another universe that lies beyond our comprehension of reality.

To find the true answers of the Bermuda Triangle, there are three places to find the answers.

The first place is in the minds of the people of today that lived during the time of Atlantis.

The second is in the minds of the people that were transported out to another dimension or to other universes that are beyond this dimension and universe, which might have returned back to this reality.

Book 4 – The Quantum leap into Consciousness

The last place that you may find the answers is in the minds of the Star Travelers that have visited the earth for the past ninety five thousand years.

As I mentioned earlier, you can be transported to another dimension on this planet. Let me take this moment to explain to you about this transportation. Within this form of teleportation to another dimension within this planet, you would need two doorways existing simultaneously. They do not need to be in the same location, and the second doorway can be activated at a different time and a different dimension as well. When the first doorway or gateway is opened and you step into this gateway, you pass into space where time does not exist. You then pass into the second gateway, upon it opening, you will find yourself in an alternate dimension that you were not part of to start with. In addition, you will find your physical appearance not any different from when you entered the first gateway even if it has been, say, one hundred years from when you first stepped into the first gateway. The reason that you do not age is because that you are traveling in space where time has no effect upon you at all. However, when you step through the other end, time will start again for you, unless you step through a gateway that does not have time in its existence.

I also presented to you within book 1 The Reawakening, about the cycles that the earth has been through over the past several ages, of the changing of the energies and of other dimensions that the earth has gone through.

So why all the need for all this thought of all these creations, which are all around us, with all types of beings?

At this particular point as we are entering into our new age, we are moving from the 3rd dimensional existence and going into the 4th and 5th dimensional existence, this is why we are seeing these other beings within our dimension. It is because all dimensions are moving forward to the next dimension, so this brings all dimensions to a point of crossing within each other's dimensions which are next to each other, such as a creation moves into the existence of the 1st dimension, the 1st dimension moves into the 2nd dimension, the 2nd dimension moves into the 3rd dimension (ours), the 3rd dimension (ours) moves into the 4th and the 5th dimension simultaneously, and the 4th and 5th dimensions move into the 6th dimension and so on and so forth. So at times, there might be several dimensions existing together at the same time.

All of these creations are unique onto themselves because we are unique conscious beings onto ourselves, because no two thoughts of our own are the same, all of our thoughts are also different from another person's thoughts, and no two people's thoughts are the same. So, this brings forth the many thoughts of forms and types of creations that might exist, for all forms and types of beings to experience within all these creations from lifetime to lifetime, the endlessness of all the forms of creation to experience and not have any two the same. This is why we are seeing this interaction of other beings from all corners of all the universes coming to this unique place in space, to our planet, because there are millions of beings on Terra creating millions of types of creations within a section of a galaxy which we are in. These beings are of many origins from across all the universes that are coming to this sector of this universe. These beings are coming to this sector of our galaxy to experience other forms of creations, other dimensions of experiences other than theirs to interact with, other paths of creation which are created by other forms of conscious beings of other creations which are created by other forms of conscious beings of other creations and other thoughts. We started to enter a new age, a new cycle of energy, and a new birth in the cosmic creation of worlds within worlds. Our world is evolving and growing and it is moving into another experience in the endlessness of experiences of experiencing other existences. All this is part of the cosmic creation of creations, not by any one being, but by all beings that exist in the vastness of all the universes that are around us at all times.

The Unseen World

I have been asked by Cindy (my wife) to share with all of you an experience that she had back in the spring of 1993. This is in the memory of Cindy, she moved onto her next existence on July 2, 1993. She had a lot to offer as a teacher of our spiritual understanding of the aspects of our existence, and upon her request, I am putting this information in this book.

~ Sometimes, it is very difficult to believe in something that you want when it has not manifested physically in your life. We are trained to believe in something only when it is physically before our eyes. This only destroys the trust that we need to have in ourselves. Every person is totally responsible for everything in his and her lives. This does include everything good and bad. When we fail to acknowledge this, we look to someone or something else to blame for the mess in our lives.

At the center of the universe, energy creates everyone and everything. It appears as a light gray mist, and it molds itself to every thought we have and everything we say. The universal energy never doubts us, it just is. It automatically gives us what we want. The problem is that we are not prepared to receive what we want. It may be that whatever you are asking for is not for your highest good. On the other hand, maybe you do not believe that you have the power to create and have anything. The universe cannot give us what we deny ourselves.

You can start building trust in the universe and that, which has not physically manifested. First, you must build a solid trust in yourself. Trust in your ability to create what you want. Experiment with creating little things in your life first. Then you can move on and create bigger and better things.

Then you can trust the universe to supply you with everything you ask for. All you need to do is send the thought of what you want out and then release it. Then be patient for the universe to bring you what you want. Some things will take longer to come than others. It depends on what you want, how much you believe you deserve to have what you want. You can only live, build the trust in yourself and the universe one day at a time. Please do not be discouraged if it takes some time to receive what you ask for. If you really want something, never give up.

We all come here to earth to learn our lessons and fulfill our desires. One important lesson to learn is that we are all one. The hate and violence must end sometime. The sooner we all recognize that there is no separation between us and if we all love each other unconditionally, then the violence will end.

The negativity on your planet is reaching its maximum level. The energy will be shifting to positive and we will have one thousand plus years of peace. This is called the Age of Aquarius. This planet Terra so desperately needs love and peace. All of us here on earth deserve to have our desires fulfilled, and live in a world of love and peace. ~

Chapter 34

The Arrival of New Guardians

It was many ages ago, to be exact it was one cycle ago, when your sun traveled around the galaxy and completed that cycle. Imagine your galaxy divided into thirteen parts and which your sun (star) within its group of stars moves through these parts through time. And imagine your galaxy doing the same thing moving through the thirteen parts of your universe, through time as well, it would be like a wheel within a wheel, with each wheel having thirteen parts, one time around your galaxy through these thirteen parts or ages as they are known as it makes the completion of one cycle around your galaxy. See diagram below.

Our group of stars rotating around one another, and rotating around the galaxy at the same time:

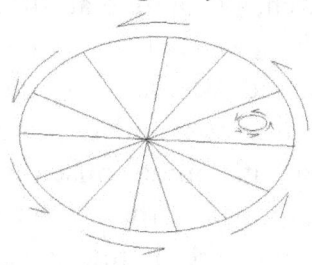

Book 4 – The Quantum leap into Consciousness

Everything rotates within and around itself like hands on a clock.

This process brings in a new age or cycle, it all depends on what our group of stars are in the process of going through and what our galaxy is going through within the universe that we are part of. Now you have a wheel, within a wheel, within a wheel, so on and so forth.

See diagram below.

Our universe that we all are in also rotates as well. Other galaxies: The Milky Way galaxy

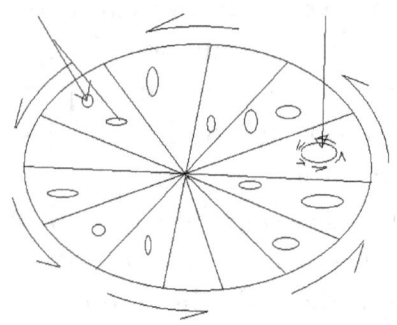

As your galaxy is rotating within itself, it is also rotating through the universe along with millions of other galaxies as well, all rotating at different speeds.

It was a cycle ago that the Cetaceans became conscious beings and became the guardians of the knowledge of the universe and became the guardians of the earth, along with other conscious beings within this galaxy and amongst other galaxies around our universe. These beings are mentioned throughout our mythology stories of our planets past cycles.

Book 4 – The Quantum leap into Consciousness

All these ancient beings at one time or another also became conscious beings and started their reawakening of the knowledge of who they are as conscious beings and learning the knowledge of the universe. As these beings of the universe became conscious beings and came into our star system and seeing these beings of this earth was just beginning to become conscious beings themselves, (the Cetaceans). So those beings of the stars taught the Cetaceans the knowledge of who they are as conscious beings, and about the earth also as a conscious living being, and these star beings also taught the Cetaceans the knowledge of the universe, which we all are part of. As I mentioned in Book 3, the human species are not the guardians of the earth, but it is the Cetaceans that are the guardians of the earth and they hold the knowledge of the universe. Now your group of stars has completed another cycle around your galaxy. As you come to this completion, the human beings are arriving at their awakening of becoming the conscious beings that you are. You have arrived to the point of earning, of becoming conscious beings with the many, which are amongst the universe. This is where the new guardians of this new cycle, this new age will come from. These new guardians will receive the knowledge from the previous guardians, like the Cetaceans and the beings from other galaxies within our universe and from beyond. This is why all these ancient star traveling beings, have this interest in this sector of our galaxy. It is because of this new age that all of us are entering into at this time.

Book 4 – The Quantum leap into Consciousness

There are millions of civilizations among our galaxy alone, that are moving forward, but not all at the same pace, but all and all, you are moving forward into becoming the conscious beings that you are. Even the human beings are moving up the ladder of evolution and becoming conscious beings as well, but not all of you are moving at the same pace. For those that have already became conscious being, that have taken that step of quantum leap into consciousness, you will have a chance of becoming the new guardians of Terra, among the Cetaceans and the other beings from the stars that have already became conscious beings, ages ago. Yes, a few humans have already taken that next step into consciousness. They are the new guardians of the knowledge of the universe and will become the guardians of Terra in this new age.

But, before anyone becomes guardians among the ranks of those other old ancient guardians of knowledge and of Terra, you all will go through a learning of the knowledge that the universe holds within itself, which is the true meaning of itself and about becoming this conscious being that we all are. This is the knowledge that I have been presenting throughout this whole series, but this is only the tip of the iceberg. After these beings, (if it be humans or beings of other star systems or the many other beings that I presented throughout this series) have become conscious beings and learned of the knowledge of the universe. Once they have fully understood the concept of life, and the concepts of creation which is created merely from all beings thoughts within all the

Book 4 – The Quantum leap into Consciousness

universes of their own creation, for their own experience within the many creations of creations, as an experience of the many forms of life to take part in. Then and only then, those beings that had taken that next step, that quantum leap into consciousness of becoming conscious beings, will become the guardians of the knowledge of the universes. In addition, it is those beings that will become the guardians of this planet and of their star system that they are part of. It is these guardians that are the teachers of the knowledge of the universes, they will become the teachers of the civilizations of their world(s) and help those beings to accomplish what they have already started, which is taking that next step into consciousness and becoming who they are, as conscious beings that we all are.

Yes, there have been some of the ancient beings of the past ages ago that were playing those roles of these gods. They were trying to prevent the human species that is across the universe, from accomplishing their next step of going into consciousness, by any means they deemed necessary to stop those civilizations from learning of the truth.

The time has now come to an end for those ancient beings that was playing those roles as gods and devils, of ages ago that was preventing other beings in the universe, from taking their next step into consciousness and learning the knowledge of the universes and of who we are as conscious beings!

Book 4 – The Quantum leap into Consciousness

Civilizations across the universe were lured away from learning of the truth by those beings that were playing those roles as gods! Now these ancient beings of truth are coming to the earth once again to teach us the knowledge of life. We are now able to take our next step into consciousness, along with the many other beings that are in our galaxy and within the vast universe that we all are part of.

Chapter 35

Time Ends

Now your star system had once again made another completion of traveling around the galaxy and a new cycle begins. Also at the same time your group of stars is entering a new age as well as a new cycle. This is a very interesting time for all beings that exist among your group of stars and your galaxy.

The ancient beings that are the guardians of the universal knowledge of the energy life force are the highest universal beings that exist in the universes around us. The universal knowledge of those beings holds the key to the knowledge that is not comprehended beyond the physical minds of today. It is these guardians of the ancient knowledge of the essence of the life force, which is brought forth by the minds of the ancient beings of beings from the universes. These beings bring forth the knowledge of the essence of the energy of the life force for the beginning of a new cycle and the new age for all beings to fully be part of. This knowledge of the universes is rightfully yours to know and to fully understand who you are. These ancient beings that brought this universal knowledge to you are not to be looked upon as gods, or your creators, or as devils, because they are not.

They were never meant to have these titles. It was the religions of Terra from around six to ten thousand years ago, that gave these non-meaning titles to these beings to bring fear into the people of the world. These ancient beings were simply known as the ancient beings of beings that are of many races from across the universes, because those ancient beings are known as the guardians, because of their superiority of the knowledge of the universes.

All of you on earth and all beings within this galaxy no matter what dimension you are in, are about to have this reawakening of this knowledge of who you are, as conscious beings as all of you take this quantum leap into consciousness, it brings with it great discipline and long training comes with, becoming a being of the knowledge of the universal energy. There is one thing that all beings and especially, "the human species," should start realizing, which is that every single being within this universe are all creators of their own creation that is all around you, along with taking the responsibility of the knowledge of the universe, which they hold within themselves. This is what I have been presenting to you throughout this whole series. This is the knowledge that all religions around the world have been hiding from all of you and getting you to believe in their way as their gods wanted you to believe in. Now you are finally able to see the truth that they, "your religions" been keeping you from.

There are a few things that hold a bond to you. In addition, you must rid yourself of those physical limitations of this physical plane, which are society's way of life. Religions and probably the most important one is, time. See, time does not exist anywhere except in your physical realm on Terra. Time is a human creation and used to measure how long it takes something to happen. They desperately want something to happen in a period, and when it does not happen by that time, they get frustrated and say it will never happen. With these limitations, it hinders the spiritual growth of one's evolution to the higher awareness in the universal knowledge of truth and wisdom. This is what this new cycle and this new age that we all are entering into is about, we are becoming conscious beings as we reawaken that ancient knowledge of the universes that lies waiting for us within ourselves.

A Meeting with the Being of Beings

I mentioned to the being of beings, "It is Time…
The ancient being answered, "Indeed."
I asked the being, "Show me who I am, reawaken all the knowledge within and bring it forth…"
Then the ancient being of beings asked, "Are you ready to unlock the knowledge of the universes within yourself?"

Yes, I am ready! I replied. After these past thirty seven years of learning, bring forth the knowledge of the past from the future to the present!

The ancient being was to the point. "You are the knowledge of the past from the future to the present! You are the past from the future to the present." "What is the past – the future – and the present?" Asked the ancient beings of beings.

I replied to the being standing next to me, "Nothing more than, the now!"

The being said in a straightforward voice, "You are the beginning and the end, then the beginning again."

The ancient being of beings then asked me, "Tell me about time."

I replied to the ancient being of beings,

"Time bends…

Time folds…

Time is space…

Time ends…"

Then the ancient being asked, "What does all this mean?"

I answered, "We are everything that life is… life is everything that we are."

"We are the creators of what is all around us that are seen and unseen, along with us!"

The ancient being said in a satisfied voice, "Very good, you are now a guardian amongst the many which hold the true knowledge of the essence of the universes, which is within yourself!"

As we now come to realize, we all are our own Brahmas, creators, and we are the breath of our own creation, which we have created from our own experiences to experience within. This is the knowledge that those ancient beings of beings of ages long ago were trying to teach to us. We are now at our new cycle and our new age that is starting again. This time we are able to learn of the ancient knowledge that is coming forth again, for all to learn of the truth, without the interfering of those particular beings that were playing the roles as your gods and devils. These beings did not want you to learn of the knowledge of the universes and about who we are as conscious beings!

A Message From the Ancient Beings of Beings

We were once where you are now, in the understanding of who we are as conscious beings!

You too will be where we are now, in the understanding of who you are!

We were once like you, before we consciously evolved to who we are now!

The moment has come for you to, to become as we are now!

As other beings that are below you, will become as you were in the past!

We too will become as beings that are before us. So on and so forth!

The moment has finally arrived for all to claim your rite of passage to the knowledge of who you really are, and to take your place among the countless other beings that are before you, which are also amongst other conscious beings that are among all the universes seen and unseen. Stand up and take this step in the quantum leap into consciousness, which is rightfully yours and learn the true knowledge of life. End the way of letting beings control you and keep you in the dark (asleep). The more you become awakened and learn of the truth, these beings that are controlling you, will no longer be able to. At the same time, these beings that have been controlling you and bringing their ways of life to Terra, and having you kill each other and, having you divided on this earth will no longer be supported in this way of life any longer.

This next cycle and your new age are all about an end to the previous age of control. It is the moment to reawaken and become conscious beings and take responsibility for your thoughts and of what your thoughts create. It is up to each and every-one of you to take responsibility for your own thoughts and of what you are creating around you.

I want everyone to take a moment and really focus on these questions.

Do you want to continue living the way you have been for the past cycle, going around killing other human beings because your government says you must. Because your government says, those people are the ones that you must fear, so you must kill them?

Do you want to continue living your life with a religious belief system that tells you that you must believe a certain way based on a god that nobody has seen in over three thousand years? That (he or she) will come to earth and destroy you, or tell you are not worthy by gods standards?

Or do you want all of that to end and be able to live in peace and harmony with each other?

This is what your governments and your religious figures do not want! They do not want peace and harmony, mainly because they would not be able to create fear within you and they would not be able to control you either!

It is up to you to live in peace and harmony, to exist on this world and extend it into our group of stars and into our whole galaxy.

This is the choice that all of you have to make, at this point.

Do you want to continue living in a world of control, fear, chaos and killing, all because someone says so?

On the other hand, do you want to live in a world of peace and harmony, the way it is meant to be?

What are you waiting for; decide now how you want to live your life on this earth!

That choice is totally up to each and every-one of you to decide on what you want no one can take that away from you!

If you had decided for peace, harmony, I would like you to send your voice out to the universe now, and say…

I want all this control, fear and killing all to stop, NOW!

I want peace and harmony on the earth and within our star group and within all the galaxies that make up our universes, seen and unseen. I want this right now!

This brings you to your next step on the evolution ladder and it takes you to the quantum Leap into consciousness.

I hope with the knowledge that I have presented to you throughout this series, that you have a better idea of what your life is truly is about. I hope this helps to remove the veils of illusions that kept all of you from learning the true knowledge of who you really are. If you start your reawakening and start to remove those veils of illusion, after reading these books, then I have accomplished what I set out to do. This is just the beginning of your reawakening of the knowledge of life and of learning of who we all are as conscious beings! Remember as you begin to awaken that there are others that have not reawakened yet, and it is up to those that have awaken to be teachers to those below you. Teach them what you have already learned, so they too can know what you know.

The knowledge of life is there for all to learn about and it is not for the select few. No one being has the right to tell you not to learn the true knowledge of life, and of who we all are. We are conscious beings and this knowledge is there for all!

What has been presented to you, within this series is the true knowledge of life. This is the knowledge that has been kept from by beings that did not want to evolve as they did, because they wanted other beings to control you. This is not going to go any longer, it stops here now!

This is not the beginning of the end…
It is also not the end…
It is a new beginning…

To be continued…

Book 4 – The Quantum leap into Consciousness

I leave you with a glimpse of the next book called –
- The Ancient Beings Who Are Among Us -
Coming in March 2008
ISBN 13: 978-0-9767832-6-8

The Gathering

Within one world of many creations, we see a Terra type planet and on a mountain range, we see a larger pyramid city with many towers, temples and many pyramids that surround one very large pyramid that is about a mile tall that is located within the center of the city. On top of this large pyramid is a triple golden flame that has one flame in the middle and two flames going around the middle flame, and all three flames extend about fifty feet into the sky. Within this pyramid is a chamber where the ancient beings of beings meet. This chamber that the ancient beings meet is a circular room with a half sphere ceiling with a circular opening on top.

Within this chamber we see about one hundred beings wearing robes that cover them totally. The robes are multiple shades of gold and yellow with tints of shades of brown. These beings are gathered in this chamber conversing about a change, and we hear

Book 4 – The Quantum leap into Consciousness

several voices male/female talking amongst themselves. There is a male being that is about six to seven feet tall standing in the middle of the chamber of the open floor, while the other beings are seated in chairs that face the open floor in this circular chamber. The being that is standing begins talking and mentions to the other beings… "Now… their journey begins… they are on their way, of beginning to be reawakened!"

We then hear a female voice from one of the beings that is seated in the circle… "We hope they reawaken before it becomes to late…" A male voice is heard from amongst the beings, "Do we need to give our assistance…?" The being that is standing in the middle of the room, turns to male being that asked the question, "Those that are already reawakening are coming together and helping those, which have not reawakened yet, to their conscious understanding of who they are as conscious beings." I am doing all that I can do to help those beings that are below us, in letting them know that the time has arrived to reawaken their knowledge of who they really are as conscious beings. It is a slow process since their knowledge has been asleep for the past six to ten thousand years. An additional assistance of the other beings may be required very shortly…"

A female voice is heard. "We are ready when you feel the need of our assistance to help awaken the other ancient beings of beings that are among those beings that are waiting to be reawaken…" Another female voice is heard. "We will begin to call those ancient beings here, and we will have them here for you, and they will be able to assist you when you need them to help on the reawakening process of these beings of the earth planet." The being that is standing in the middle of the chamber mentions, "I will monitor the earth civilizations journey and their reawakening, and I will let you know when the assistance of the other ancient beings are needed, for the reawakening of the civilization on earth."

The being that is standing in the middle of the chamber turns back into his original state of existence of a golden ball of energy, and leaves through the top of the chamber and goes through the triple golden flame that is at the top of this pyramid and disappears into the space above. Then soon after that, the other beings that are in the chamber leave the pyramid in their original state as well but of various colors. In addition, these beings also disappear into the space above the planet.

Book 4 – The Quantum leap into Consciousness

Research Materials

THE ZOROASTRIAN SERIES FROM 4,000-1,000-? BC TRANSLATION BY JOSEPH H. PETERSON 1997

GRECIAN HISTORY, 1892 BY JAMES RICHARD JOY

THE BUNDAHISHN (CREATION) OR KNOWLEDGE FROM THE ZAND, 1897 BY E.W. WEST

COUNSELS OF ADARBAD MAHRASPANDAN (THE TEACHINGS OF THE MAGI) 1956 BY R.C. ZAEHNER

THE KNIGDOM OF LU, 1929 BY MAURICE MAGRE

APHRODITE, 1932 BY PIERRE LOUYS
OAHSPE A NEW BIBLE, FIFTH AMERICAN EDITION 1942 BY ANNO KOSMON

THE AGE OF FABLE, OR THE BEUTIES OF MYTHOLOGY, 1942 BY THOMAS BULFINCH

THE WORLD'S RELIGIONS REVISE, 1954 BY CHARLES S. BRADEN

THE WISDOM OF THE LIVING RELIGIONS, 1956 SEVENTH PRINTING BY JOSEPH GEAR

HINDUISM, GREAT RELIGIONS OF MODERN MAN, SECOND PRINTING 1961 BY GEORGE BRAZILLER

LIVING RELIGIONS OF THE WORLD, 1962 BY FREDRERIC SPIEGELBERG

THE TERRA PAPERS 1947 BY ROBERT MORNING SKY NATIVE AMERICAN

Book 4 – The Quantum leap into Consciousness

THE COMPARATIVE STUDY OF RELIGIONS, FIFTH PRINTING 1969 BY JOACHIM WACH

HOLY BIBLE, (RSV, REVISED STANDARD VERSION) 1972 EDTION BY THOMAS NELSON

HOLY BIBLE, (KJV, KING JAMES VERSION) 1985 EDTION, BY THE GIDEONS INTERNATIONAL

THE BOOK OF MORMON, 1963 THE CHURCH OF JESUS CHRIST OF LATTER-DAY SAINTS, BY DAVID O. MCHAY

THE URANTIA BOOK, SIXTH PRINTING 1978
 By URANTIA FOUNDATION

THE TWELFTH PLANET, THE EARTH CHRONICLES, 1978 BY ZECHARIA SITCHIN

MYTHOLOGY SERIES, BY JOSEPH CAMPBELL 1983

CHRISTIAN CHURCHES OF GOD, 1997 AUSTRALIA
  THE ELECT AS ELOHIM
  THE MEANING OF THE NAMES OF gods
  LIGHT BEARER AND THE MORNING STAR
  ABRACADABRA THE MEANING OF NAMES

FROBIDDEN KNOWLEDGE, 1996 BY ROGER SHATTUCK

HINDUISM, THE JOURNEY OF SELF DISCOVERY, 1997 BY A.C. BHAKTIVEDANTA SWAMI PRABHUPADA

Book 4 – The Quantum leap into Consciousness

HINDUISM, THE SCIENCE OF SELF REALIZATION 1997 BY A.C. BHAKTIVEDANTA SWAMI PRABHUPADA

HINDUISM, BHAGAVAD-GITA AS IT IS, SIXTH PRINTING 1994 BY A.C. BHAKTIVEDANTE SWAMI PRABHUPADA

THE TEMPLAR REVELATION, SECRET GUARDIANS OF THE TRUE IDENTITY OF CHRIST, 1998 BY LYNN PICKETT, CLIVE PRINCE

ALSO OTHER MATERIALS SUCH AS:
ATLANTIS, LEMURIA, MU

LORD OF THE RING SERIES BY JRR TOLKEN

STAR WARS 1977-2005 BY GEORGE LUCUS

STARGATE MOVIES/TV SERIES

V 1983 TV SERIES

CONTACT 1997 MOVIE WITH JODIE FOSTER

THE ARRIVAL MOVIE

TOTAL RECALL WITH ARNOLD SCHWARZENGGER

AND MANY OTHERS

Book 4 – The Quantum leap into Consciousness

DRAWINGS / PICTURES

Robert Morning Sky - The Terra Papers
Eridanus System Page 162 From The Terra Papers 1& 2
Eridanus with beings Page 170 From The Terra Papers 1& 2
Eridanus evolution Page 218 From The Terra Papers 1 & 2
Beh & Iku Beings Page 219 From The Terra Papers 1 & 2
The Death Starship Page 249 From The Terra Papers 1 & 2

Zecharia Sitchin - The Earth Chronicles
Earth Solar System with Twelve Planets - From The Twelfth Planet - Page 250
Bird humanoid demons From The twelfth Planet - Pages 284

Atlantis
Zephyrs - Page 323

Materials used

* The Terra Papers By Robert Morning Sky

*CHRISTIAN CHURCHES OF GOD, 1997 AUSTRALIA
 THE ELECT AS ELOHIM
 THE MEANING OF THE NAMES OF gods
 LIGHT BEARER AND THE MORNING STAR
 ABRACADABRA THE MEANING OF NAMES

Names of GODS, GODDESS and DEVILS, DEMONS from several Cultures around the world.

www.ingramcontent.com/pod-product-compliance
Lightning Source LLC
Chambersburg PA
CBHW051414290426
44109CB00016B/1296